Discovering the Five Elements One Day at a Time

A Chinese Medicine Guide to Healthy Living

By Janice MacKenzie, with Sara Steele
Illustrations by Sara Steele

Wind Palace Publishing, 14 Chapel Road, New Hope, PA 18938
Email: Acujanny@comcat.com

Library of Congress Control Number: 2002109281
ISBN Number: 0-9613584-9-1

Cover Art:
Revival, ©1988, 2002 by Sara Steele

Interior Art:

Na Pali Coast III, watercolor ©1996, 2002 by Sara Steele
Private Collection.

First Crocuses, watercolor ©1984, 2002 by Sara Steele.
From the collection of Peter Wescott.

Sunflowers, watercolor ©1995, 2002 by Sara Steele.
From the collection of Melinda Fudge and Tim Smith.

Comice Pears, watercolor ©1997, 2002 by Sara Steele.
From the collection of Manon Floquet and Becky Lee.

Staghorn Fern, watercolor ©1996, 2002 by Sara Steele.
From the collection of Margaret Krebs.

Pat's Daylilies, watercolor ©1993, 2002 by Sara Steele.
From the collection of Jim Cost.

Book Design by Janet Gala
Cover Design by Janet Gala and Sara Steele

Printed and bound in the United States.

Dedication

This book is dedicated to

my mother, Marjorie May Grimm MacKenzie,
who gave me the Earth that I stand upon
and taught me to love life;

and to my grandmother, Helen Bogue Grimm,
who taught me to accept people
and to always see the best in them.

Two Things of Opposite Natures Seem to Depend

Two things of opposite natures seem to depend
On one another, as a man depends
On a woman, day on night, the imagined

On the real. This is the origin of change.
Winter and Spring, cold copulars, embrace
And forth the particulars of rapture come.

Music falls on the silence like a sense,
A passion that we feel, not understand.
Morning and afternoon are clasped together

And north and south are an intrinsic couple
And sun and rain a plural, like two lovers
That walk away as one in the greenest body.

In solitude the trumpets of solitude
Are not of another solitude resounding;
A little string speaks for a crowd of voices.

The partaker partakes of that which changes him.
The child that touches takes character from the thing,
The body, it touches. The captain and his men

Are one and the sailor and the sea are one.
Follow after, O my companion, my fellow, my self,
Sister and solace, brother and delight.

- Wallace Stevens

Acknowledgments

Creating a book takes many hands and minds. I would like to acknowledge the many people who have helped, either directly or indirectly, to bring this book into being.

First and foremost, I want to thank Sara Steele—who was there at the very beginning, and who was in fact the book's inspiration. In addition to her beautiful paintings, she contributed countless ideas and suggestions, much early editing, and hours of discussion about the elements and the possibilities for this daybook.

Without her, this book would not have been.

Other people I'd like to thank who have helped directly with this book are: Jenny Beer, for her excellent editing and creative suggestions; Jim Campbell, for much-needed encouragement and technical assistance; Janet Gala for her elegant design and typesetting; and Donna Greenberg for sharp-eyed copyediting and proofreading.

Thanks are also due to Emily Sell at Shambhala Press, for her encouragement, and Cary Brosius, for a much-needed lift at a low point in the process.

Most of the material in this book comes directly from the teachings of Professor J.R. Worsley and the teaching staff at the College of Traditional Chinese Acupuncture (U.K.), as well as the teaching staff at the Traditional Acupuncture Institute in Columbia, Maryland. They were all my teachers in this wonderful tradition of healing, but I particularly want to thank Dianne Connelly, for inspiring me and expanding my awareness of my own potential, and Bob Duggan, for guiding my steps in the transformation process of becoming a practitioner.

I also want to thank Erica Lazaro, Haig Ignatius, Charlotte Kerr, Cyrie Barnes, Mary Ellen Zorbaugh, and the rest of the staff at TAI for all of their support and advice early in my career.

There are many teachers and acupuncture writers who I am particularly indebted to: Simon Mills; Ted Kaptchuk; Peter Eckman; Lonny Jarrett; Leon Hammer; Kiiko Matsumoto; Claude Larre and Elisabeth Rochat de la Vallee; Mark Seem; and Cara Frank—all have helped me understand the Five Elements and healing more deeply.

I want to acknowledge all of my professional colleagues in the Acupuncture Society of Pennsylvania and the Association for Professional Acupuncture in Pennsylvania; also, I need to thank my two supervising physicians all these years: Joseph Kipp and Sal D'Angio.

I especially need to thank all of my patients, who have provided me with continued learning about healing and the Five Elements, and all of my students, especially Sara Post Lee, for sharing with me her own list of exercises.

I wish to acknowledge Margaret Wagner, in particular, who provided me with much-needed material support at a critical time.

And of course, I want to thank my family, for always being there: Sue, Bob, Jody, Matt, Pam, Becky, Ted, Theresa, Hank, Andrew, Jill, Ron, Michelle, Brian, Ralph and Gail—and Mom, in spirit.

Most of all, I want to thank my extended family of friends who have believed in me and supported me all these years: Karen Beatty; Helynn Lindsay; Jim Campbell; David Karpoff; Lynn Mitchell; Brenda Jones; Linda Quaste; Joyce Goldberg; Janet Sweeney; Claudia Balant and Laura Ansill; Ann Mintz and Cliff Wagner; Diana Post; Lorna Lee; Paulette Pettorino; Susan Paul; Nancy Post; Donna Poyer; Joe Mills; Greg Artzner and Terry Leonino; Chris Rietz and Debra Huxtable; Yoni Silberman; Andi Coyle; Blaize Malone; Miriam Kanev; Rose Meyers; Melissa Craighead; Loren Crabtree; Mary McCabe; and Gail Huguet.

Finally, my thanks to Rolly and the Australian Kelpies, Keli and Django—who make it all possible.

Introduction

Health is more than the absence of disease, and well-being is more than the absence of symptoms. The Chinese concept of true health has to do with a state of balance and harmony, both internally and with the world at large. To understand more about this state of harmony, it is necessary to understand a bit about the Chinese world view and philosophy.

A cornerstone of Chinese thought is the "Tao"—which means "the Way." The Tao is a very difficult, if not impossible, concept to translate, but means something like "the way things naturally go," and contains the sense of the immutable laws of the universe. To the Chinese, the highest virtue was to be in harmony with the Tao. Since humans are perceived as microcosms of the larger universe, it follows that to be in harmony with the Tao means to adjust oneself to reflect more perfectly the laws of the universe.

One of the primary laws is the interplay of forces known as Yin and Yang. These words refer to the underlying duality of Nature, with the closest metaphors being water and fire. Yin is like water because it is cold, dark, sinking, reflective, receptive, contracted, quiescent, and still. It correlates with the moon, nighttime, the earth, the female, winter, and the interior. Yang is like fire because it is hot, bright, rising, active, dynamic, expansive, and moving. It correlates with the sun, daytime, the heavens, the male, summer, and the exterior. The unending combinations of these two forces create the known universe.

In China, the laws of the universe are based on observation of Nature, particularly the changes of the seasons. The seasons are seen as energetic movements in Nature, which affect all living things and are reflected in their behavior. Plants grow in the spring, flower in the summer, bear fruit in the late summer, lose their leaves in the fall, and die down to the roots in the winter. Animals bear their young in the spring, mate in the fall, and hibernate in the winter. The weather changes with each new season, and different foods are available to eat. In a temperate, agrarian culture, each season had its particular activities: thus, one had to plant in the spring and reap in the fall, not the other way around!

By observing all of these things, the Chinese discerned five basic movements or phases of Nature, which they linked to the seasons.

These five phases are called Wood, Fire, Earth, Metal, and Water, and are linked, respectively, to Spring, Summer, Late Summer, Fall, and Winter. The inclusion of a fifth season (Late Summer) makes Chinese philosophy distinctly different from other systems, most of which were organized into four elements and four seasons. All of Chinese philosophy and medical theory are grounded in this law of the five elements.

Living in harmony with these five phases, then, was the way to health, and some of the earliest known Chinese writings were about just how to do that. The most famous and revered is a book entitled *Huang Ti Nei Ching Su Wen*, or *The Yellow Emperor's Classic of Internal Medicine*, written sometime in the 2nd century B.C., but compiled from traditions much older. To this day, the *Nei Ching* (hereafter referred to as *Nei Jing*, in the Pinyin spelling) serves as a major reference text for students of Chinese medicine. It details the many associations—physical, emotional, and spiritual—that the Chinese made to each element and season. This daybook uses many quotations from the *Nei Jing* as a springboard for explaining different concepts. Also in the *Nei Jing* are specific rules for human behavior in the five seasons. With some allowances for culture and era, these rules are still remarkably applicable today.

The language of the *Nei Jing* is obscure, poetic, and terse. Explaining this material in plain English is only partly possible. I amplified the explanations with concrete examples and stories based on my 20 years of experience as an acupuncture practitioner, as well as the experiences of my teachers and colleagues, who practice acupuncture here in the United States with primarily American, not Chinese, patients.

Since the bulk of this daybook is based on these five elements, it is essential to outline what they are. What follows is a brief synopsis of the five elements, or phases, and their corresponding seasons:

WATER

Water is the name given to the energy of Winter. It is wet and cold, sinking and receptive, (like the depths of the ocean or the still darkness of a winter's night). After the harvesting and letting go of the Fall, all things go inside in Winter, or die down to their roots. It is a time of seeming non-activity, of quiescence, when ground water is stored up in the earth to nourish the new growth the following Spring.

We experience this energy most in our old age, when the activity of our lives ebbs and we reflect over the past, remembering, collecting, and storing up the essence of this life in preparation for the next. But, we also experience this energy every day in the quiet times, every night when we sleep, and every year during our Winter's rest. This resting phase, a time for replenishment and renewal, is absolutely essential for a healthy life.

The activity most appropriate to Water and Winter is actually no activity—a difficult concept to comprehend, since we Americans value activity much more than we do rest. Learning to harmonize with the energy of this season is probably the single biggest gift you can give yourself. In a culture founded on the Puritan work ethic, a philosophy that advocates the virtue of rest is needed, indeed! Only if we allow for periods of rest in our daily, weekly, and yearly cycles will we truly be in balance and harmony with the Tao.

WOOD

Wood is the name the Chinese gave to the energy of Spring. It is explosive, fast-moving and powerful, just like the growth of plants and trees in the Springtime. Although slow, inner transformations take place all winter inside the buds, roots, and seeds, in Spring this growth becomes rapid and outward. New green shoots of grass bursting up through the thawed earth, pliant yet strong enough to crack concrete, describe the nature of Wood energy.

Since we are a part of Nature, we also experience this energy of Wood. We are born by a powerful push from our mothers' wombs, and thus, begin two decades of intense and rapid growth. During childhood, we express many of the qualities the Chinese ascribe to Wood—we are rooted and growing, flexible, creative, hopeful, explosive, dynamic, assertive, spontaneous, and experience a free flow of emotions. If we are healthy, we grow directly from the roots of our essence, and create our own identity by asserting ourselves in the world.

To be in harmony with this energy of Wood in the Springtime, allow yourself to experience this birth and rapid growth. Activities for the season might include beginning new projects, planting seeds, creating something, or exercising, to express some of this explosive and dynamic energy.

FIRE

The energy of the Summertime is Fire. It is heat and light, the warmth of the sun, and the long, light-filled days of summer. Fire is expansive and kinetic, a metaphor for the life force itself. The growth that began so powerfully and rapidly in the Spring now reaches a peak of lush maturity, as all of Nature flowers and begins to bear fruit.

We experience this energy most powerfully in the summertime of our lives—in young adulthood, the time of our sexual maturity and the fuller development of our personalities. From the branches of our emerging identity we put forth the flowers of expression. It is then that we experience relationship—the sharing of expression with others, both socially and intimately. As adults, if we are healthy and our lives allow it, we experience Fire as expansion, communication, expression, connectedness, love, sexuality, and joy. We are warm, happy, and loving, with a capacity to enjoy life, as we reach our physical, mental, and emotional maturity.

Activities appropriate to Summer and Fire are: continuing projects begun in the Spring; cultivating our gardens and watching them flower; communicating and relating to others; expressing ourselves, our ideas and emotions to a broader audience; connecting to others in an intimate way; and having "fun in the sun."

EARTH

Earth is the name given to the energy of Late Summer. In the yearly cycle, it is the short, transitional season between Summer and Fall—the season of the harvest.

This season is a time of intense metamorphosis in Nature, a time of fullness and ripeness, richness and abundance. This is Mother Nature at her most bountiful—the days are warm, the nights are cool, and there is plenty of good food to eat. If there's been a good harvest, we feel content and secure that we will be provided for in the Winter months ahead. This is the stillpoint, that rich moment of total perfection before the slow descent into Fall and Winter. It is like a sigh of contentment, the satisfaction that follows achievement, the security of abundance, peace, and plenty.

We experience this energy in the middle of our lives—our "productive years," when we raise children or create a body of work, make a contribution to our field, or produce something tangible. We are more stable than in our youth; we create a home, a center from which to operate, and we harvest the rewards of our labors. This is a time of nurturing—a time when our thoughts turn to nurturing the next generation. It is no coincidence that this season is most closely associated with "Mother" earth—the primary nurturer is the Mother, and so we need to "mother" something at this phase of our lives. During this time we experience the pleasure of nurturing others and of being nurtured by the abundance we've created. We've learned how to transform our experience, energy, and ideas and make them manifest on the material plane.

Activities appropriate to the season include: finishing the projects begun in the Spring; reaping the rewards for our labors; harvesting the fruits and vegetables from our gardens; nurturing those around us with food, touch and listening; making our homes more comfortable; and producing something with our hands.

METAL

Metal is the name given to the energy of Autumn. Like the mineral ores, salts, and gems of the earth, Metal energy represents strength, structure, and quality. The minerals of the soil provide the richness that nourishes living things, and the metallic ores provide the materials for structural strength and for conduits through which communications flow.

On the functional level, Metal is the energy of letting go, of losing all that is inessential. Like the trees as they shed their leaves, it is a paring down to the bare bones, so that you can see the inner structure of the naked branches. As the year slows down to prepare for Winter's rest, so we turn inward, pause, and take stock of how far we've come in the year's growth. Sometimes we feel a sense of loss or melancholy as we let go of the year, especially if we don't feel that we've accomplished all that we set out to do in the Spring. If it's been a good year, then this time of harvest and evaluation can create a feeling of completion and perfection, a solid sense of our own value and worth.

We experience this energy mostly later in life, when the children are grown, or when our career goals have been achieved. It's then that we begin to really look at and evaluate the quality of our lives, when we measure our worth and look for the meaning of it all. This tends to lead to a spiritual or philosophical focus, and often at this time we begin to follow a spiritual path.

Activities appropriate to Fall and Metal are: evaluating the projects we've completed this year; bedding the garden down for the Winter; cleaning house and throwing out or recycling everything inessential; spending some time grieving over losses experienced over the year; seeking inspiration for our spiritual side; writing in our journals and recording our dreams to explore our inner lives.

Element Chart

Category	Water	Wood	Fire	Earth	Metal
Color	Blue/Black	Green	Red	Yellow	White
Season	Winter	Spring	Summer	Late Summer	Fall
Climate	Cold	Wind	Heat	Humidity	Dryness
Emotion	Fear	Anger	Joy	Sympathy	Grief
Part of Body	Bones	Muscles	Circulation	Flesh	Skin
Tissue	Head hair	Nails	Complexion	Lips	Body hair
Organs	Kidneys Bladder	Liver Gall Bladder	Heart Small Intest. Pericardium Triple Heater	Spleen Stomach	Lungs Large Intest.
Sense Organs	Ears	Eyes	Tongue	Mouth	Nose
Sound of Voice	Groan	Shout	Laugh	Sing	Weep
Taste	Salty	Sour	Bitter	Sweet	Pungent
Time of Day	3–7 p.m.	11 p.m.–3 a.m.	11 a.m.–3 p.m. 7–11 p.m.	7–11 a.m.	3–7 a.m.
Activities that drain	Standing	Walking	Talking	Sitting	Lying Down
Activities that support	Resting Receiving motivation	Exercise Team sports	Being loved Laughing	Receiving nurturing	Being valued Being inspired

Category	Water	Wood	Fire	Earth	Metal
Strengths	Motivating Generating Reflecting Allocating Containing Limiting Energizing	Planning Organizing Strategizing Decision-making Scheduling Clarifying Analyzing Visioning	Leading Expressing Appreciating Sorting Communicating Networking Social/Hosting Coordinating	Supporting Producing Integrating Nourishing Assimilating Holding Distributing	Receiving Balancing Ordering Eliminating Evaluating Evolving Inspiring
Daily Activities	Resting Private time Sleeping Meditating	List-making Working Creating Reading Exercising	Playing Social Time Talking Dancing Sex	Nurturing Self-care Eating Cooking Care for others	Discarding Praying Cleaning Eliminating
Common physical signs of imbalance	Tired Back pain	Jumpy Muscle pain	Hot or cold Blood pressure	Overweight Indigestion	Tense Breathing problems
Common mental signs of imbalance	Dullness Ambitious	Judgmental Negative	Confused Scattered	Obsessive Ruminating	Critical Vapid
Common emotional signs of imbalance	Anxious Depressed	Irritable Defensive	Manic Shy	Insecure Needy	Rigid Despairing
Common spiritual signs of imbalance	Lack of purpose Lack of will	Lack of hope	Alienation Amorality Cruelty	Lack of center Selfishness	Pride Unethical behavior

How to Use this Book

This book is divided into 5 sections, each one representing one of the 5 Chinese seasons, and explaining the corresponding element and its associations. Each of the 365 daily pages contains a mixture of quotations from the Chinese classics, poems, information about the Element, and an exercise that you can do to stay healthy in that season. The poems are there because they are appropriate to the season and illuminate some aspect of the Element.

At the bottom of each daily page is a diagram representing the five elements, and a blank section for you to record your own thoughts and reflections concerning the day, especially the sense of balance and energy that you experienced that day.

The diagram shows the five elements in a circle, representing the natural flow of energy around the circle of the seasons. You can monitor your own energy by coloring or marking the circle that best represents your energy that day. In this way, the pages become a kind of energy diary. Over time, you can look back and see which element predominates, and get a visual sense of the flow of energy in your life.

(Write your own thoughts and reflections here)

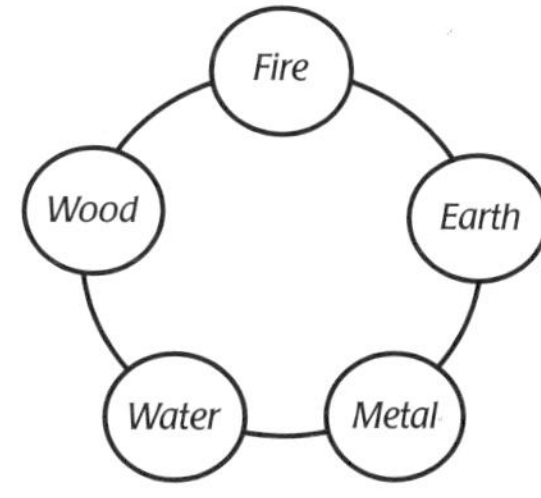

Reflections

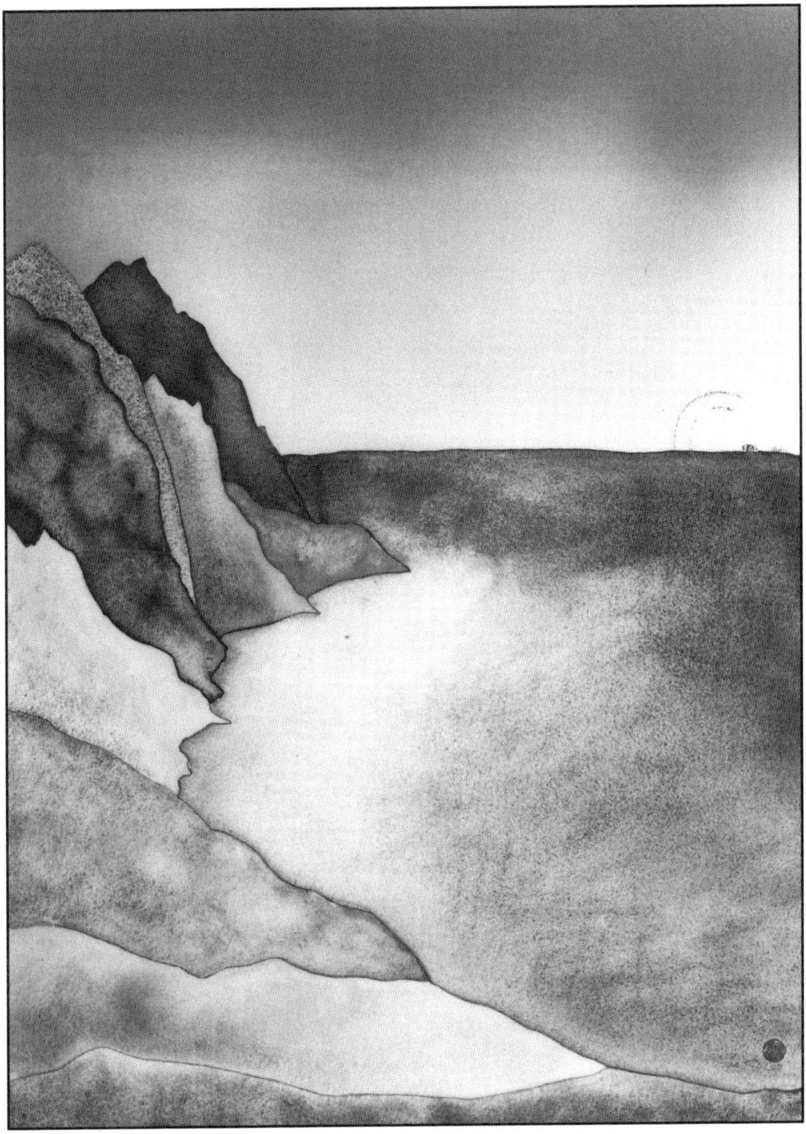

Na Pali Coast III, Watercolor © 1996, 2002 Sara Steele

WINTER

水

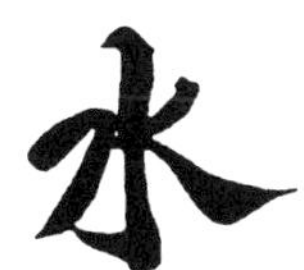

Winter/Water

> *"The three months of Winter are called the period of closing and storing. Water freezes and the Earth cracks open."*
>
> *"The [mysterious] powers of Winter create the extreme cold in Heaven and they create water upon earth. Within the body they create the bones, and of the orifices they create the kidneys (testicles). Of the colors they create the black color...they give to the human voice the ability to groan and to hum."*
>
> **- Nei Jing**

Water is the name given to the energy of Winter. It is fluidity and flow, the ceaseless movement of the tides, the rise and fall of the waves. All life begins in the sea—as we all begin life in the waters of our mothers' wombs. Our bodies are 78% water. Without water, we would die in a matter of days. Water is always changing form, taking the shape of whatever container it is in. It is the perfect expression of Yin - wet and cold, sinking and receptive, like the depths of the ocean or the still darkness of a winter's night.

The Water energy in our bodies governs all of our fluid systems —it is the medium for our blood and lymph circulation, our tears, sweat, saliva, urine, and sexual secretions. The harmonious movement of this fluid is very important for health. Problems with dryness, or swelling and edema, could point to an imbalance in Water energy.

It is no surprise that the organs associated with Water energy are the Kidneys and the Urinary Bladder. The Urinary Bladder's job is to "store the overflow," according to the *Nei Jing*. The Kidneys' role is to move the fluids around in our bodies so that we have lubrication and fluidity where we need it—as the classics say, "The kidneys are like the officials who do energetic work." The Kidneys are also perceived as storing the Vital Essence, or Jing—the internal reservoir of the life force itself. This energy also directs the whole course of our lives, from birth to death, and is what links us with our ancestors and our children—what we in the West might call genetic inheritance —but which encompasses much more in Chinese thought.

Mentally, Water energies have to do with the flow of thoughts and ideas, the "stream of consciousness" that underlies our focused awareness. It is linked with Jung's "collective unconscious"—the storehouse of archetypes and group memories that are the fertile substratum to our individual conscious minds. Water is the Zen idea of "no-mind" reached in meditation—a receptive, open, timeless awareness. Dreaming, the play of images in our nighttime consciousness, is also associated with Water, and can be so much more vivid and fluid than our daytime wakeful mind.

Fear is the emotion connected with Water. This can be a healthy expression of the body-mind-spirit in an appropriate situation—for example, if one were being attacked by a vicious dog! However, a chronic low level of anxiety and dread, a sense of gloomy foreboding or negativity, saps one's energy. If we feel overwhelmed, inundated, or frozen with fear, it is usually a sign that we are not flowing in our lives and that our Water energies need balancing.

Spiritually, Water energy has to do with our will power and ambition. This aspect of the life force is that which drives us forward—it is the "Will of Heaven" acting in us to achieve something. When our Water energy is clear and flowing, and we are connected to our own Essence, then our will power and drive are strong. Someone cut off from his Essence, or one whose personal force in life is weak, may find it difficult to harness the will to achieve anything in the world, or might get pushed around by someone else's will.

Another spiritual aspect of Water is that of faith. As in the Winter we assume that Summer will come again, so in our lives we must ride on the tides of change, through the cycles of the seasons, and the rhythms of life—trusting that the good times always follow the bad, that Spring always comes after Winter, that there is a pattern and cycle to all of life.

January 1

"The [mysterious] powers of Winter create extreme cold in Heaven and they create water upon earth."

—Nei Jing

Winter is the season connected to the Water element, and it is fitting that we begin the calendar here, since it is here that all life begins. In the coldest month of Winter, when all Nature appears to be dead and still, the seeds of the new growth are germinating in the earth. The potential for new life is already here, waiting for the right time and temperature to make itself manifest. In human life, this is likened to the time before birth—a time when all is potential but nothing is actual.

The dark, inactive time of Winter gives a needed rest to the trees, animals, and soil. Humans and animals alike die without sleep. The snows and rains of Winter store up groundwater to be used by the new plants in Spring. This time of rest allows us to gather our Water energy for Spring renewal.

Exercise

Take a nap in the late afternoon, as the sun is going down. Allow yourself to rest and gather energy.

Write your reflections . . .

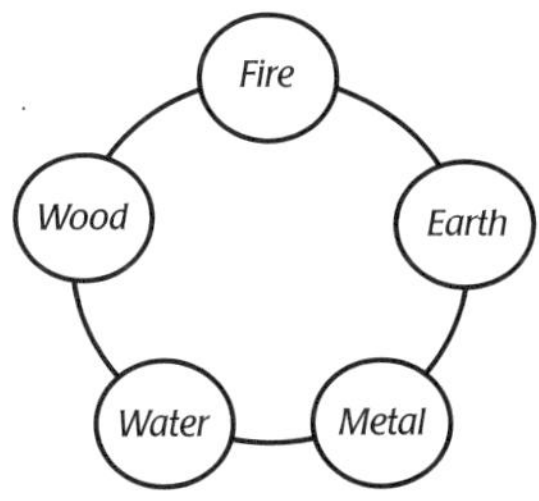

Reflections

January 2

Winter tests our will to survive—to live through the cold and storms and make it to Springtime. It is a time of waiting—waiting to be born or waiting to die. Inside, many small transformations are happening in preparation for the next stage. This waiting time allows us to gather force for the movement of birth or death.

Perhaps this is the reason that New Year's resolutions are so hard to put into practice: the energy of Winter is about waiting, not about action.

According to the Book of Rites, *Yue Ling* (an ancient Chinese classic), the core of Winter is the moment when tigers mate, and also the necessary period to store seeds in darkness for germination. It is the time for the mysterious gathering of water inside the earth, ready to receive the impulses of Heaven.

Exercise

Stay home for one day, and be still. Speak as little as possible and have silence in your house. What happens when you try to do nothing? Can you feel the inner transformations?

Write your reflections . . .

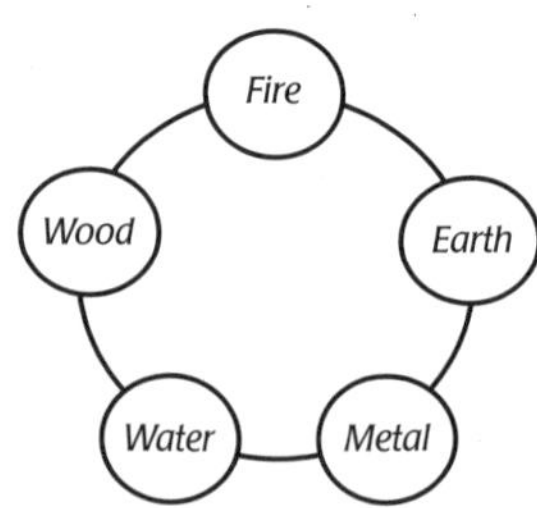

January 3

"Black is the color of the North..."

- Nei Jing

In the *Nei Jing*, the color associated with Winter and the Water element is black, but more recent texts give the color as blue. Both are colors of cold, darkness, and death—the essence of Winter energy. We have phrases in our language that illustrate these connections: "so cold her lips were blue;" "blue with cold;" "I feel blue;" "in a black mood;"and "a black depression."

These colors call to mind two of Nature's phenomena that are blue and black; the sky is blue, but if you travel out of the Earth's atmosphere, the color of limitless space is black. The ocean is blue on the reflected surface, but if you go into the depths, it is black and lightless.

Exercise

Wear Winter colors for a day of silence and invisibility.

Write your reflections . . .

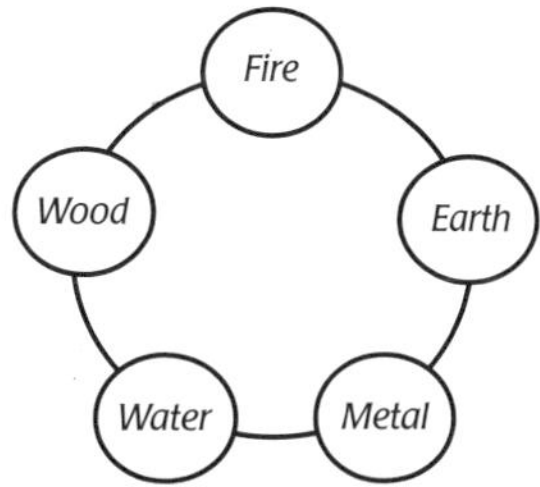

Reflections

January 4

On a snowy day, the shadows are blue, the wet tree trunks black against the snow. The connection of color and seasonal energies shows up in many ways in our human lives as well as in nature. In someone with a Water imbalance, it might show up as a blue-black hue around the face, especially around the eyes; or there might be a marked preference for blue or black clothing. Or, contrarily, someone may refuse to wear blue and black and not want those colors around. A strong preference or aversion to blue and/or black could indicate an imbalance in the Water element.

In choosing which colors to wear each day, we are often guided by unconscious assumptions or associations with colors. For example, we might choose dark blue or black because we think those colors are more "conservative," or because we feel they don't make us stand out in the same way that the color red would. A lot of people, especially in big cities, wear black because they think it is sophisticated or "cool."

Exercise

Look today at the faces and clothes of those who pass by —are they Water people?

Write your reflections . . .

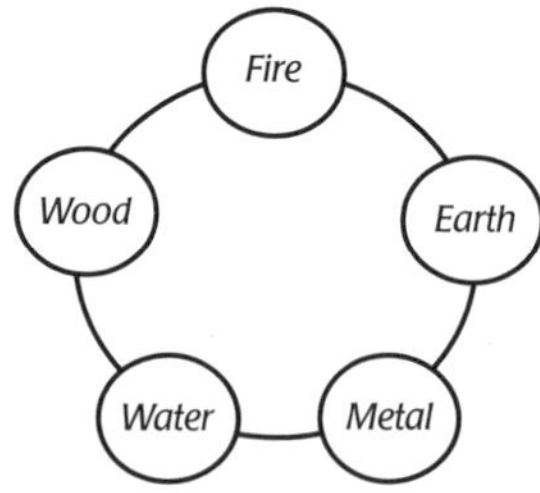

Reflections

January 5

"Extreme cold is created in the North..."

- Nei Jing

The character for North, <u>bei</u>, (北), tells something about the Chinese understanding of this direction. Two halves face away from each other, back to back, with no communication. This shows the separation of Yin and Yang in Winter; the movement is one of separation and exile. In central China, when people were exiled, they were driven toward the North. The Great Wall was built to guard against the North.

Also, the ancient Chinese believed that the North was the region where the ten thousand things withdrew and hid during the Winter. However, this was because the North was actually their origin, so the North is also the direction of the underlying and original unity of all things. This idea of being simultaneously the beginning and the ending of something is carried through in other aspects of Water; for example, in the association with both birth and death.

Exercise

Find a window facing North, and spend half an hour just sitting in a chair facing that direction.

Write your reflections . . .

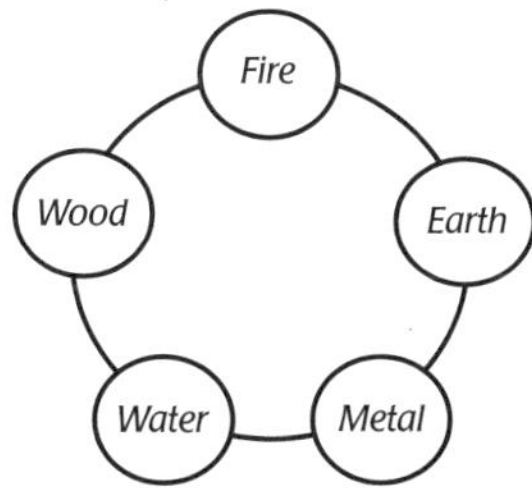

Reflections

January 6

The *Nei Jing* says that "The North is the region of storing and laying by." The extreme cold and long Winters in northern China dictated that the people of the North needed to store up as much food as possible to last until Spring; thus, the association of the direction of North with the concepts of storing and gathering. This storing is really on many levels: Water is stored up in the earth; animals and people gather food to last the Winter; and your body stores energy, by craving solid, hearty, warm foods, to be called upon to fuel the new growth in the Spring.

Many people complain that in the Winter they feel tired and sluggish, and that they tend to gain weight—often going on stringent diets to try to lose it. Perhaps this is just our bodies' natural shift into storing mode for the Water season, and we should cooperate with Nature's plan rather than resisting it.

Exercise

Today, find at least a half-hour in your schedule when you can just lie down and rest. When you lie down, imagine that you are an empty lake or reservoir, slowly being filled with water from several streams. Feel your body gathering and filling, storing "water" in your cells for future use as energy.

Write your reflections . . .

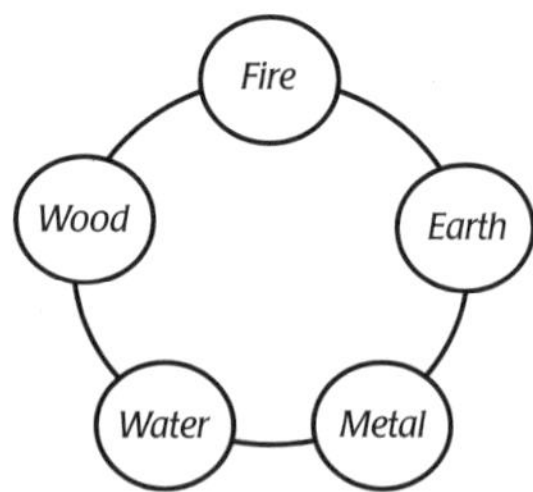

Reflections

January 7

"The [mysterious] powers of Winter create extreme cold in Heaven ..."

- Nei Jing

The climate of cold is associated with the season of Winter and the element of Water. This goes beyond the obvious fact that, of course, the temperatures in Winter are cold. "Cold" here is associated with the ideas of contraction, immobility, frozenness, shrinking in, consolidation, and hardening. The ideogram for cold is han, (寒), which represents a man inside straw under a roof, with the idea of freezing. This depicts the time of winter when people huddle together inside under the straw, to make sure they don't freeze.

The ideogram points to the correct conduct in this type of climate or weather. As the *Nei Jing* says, "People should try to escape the cold and they should seek warmth."

Exercise

Huddle under a quilt with company or with a good book. Let the warmth into your bones.

Write your reflections . . .

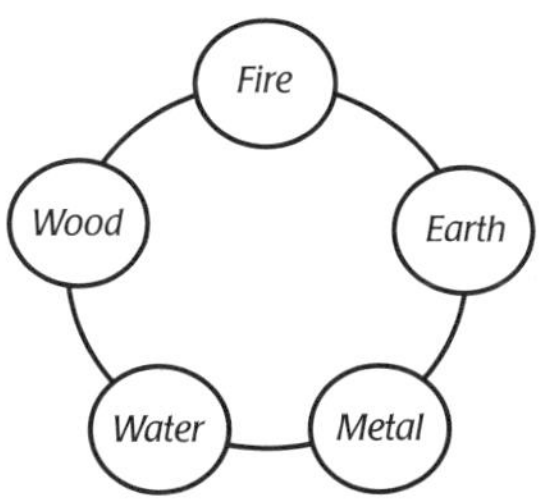

Reflections

January 8

During Winter, our bodies reflect the contracted, immobile state of "cold." Sometimes cold penetrates so deeply that certain parts of our bodies remain contracted, even after Winter is over—we can experience a "frozen" shoulder or stiff, contracted muscles, arthritis, or aching joints. On the mental level, too, we can become static and contracted, afraid to make a move. Emotionally, we can experience an inner coldness and contraction, difficulty in "warming up" to people or in "coming out of our shells." All of these things show a condition of coldness and could point to an imbalance in the Water element.

Exercise

Only do this one if you are in good health! On a really cold day, step outside for just 2 minutes without your hat and coat (or less if the day is windy)! Feel how your muscles get tense and contract as they try to hold your body heat inside. Note how your chest constricts as you breathe more shallowly in the cold air. Then go back inside and do something to warm up quickly—jump into a hot bath or shower, sit by a roaring fire, stand on a heating grate, or just pull the bed covers over your head. As your muscles relax, acknowledge the powerful effects of cold on your body.

Write your reflections . . .

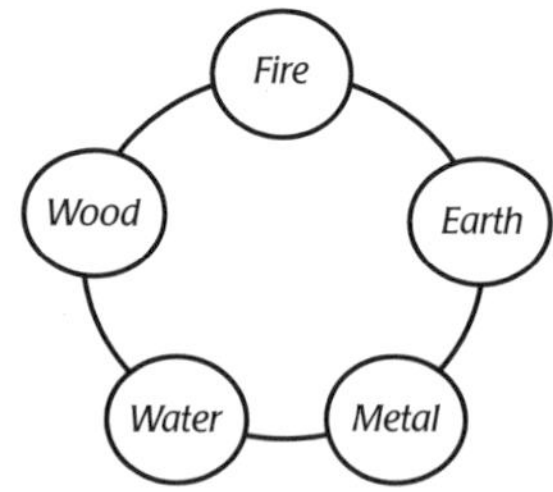

Reflections

January 9

"...the kidneys are like the officials who do energetic work, and they excel through their ability and cleverness."

- Nei Jing

The Kidneys (and their sister organ, the Urinary Bladder), are the organs associated with the Water element. In Chinese medical thought, each organ is pictured as an Official in a Kingdom, with specific duties to perform for the good of the land. The Kidneys are seen as a kind of powerhouse, a dynamo that drives all of the activity of the body-mind-spirit, as well as a storehouse of energy. Professor Worsley calls the Kidneys " The Storehouse of the Vital Essence." The Kidneys store your life force, especially that aspect of the life force that has to do with the energy you receive from your ancestors. They are associated with your very beginnings, and house the essence of who you are. When the Kidneys are depleted, your Storehouse supplies are running low, and you can experience fatigue, lethargy, and a lack of vitality.

Exercise

Dig out your photo albums, and look at pictures of your ancestors. What essence has come down to you through them?

Write your reflections . . .

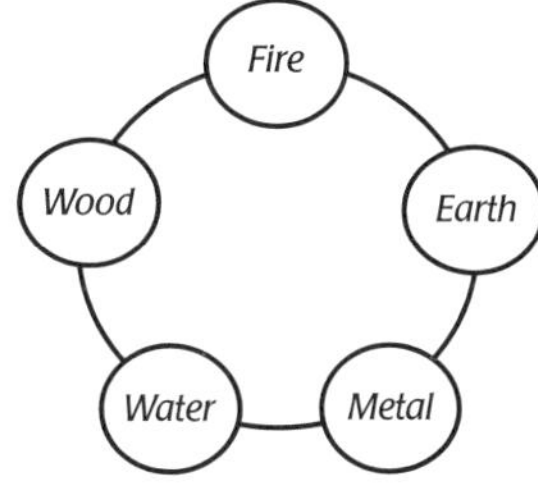

Reflections

January 10

The Kidneys also regulate all of the fluid metabolism of our bodies. Each cell is bathed in fluid, and this fluid flows throughout the body, carrying nutrients and messages, lubricating joints, and carrying away waste materials to be collected and excreted as urine. When something goes wrong with the Kidney official, wastes or too much fluid begin to pile up in the body, collecting in joints and creating blockages called arthritis, or swelling in tissues as edema, or blocking up the Kidneys themselves, causing hypertension. In general, any time that a life process seems to be suffering from a lack of fluidity or lubrication, we must look to the Kidneys to see what is the matter.

Exercise

Observe the different forms of water in Nature: lakes; streams; oceans; puddles; raindrops; snow; ice; fog and frost. Notice its quality of flow or stillness, and how it differs at different times of day. These same qualities can be manifested in your own Water energies. Do you feel the calm stillness of a frozen pond in Winter? Or the rushing of a flooding river in a January thaw?

Write your reflections . . .

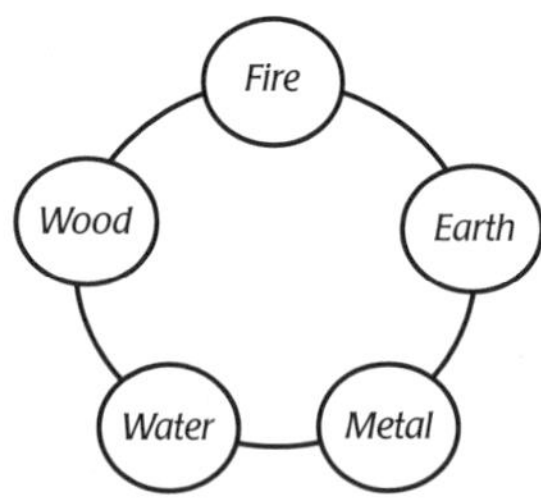

Reflections

January 11

"... the groins and the bladder are like the magistrate of a region or a district; they store the overflow and the fluid secretions ..."

- Nei Jing

The Urinary Bladder is another organ associated with the Water element. As an organ that eliminates fluid, the bladder serves an excretory function, and prevents the body-mind-spirit from being poisoned. A key characteristic of the Bladder official is its ability to be flexible and adaptable, to expand or contract with different amounts of fluid, and to know when to eliminate them. This adaptability is significant on every level; someone with an imbalance in the Bladder official might be totally unable to adapt to change or new situations, fearful, depressed, or unable to cope. Also, someone who is not able to store or hold energy, who "pisses it away,"could be manifesting an imbalance in the Bladder official.

Exercise

What do you need to eliminate? To hold in for now?

Write your reflections . . .

Reflections

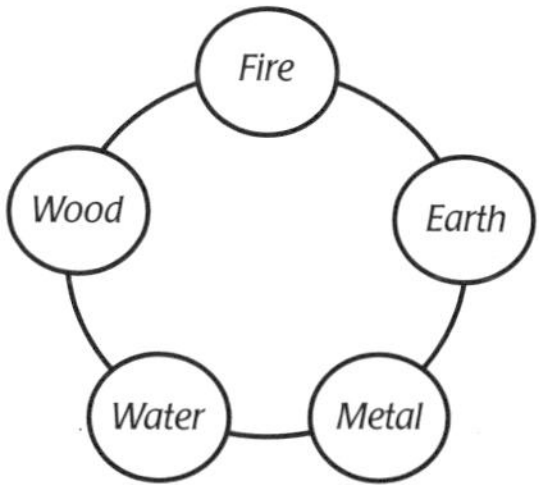

January 12

"Water—the ace of elements. Water dives from the clouds without parachute, wings or safety net. Water runs over the steepest precipice and blinks not a lash. Water is buried and rises again; water walks on fire and fire gets the blisters. Stylishly composed in any situation —solid, gas or liquid—speaking in penetrating dialects understood by all things—animal, vegetable or mineral—water travels intrepidly through four dimensions, *sustaining* (Kick a lettuce in the field and it will yell "Water!"), *destroying* (The Dutch boy's finger remembered the view from Ararat) and *creating* (It has even been said that human beings were invented by water as a device for transporting itself from one place to another, but that's another story). Always in motion, ever-flowing (whether at steam rate or glacier speed), rhythmic, dynamic, ubiquitous, changing and working its changes, a mathematics turned wrong side out, a philosophy in reverse, the ongoing odyssey of water is virtually irresistible."

Tom Robbins,
Even Cowgirls Get the Blues

Exercise

Bundle up and go for a long walk by a lake, river, stream, or ocean.

Write your reflections . . .

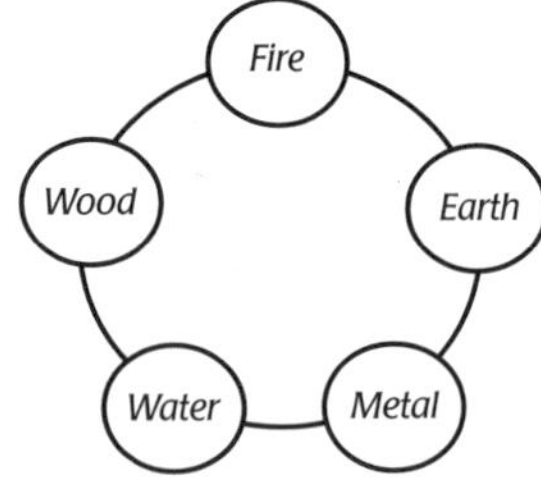

Reflections

January 13

"... and among the emotions they create fear."

- Nei Jing

Fear is the emotion associated with the Water element. As one of the five primary emotions, it is not in and of itself negative. There is a healthy fear, which is the body-mind-spirit's reaction to physical danger. When you see a snarling dog, or a truck bearing down on you, fear stimulates you to take action to save yourself—namely to run, jump, or hide! In Western terms we would say that the danger stimulated your adrenal glands to secrete adrenaline, which precipitated a "fight-or-flight" response in your body. (It is interesting that the adrenal glands sit on top of the Kidneys, organs associated with the Water element.)

When fear becomes a chronic response to everything—not just life-threatening situations—it becomes anxiety, pervading all of life, underlying every action and thought. When this happens, we speak of an imbalance in the Water element—we've become stuck in one emotion whether it matches the situation or not , and can't seem to move on.

Exercise

Make a list of all the things you used to be afraid of that you're not afraid of anymore. How did you conquer your fear?

Write your reflections . . .

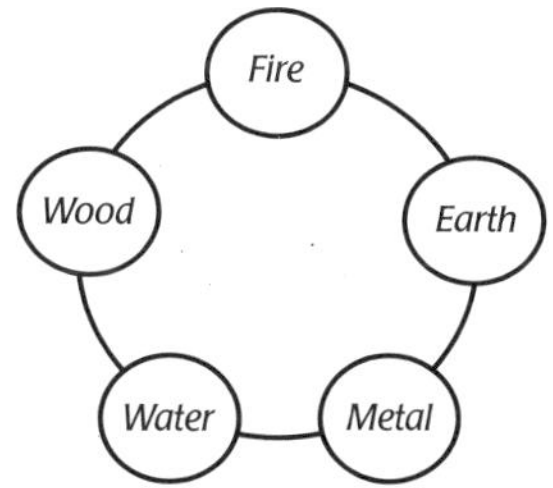

Reflections

January 14

Sometimes, anxiety is a feeling of being overwhelmed by life's circumstances, not being able to "keep our heads above water," of having insufficient resources to do what we need to do. The fear can manifest as debilitating panic attacks.

The Su Wen, Chapter 39, says "Fear makes Breaths go down." Noted Chinese scholar Elizabeth Rochat de la Vallee explains that this means that the movement of fear is downward. We can see this in cases of fright when someone becomes incontinent with fear, i.e., "wets his pants." But in cases of chronic fear, this can lead to a weak bladder, a sense of things dropping out from under one's feet, because there is not enough energy in the Water element to stop the downward movement.

Exercise

Where in your body do you feel fear? What do you usually use to counter or balance it? For some people, it's taking deep breaths; for others, it's eating or drinking something, or asking someone else for reassurance. Try this: the next time you feel anxious, spend a few minutes massaging your back over the kidney area, until the friction makes your back feel warm.

Write your reflections . . .

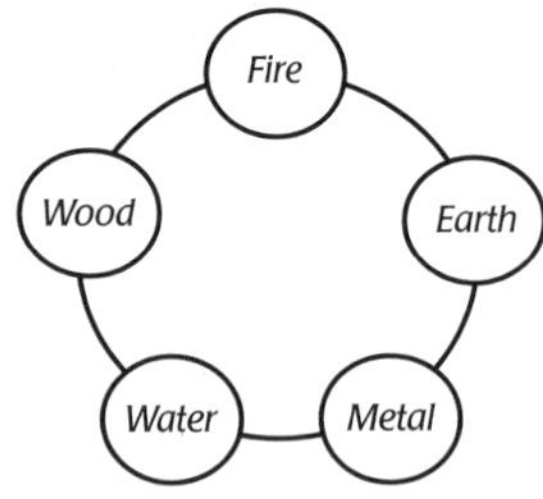

Reflections

January 15

The body has daily cycles, as well as seasonal ones, which the ancient Chinese mapped out many centuries ago. They discovered that each two hour period of the day was the peak for one organ and the low time for another. For the Water organs of the Urinary Bladder and the Kidneys, the peak times are from 3-5 p.m. and 5-7 p.m., respectively.

We experience this movement into Water energy differently, depending on the state of our own Water energies. If we are healthy, then we feel a greater capacity for stillness and meditation during these times, a quiet withdrawing of energy from the outer world, and a deepening of our energies inward. If we are out of balance in Water, then we might feel these as times of low energy, fatigue, scattered thoughts, irritability, tearfulness, and strain.

For those who work 9-5 jobs, those last two hours from 3-5 are often the hardest, as we struggle to keep going until quitting time on exhausted reserves. Then, the hours from 5-7 include commuting home, sometimes long distances, cooking dinner, and coping with family responsibilities—all during the time intended by Nature for refueling and replenishment.

Exercise

Sometime between 5 and 7 p.m., sit quietly in a comfortable chair, close your eyes, and allow yourself to "just" rest. Be aware that even at rest, your body is humming with activity and your mind is brimming with thoughts.

Write your reflections . . .

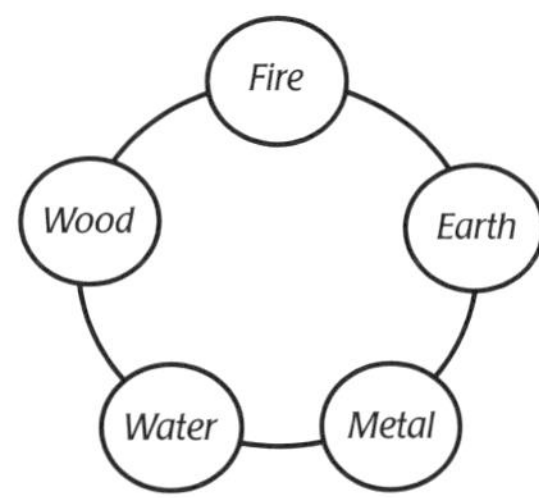

January 16

There are two times of life associated with the Water element—the time spent in the womb, and old age. We swim in the amniotic fluid for nine months until the moment of birth, which is the passage from Water into Wood. The Chinese believe our consciousness in the womb is still very diffuse; it's like the undifferentiated sensate awareness of a fish or animal. In this dreamy space, great transformations are happening, as our bodies are built out of the elements provided by our mothers' bodies, but we are unconscious of them.

Old age is a return in some ways to that kind of awareness—a letting go of the ego and a sinking back into this undifferentiated awareness of being. The difference is that in old age, we have a lifetime of experiences to reflect upon, and we are conscious of the transformations of aging happening to our bodies. If we are lucky, the letting go is a spiritual process that brings us back to a universal oneness, an acceptance of our life on earth and of our own death and dissolution. In this Winter of our lives, we slow down and enter into the same timelessness of the womb, as we prepare to be born into another dimension.

Exercise

Spend some time in quiet reflection of your life. Think about yourself being born, and picture yourself at all the stages of growing up, right to the present day. Could you accept your life if it ended tomorrow?

Write your reflections . . .

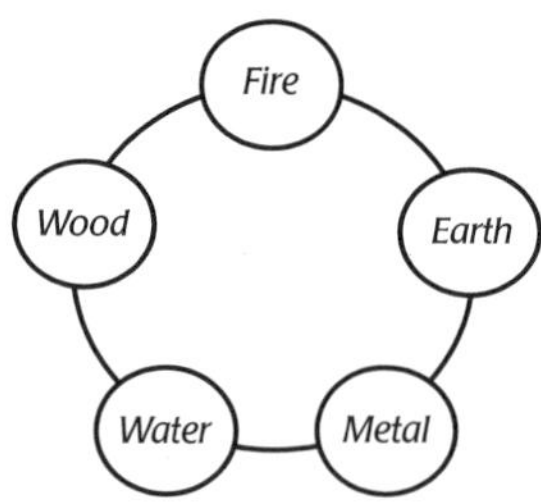

January 17

"The force that through the green fuse drives the flower/ Drives my green age."

- Dylan Thomas

Chapter 8 of the Ling Shu (a part of *The Nei Jing*) says, "...The will resides in the energies of the kidneys." The Chinese idea of will and will power has fascinated me ever since I first heard Chinese scholars Claude Larre and Elisabeth Rochat de la Vallee talk about it. Here we come close to the central mystery of human life—the force that drives us to live, to do, to create, to achieve. This will is intimately connected to and arises out of our Kidney Essence—so that, if we are healthy, what we do flows out of who we are. Phrases like "strong-willed," "weak-willed," "the will to live," and "I need will power," all express our American conception of will—which makes of the will a conscious process that should be in our control.

In the Chinese conception, the will (*zhi*) is more an unconscious blending of energy, essence, and motivation—a force that is coming through us but is not necessarily of us. The Chinese speak of the "Will of Heaven" as a force that comes from our ancestors and from Heaven, that enters us through our Kidneys and then manifests in our actions.

Exercise

When you get up in the morning, think about what you "will" for the day. In the evening, consider how easy or hard it was to achieve your will.

Write your reflections . . .

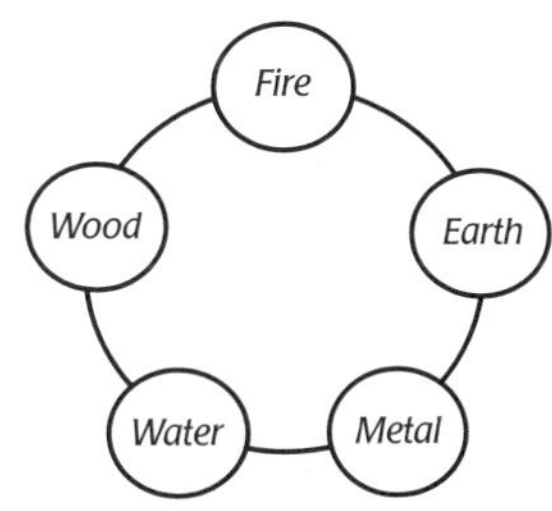

January 18

"Willpower, zhi, is of course, specially connected with the kidneys...Zhi is like a tension or an intensity of life, taut and intent on a certain direction... In the ideogram zhi we can see the power of the tension of life, and this is a specific aspect of the kidneys: tension, foundation, attention and the passage to knowhow."

- Elisabeth Rochat de la Vallee,
***The Kidneys*, p. 71**

The more closely we can harmonize our own individual wills with the Will of Heaven, the more powerful our actions will become. When there is no friction between the Will of Heaven and our own small, human will, then we flow smoothly through life, with the power of an ocean behind us.

Discovering the Will of Heaven is a process of knowing ourselves at the deepest level. For most of us, this means spending time in contemplation or meditation. When we know who we are, then we know what we must do to achieve the Will of Heaven, and how to harness our own will power to do it.

Exercise

Use your will power today to do something that is difficult.

Write your reflections . . .

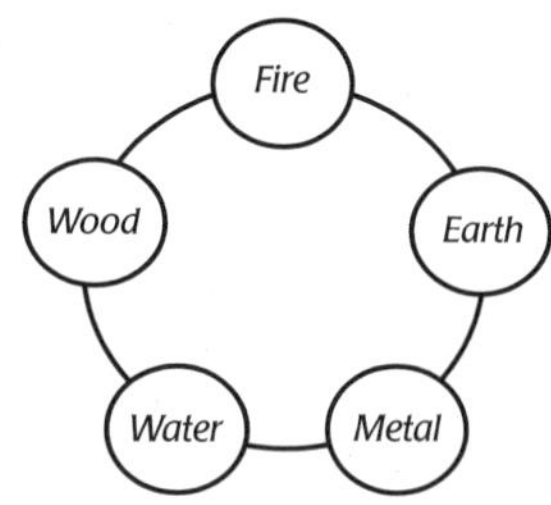

Reflections

January 19

"...and the kidneys strengthen the bones and the marrow;"

"The lowest of the viscera are the kidneys, thus the kidneys harbor the force of life of the bones and the marrow."

- Nei Jing

The Water element governs the bones and the bone marrow. As water tends to sink to the lowest level and is associated with the depths, so our bones are the deepest layer of our bodies, the solid framework that provides form and strength, and upon which the other tissues of our bodies are layered. All of the bones, including the teeth, skull, and spine, are fed by the energy of the Kidneys and Bladder. Any weakness in that energy can manifest in problems in the bones, including symptoms such as osteoporosis, soft or loose teeth, bone spurs, osteoarthritis, etc.

Exercise

Make an infusion of what herbalist Susun Weed calls "Bonny Bony Brew:" Place one ounce of dried nettle, 1 tablespoon of dried horsetail and 1 tablespoon of dried sage in a quart container; fill with just-boiled water, cap and let brew for at least four hours or overnight. Strain and drink as is or heat and add honey. Each cup contributes as much calcium as a cup of milk.

Write your reflections . . .

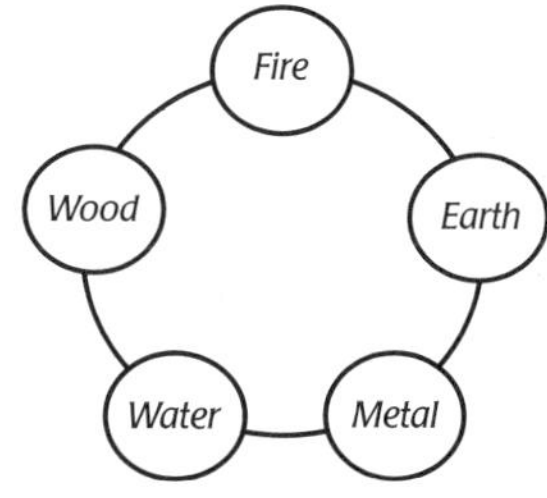

Reflections

January 20

"....its disease is located within the bones..."

- Nei Jing

Within the bone is the bone marrow, which is the deepest layer of the bone. Marrow creates new cells, which provide nourishment and replacement, continually renewing us. Although the Chinese had no way of knowing that red and white blood cells were created in the marrow, centuries ago they wrote that the kidneys govern the storage of the life force in the bones and marrow. Here, we see another example of the accuracy of their observations. Thus, from our depths, from the very marrow of our bones, we are continually being renewed.

English is full of sayings that express this connection between the bones and the depths: "I feel it in my bones" means we feel something very deeply, intuitively. "Even my bones hurt" indicates a serious illness. When patients tell their doctors that they feel "cold to the bone," or that "even my bones feel hot," it's an indication that the Kidneys or the Water energy needs attention.

Exercise

Warm your bones by adding cinnamon or ginger to hot cereal.

Write your reflections . . .

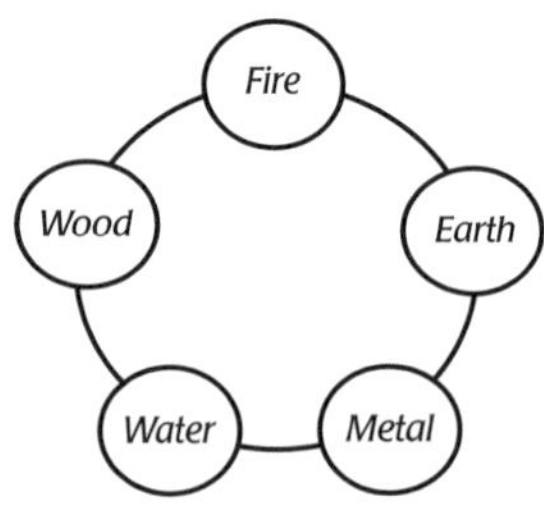

Reflections

January 21

"The condition of the hair on the head shows when the [kidneys] are in a splendid and flourishing condition."

- Nei Jing

Have you ever wondered why sometimes your hair feels soft and has a lustrous shine, and other times it feels brittle and dry like straw? It's not necessarily your shampoo—the condition of your head hair reflects the condition of your Water energy. If your Kidney energy is healthy, then your hair will be healthy and flourishing also; if your Kidney energy is weak, your hair might be scanty, dry or split. You can use the condition of your head hair—its texture, thickness, and rate of growth—to diagnose the health of your Water energy.

Many men, and some women, go bald as they get older. The Chinese would explain this by saying that, as we age, we use up our Kidney Essence in the stresses of living. When the Kidney Essence no longer nourishes the head hair, then the hair thins and we begin to go bald.

Exercise

Rinse your hair with a dilute infusion of chamomile and rosemary for hair luster and scalp health. Rub several drops of jojoba oil on brittle hair ends to protect them.

Write your reflections . . .

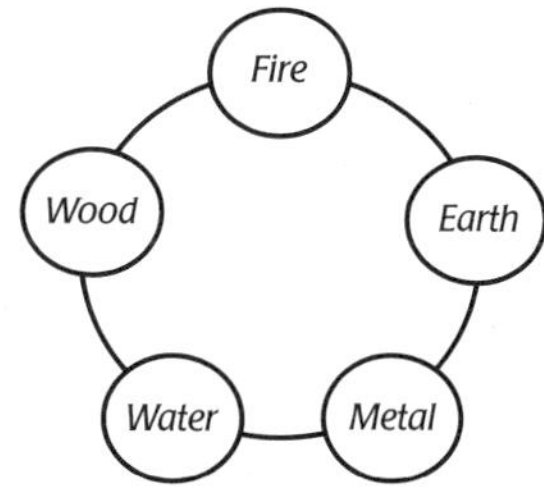

January 22

There's a certain Slant of light,
Winter Afternoons -
That oppresses, like the Heft
Of Cathedral Tunes -

- Emily Dickinson

Late afternoon, from 3 p.m. to 7 p.m., is when the energy of Water is most prominent, especially so in Winter, the season of Water. If your Water energy is depleted, then winter late afternoons could emphasize for you that depletion, and you can really feel your exhaustion on a deep level.

The early darkness can add to your feeling of oppression, or depression. Many people are afflicted with something called Seasonal Affect Disorder, or S.A.D., which is brought on by the limited sunlight in the Winter months. If you feel depressed or exhausted in the late afternoons, perhaps it is a signal from your body-mind-spirit that your Water energy needs to be replenished.

Exercise

Tonight, build a fire in the fireplace. If you don't have a fireplace, put several candles on a tray and light them, then turn off the lights and watch the candles burn.

Write your reflections . . .

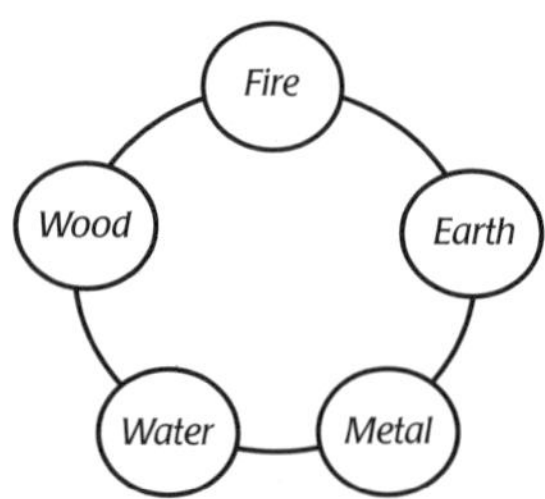

Reflections

January 23

"The kidneys rule over the ears."

- Nei Jing

The ears are the sense organ connected to the Water element. Hearing is one of the earliest sense faculties developed—it is already functioning in utero, in the waters of the womb. This further reinforces its connection to the Kidneys, which influence embryonic development in the aquatic environment of the developing fetus. The ability to hear sounds underwater points to another primary connection with the Water element—water is a good conductor of sound. In the inner ear, the canals are filled with fluid, and our hearing depends on the right amount of water being there.

When, for various reasons, the fluid in the inner ear is insufficient or in some other way disturbed, then various symptoms can result, including: vertigo, dizziness, lack of balance and equilibrium, tinnitus, sounds like a waterfall in the ear, and certain kinds of deafness. Many of these symptoms are more common in older people; the Chinese believe that as you age you gradually lose your Kidney Essence, an aspect of your life force that is housed in the Kidneys. Aging, therefore, is a kind of "drying up" of all bodily fluids, including the fluid in the ears.

Exercise

Listen to Handel's *Water Music*. Imagine the sound waves vibrating the waters of your inner ear.

Write your reflections . . .

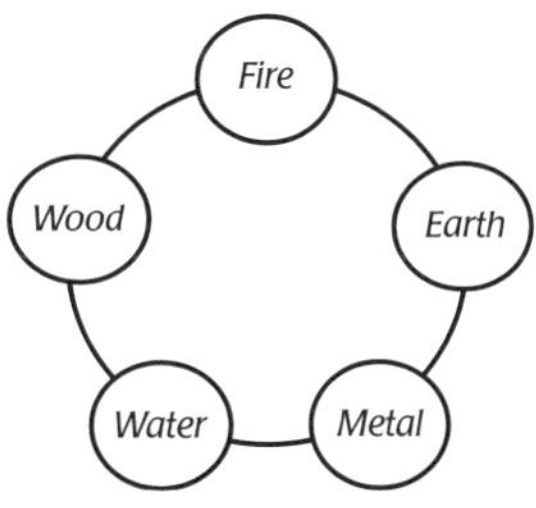

Reflections

January 24

"When I kept silence, my bones wore away
through my groaning all the day long
for day and night thy hand was
heavy upon me;
My sap was turned as in the droughts of summer."

- Psalm 32:3

The sound of voice associated with the Water element is groaning. In some texts they also include moaning, sighing, and humming as sounds of the Water element. This sound goes hand-in-hand with exhaustion, and also with fear. If we listen to our own voices when we are tired, we'd be surprised at how many times we sigh, and how gravelly and, in general, more "groaning" they are. It is as if there is not enough energy even to speak with any force. The same thing happens when we are afraid—our voices will unconsciously groan and moan with fear.

Exercise

Listen to the voices of your friends and family today. Hear how they sound by the end of the day.

Write your reflections . . .

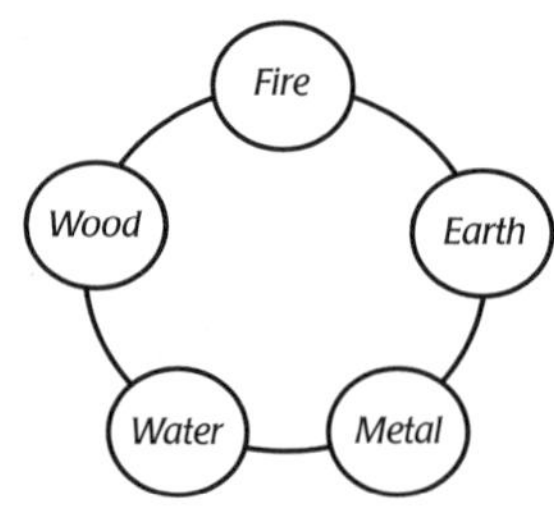

Reflections

January 25

In someone whose Water energies are imbalanced, the voice will continually moan and groan, even when speaking of happy things. Usually, this person would be surprised to be told that his or her voice was groaning. This kind of voice makes you tired to listen to it. People whose voices groan are probably mystified as to why people seem bored by their conversation or routinely cut them off. For people of more energetic temperament, this type of voice can be extremely irritating.

An interesting note here is that the character that has been translated as "groan" or "sigh" is shen—which has the same pronunciation as the ideogram for the Kidneys. Shen means to spread out and extend. Since the Chinese believe that the Kidneys function to grasp the Breath, then when there is blockage, the "sigh" is the way we extend the breath. In other words, a weakness in the Water energy will block the surging up of the Breaths. The reaction to this blockage is the sigh—a large and long respiration to help the Breaths circulate again.

Exercise

Sleep at least eight hours every night this week. When you arise, practice taking deep, full breaths for at least five minutes. How do you feel by the end of the week?

Write your reflections . . .

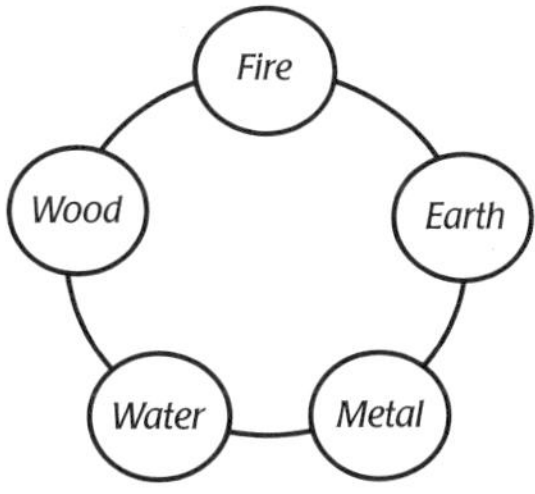

Reflections

January 26

"Extreme cold is created in the north. Cold creates water, and water creates salt. Salt nourishes the kidneys..."

"...and the kidneys crave the salty flavor."

- Nei Jing

The taste associated with Winter and the Water element is salty. This taste is such a basic taste that we almost don't need to describe it; other than the sweet taste of mother's milk, it's probably the first taste we experience as infants in the form of our own tears. All of our bodily fluids contain salt, including blood, sweat, and tears. This substance has an essential role in many physiological processes, especially in muscle metabolism. Probably, this is because all life comes from the sea, and partakes of its briny nature. It's no surprise that something so basic and fundamental to life would be connected to our deepest and most fundamental energy, our Water.

Exercise

Buy some good sea salt, which has been extracted by sunshine. Use it this month instead of regular table salt, which has been refined through heat processing, bleached, and mixed with chemicals to make it flow easier.

Write your reflections . . .

Reflections

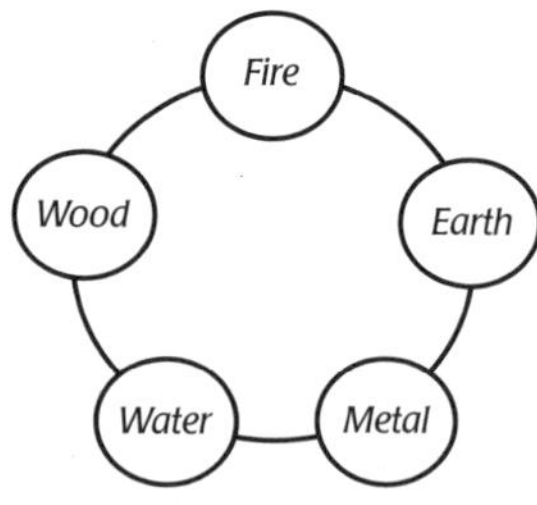

January 27

The character for salty is <u>xian</u> (鹹), which is composed of two parts: the left part has two strokes crossing with four dots inside, representing a rock and four grains of salt; the right part has the meaning to bite or to wound with the mouth. Pure table salt can have a slightly biting effect on one's tongue, so perhaps this is what was intended!

The *Nei Jing* says: "... (Sick) kidneys have the tendency to harden; then one should eat bitter food to strengthen them. One uses bitter food to supplement and to strengthen them and one uses salty food to drain them and to make them expel ...the salty flavor has a softening effect." In Chinese herbal medicine, herbs with a salty taste are used to soften lumps in the body, i.e., kelp and other seaweeds are used medicinally to treat goiter.

Each taste has a specific effect on the body if taken in excess: "Hence if too much salt is used in food, the pulse hardens, tears make their appearance and the complexion changes." A craving for the salty taste could indicate an imbalance in your Water energy.

Exercise

Today, eat some of the edible seaweeds such as nori or hijiki, instead of potato chips, if you crave something salty.

Write your reflections . . .

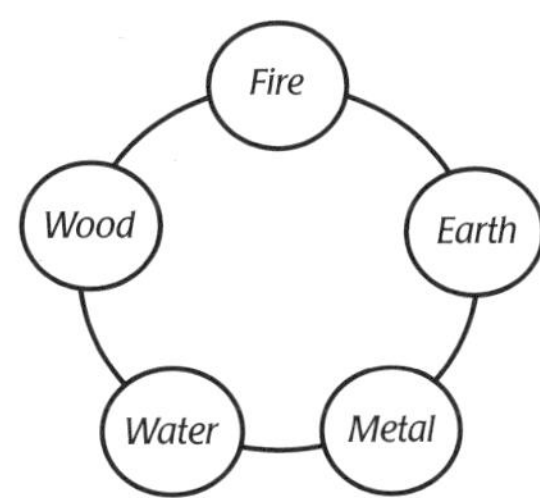

Reflections

January 28

"...the kidneys crave the salty flavor...One uses bitter food to supplement and strengthen them and one uses salty food to drain them and to make them expel."

- Nei Jing

Chinese medicine has always used specific foods to strengthen and nourish specific organs of the body. As the *Nei Jing* says: "The five grains act as nourishment; the five fruits from the trees serve to augment; the five domestic animals provide additional benefit; the five vegetables serve to complete the nourishment. Their flavors, tastes and smells unite and conform to each other in order to supply the beneficial essence (of life)." The specific foods associated with the salty taste, the Kidneys and the Water element are: "Large beans, pork, chestnuts, and coarse greens..." When we eat a lot of these foods, as well as others associated with the Water element, we are consciously nourishing that element within us.

Exercise

Cook some red aduki beans, black beans, or kidney beans with millet or buckwheat for a nutritious winter meal.

Write your reflections . . .

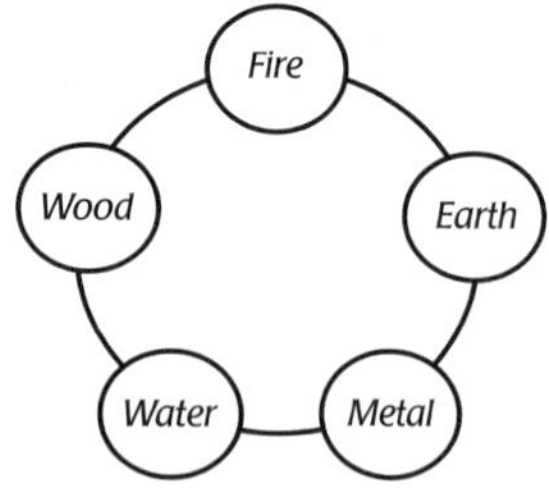

Reflections

January 29

There are many schools of thought when it comes to using foods to cure illness or to support different organs. Henry Lu, in *Chinese System of Food Cures*, writes that foods with an "inward movement" are good in winter. Foods with an inward movement can ease the bowels and reduce abdominal swelling. These foods have a cold energy and can be of two different flavors—bitter or salty. Clams (salt and freshwater), crabs, hops, kelp, lettuce, salt, and seaweed are all foods that create this inward movement.

In addition, salty foods have the specific action in the body of softening hardness, and, thus, are useful in treating tuberculosis of the lymph nodes and other symptoms that involve the hardening of muscles or glands. Other foods classified as salty and, therefore, nourishing to the Kidneys, are: abalone; barley; chives; clams; crabs; cuttlefish; duck; ham; kelp; milk; oysters; pork; seagrass; and seaweed. Finally, there are additional foods that are neither salty nor cold, yet are traditionally believed to act on the Kidneys: black sesame seed; black soybean; caraway; carp; chicken egg yolk; cinnamon bark; cloves; dill seed; fennel; grape; grapefruit peel; mutton; plums; stringbeans; tangerines; and walnuts.

Exercise

Eat a handful of walnuts today, or bake a loaf of date-nut bread.

Write your reflections . . .

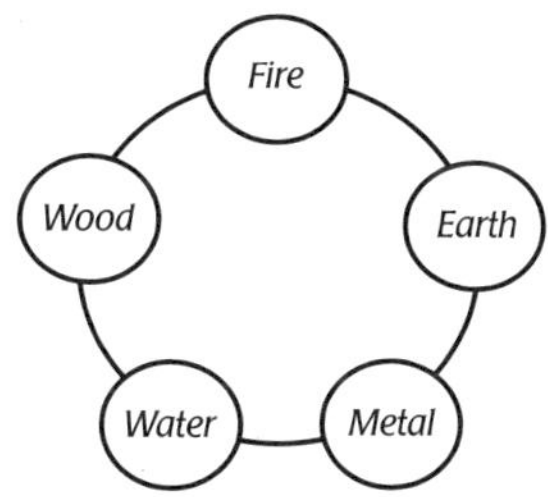

Reflections

January 30

"Black is the color of the North... and its smell is putrid..."

- Nei Jing

The odor associated with the Water element and the season of Winter is putrid (although the *Nei Jing* calls it "rotten and evil"). This is an odor that can be detected on someone who is out of balance in their Water energies, and it can sometimes be quite strong. It is not body odor but a distinct smell having to do with the state of balance of the Kidney and Bladder energies. It is often subtle and is usually disguised by perfumes, soaps, and deodorants.

Odors are very difficult to describe, so it is usually necessary to liken them to smells with which most people are familiar. Putrid can smell "like stagnant water," "like stale urine," or "like a faint whiff of ammonia." All of these connections are very apt, since stagnant water and urine are very clear metaphors for blocked Water energy, and since urine is definitely connected to the Kidneys!

Exercise

Practice smelling for the Element odors by sniffing the backs of peoples' necks when you hug them.

Write your reflections . . .

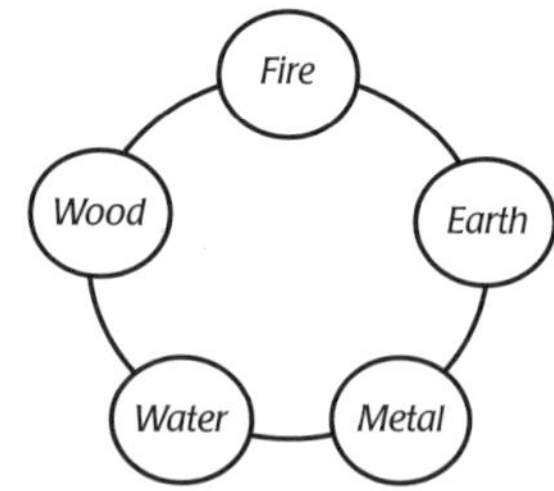

Reflections

January 31

"...in regard to the kidneys the secretions become spittle."

- Nei Jing

The fluid secretion associated with Winter and the Water element is spittle, or saliva. The Chinese considered saliva to be two distinct secretions, produced by and related to two different energies, Earth and Water. The saliva associated with Water has to do with the teeth, which makes sense because the teeth are governed by the Water element. This saliva bathes your teeth and gums continuously, lubricating the processes of eating, chewing, swallowing, and speaking. Dryness of the mouth, the oversecretion of saliva, or drooling are all symptoms that could point to an imbalance in the Water energy.

In the Winter season, you may notice a change in the amount or consistency of your spittle—indoor heating tends to be very drying of all secretions. It may be necessary to drink more fluids to counteract this drying tendency, and also to avoid drying foods that could promote the drying up of bodily fluids, such as coffee and wine. The saliva constantly washing your mouth rinses away bacteria and protects your teeth and gums from disease.

Exercise

Drink eight 8-oz. glasses of water today.

Write your reflections . . .

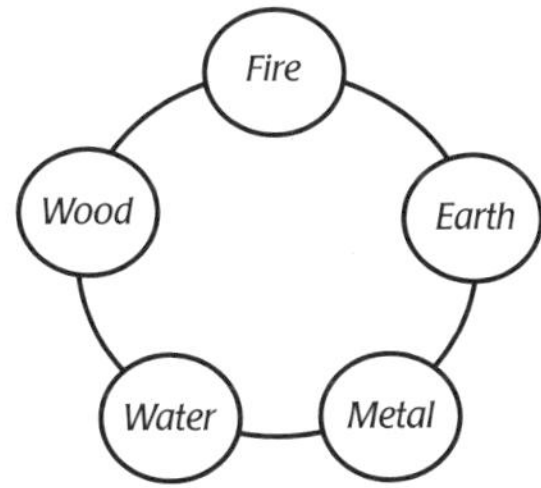

Reflections

February 1

Stopping by Woods on a Snowy Evening

Whose woods these are I think I know.
His house is in the village though;
He will not see me stopping here
To watch his woods fill up with snow.

My little horse must think it queer
To stop without a farmhouse near
Between the woods and frozen lake
The darkest evening of the year.

He gives his harness bells a shake
To ask if there is some mistake.
The only other sound's the sweep
Of easy wind and downy flake.

The woods are lovely, dark and deep.
But I have promises to keep,
And miles to go before I sleep,
And miles to go before I sleep.

- Robert Frost

Exercise

If you don't live where there's snow, take a trip north for a vacation. Walk in the snowy woods and come in to a roaring fire.

Write your reflections . . .

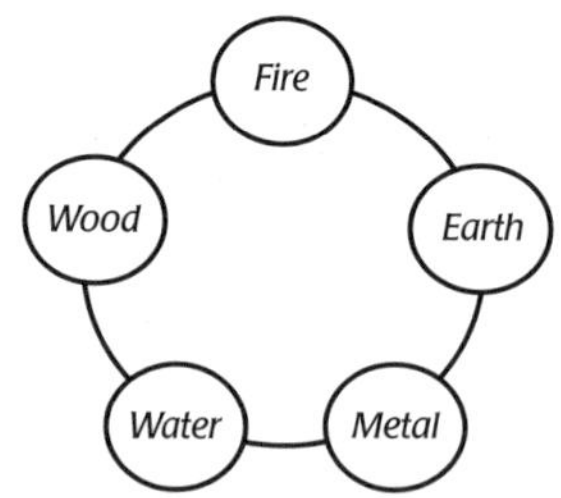

Reflections

February 2

The Symptoms of Inner Peace

Author Unknown (but still very much appreciated)

1. A tendency to think and act deliberately, rather than from fears based on past experiences.
2. An unmistakable ability to enjoy each moment.
3. A loss of interest in judging others.
4. A loss of interest in judging self.
5. A loss of interest in conflict.
6. A loss of interest in interpreting the actions of others.
7. A loss of ability to worry.
8. Frequent, overwhelming episodes of appreciation.
9. Contented feelings of connectedness with others and nature.
10. Frequent attacks of smiling through the heart.
11. Increasing susceptibility to kindness offered, and the uncontrollable urge to reciprocate.
12. An increasing tendency to allow things to unfold, rather than resisting and manipulating.

Exercise

When you come upon a saying of true wisdom, write it on a piece of paper and tape it to your mirror.

Write your reflections . . .

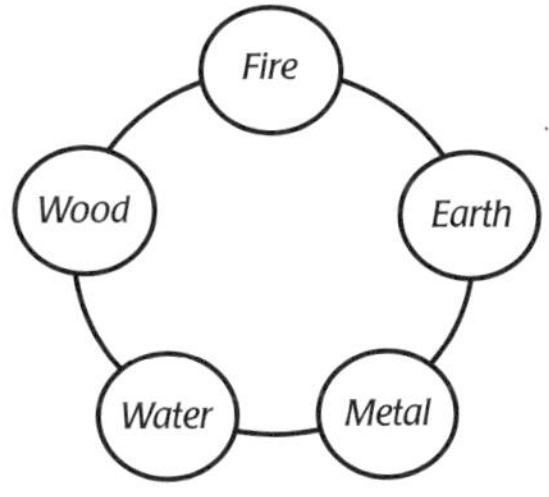

February 3

"The three months of Winter are called the period of closing and storing....

"The kidneys....are the natural organ for storing away...."

- Nei Jing

In Winter, you should rest as much as possible in order to store up energy for the following Spring. In this, take your cue from Nature, where Winter is when much of life hibernates and goes underground. This time of storage is an essential aspect of life, which cannot be ignored if you want to have good health: "Those who disobey (the laws of Winter) will suffer an injury of the kidneys (testicles); for them Spring will bring impotence, and they will produce little."—*Nei Jing*. Many of us have had the experience of greeting Spring with groans instead of cheers because we don't have the energy to respond to that quickening.

Exercise

Go into your basement and take inventory of what you have stored there. If you don't have a basement, take inventory of your biggest closet. Does what you have stored represent an asset or a liability?

Write your reflections . . .

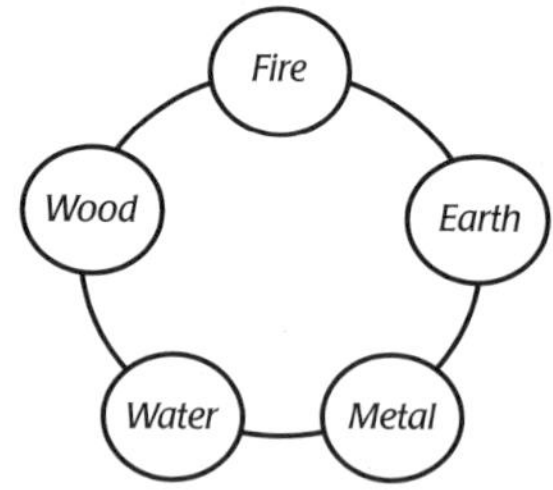

Reflections

February 4

In addition to our ordinary energy, our Kidneys house our Essence—the special, pre-natal energy that is the well or source governing birth, growth, reproduction, and development. This Essence determines our basic constitution, strength, and vitality, and is the basis of sexual life, including the formation of sperm in men and ova in women. It determines the rate of our growth and development into sexual maturity, and the timing of everything from the loss of baby teeth to the onset of old age. When this energy is depleted, it is necessary to do more than rest to replenish it. Good diet, herbs, and special energy-building exercises such as qi gong or tai chi are necessary to create and store Essence.

Exercise

Stand with your feet a shoulder-width apart, toes pointing forward, knees slightly bent. Let your hands hang loosely by your sides and drop your shoulders. Imagine that, like a puppet, your whole body is hanging, suspended by a string from the ceiling. Breathe calmly and naturally. Stand for up to five minutes—at first, it may be difficult to do even two minutes! This simple exercise is the basis for many energy-storing practices of the Chinese masters.

Write your reflections . . .

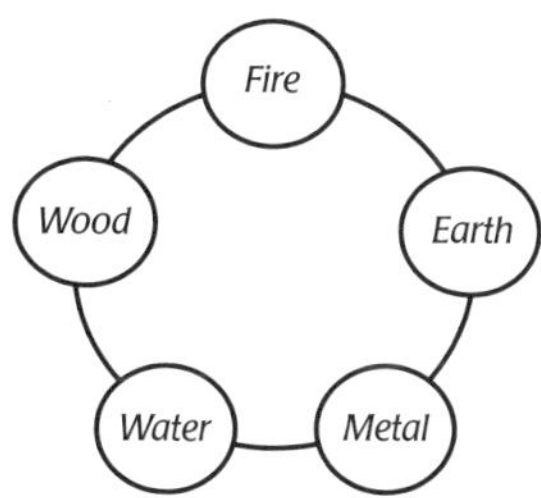

February 5

In February
All of a sudden there's a lot more light
And it's a warm light - snow melts off the roof,
The first lambs are born in the barn cellar,
The hens start laying, the mare comes into season,
And I notice that the geraniums at the window
Have pushed their stalks up eight inches
And covered them with brick-pink blossoms.

Every day I wake up earlier
And my bones crack as I sit up and stretch.
When I poke my boot through a drift in the field
I find clover growing green beneath it.
Now the sap is running
And when I drive my sleigh up to the wood lot
I see three young maple bushes
Deeply scored with new bear scratches.

Oh warm light,
Couldn't you have waited a little longer?
How safe we were in the dead of winter,
How gently we dreamed,
How beautiful it was to sleep under the snow!

- Kate Barnes, *Talking in your Sleep*

Exercise

Look for some early signs of Spring. Are you happy about them, or do you also want them to wait a little longer?

Write your reflections . . .

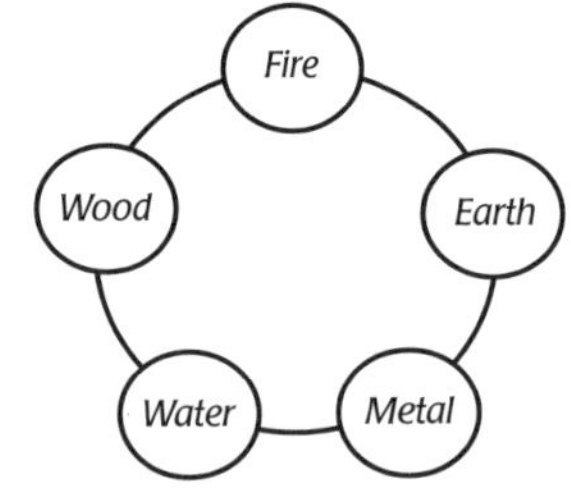

Reflections

February 6

"...to stand up for a long time is hurtful to the bones..."

- Nei Jing

The *Nei Jing* talks about the "five exertions" that are hurtful to the body. These are five common activities, which, if done to excess, can cause imbalances in the system and ultimately harm one of the five "organs" or energetic spheres of the body. In the case of the Water element, standing for a long time can be hurtful to the bones. This does not mean that waiting in line for a long time or going to a cocktail party will harm you, but perhaps working a job that requires you to stand for eight hours a day could.

This makes sense if you think about what happens to your body when you are forced to stand for a long period of time. For most people, this means they begin to notice their backs hurting. The lower back is home of the Kidneys, the organs associated with the Water element.

Exercise

Get up earlier than usual and do 10 minutes of stretching exercises.

Write your reflections . . .

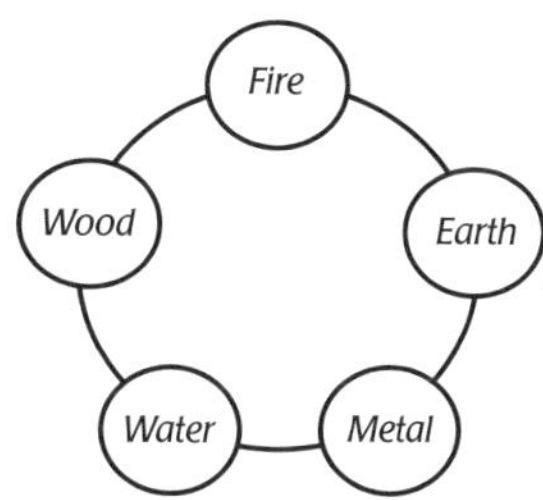

February 7

Prolonged standing can drain the energy from the Kidney and Bladder meridians, which run across the lower back and down the legs. Eventually, if someone is forced to stand for work over a period of months or years, he or she can develop back problems such as compressed discs in the lower spine, or sciatica. On a deeper level, if the Kidney energy becomes drained, it will fail to nourish the bones, and the bones will become weak and brittle.

Try to vary your activities throughout the day so that you don't spend the majority of your time doing any one thing. If your job requires standing for long periods, make sure you sit down, walk, or even lie down on breaks to create more balance. When you are standing, try to vary your posture and positions as much as possible to allow for better circulation of energy in the body.

Exercise

Practice yoga poses that stretch the spine and, therefore, also stretch the Bladder meridian. A yoga proberb says, "You are as young as your spine is flexible."

Write your reflections . . .

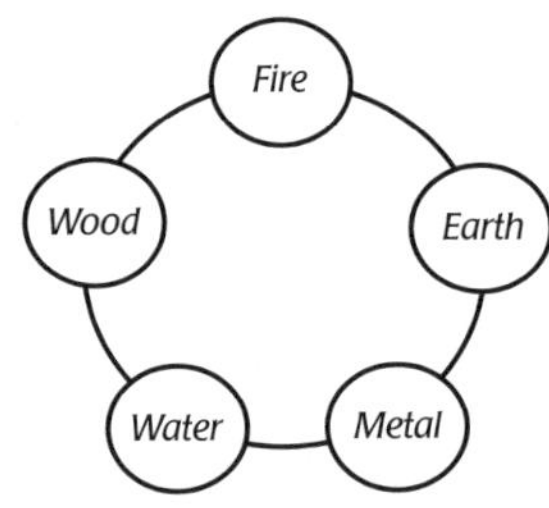

Reflections

February 8

There is an old Taoist healing practice that uses the breath and certain specific sounds to maintain balance in the different organs of the body. Mantak Chia, a Taoist master teaching in the United States, calls this practice "The Six Healing Sounds," and says that doing these exercises every day will enhance energy flow through the organs, relax tension, and enhance the smooth running of the body.

Each sound is associated with a season of the year and with its corresponding organ. For Winter (and for the corresponding organ of the Kidneys), the exercise is as follows:

1. Sit upright in a chair, with feet on the floor.
2. Pull legs together and lean forward, clasping your hands around your knees. Lift your head up slightly, staring upward. Keep elbows straight. Inhale.
3. Pull abdomen tightly in (toward the kidneys) as you exhale. Make the sound Woooooooo with rounded lips, as if you're blowing out a candle.
4. When you've fully exhaled, sit erect, close your eyes, put your hands on your thighs, palms up, separate your legs, and breathe normally, concentrating on your kidneys.

Write your reflections . . .

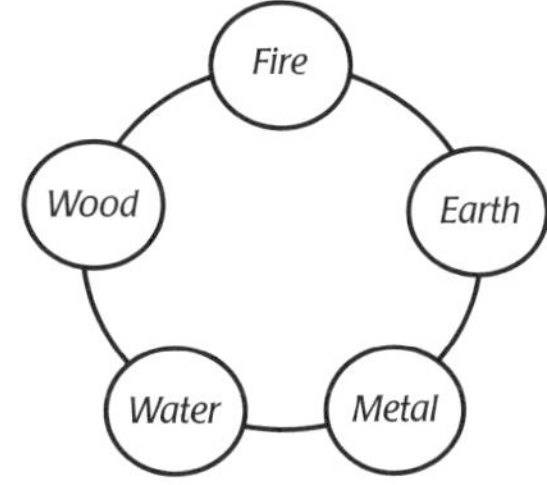

February 9

A Time of Waiting

The moment comes when my sound senses
Warn me to keep the pot at a quiet simmer,
Conclude no rash decision, enter into
No random friendships, check the runaway tongue
And fix my mind in a close caul of doubt -
Which is more difficult, maybe, than to face
Night-long assaults of lurking furies.

The pool lies almost empty; I watch it nursed
By a thin stream. Such idle intervals
Are from waning moon to the new - a moon always
Holds the cords of my heart. Then patience, hands;
Dabble your nerveless fingers in the shallows;
A time shall come when she has need of them.

- Robert Graves

Exercise

If you have to wait for something today, imagine that the "idle interval" is a gift of time for storing up energy for when you have need of it.

Write your reflections . . .

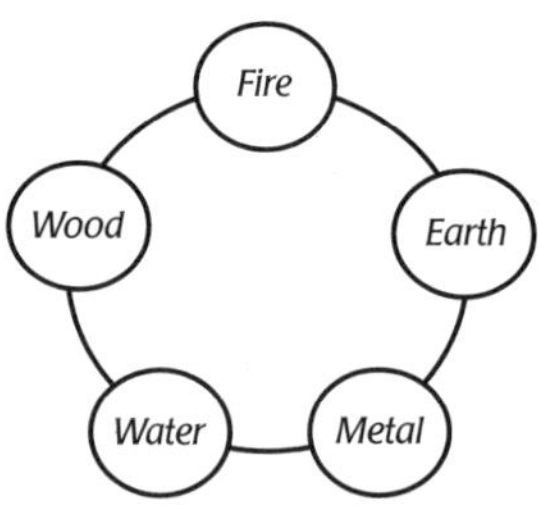

Reflections

February 10

Under heaven nothing is more soft
and yielding than water.
Yet for attacking the solid and strong,
nothing is better;
It has no equal.
The weak can overcome the strong;
The supple can overcome the stiff.

- Lao Tzu,
Tao Te Ching

This quote from the Chinese classic, the *Tao Te Ching*, is poetry that operates on several levels at once. On one level, it is stating the well-known natural fact that water can wear away stone. On another level, it is talking about the application of this principle in human affairs. It suggests that a soft and yielding approach can actually prevail over a strong or "stiff" one. We have all seen in practice how sometimes, a person who approaches a problem or confrontation in a conciliatory way will win over his opponent, while someone who is hard and unyielding will just run into a wall.

Exercise

Read the *Tao Te Ching* to learn about the concept of yielding. Or better yet, sign up for a class in Tai Chi.

Write your reflections . . .

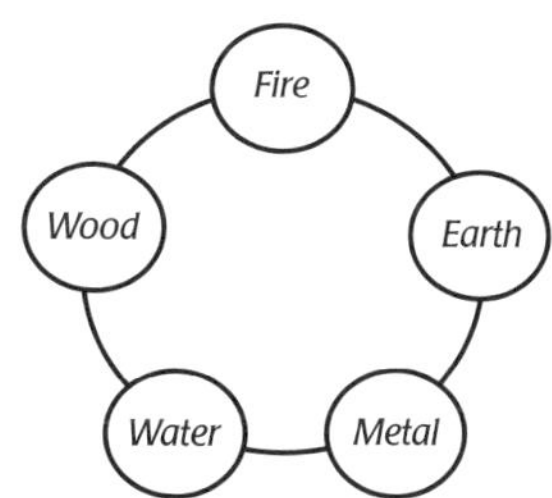

Reflections

February 11

The "yin" or "watery" approach to conflict is also the basis for some of the Chinese martial arts, such as Tai Ch'i Chuan, in which the true Master is one who is the most "soft" and yielding, and yet who cannot be pushed over. These ideas are very foreign to our Western ears, since here in the West we believe in bigger, stronger, harder, more powerful, more aggressive. Many people have been confounded to see big, strapping American men being tossed around a room by tiny, frail-looking old Chinese Tai Ch'i masters, who themselves seem to elude all efforts to push or hit them. Here, we see the superior strength of Water in being soft and yielding, yet able to overcome the "stiff." Focusing on being soft and yielding can put us in touch with this unique aspect of Water energy in ourselves.

Exercise

Do this with a partner: stand and face each other about a foot apart, knees slightly bent, with your arms at your sides. Take turns reaching out with one hand and trying to push the other person's shoulder, while the person being pushed tries first to be "stiff" and then to be "soft and yielding."

Write your reflections . . .

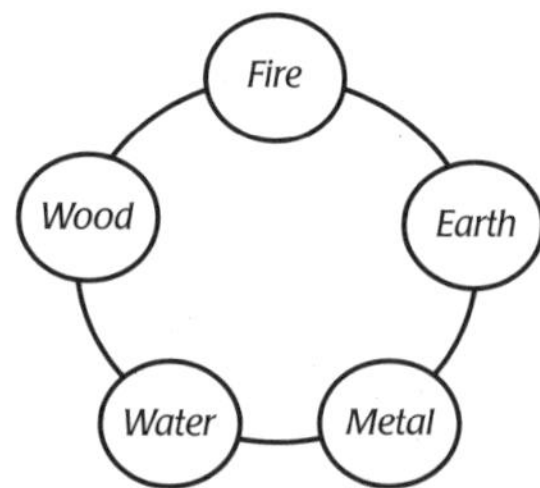

Reflections

February 12

Water, water, see the water flow
Glancing, dancing, see the water flow
Oh, river of changes, teach me the lesson
of flowing.

- Incredible String Band,
The Hangman's Beautiful Daughter

At one time or another, we have all felt the need to "Stop the world—I want to get off!" It seems that time and events are moving too rapidly, and we are not able to change quickly enough to keep up with them. When our Water energy is depleted, we are more likely to feel this need to resist the flow, the tides of time. The lesson of "going with the flow" is one that is difficult, with our need to plan, to control things, to keep things predictable; or alternatively, our eagerness to "get on with it," to be efficient and busy, to "push the river." Just allowing ourselves to flow with the situation is not an option that many of us consider.

Exercise

Today, take the path of least resistance, like water, and flow with what life brings you.

Write your reflections . . .

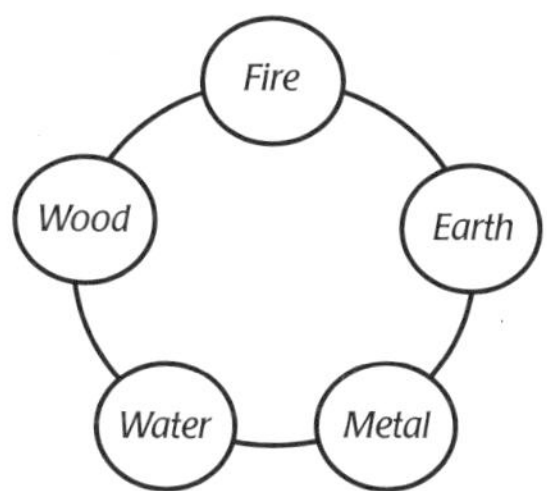

Reflections

February 13

In *The Immense Journey*, Loren Eisley describes allowing himself to float on his back down the Platte River in the western United States, feeling himself to be one with the river:

> *"I had the sensation of sliding down the vast tilted face of the continent. It was then that I felt the cold needles of the alpine springs at my fingertips, and the warmth of the Gulf pulling me southward. Moving with me, leaving its taste upon my mouth and spouting under me in dancing springs of sand, was the immense body of the continent itself, flowing like the river was flowing, grain, by grain, mountain by mountain, down to the sea."*

Exercise

Dress warmly and go walking by the nearest stream or river. Drop a winter twig in the water and watch it out of sight, imagining its journey to the sea.

Write your reflections . . .

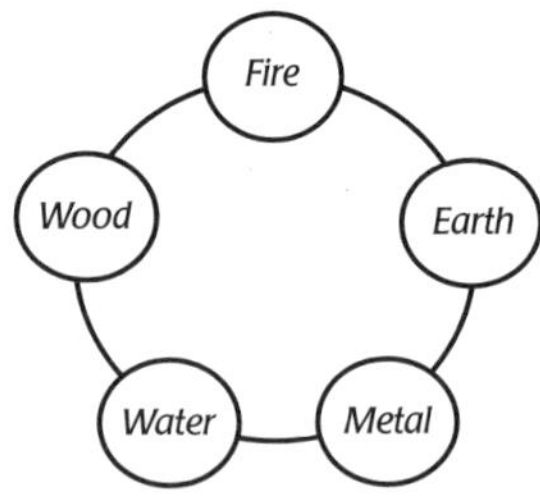

Reflections

February 14

"Many of us spend time and energy trying to be something that we are not. But this is a move against soul, because individuality rises out of the soul as water rises out of the depths of the earth."

- Thomas Moore,
Care of the Soul

One of the spiritual dilemmas of an imbalance in the Water element is a lack of purpose in life. Because the Kidneys, the Yin organs of the Water element, store the Essence, they also are associated with what is deepest and most essential in us. The Chinese say that the Kidneys are the root of vital destiny for each particular life in its becoming, and if we are in touch with our own Essence, our purpose in life is clear—it is to live out the destiny inherent in our natures. An acorn can only become an oak tree—it cannot change its mind or decide that being a willow tree is better. Humans have the capacity to choose a course; in the richness of choice and possibility, we can forget that becoming a "tree" is what life is all about.

Exercise

Do you know your life's purpose? Can you articulate what that is?

Write your reflections . . .

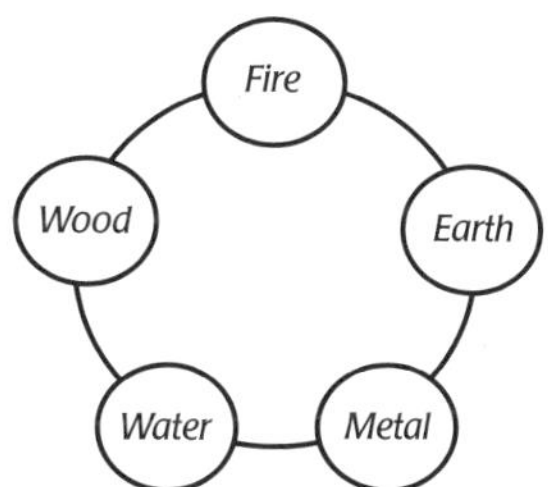

Reflections

February 15

Many people nowadays are cut off from their own deepest essence. Trapped by busyness and a modern lifestyle centered around acquisition and consumption, they never dip below the surface to experience their own essential selves. Decisions about career, how to spend their time and energy, and what is important and valuable are based on superficial criteria such as money, prestige, and "what the neighbors think."

When we know and live out of our true essence, then our purpose becomes clear. For example, if I know that in my essence I am sensitive and empathetic to other people's pain, I am closer to my true purpose if I become a doctor or nurse than I am if I become an accountant or a policeman. On the other hand, if in my essence there is a passion for justice and a strong belief in fairness, my purpose might be fighting for some cause. When you know yourself, the path that resonates becomes more clear.

Exercise

Think deeply and come up with one word that defines your essence.

Write your reflections . . .

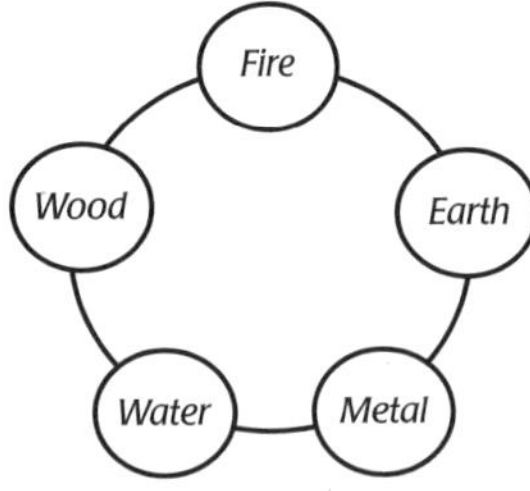

February 16

The woods are lovely, dark and deep,
But I have promises to keep,
And miles to go before I sleep,
And miles to go before I sleep.

- Robert Frost

Many of us have felt, like Frost, the beauty and peacefulness of snow-filled woods and the pull toward a deep, dreamless "sleep," far from the responsibilities and pressures of our lives. Sometimes, on winter days especially, we'd like to just curl up and hibernate, like the bears and squirrels. In the hectic pace of modern life (we "have promises to keep"), when can we allow ourselves the luxury of sinking down into our deepest selves, the peaceful abode of our essence? Here is our connection to existence, to past and to future, and to our deepest hopes and dreams. When we can bathe in this deep, watery space, we can be filled from the inexhaustible wellspring of life, and come up replenished, refreshed, and re-inspired with new ideas and new energy.

Exercise

Take a luxurious bubble bath, or add some essential oil of lavender to your bath water to relax and refresh your senses.

Write your reflections . . .

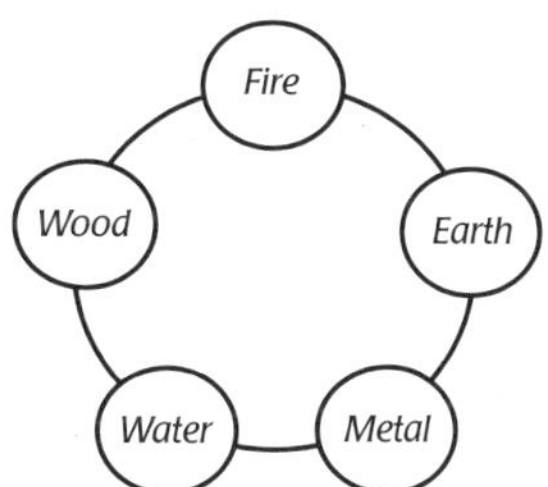

Reflections

February 17

Obviously, none of us can really hibernate all winter, so we need to develop ways of integrating rest and replenishment into our daily lives. This means more than just collapsing into bed, exhausted, every night after working 12- or 14-hour days.

One way is to schedule a regular "time-out" for yourself during the day, in which you allow yourself to "tune out" all of the demands, promises, schedules, and lists, and just sink into yourself. You could simply take a nap, or put on headphones and listen to music, or meditate, or pray. But these moments of deep peace will give you the stamina to travel the "miles to go before I sleep."

Exercise

Allow yourself to take a nap sometime today. Give yourself permission to rest on your journey of miles and promises.

Write your reflections . . .

Reflections

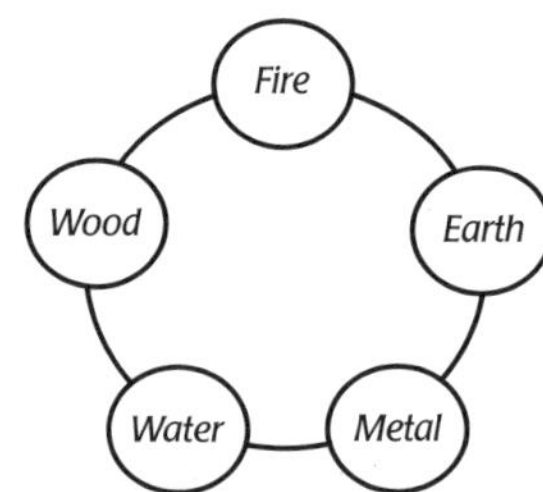

February 18

To make a prairie it takes a
clover and one bee -
One clover, and a bee,
And revery.
The revery alone will do
If bees are few.

- Emily Dickinson

When you're feeling "dry," when ideas won't flow and you can't force your mind to come up with new solutions, try quieting your mind in meditation. As you try to still the ceaseless flow of thoughts and images, they may actually become more intense, at first. As you tap into the "fertile void," you open yourself up to the boundless ocean of thoughts and ideas that your focused striving has prevented you from reaching. Here, new ideas arise spontaneously, with no effort, because it is a law of Nature that out of Water comes Wood —that new life will always rise up in the Spring, nourished by the Waters of Winter.

Exercise

Sit in a comfortable position with your back straight and your eyes lightly closed, having loosened any tight clothing. Focus your attention on your breathing, and follow the cycle through inhalation and exhalation, noting the points at which one phase changes into another.

Write your reflections . . .

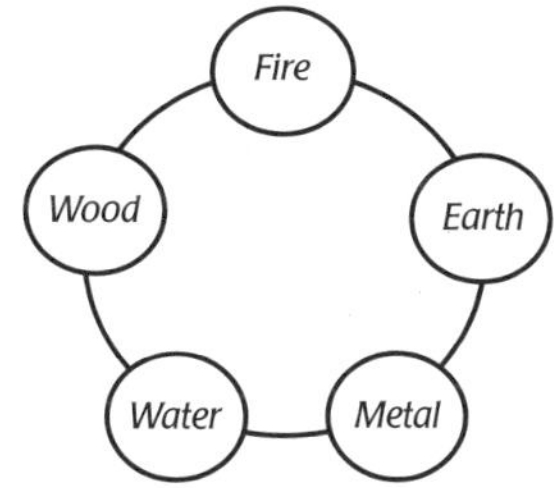

Reflections

February 19

"You do not need to leave your room. Remain sitting at your table and listen. Do not even listen, simply wait. Do not even wait, be quite still and solitary. The world will freely offer itself to you to be unmasked, it has no choice, it will roll in ecstasy at your feet."

- Franz Kafka

Every writer and creative artist knows the value of fallow times, the times between creations when it seems that nothing is happening, or the time just spent doodling or staring into space. As Somerset Maugham said, "The hardest thing about being a writer is explaining to your wife that when you're just sitting and staring out the window, you're working!" During these quiet moments, we connect with the fullness of our potential, to the realm where all thoughts and ideas have their origin. Be patient during these Winter times, with others as well as yourself, to allow your mind to be bathed and revitalized in that Water, and then trust that Spring will come.

Exercise

Spend one day without the radio, T.V., or stereo on. Allow your house or apartment to be silent. Notice how you feel.

Write your reflections . . .

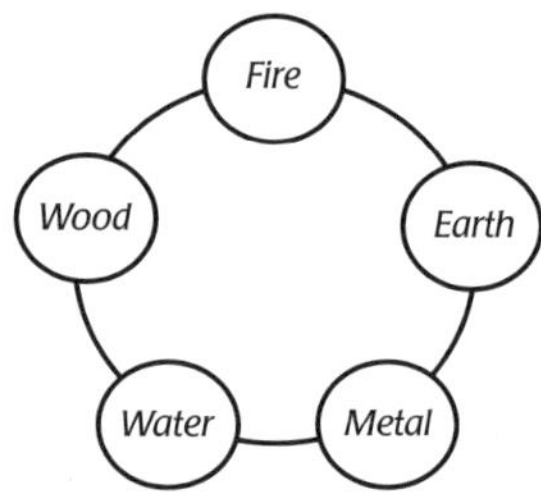

Reflections

February 20

All things by immortal power
Near or far
Hiddenly
To each other linked are
That thou canst not stir a flower
Without troubling of a star.

- Francis Thompson

I watched an acorn fall into a pool. The ripples spread out in a perfect circle, and moved quickly across the surface of the water, expanding out and out until every square inch of the surface of the pool had been touched, all the way out to the walls. When the ripples hit the closest wall, they bounced back and began a counter-ripple moving in the opposite direction, as the same thing happened to the ripples reaching the opposite wall—so that soon there were ripples and counter-ripples meeting and crossing from all four directions. So much movement and activity from one little acorn! A complex web of ripples in a beautiful moire pattern filled the pool for a while, then gradually subsided back to stillness.

Exercise

Drop a pebble into a still pond, and watch the ripples. Or go outside on a clear, cold night and look at the stars.

Write your reflections . . .

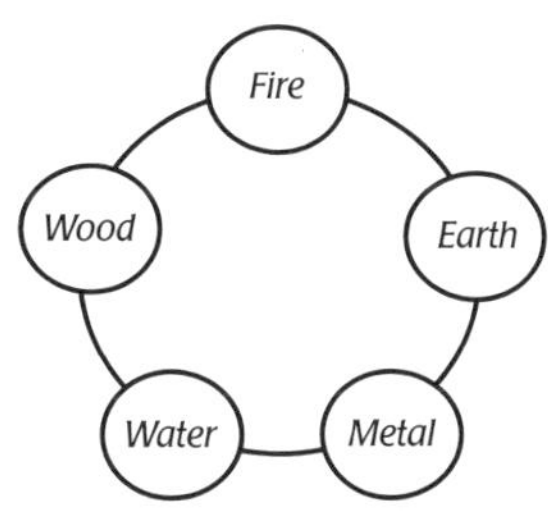

February 21

"Water sets the example for the
right conduct under such circumstances.
It flows on and on, and merely fills up
all the places through which it flows;
it does not shrink from any dangerous spot
nor from any plunge, and nothing can make it
lose its own essential nature."

- *I Ching*, Hexagram 29, K'an

Water energy is infinitely adaptable, "filling up all the places" —yet it retains its own essential nature. In our lives, we are often called upon to adapt to changing circumstances, to different conditions, and yet, we want to keep our individual integrity. This quotation shows that if we remain true to ourselves, to our own essential natures, we can flow through "any dangerous spot." Like Water, we can flow into many differently shaped containers, yet still be Water. This contradictory ability to be flowing, yet retain integrity, is the strength of the Water person.

Exercise

Imagine that you are stranded on a desert island. What three things do you absolutely need to have with you?

Write your reflections . . .

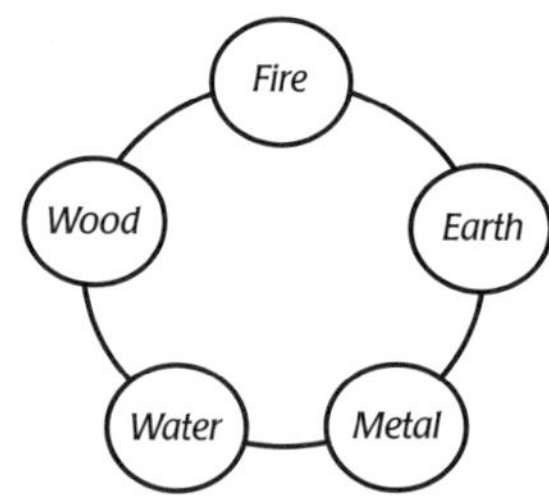

Reflections

February 22

"...for verily I say unto you, If ye have faith as a grain of mustard seed, ye shall say unto this mountain, Remove hence to yonder place; and it shall remove; and nothing shall be impossible unto you."

- St. Matthew, 18:20
King James Version

Faith is the spiritual quality of the Water element. Like water, faith is deep, enduring, and unchanging. It abides when all logical reasoning tells us the opposite. It is implacable in the face of adversity, attack, and belittlement. It is a stubbornness of the heart to believe against all odds.

Faith implies a resonance at the deepest level of our beings with the rightness of a particular belief. But how many of us in this culture have ever delved into this deepest level? Only by experiencing the depths of our beings, can we know what is true for us, and what there is for us to have faith in.

Exercise

Get up at dawn and watch the sun rise. Watch what happens to the frost.

Write your reflections . . .

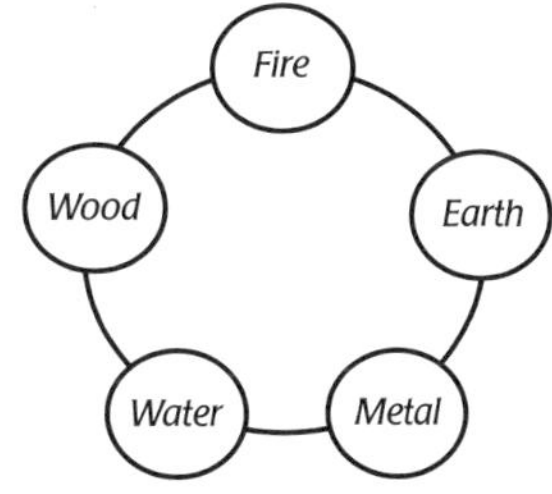

February 23

We think of the word "faith" mostly in connection with religious feelings—witness the Biblical quote on the preceding page. There are many other sayings about faith in the Christian tradition: "O ye of little faith;" "Faith, hope, and charity;" "Faith of our Fathers;" etc. Many of us profess to have no feelings of religious faith—it's not so much that we've <u>lost</u> our faith, as that we've never really had it to begin with.

To be "faithful," to "keep faith with" someone, implies that we stick by them, no matter what. Like water in a mountain lake, faith is clear to the bottom. It has the quality of longevity, of lasting—and these are qualities that are traditionally associated in Chinese thought with the Kidneys, the organs of the Water element. It also has the connotation of great power and strength, as in the phrase, "Faith can move mountains." The power of faith in healing is legendary—in one famous story from the Bible Jesus heals a blind man and says, "Thy faith hath made thee whole."

Exercise

Think of three things you have complete faith in.

Write your reflections . . .

Reflections

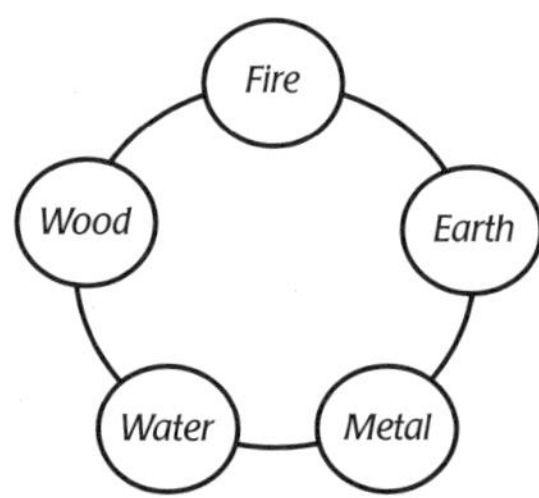

February 24

"Mighty oaks from little acorns grow."

- Anonymous

This quote is a perfect one to illustrate the power of the seed—that an acorn, which is a tiny, self-contained unit, has within it the power and potential to become a mighty oak. The energy of Water is like the energy of a seed—it is all potential, with very little manifesting. In the winter, all we have are the seeds of future growth—we must wait for spring to see anything above ground.

The Chinese think of a baby in its mother's womb as a kind of seed. Everything is present at the moment of conception for who the future human being will become—all that is needed is time and proper nurturing for the baby to grow into an adult. The unique combination of qualities that make up each person are already there in the "seed," and the living of one's life is the way that each person's potential becomes actualized.

Exercise

What is your lifetime's ambition—and why?

Write your reflections . . .

Reflections

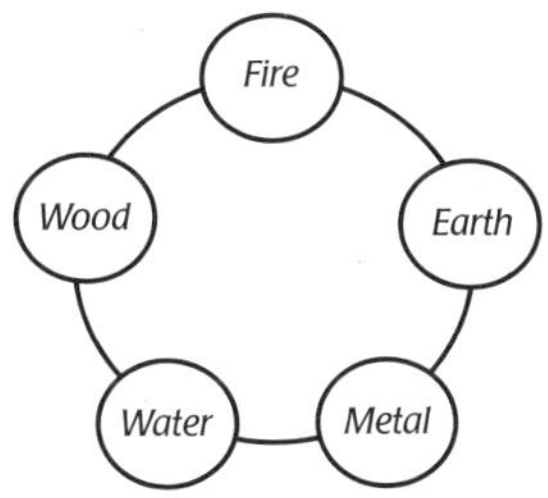

February 25

The unique thing about being human is that we get to have some control and choice in the manifesting of our potential. An acorn has no choice but to become an oak tree, and a puppy has no choice but to become a dog, with the same instincts as all other dogs. But a human being has an enormous potential to become many things, and we get to choose which aspect of our potential we grow into.

Of course, any gardener knows that a seed needs the right soil, the right amount of water, the proper temperature, and sunlight in order to thrive. We all know the Biblical story of the seeds that fall on stony ground, or that are eaten by birds. Most seeds do not get to grow, and not all human beings get to live out their potential. But it is important to recognize that there is tremendous power in the potential of a seed, and this is the power of the Water element.

Exercise

Draw up a family tree, as far back as you know; note on it how old your ancestors were when they died, and what illnesses were prevalent. This gives you an idea of the nature of your "ancestral qi."

Write your reflections . . .

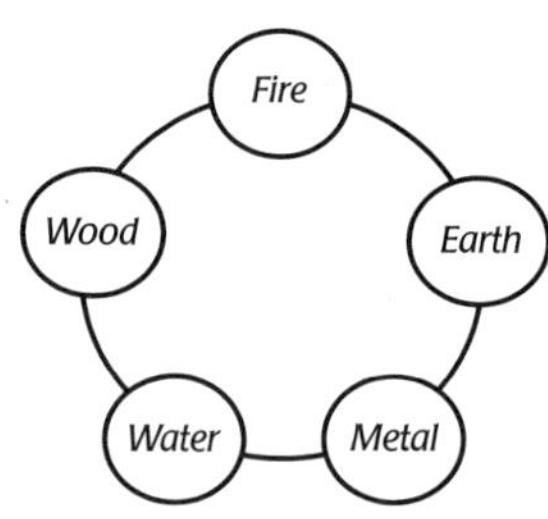

Reflections

February 26

"...and of the musical notes they create the note yu (羽)..."

- Nei Jing

The musical note corresponding to the Winter season and to the Water energy is yu, one of the five notes in the Chinese scale. A musical note, like a particular smell, cannot be explained in words—we can only get the flavor of it by likening it to another sound in nature with which everyone is familiar. Yu is said to correspond to "cloudbursts or rain in spring and summer."

Chinese historians trace the origins of the five notes to the ancient practice of war divination used to ascertain the state of the armies before battle. In this system, each sound quality represented a different aspect of the army's energy or qi : "If it is yi (yu), the soldiers are soft and little glory will be gained."

Exercise

Play a recording of a rainstorm and notice how you feel.

Write your reflections . . .

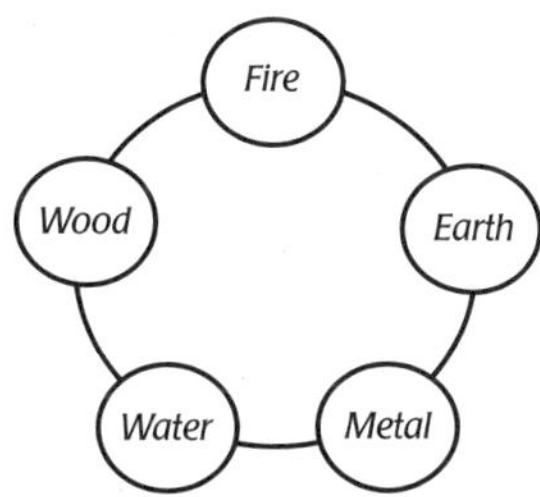

Reflections

February 27

The skin head drum is the instrument associated with winter: "In winter, the most solemn ceremony was the solstice and the drum was central to it. However, the drum also gave the signal to advance in battle." Thus, the tones of the instrument produced certain emotional and martial effects: "The sound of the stand-drums and the tambourines is rowdy. Boldness (of spirit) sets up (physical) activity. Physical activity sets the people marching. When the man of breeding listens to the sound of drums and tambourines he thinks of great generals leading out armies."

The knowledge that specific tones can produce standard associations or moods can be used for healing as well as for war divination! In fact, the use of music for healing is an ancient practice, but more recently people have been experimenting with using single tones or frequencies to stimulate healing of specific parts of the body. Recordings are now available of music based on these principles, to enhance the proper circulation of qi in the body and to counter diseases related to the different changes of seasons.

Exercise

Find one of these recordings and play the section for Water. A good one is *Elements of Rejuvenation*, by Merlin's Magic, distributed by Inner World Music, USA.

Write your reflections . . .

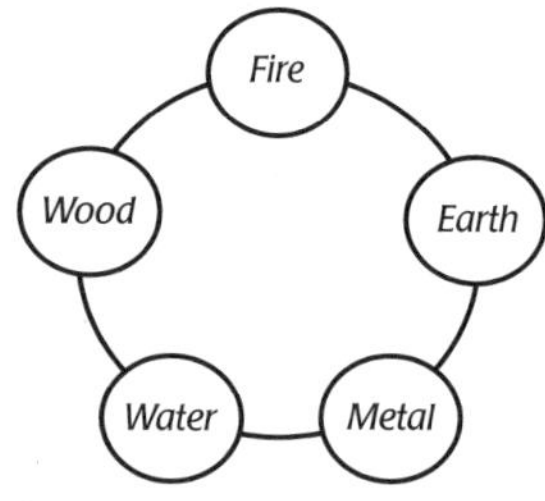

Reflections

February 28

"In terms of overall morphology, the Water hand is short and spatulate, with short fingers."

- Yves Requena,
Morphotypological Hand Diagnosis in Acupuncture

One of the things that a Chinese doctor examines is the shape of the hand. Each of the five elements has a particular shape of hand associated with it, and the Water hand is short with short fingers and puffy skin. In fact, the skin of the Water hand is loose and soft, on the back of the hand as well as on the palm, and often feels moist as well. The underside of the fingers is puffy and soft, and the whole hand has a limp, almost boneless feeling. If your hand is shaped like this, it says that you have an inherited Water constitution.

Exercise

Look at the shape of your hand, the shape of the palm, the length of the fingers, and your fingernails. Do you have a Water hand? Compare it to the hands of your family and friends.

Write your reflections . . .

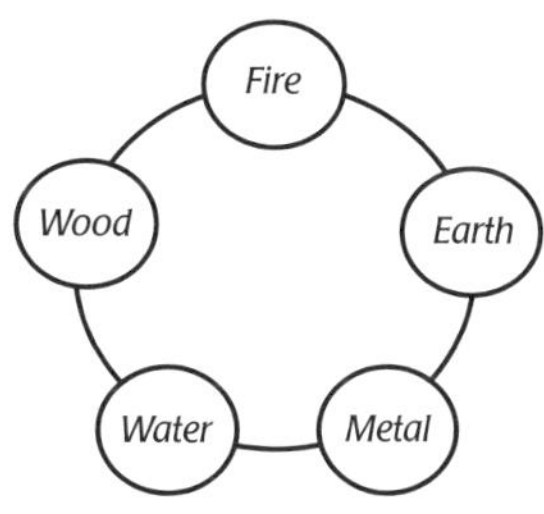

February 29

Puffiness of the skin of the hand gives the impression of an overabundance of skin tissue, a "bagginess," which is particularly noticeable at the knuckles; instead of protruding as knuckles, the bones recede into a paradoxical hollow. If the skin is pinched between thumb and forefinger, then released, the fold of skin will remain pinched and upright. Another characteristic specific to the Water hand is the flatness of the distal phalanx. From the final joint to the base of the nail, the skin is flat and wrinkled, with a curtain-like fold on either side of the base of the fingernail. The wrinkles tend to darken the distal phalanx, which can look quite brownish in color. This is especially noticeable on the little finger.

The Water fingernail is short and flat. Its shape is that of a trapezoid, with the short base toward the hand and the rest of the nail fanning out from it. This fan-shaped growth makes the white at the tip of the nail resemble a crescent moon. In addition, the nail is often soft and fragile, which leads people with Water hands to cut their nails short. If the nail does grow long, it tends to curve downwards slightly as if to protect the end of the finger.

Exercise

If you or someone close to you has a Water hand, notice how many other correspondences to Water energy match up.

Write your reflections . . .

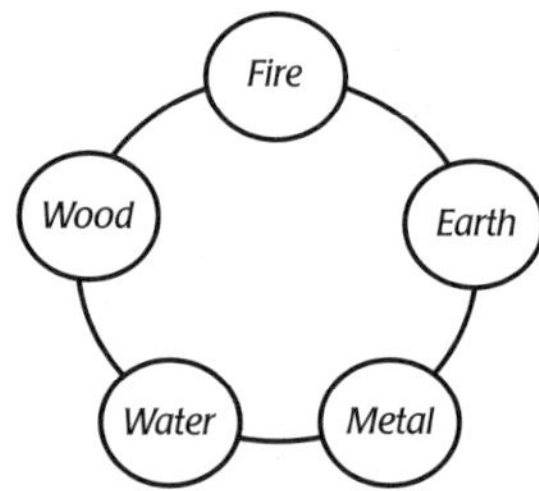

Reflections

March 1

In Winter, the functions of the Kidney and Bladder officials are emphasized. One of the key words used to describe the function of the Bladder is adaptability. If we think about what the physical bladder actually is, it is easier to understand this connection. The bladder is a receptacle, a sac-like, flexible but muscular bag, which receives a continuous dribble of urine from the kidneys. As the urine flows in, the walls of the bladder stretch to store it, until a certain limit is reached. Then the urge to pass the urine, to empty it out of the body, is felt. An average bladder can hold about a pint of urine without serious discomfort.

This quality of adaptability extends to other levels of our being. If personal flexibility is blocked, symptoms may show up in other parts of the body-mind-spirit. For example, sexual intercourse requires flexibility, so problems such as frigidity and impotence could indicate a problem in being expansive. On the mental level, narrow-mindedness may indicate a blocked Bladder meridian.

Exercise

Learn one yoga pose and practice it daily for a week.

Write your reflections . . .

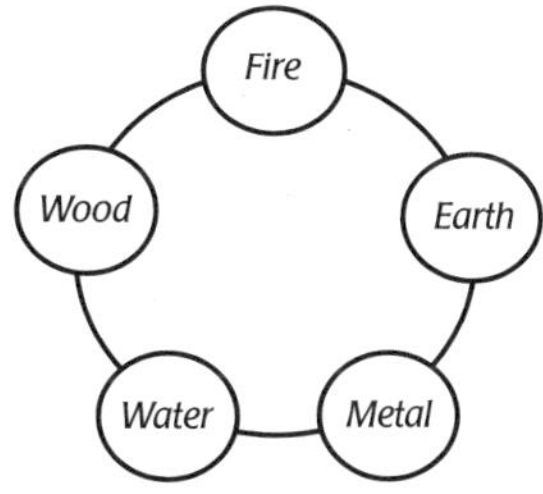

March 2

The highest form of goodness is like water.
Water knows how to benefit all things
without striving with them.
It stays in places loathed by all men.
Therefore, it comes near the Tao.

Hesitant like one wading a stream in winter;
Timid like one afraid of his neighbors on all
sides;
Cautious and courteous like a guest;
Yielding like ice on the point of melting;
Simple like an uncarved block;
Hollow like a cave;
Confused like a muddy pool;
And yet who else could quietly and gradually
evolve from the muddy to the clear?
Who else could slowly but steadily move
from the inert to the living?

- Lao Tzu, *Tao Te Ching*

Exercise

Drink cool water by taking one sip at a time, savoring it, and then swallowing.

Write your reflections . . .

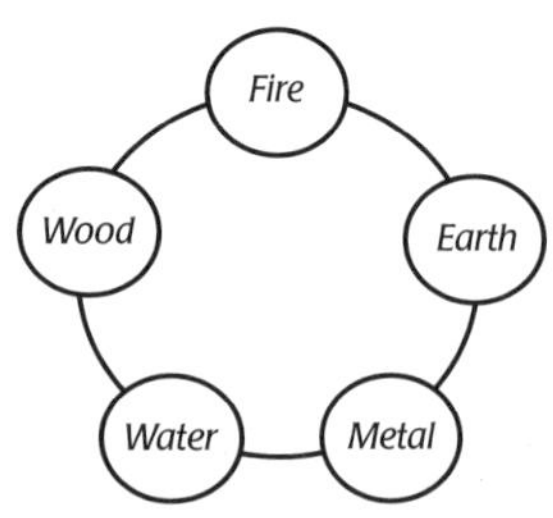

Reflections

March 3

"A healthy person is one who is receptive yet knows her own limits."

- Dianne Connelly

Another function of the Bladder official is that of setting limits. There is a certain amount of flexibility in how much an individual bladder can comfortably hold, but when the limit is reached, the urge to release becomes uncontrollable.

Someone who is rigid, inflexible, contracted or afraid may reach his or her limit very quickly. This person cannot cope with much—he or she reaches a saturation point and then becomes overwhelmed. On the other hand, someone who takes on too much, who allows herself to be talked into things or be intruded upon by others even when she is busy, may not be setting appropriate limits for herself. Knowing your limits enables you to store energy when necessary and to spend it only when appropriate.

Exercise

Go away for the weekend—by yourself. Spend all of the time in your own company.

Write your reflections . . .

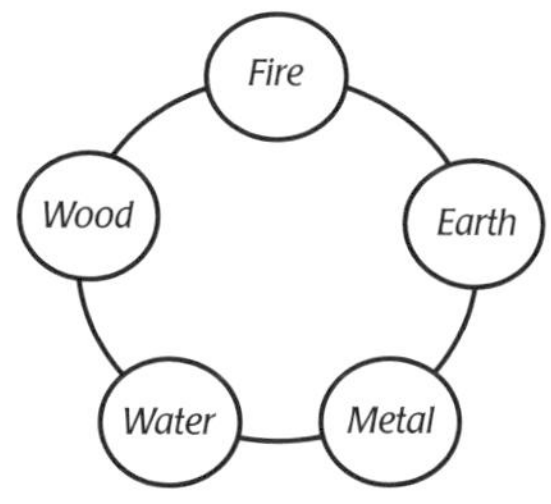

Reflections

March 4

"When the bladder does not function efficiently,
it causes retention of urine;
when it functions without restraint,
it causes copious urination."

- Nei Jing

The Chinese recognized that an imbalance in the functioning of any particular organ or meridian could cause specific physical symptoms. For example, in the quotation above, they clearly delineate specific symptoms pertaining to urination caused by a dysfunction in the Bladder. Another physical symptom related to an imbalance in the Bladder's functioning is low back pain; it makes sense if you realize that the Bladder meridian crosses the lower back several times. Furthermore, the back pain may be from low energy in that meridian, due to the Bladder not fulfilling its function of storing energy. Dry eyes can be another symptom, and again, the Bladder meridian begins in the inner corner of the eye—the dryness could indicate an imbalance in the fluids that the Bladder is supposed to regulate.

Exercise

Tone your bladder and kidneys by drinking a cup of dandelion leaf and kava-kava tea.

Write your reflections . . .

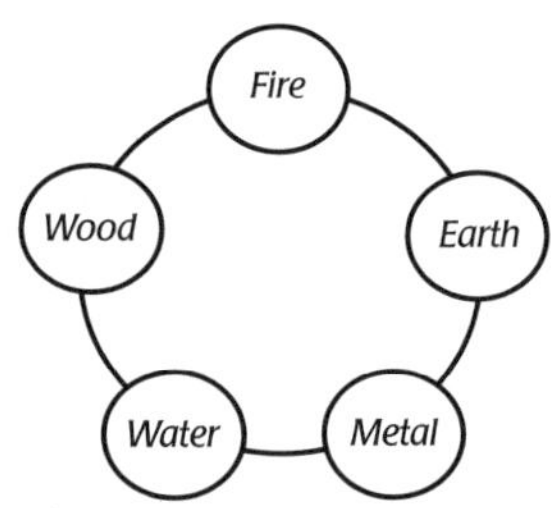

Reflections

March 5

"...the kidneys cause deficiencies which in turn cause sneezing and running at the nose..."

- Nei Jing

There are many physical symptoms that are associated with an imbalance in the Kidneys. Although the root cause of these symptoms may lie elsewhere, nevertheless, there is a correlation between the functioning of the Kidneys and certain physical problems. Many of these symptoms come from a deficiency of energy, which is indicative of the Kidneys not storing up enough energy, for example: exhaustion; impotence; weak sexual energy; ringing in the ears; lumbago; vertigo; and chronic prostate problems. The quotation above indicates that a deficiency in Kidney energy can also lead to problems with the immune system, leading to allergies, rhinitis, and asthma.

Exercise

Stay warm. Conserve your resources by wearing warm clothing and taking in warm food and drink.

Write your reflections . . .

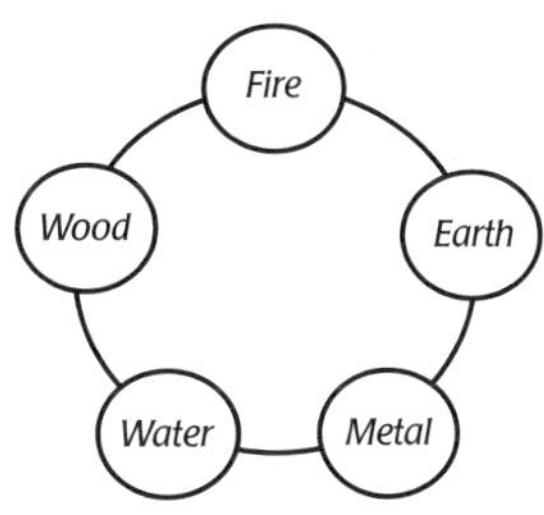

Reflections

March 6

"The kidneys (testicles) call to life
that which is dormant and sealed up;..."

- Nei Jing

The Chinese recognize the role of the Kidneys in energizing and generating life. They believe that the Kidneys house the "ancestral qi," or the energy that is passed on from generation to generation (we might call this our genetic inheritance). They link the Kidneys with the sexual organs, believing that they both store life energy and contain the potential for the propogation of new life. Thus, the Kidneys are the organs in charge of sexual energy or drive, and also, by extrapolation, the capacity to energize the entire body-mind-spirit. The Kidneys can be likened to an electric generator, or to a car battery, filled with potential energy, which just needs to be tapped and harnessed in order to be used.

Exercise

How much potential energy do you think you have - a lot or only a little?

Write your reflections . . .

Reflections

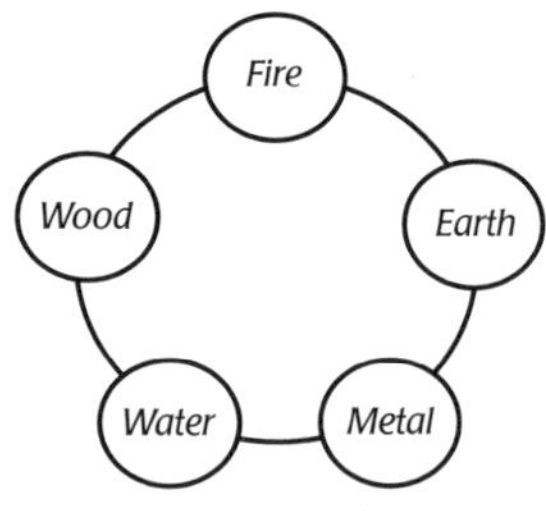

March 7

"...and the kidneys harbor will power and ambition."

- Nei Jing

Ambition can be seen as the force that drives us, that makes us want to achieve our goals, to rise or to attain. The dictionary defines ambition as "an ardent desire for rank, fame, or power; the desire to achieve a particular end." It is an ambiguous word in our culture—a positive or a negative attribute, depending on who is applying it, and in what context. For example, of someone who is lazy, lackadaisical, and aimless in life we might say, "He has no ambition." On the other hand, we might say of a ruthless business executive, "He has a lot of ambition." In the first instance, ambition is seen as a positive quality that is lacking; in the second, it's a negative quality that is too present. A balanced Water energy gives us a balanced ambition—enough drive to achieve our goals, without overshadowing other aspects of life.

Exercise

List three things you want to achieve this week.

Write your reflections . . .

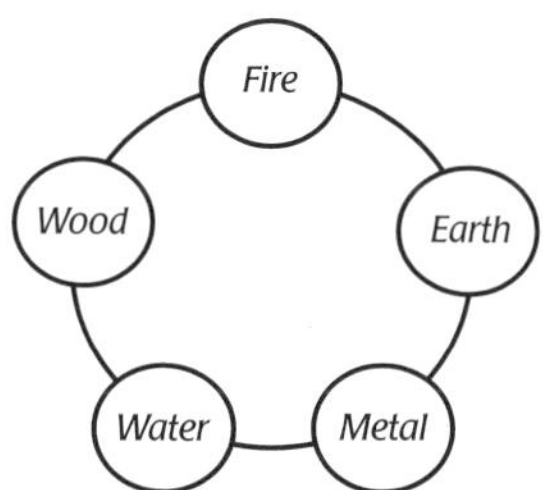

Reflections

March 8

The Chinese view ambition as a natural force emanating from the Kidneys, which is inherent in all of us. They make no moral judgment about how much ambition a person has; the important thing is to fulfill your ambitions fully, to make the most of what you were given by Heaven. If you have large ambitions, then in the Chinese view, it is your destiny to try to achieve them. If you have little ambition, that is o.k. too—you must just live within the limits of your energy.

Chuang Tzu, a famous Taoist sage, wrote:

> *"When we look at things in the light of Tao,*
> *Nothing is best, nothing is worst.*
> *Each thing, seen in its own light,*
> *Stands out in its own way....*
> *Fine horses can travel a hundred miles a day,*
> *But they cannot catch mice*
> *Like terriers or weasels:*
> *All creatures have gifts of their own."*

Exercise

What is your unique gift?

Write your reflections . . .

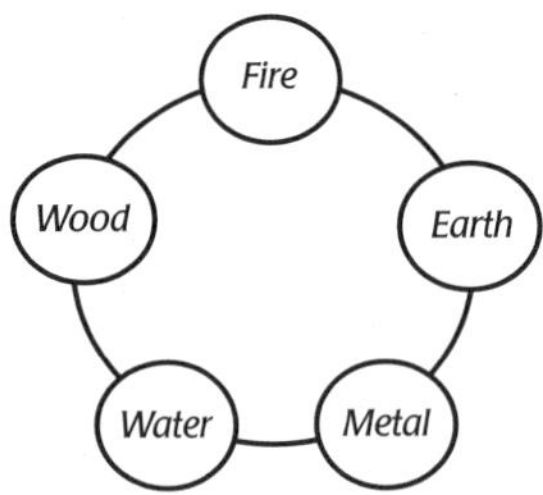

Reflections

March 9

"The [mysterious] powers of Winter create the extreme cold in Heaven and they create water upon earth....
In times of excitement and change they create trembling....."

- Nei Jing

The power granted by Water is the capacity to create trembling. This physical reaction can be just a momentary release of pent-up tensions, or it can be a constant accompaniment to chronic illness. Anyone who has ever experienced strong fear has felt the accompanying trembling and shaking. Any sudden shock, accident, or emotional jolt can produce shaking, trembling, and shivering, which physiologically has to do with the sudden release of hormones from the adrenal glands into the bloodstream. The adrenals just happen to be right next to the Kidneys in the body!

Exercise

When you go to bed at night, appreciate the warmth of your blankets.

Write your reflections . . .

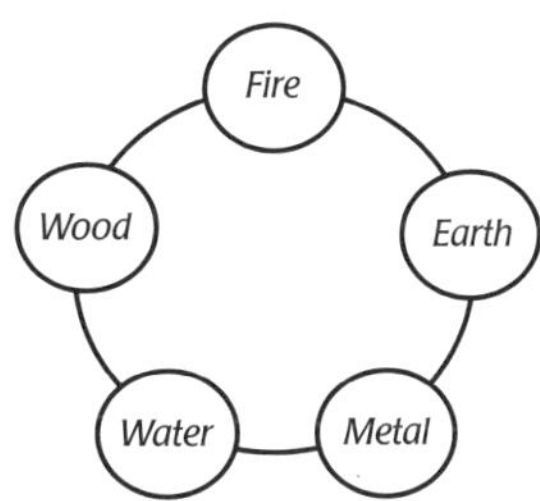

Reflections

March 10

While trembling makes someone feel weak, it is actually the way the body prepares to deal with a traumatic event. The shivering raises the body's heat production to as high as five times normal, by increasing muscle metabolism. Thus, the trembling and shaking serve to jump-start the body into a higher level of functioning, for a quick response to an emergency.

Chronic illnesses that are accompanied by trembling, such as Parkinson's disease and hyperthyroidism, also manifest ways in which the body's Water element can be out of balance. When there is a deep deficiency of the body's natural resources, then other aspects of the body will reflect that deficiency; in this instance, a chronic depletion of the body's Kidney energy can lead to symptoms of tremors in the muscles.

Exercise

If you've caught a chill, eat some hot soup or make a cup of cinnamon tea to warm up your insides. Cinnamon is also used medicinally in China to warm and tonify the Kidneys.

Write your reflections . . .

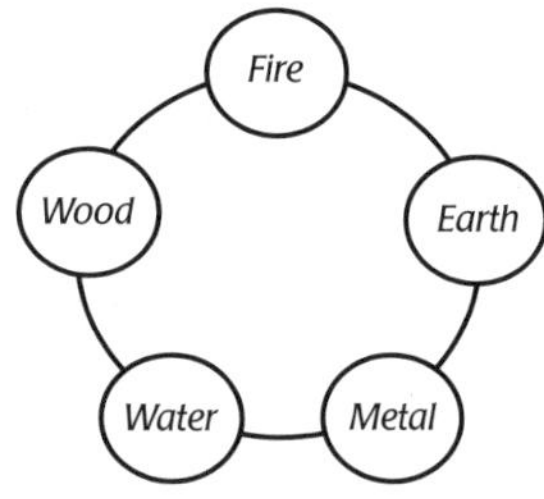

Reflections

March 11

The Winter is a time of year when it is common for people to experience the feeling of being overwhelmed. People phrase it as "It's all just too much!" or "I'm in overwhelm up to my eyeballs!"or "I feel like I'm drowning!" It's a sense of having too much to do and not enough time to do it. It leads to a feeling of being out of control of one's own life, of being engulfed or washed over by a tidal wave of responsibilities, and ultimately, of being exhausted by trying to keep up.

For most of us, Winter is a time when we feel our internal resources dwindling. Without adequate rest and warmth, it is easy to feel that we won't have enough resources, either physical, mental, or emotional, to get through the Winter. Instead of swimming and playing in the ocean, we are submerged and overwhelmed by the waves, tumbling out of control. This is what happens when our Water energy is not equal to the demands we put on it. The feeling of being overwhelmed, therefore, is a symptom that tells us our Water energy is out of balance.

Exercise

Calculate your financial assets. How much to you have on reserve for a rainy day?

Write your reflections . . .

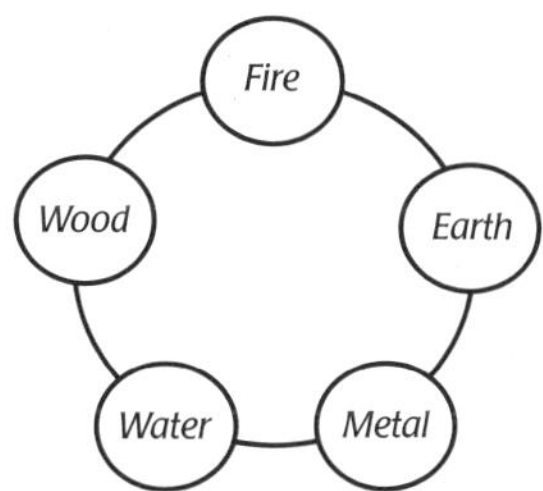

March 12

"...when Yin is flourishing then there occur dreams, as if one had to wade through great waters, which cause bad fears..."

- Nei Jing

Dreaming is a Yin activity because it occurs at night when we are asleep, in a Yin state. Dreaming of water can often be an indication of the quality of the dreamer's Water energy within. To dream of tidal waves or floods can point to being overwhelmed by anxiety, while to dream of dry stream-beds or strangely shallow waters could point to a lack of resources in one's life. Dreams are one of the ways we can tap into our deeper selves on a daily basis.

One patient dreamed of vast areas of very marshy ground—this patient suffered from interstitial cystitis! Another patient dreamed of a stream that flowed out of his fireplace, then slowed down to a trickle; he knew in the dream, however, that it would resume at 4:00 p.m. —exactly during Kidney time in the Chinese clock!

Exercise

Keep a journal by your bedside and write down your dreams.

Write your reflections . . .

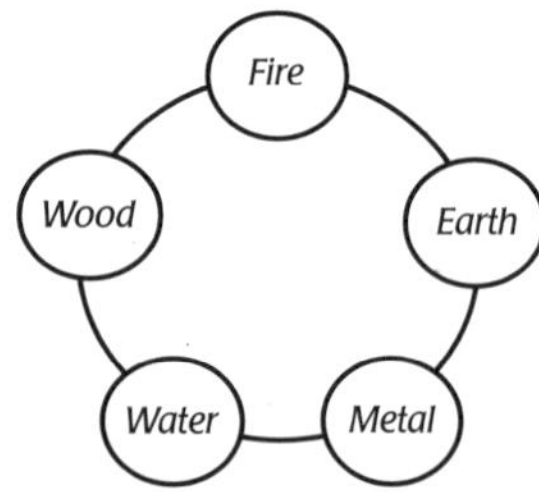

Reflections

March 13

"Ch'i Po said: 'The present generation must respect the poisonous medicines, which assault the diseases within their bodies, and they should hold in awe acupuncture and treatment with moxa, which cure the diseases of the external body.'

The Emperor asked: 'When the body is worn out and the blood is exhausted, is it still possible to achieve good results?'

Ch'i Po replied: 'No, because there is no more energy left.'

The Emperor inquired: 'What does it mean, there is no more energy left?'

Ch'i Po answered: 'This is the way of acupuncture: if man's vitality and energy do not propel his own will his disease cannot be cured.

'Nowadays vitality and energy are considered the foundation of life; in order to keep them flourishing they must be protected and the life-giving force must rule. When this force does not support life, its foundation will dissolve, and how can a disease be cured when there is no spiritual energy within the body?'"

- Nei Jing

Exercise

Take time for some inner practice, like yoga, Tai Chi, meditation, or prayer.

Write your reflections . . .

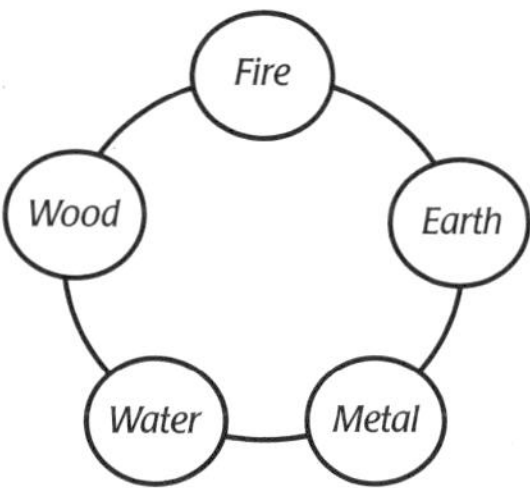

Reflections

March 14

golden ochre grasses
against the rosy snow
blue shadows of the trees
stretching over the pure fields
in the late afternoon
winter sunset light -
warm from walking
I stand in the lonely road
hearing only my own breath
inside my hood, and the calling
of a distant crow -
loving the silence
the blessed pause
before Spring

- Janice MacKenzie

Exercise

Spend 15 minutes outside each day this week.

Write your reflections . . .

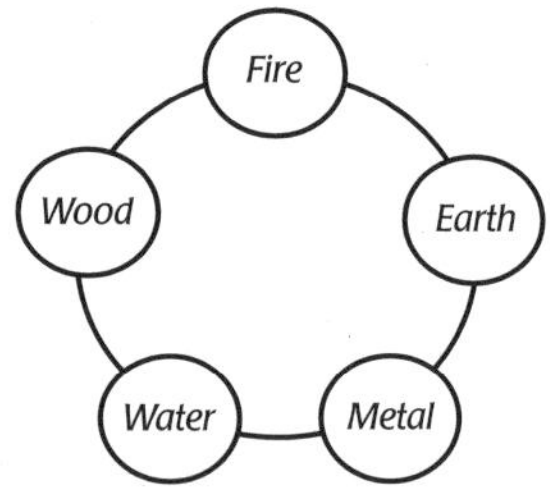

Reflections

First Crocuses, watercolor

SPRING

Spring/Wood

"The three months of Spring are called the period of the beginning and development of life. The breaths of Heaven and Earth are prepared to give birth..."

"The East creates the wind; wind creates wood; wood creates the sour flavor; the sour flavor strengthens the liver; the liver nourishes the muscles; the muscles strengthen the heart; and the liver governs the eyes."

- Nei Jing

Wood is the name the Chinese give to the energy of Spring. Like the new green shoots poking out of the ground, it is tender and flexible, but also vibrant and dynamic. Wood is the energy of birth and creation, of the rapid growth of plants and trees in the Springtime. It is the powerful urge to push forward into life.

In our human lives, Wood is our power to be born and to grow, and it is therefore linked with the energy of childhood. A child embodies many of the qualities of Wood—spontaneous, assertive, creative, and energetic—and represents Wood's association with the beginning of things. If our Wood is healthy, we grow straight and tall, with a free flow of energy from our roots to our furthest branches.

Hopefully, our circumstances allow us to grow in ways consistent with our innate potential. Depending on the choices and decisions we make, we can end up manifesting our potential in the world or we can end up stifled and unfulfilled. Our lives can be stunted, like a tree that receives little sun or too little water, or twisted, like a tree subjected to constant wind. Thus, all of the elements must be in harmony for Wood to be healthy, but first of all, the Wood itself must be strong —the energy for growth, learning, and creativity must flow.

The Wood energy in our bodies governs our growth and the structures that support us physically—specifically, our trunk, limbs, and joints. It also governs muscles, tendons, and ligaments, so that the physical ability to move, to be flexible, and to have strong muscles is governed by the healthiness of our Wood. Problems with muscle weakness or stiffness could point to an imbalance in Wood energy.

The organs associated with Wood are the Liver and Gall Bladder; thus, our digestion and overall metabolism are dependent on healthy Wood functioning. The classics say that the Liver nourishes the eyes; thus, our eyes and our vision are connected to Wood, too. In addition to physical vision, our capacity to visualize, to envision the future, and to have a vision for our lives has its origin here.

Mentally, the Wood energies have to do with the ability to plan and make decisions. Our mental clarity, the ability to organize our thoughts and to make clear judgments, all come from Wood. Confused or fuzzy thinking, or the inability to make decisions, might point to a Wood imbalance. On the other hand, excessive Wood can lead to too much thinking and analyzing, trying to organize everyone else's lives, and living too much in the future instead of in the present.

The emotion connected to Wood is that of anger. Excessive anger, lingering resentments or, conversely, the inability to express anger appropriately, all point to an imbalance in Wood. Repressed anger can lead to a host of physical and mental illnesses, including ulcers, gall bladder disease, migraines, and depression.

Spiritually, the Wood element gives us the capacity to feel hope. It gives us the desire for life, and the ability to look forward to the future. The classics say that the Liver houses the soul. Wood grants us the power of renewal—of a rebirth every Spring.

If allowed to flourish, Wood energy will enable us to grow, to learn, and to forge an identity. Only if this energy has been allowed to flow freely will we truly be ready for the next phase in the cycle, the Fire phase, or energy of Summer. Once identity has been created, the next step is the sharing of expression with others—the capacity for relationship.

March 15

"The east wind arises in Spring...
The East creates the wind; wind creates wood;.."

- Nei Jing

The first signs of Spring are often the tiny green shoots poking out of the bare, winter ground. Because of this natural connection between Spring and green growing things, the attributes of Spring are linked with Wood energy. Wood energy is about birth, growth, beginnings, renewal, creativity, planting seeds, visioning, and planning the future. In Spring, we plant our gardens, begin new projects, and "put out new leaves" on old ones. The newness of Spring inspires our visions of the future. Wood energy is dynamic and quick-growing, determined, yet vulnerable and flexible—like a blade of spring grass.

Exercise

Take a walk in Nature and observe the new green grass and the budding and leafing out of the trees.

Record your visions . . .

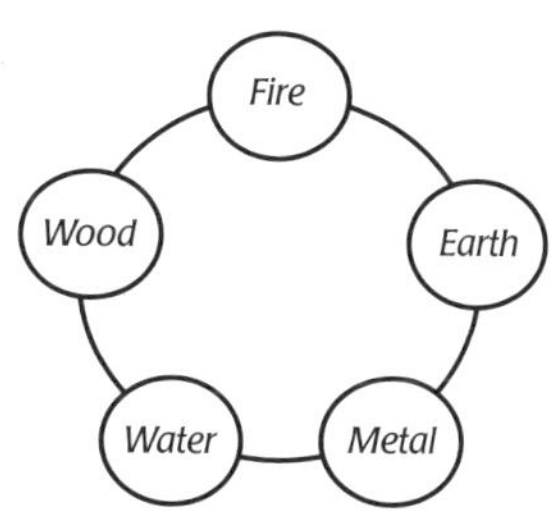

March 16

The actual first day of Spring in China is usually February 4, according to the solar calendar. Called Li Ch'un, or the Beginning of Spring, it relates to the start of the agricultural cycle. It is often symbolized by a picture of a cow being led by a young boy. This Spring Festival Cow harkens back to a Shang dynasty ritual, which was to sacrifice valuable cows to insure a prosperous year.

Spring gives our Wood energy a boost each year. We may feel an extra measure of creativity and energy for beginning new projects. When our Wood energy is strong, our lives are both rooted and growing. When our Wood energy is weak or imbalanced, we are stuck, incapable of growth or renewal. We can be stiff and inflexible, like an old tree trunk, or weak and withered as an uprooted plant.

Exercise

Clear away deadwood and weeds, turn the soil over and plant seeds in your garden.

Record your visions . . .

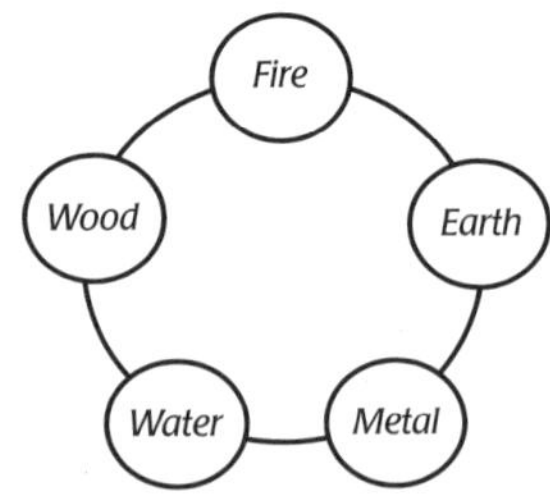

March 17

"Green is the color of the East..."

"The supernatural [powers] create wind in Heaven and they create wood upon earth...Of the colors they create the green color..."

- Nei Jing

Green is the color associated with the East, with Wood, and with Spring. How startling the vibrant new greens of Spring are, after the drab grays and browns of Winter! This color certainly signifies something come alive, something new and innocent. We say that someone is "still green" or a "greenhorn" to indicate inexperience and naivete. The Chinese characters for "green" plus "years" mean "adolescent." The fresh, new shoots of Spring are often fragile, in spite of their vivid green color. The impulse to grow in them is so strong that it makes up for their vulnerability. We are most like Wood when we have that power combined with that flexibility.

Exercise

Wear something green today to signify your strength and openness to new experience.

Record your visions . . .

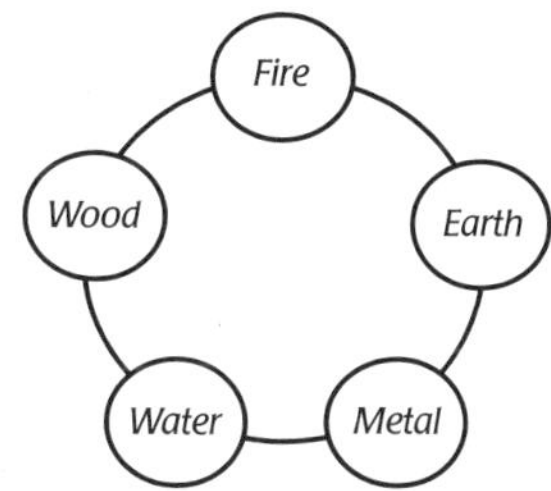

March 18

The connection of green with the element of Wood has further applications when we talk about a person's health. Just as Water imbalance manifests itself with blue tones, so too does Wood imbalance show as a greenish hue around the eyes and mouth, and the person may have a strong liking for or an aversion to green clothing and furnishings.

Another correspondence with green and with Wood energy is that Wood is associated with the emotion of anger, and we have many phrases that acknowledge that connection: "green with jealousy," "turning green with envy," and "green around the gills." The next time you are around someone who is really angry, look at him or her with your peripheral vision, and see if you can detect a flash of green around his or her face.

Exercise

Assess your week's laundry - what colors appear most often? What colors aren't there?

Record your visions . . .

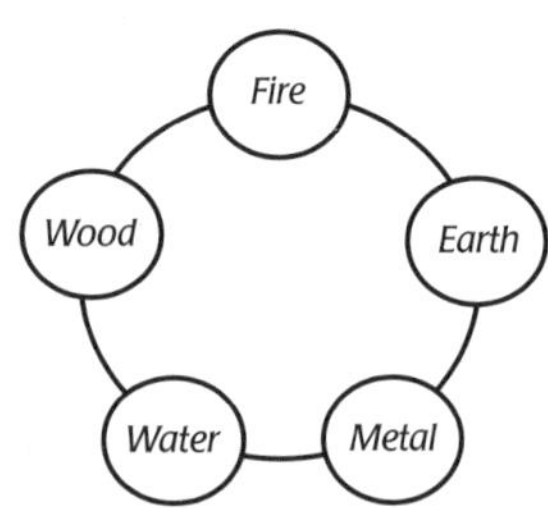

March 19

"The east wind arises in the Spring..."

- Nei Jing

The connection of the direction East with the season of Spring goes back for thousands of years before the writing of the *Nei Jing*. The knowledge of these correspondences was taken for granted by the writers of the *Nei Jing*, but for us in 21st century America, they need some explanation.

In ancient China, each season was thought to originate from a different point of the compass. Because the sun rises in the East, beginning the day, and because Spring is the beginning of the agricultural year, it seems like an obvious connection to make. Elsewhere in the *Nei Jing* it says: "At the end of one year the sun has completed its course and everything starts anew with the first season, which is the beginning of Spring." Also, "Beginning and creation come from the East." Thus, the starting point of the yearly cycle was made out to be Spring, and the direction of beginnings was labeled the East.

Exercise

Get up for sunrise. As you face East, contemplate what you plan to begin soon.

Record your visions . . .

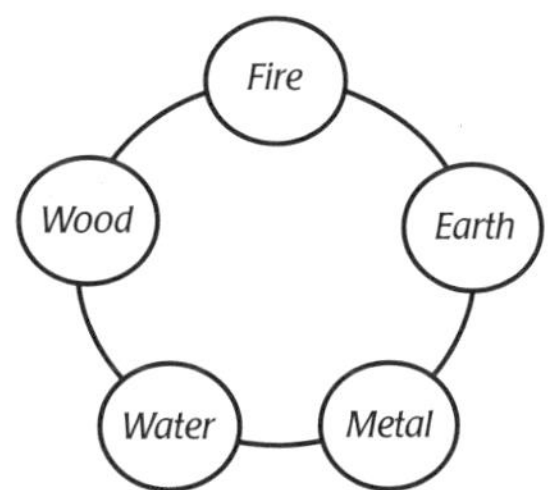

March 20

In the *Nei Jing* it says that disturbances in the throat and neck came out of the wind from the East. As an acupuncturist, I have certainly seen my share of people with head colds and stiff necks from being out in a brisk March wind—although we rarely have East winds here. There are acupuncture points on the head and neck named "Wind Pond" and "Wind Palace," which are said to be points where wind can penetrate the body and cause various diseases. It's well-recognized among acupuncturists that of all the seasons, the Spring winds are the worst in terms of making people sick. Thus, it is good advice to wear windbreakers, scarves and hats to protect yourself from the wind, especially in the Spring, and especially if it's from the East!

Exercise

Fly a kite or hang up a windsock. Be sure to protect your throat and neck, even if the wind is warm.

Record your visions . . .

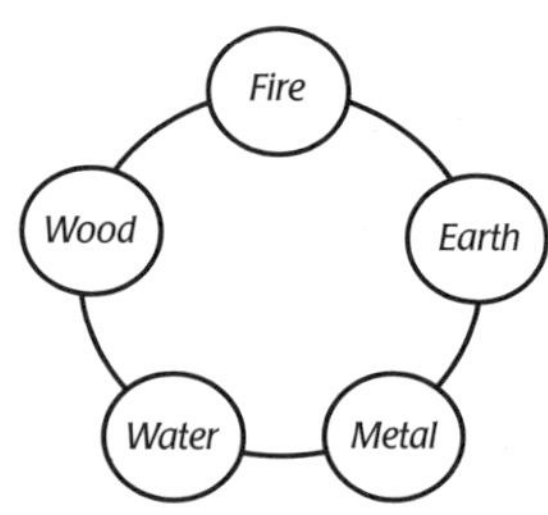

March 21

"...the liver has the functions of a military leader who excels in his strategic planning;..."

- Nei Jing

One of the two organs associated with Wood energy is the Liver. The Liver official is the planner of the body-mind-spirit. As the "architect of the universe," the Liver provides the overall organization and direction for a person's life, as well as the daily plans for accomplishing tasks and goals. The Liver is a very busy official, and is working all the time, even in sleep. In fact, the peak time for the Liver official is from 1:00 a.m. to 3:00 a.m., so a lot of planning is happening during the night, preparing for the next day—maybe keeping you awake if it is an important issue or event.

The Liver official can be compared to someone who draws up plans to build a new house. You may have all of the materials you need and the land to build it on and the workmen to do the labor, but without a plan nobody knows what to do first, or what a successful completion is supposed to look like.

Exercise

Plan a new project; start with a picture of what the outcome will be.

Record your visions . . .

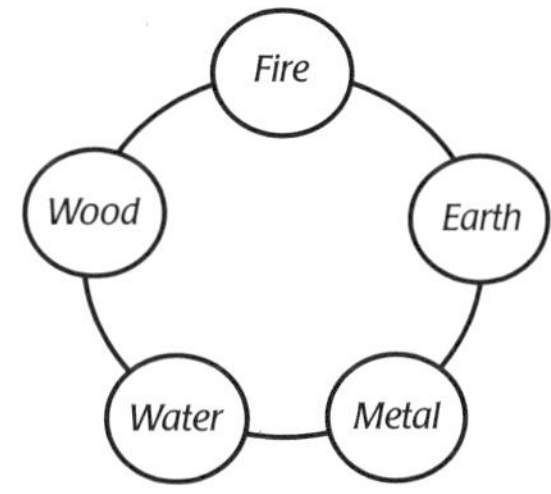

March 22

In Spring the Planner is busy making all of his plans for the year. This is the time for laying out the garden, fighting a war (after winter thaw), reorganizing the house and barn. It is very important that the Liver function well at this time because the plans that we make in the Spring determine what happens the rest of the year.

It is also important to be in harmony with the design of Heaven, according to the Tao. This harmony provides a kind of serenity or peacefulness, which is the virtue of a smoothly functioning Liver.

This sense of harmony and coordination extends from the spiritual down to the physical—since Wood energy controls the muscles, tendons, and ligaments, it also controls our physical coordination. Anyone who is having a problem with coordination, either by being spastic or being overly tense and stiff, could be manifesting a symptom related to the Liver official.

Exercise

List your goals for today, and organize the list in a way that makes sense to you. Feel the satisfaction as you check off goals when they are accomplished.

Record your visions . . .

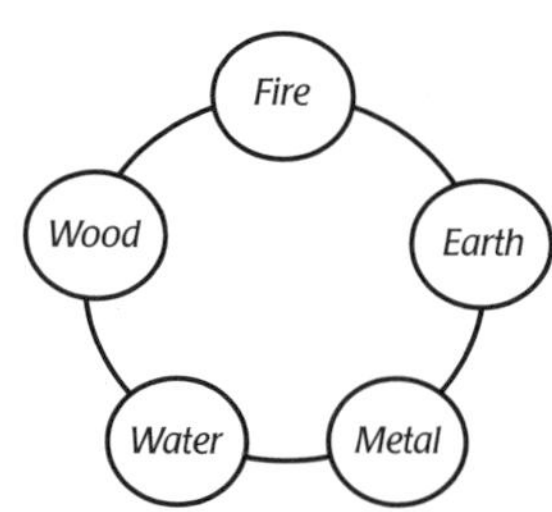

March 23

"The liver causes utmost weariness....it brings forth animal desires and vigor."

- Nei Jing

When the Liver official is out of balance, many aspects of our lives begin to go awry. A lack of capacity for planning and envisioning a future can lead to everything from poor eyesight (physical level) to suicidal despair (emotional/spiritual level). In between are many other manifestations of Liver imbalance, including poor organization, over-scheduling, and workaholism.

Because of the Liver's connection to "animal desires and vigor," it is implicated in many modern conditions, such as Chronic Fatigue Syndrome and chronic mononucleosis, where one of the primary symptoms is fatigue. The "utmost weariness" of a Liver imbalance can be lifted by acupuncture treatment; after a treatment on her Liver points, one patient said, "I feel almost like my old self again!"

Exercise

Gently stretch your neck, the sides of your torso and your legs. This will stimulate the Liver and Gall Bladder meridians.

Record your visions . . .

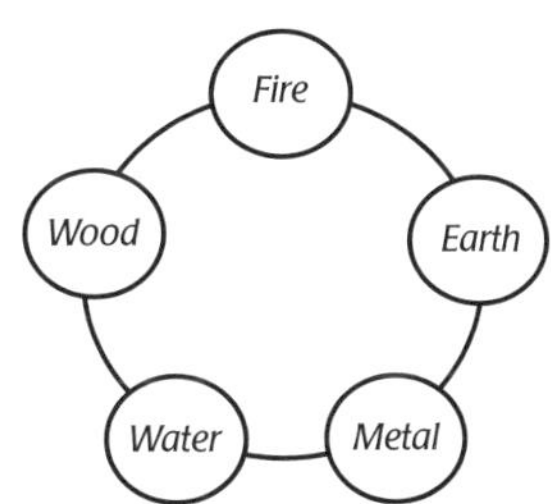

March 24

*"...the gall bladder occupies the position of
an important and upright official who excels
through his decisions and judgment;..."*

- Nei Jing

The second organ associated with Wood energy is the Gall Bladder. The Gall Bladder is the Decision Maker of the body-mind-spirit. This official gives us the capacity to make wise judgments and to make decisions from the most mundane level to the most profound level. How could we function without the Gall Bladder? We wouldn't know whether to go left or go right, stand up or sit down, have the cheeseburger or the tofu burger, love one person or another, live in Connecticut or Kansas, etc.

A sense of direction or decision animates every movement. On a strictly physical level, indecision could mean a total lack of coordination, since the muscles and ligaments need to decide when or how far to move. If you can't decide which foot to move when, then you'll have a difficult time walking.

Exercise

List all the micro-decisions you made in the last 10 minutes.

Record your visions . . .

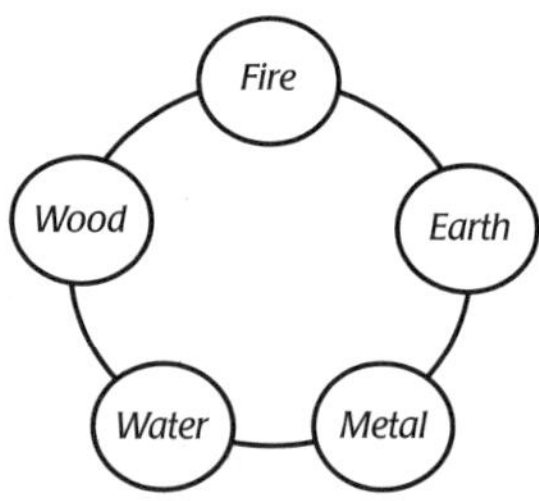

Visions

March 25

The Chinese classics state that the Gall Bladder was the one and only official ordained never to have any impurities passing through it. On a physiological level, they thought the bile to be a pure substance, since it is totally manufactured by the body with no waste products from other parts of the body or from outside the body included in it. Thus, the Gall Bladder official, since it stores only "pure" bile, is itself pure—the "upright" official—and thus makes only pure judgments.

If the Gall Bladder is functioning properly, decisions and judgments will be clear and pure. When the Gall Bladder is malfunctioning, or when there are a lot of impurities in the body, toxins can build up in the gall bladder in the form of gall stones. On a mental or spiritual level, this would mean an inability to make good judgments or decisions. Someone who is overly judgmental could be manifesting an imbalance of the Gall Bladder official, as could someone who uses poor judgment about something.

Exercise

Who do you feel judged by, and who do you judge?

Record your visions . . .

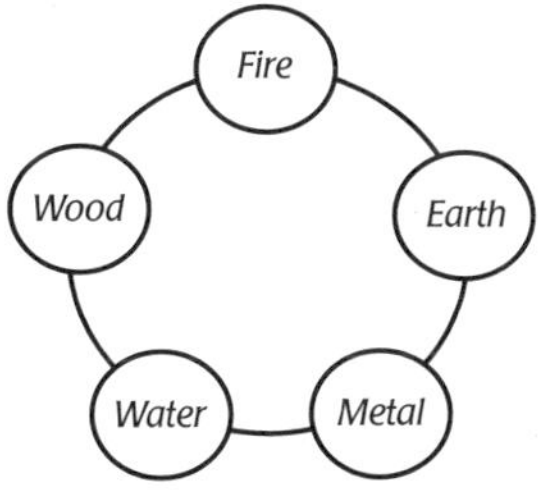

March 26

When the Gall Bladder official is out of balance, the body-mind-spirit begins to make all kinds of bad decisions. On a physical level, the body begins to over-react to harmless substances (allergies), while on the mental level, you can experience chronic lateness or fanaticism about time, hesitating too long and missing your opportunity, or "going off half-cocked." Emotionally, you can have poor judgment about people and end up being taken advantage of, or being suspicious of others.

Some American acupuncturists associate the Gall Bladder official with the corpus collosum, a large fibrous bundle in the brain that connects the right and left cerebral hemispheres. These two hemispheres are specialized for two different modes of thinking—analytic and intuitive. Using both of these hemispheres fully gives you perspective, a virtue of a healthy Gall Bladder. Using only one or the other half of the brain makes you very one-sided in your thinking, unable to experience other points of view.

Exercise

Decide to be different today. If you are usually talkative, be quiet. If you are usually quiet, greet strangers and talk to people in the supermarket or wherever you go.

Record your visions . . .

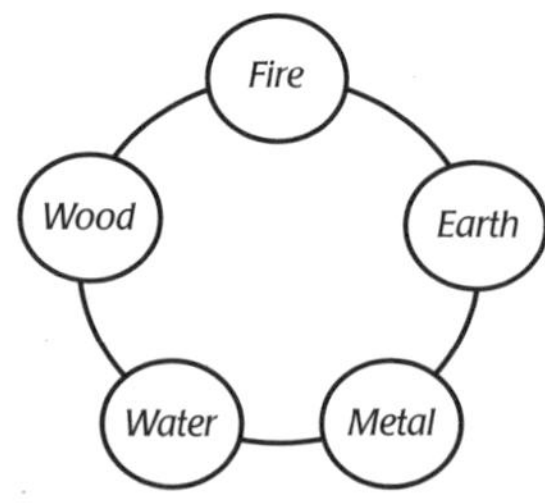

March 27

Through the weeks of deep snow
we walked above the ground
on fallen sky, as though we did
not come of root and leaf, as though
we had only air and weather
for our difficult home.

But now
as March warms, and the rivulets
run like birdsong on the slopes,
and the branches of light sing in the hills,
slowly we return to earth.

- Wendell Berry

Exercise

Get some seeds or breadcrumbs, go to the nearest park, and feed the birds.

Record your visions . . .

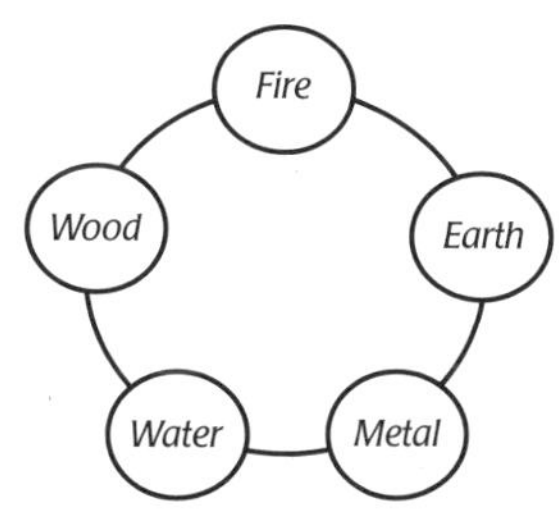

March 28

"...of the emotions they create anger.'"

- Nei Jing

Anger is the emotion associated with Wood. The Chinese say that "anger is injurious to the Liver..." Modern American psychology would say that anger is a natural expression of the life force—which is healthy when it is in response to an appropriate situation, is allowed to be expressed, and is then released and forgotten. Anger that is held in, repressed, or held onto is unhealthy and begins to have negative consequences for one's overall well-being.

Learning when and how to get angry is one of the difficult tasks of childhood. (What would society be like if we all had 2-year-old style tantrums every day, for instance!) Many people have learned to contain their anger so completely that they don't feel angry even when they should. This lack of anger is as much an indicator of an imbalance as is the constant feeling of anger and irritation that can come from blocked Wood energy.

Exercise

Vent your anger in a constructive way: punch a pillow, chop firewood, spring a mile, write a letter to your congressperson.

Record your visions . . .

Visions

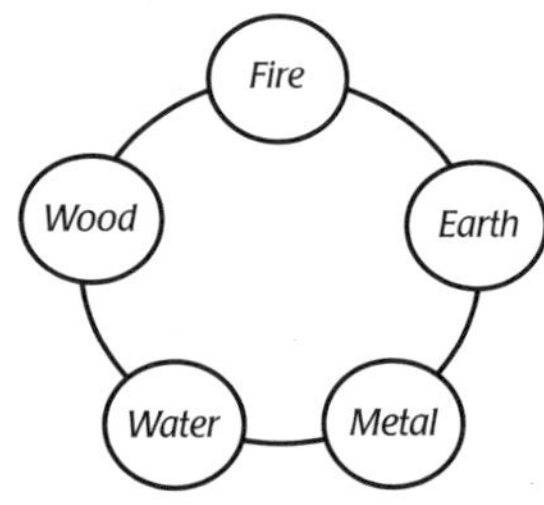

March 29

Wood energy functions at its peak from 11 p.m. to 3 a.m. The Gall Bladder is at its peak from 11 p.m. to 1 a.m., and the Liver from 1 a.m. to 3 a.m. It may seem strange to think of the Wood energy, with all of its creativity, decision-making and planning, having its peak late at night—but actually, that's when we should rejuvenate those functions, since they are active all of our waking hours. If you are awake at that time, you may notice that your mind is better able to think and organize material than during the day. Students who are writing term papers are familiar with this phenomenon—the ability to do their best writing after midnight.

This connection is used to diagnose a Wood imbalance when someone's symptoms change during that time of day. People with insomnia report being awake until 3 a.m., then suddenly find they fall asleep. Someone with arthritis pain may feel a temporary exacerbation of the pain during those hours, only to have the pain recede at 3 a.m.

Exercise

Map 24 hours today to notice when your body or mind or mood shifts.

Record your visions . . .

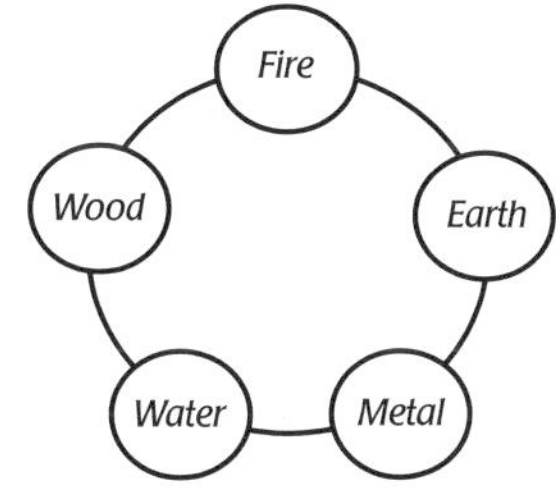

March 30

"Now as I was young and easy under the apple boughs
About the lilting house and happy as the grass was green,
The night above the dingle starry, Time let me hail and climb
Golden in the heydays of his eyes..."

- Dylan Thomas, *Fern Hill*

Childhood is the time of life associated with Wood. Looking at children playing gives us a good picture of what the Chinese meant by Wood energy—children are bursting with energy, and need to move about; they are spontaneous, playful, creative; their emotions change rapidly; their energy is fitful, like the wind; they are flexible and supple; they love exploring, learning, and pushing constantly against limits; they love action and have great determination. Yet, they are also soft, vulnerable, tire quickly, and are easily hurt. All of these qualities describe Wood energy at any time of life, in any season.

Exercise

Skip stones, play catch or tag with a friend to relive the playfulness of childhood.

Record your visions . . .

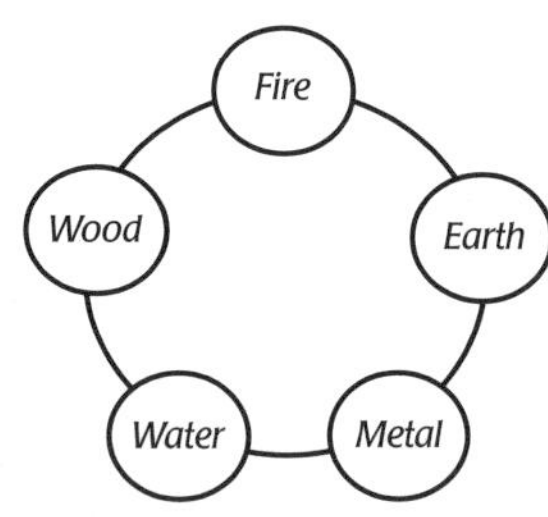

March 31

A Light exists in spring
Not present in the Year
At any other period -
When March is scarcely here

A Color stands abroad
on Solitary Fields
That Science cannot overtake
But Human Nature feels.

It waits upon the Lawn,
It shows upon the furthest Tree
Upon the furthest Slope you know
It almost speaks to you...

- Emily Dickinson

Exercise

Open your shades or curtains in the morning, to let the light help you wake up.

Record your visions . . . .

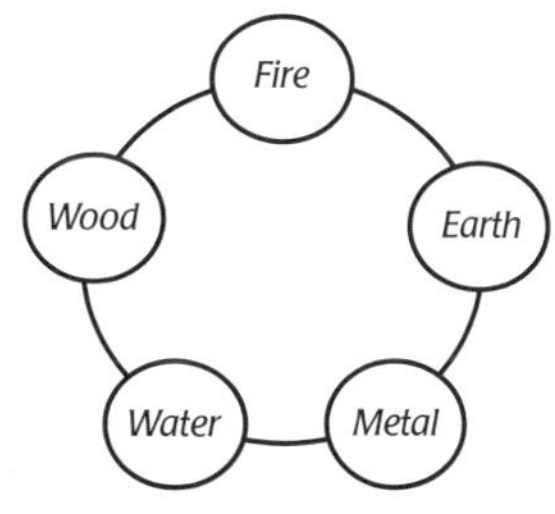

April 1

in Just-
spring   when the world is mud
-luscious the little
lame balloonman

whistles   far   and wee

and eddieandbill come
running from marbles and
piracies and it's
spring

when the world is puddle-wonderful

the queer
old balloonman whistles
far   and   wee
and bettyandisbel come dancing

from hop-scotch and jump-rope and

it's
spring
and
the
goat-footed

balloonMan   whistles
far
and
wee

- e. e. cummings

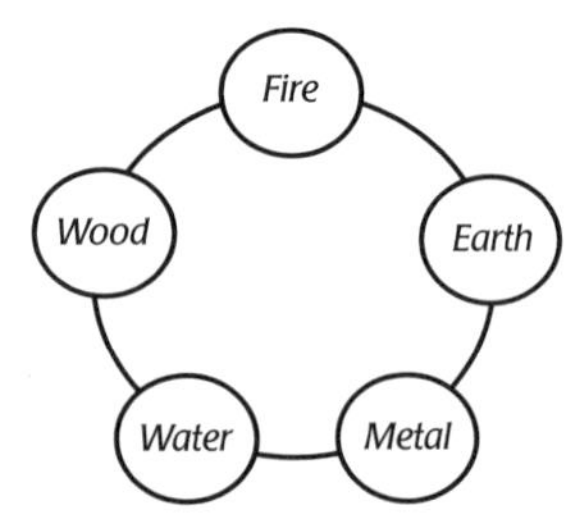

April 2

Hope is the spiritual quality associated with the Wood element. It is linked with the Wood's capacity for vision and its orientation to the future. "Hope springs eternal," and indeed, the feeling of hope is accentuated in the Spring, the season of Wood. It is part of the cyclic nature of our experience that every Spring brings us a renewal of hope for the coming year. When we feel no hope, not even in the Springtime, then we know truly that our Wood energy is out of kilter.

Some people have been disappointed so many times that they squelch stirrings of hope in themselves and are cynical to others who express it. They may, in fact, be so deadened in their Wood energies that they are hopeless—and their bodies will express that. There is an acupuncture point on the Liver meridian named the "Gate of Hope," and it is located on the rib cage just below the lungs. When this point is treated, it can release a tremendous boost of hopeful energy. Hopefulness is often lurking underneath our despair, wanting to send up its green shoots.

Exercise

Next time someone says something despairing or hopeless, don't try to persuade them otherwise. Just agree: "It really is completely hopeless, isn't it?" Most people will then argue with you—thus surfacing the hopefulness that is as natural to us as breathing.

Record your visions . . .

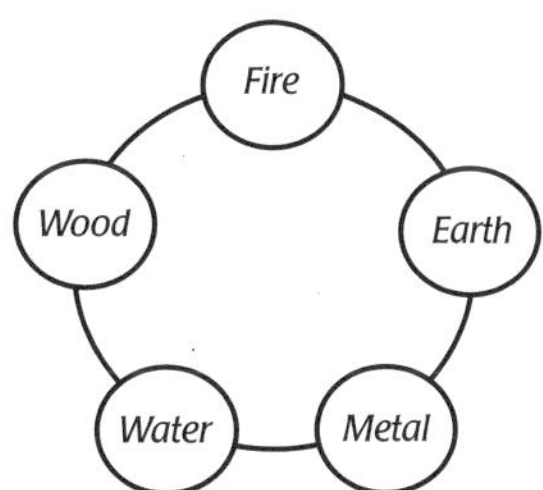

April 3

Hope is the thing with feathers
That perches in the soul,
And sings the tune without the words
And never stops at all,

And sweetest in the gale is heard;
And sore must be the storm
That could abash the little bird
That kept so many warm.

I've heard it in the chillest land,
And on the strangest sea;
Yet, never, in extremity,
It asked a crumb of me.

- Emily Dickinson

Exercise

List three things you hope for in the year ahead.

Record your visions . . .

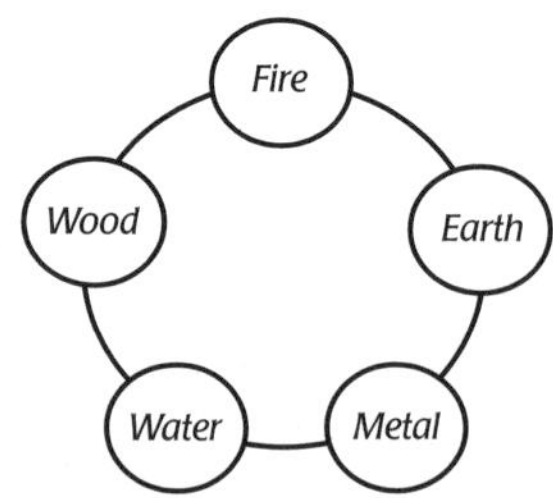

April 4

"The supernatural [powers] create wind in Heaven and they create wood upon earth. Within the body they create the muscles..."

- Nei Jing

The muscles, along with the tendons and ligaments, give us the ability to move, and so it is appropriate that they are governed by Wood energy—the energy that is the most dynamic. When our Wood energy is balanced, we move easily and spontaneously. We can also let go and relax completely. When the Wood energy is not balanced, we may experience severe and chronic muscular pain, cramping, spasms, soreness and swelling, and inflammation—with Western diagnostic names such as tendonitis; bursitis; arthritis; back spasms; "pulled muscles;" tennis elbow, etc. Or, our muscle tone may be flaccid, coordination poor, joints stiff or paralyzed. In all these cases, the Wood energy is not flowing and movement is impeded.

Exercise

Lift weights, and feel the pleasurable sense of your muscles working.

Record your visions . . .

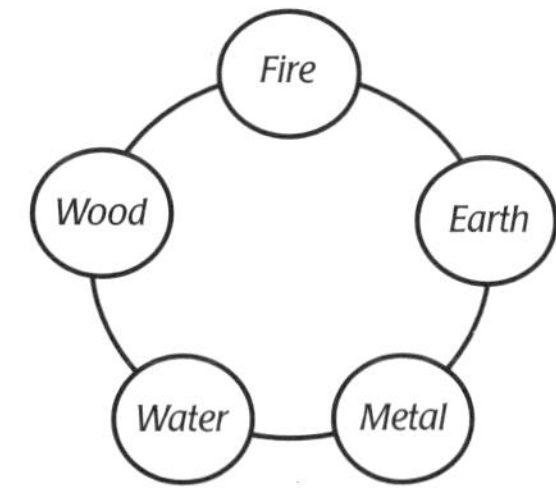

April 5

"Great ideas originate in the muscles."

- Thomas Edison

Healthy muscles permit movement; regular movement keeps your muscles healthy. To extend that feedback loop metaphor a bit, you could say that healthy Wood energy allows for movement, and regular movement keeps your Wood energy healthy. When we don't get regular exercise, our Wood energy begins to dam up, clogging some muscles and under-nourishing others. Ultimately, we experience a chronic stagnation and fatigue. Conversely, regular exercise moves the energy and blood through the muscles and tendons, eliminating stagnation and enhancing vitality. (Exercising gives one energy.) Thus, the healthiness of our muscles is a good indicator of the balance in our Wood energies. And healthy Wood energies allow for the flow of creative ideas.

Exercise

Add one to two cups of epsom salts to your bath to relieve sore muscles. Lie back in the bathwater, close your eyes and let your creative mind flow.

Record your visions . . .

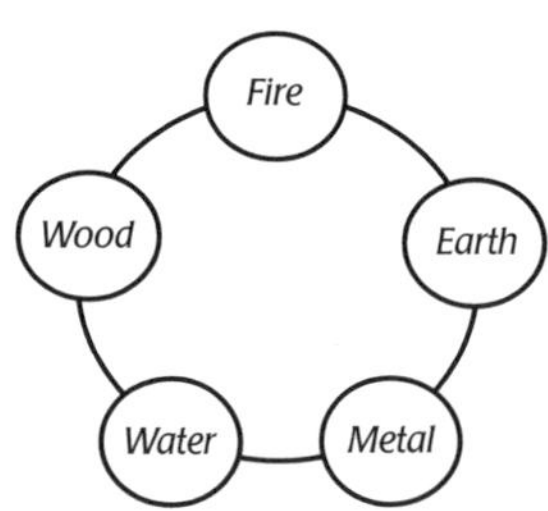

April 6

"The condition of the finger and toe nails shows when the liver is in a splendid and flourishing condition."

- Nei Jing

The nails of the fingers and toes are the most easily visible signs of the condition of the Wood energy. When Wood energies are off, the nails often change before any other symptoms appear. These changes can be anything from ridges and striations to splitting, peeling and thickening, to changes in color, spotting, and blackening.

If our nails change suddenly, if they have developed small vertical ridges, for example, then we must ask ourselves what might be affecting our Wood energy. Perhaps there are too many substances in our diets that are affecting the Liver, such as coffee; alcohol; cigarettes; chocolate; or fatty foods. Or, maybe we are in stressful work situations, or are holding onto some anger. Our nails are telling us that we need to change something in our lives in order to keep our Liver, and our Wood energy, in a "splendid and flourishing condition."

Exercise

Get a manicure. Ask your manicurist what she/he thinks of the condition of your nails.

Record your visions . . .

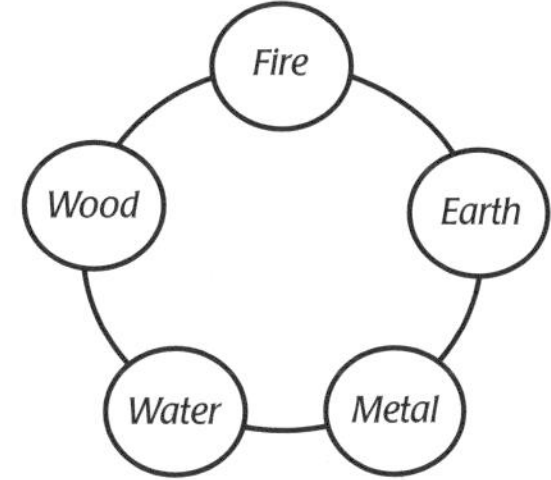

April 7

"...and the liver governs the eyes."

- Nei Jing

The eyes are the sense organ connected to the Wood element. Since the functions of the Liver and Gall Bladder are planning and decision-making, we need "vision" in order to do either of them. A deep pathway of the Liver meridian brings energy to the back of the eye. Thus, any problems with physical vision, including blindness, astigmatism, near or far-sightedness, blurry vision, cataracts, seeing double, and painful, tired eyes could be pointing to an imbalance in Wood, or a problem with the Liver or Gall Bladder.

Our vision often correlates with how we plan or make decisions. One example is a woman with double vision who worked as a mediator—she saw too many options and was therefore indecisive with her clients. Good vision can mean clear decisions.

Exercise

Obtain one of those buckwheat and lavender eye pillows. Place it over your eyes when you lie down for a nap. Notice how it makes your eyes feel. Are decisions easier?

Record your visions . . .

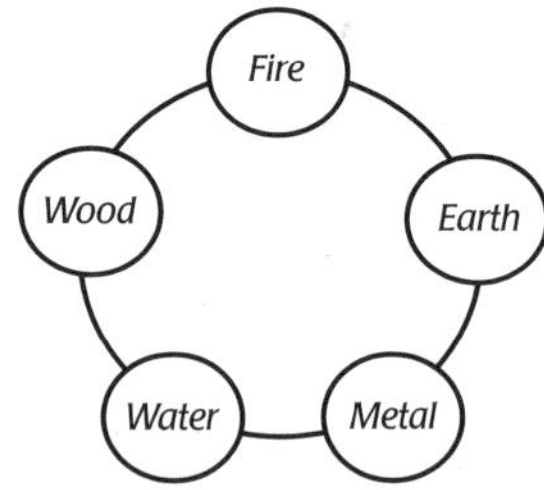

Visions

April 8

"The eyes see the darkness and mystery of Heaven and they discover Tao, the Right Way, among mankind."

- Nei Jing

Physical vision is linked to metaphorical vision—the capacity to "see the darkness and mystery of Heaven" and "discover Tao, the Right Way, among mankind." When someone has difficulty envisoning things, or has no "vision" for his life, we can say he has an imbalance of the Liver, even if his physical vision is perfect. When leaders are accused of having a "lack of vision," or of being "short-sighted," or of "turning a blind eye" to some problem, they are also manifesting an imbalance in Wood. Our wood energy is healthy if our vision is clear and unobstructed, and our perceptions, plans, and decisions are balanced and accurate.

Exercise

Take a course in photography, or just take your camera out and try to see with new eyes.

Record your visions . . .

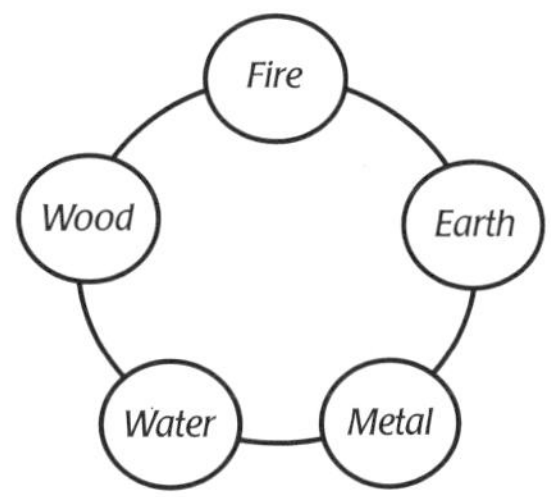

April 9

"...now the eyes of my eyes are opened..."

- e.e. cummings

Some Lakota Sioux tribes do a vision quest to mark the transition to adulthood or to seek direction and guidance. The person fasts and purifies him or herself, then goes up a mountain or into a wild area for several days to wait for a vision. This vision would serve as the guiding principle of that person's life. If there was a vision of horses, for example, then perhaps that person would be a horse-tamer. A vision of arrows could indicate a hunter or an arrow-maker.

Exercise

Consider making a vision quest this Springtime. Take a few days to go off someplace alone, and spend the time as much as possible outdoors, trying to be receptive to the observations and ideas that come. Record your experiences, thoughts, and feelings at the end of each day. When you come home, show your vision to a trusted friend, counselor, or therapist for help in interpretation.

Record your visions . . .

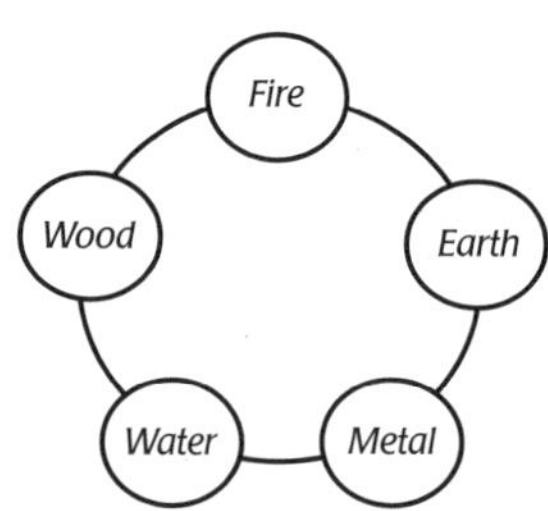

April 10

The extreme delicacy of this Easter morning
Spoke to me as a prayer and as a warning.
It was light on the brink, spring light
After a rain that gentled my dark night.
I walked through landscapes I had never seen
Where the fresh grass had just begun to green,
And its roots, watered deep, sprung to my tread;
The maples wore a cloud of feathery red,
But flowering trees still showed their clear design
Against the pale blue brightness chilled like wine.
And I was praying all the time I walked,
While starlings flew about, and talked, and talked.
Somewhere and everywhere life spoke the word.
The dead trees woke; each bush held its bird.
I prayed for delicate love and difficult,
That all be gentle now and know no fault,
That all be patient—as a wild rabbit fled
Sudden before me. Dear love, I would have said
(And to each bird who flew up from the wood),
I would be gentler still if that I could ...

- May Sarton
Collected Poems

Exercise

Grab your umbrella and go for a walk in the rain. Notice the new green growth soaking up the rain and poking out of the wet soil.

Record your visions . . .

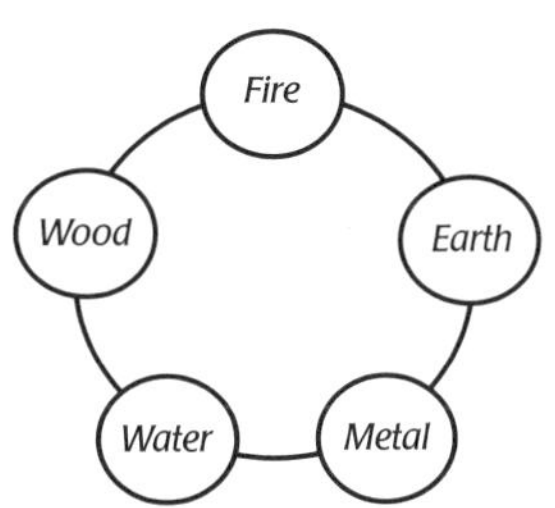

Visions

April 11

"...and they give to the human voice the ability to form a shouting sound."

- Nei Jing

The sound of voice associated with the Wood element is shouting. When someone is angry, his voice will often become louder, more forceful, and penetrating. We instinctively react to this aggressiveness in someone who is angry when we say, "Don't raise your voice at me!" A shouting voice is difficult to ignore—it gets attention.

In someone whose Wood energies are imbalanced, the voice may have a shouting quality, even when there is no anger present. This is not necessarily a matter of loudness—someone's actual decibel level may be normal, but there is an insistent, demanding quality to the voice, which almost seems to attack you. Often, the person doesn't hear his own voice, and will tell you, "I'm not shouting." Just as the groaning voice of a Water imbalance can make a listener tired, so the shouting voice can lead to irritation—leaving the shouting person mystified as to why people are always getting angry with him.

Exercise

Think of the people whose voices seem loud or unpleasant to you. Can you see a reason why they might be angry?

Record your visions . . .

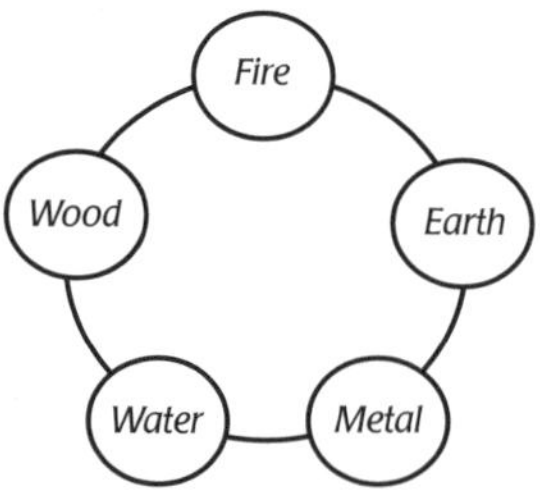

Visions

April 12

Sometimes, instead of shouting, a person with a Wood imbalance will do the opposite of shout—the voice quality will be soft, uninflected, lacking in emphasis and dynamism, almost a whisper. This voice quality, called "lack of shout," can indicate a deficiency of Wood —the inability to be assertive, even with one's voice. People with this voice quality are always being told to "speak up!"—and, like those who shout, they are unaware of how their voice is coming across to others. Or, if they are aware, they cannot raise or sustain a more assertive tone.

Exercise

Tape a number of people talking into a tape recorder and then listen to the different voices without the distraction of their presences. Or listen to a TV or radio talk show. Listen for the shout or the groan or the whisper.

Record your visions . . .

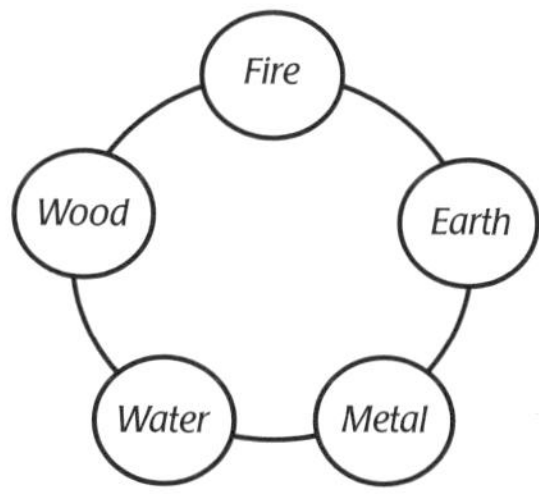

April 13

"A whine is anger passing through too small an opening."

- Graffiti on a wall

Everyone gets a chuckle out of this quote. When someone is angry but doesn't feel able to resolve or deal with it, it causes a constriction that comes out as a whine. Often this is a sign of feeling powerless or subordinate. When a child is told, "Stop whining!," it creates yet further constriction. If this pattern persists for too long, it can lead to physical problems of constriction as well, including chronic sore throats, tension in the abdomen leading to poor digestion, and tension and stiffness in the muscles.

Exercise

Driving down the highway, sing or shout at the top of your voice. Make as much noise as you possibly can.

Record your visions . . .

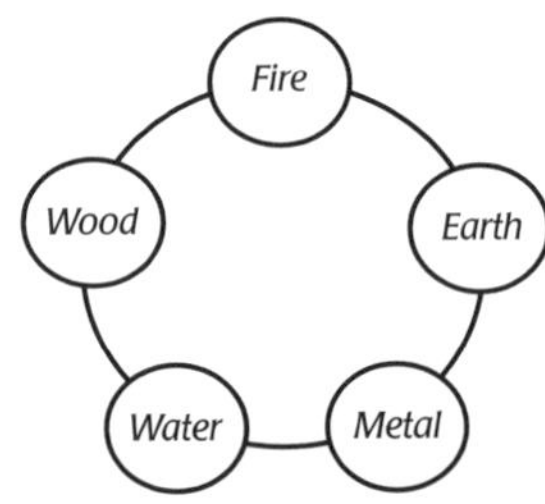

Visions

April 14

When anger is repressed, it constricts the energy of the Liver and Gall Bladder—which the Chinese call "constrained Liver qi." Because the Liver is in charge of the smooth flow of energy and emotions in the entire body, its constraint creates a myriad of problems. The constraint is usually felt in the throat, the solar plexus, the back of the neck and upper shoulder area, the jaw, or the hips. These are all areas energized by the Liver and Gall Bladder meridians. If you feel tightness or tension in any of these areas, then you may be experiencing "constrained Liver qi."

Although there are ways of treating "constrained Liver qi" with acupuncture, herbs, and massage, we can work on it ourselves with breathing and relaxation exercises, and by expressing any anger we are holding in. If we can turn our "whine" into a roar, even if not directly to the person we are angry at, we will probably feel much better.

Exercise

Play your favorite CD or tape in a private room, turn up the volume, and dance. Practice roaring.

Record your visions . . .

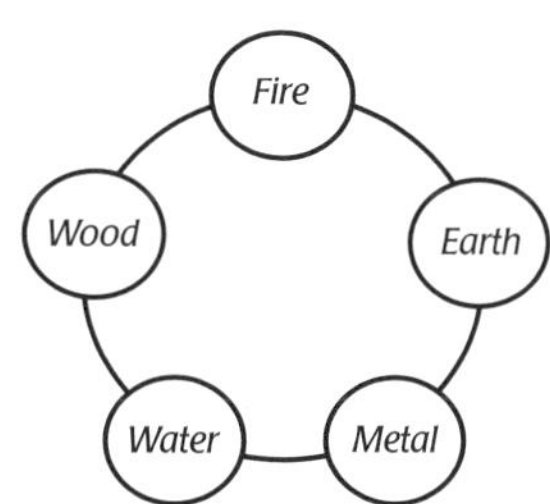

April 15

George Leonard, in his book, The Silent Pulse, talks about the concept of "soft eyes." He states that for most of us in American culture, normal vision entails focusing the eyes on specific entities, giving them shape, cultural meaning, and name. This kind of seeing he labels "hard eyes," because it is basically analytical, separating figures from the background and drawing sharp edges around objects. "Seeing with hard eyes is a positive act; it requires reaching out into the world. With hard eyes we can read the fine print." The Planner needs hard eyes.

"Soft eyes" is a receptive visual mode, synthesizing rather than analytical. It involves letting the visual world come in rather than reaching out to grab it. With soft eyes we can perceive a whole field of vision in terms of the energy and motion that make it up, rather than perceiving the collection of objects that exist within it. There is less than the usual distinction between figure and background; peripheral vision is enhanced, the depth of field appears to be greater, and colors seem remarkably vivid. The Visionary needs soft eyes to see the whole field.

Exercise

Take a walk in the woods and look at the trees with soft eyes. Notice the texture of the bark, the way the branches come out of the trunk, as well as the leaves.

Record your visions . . .

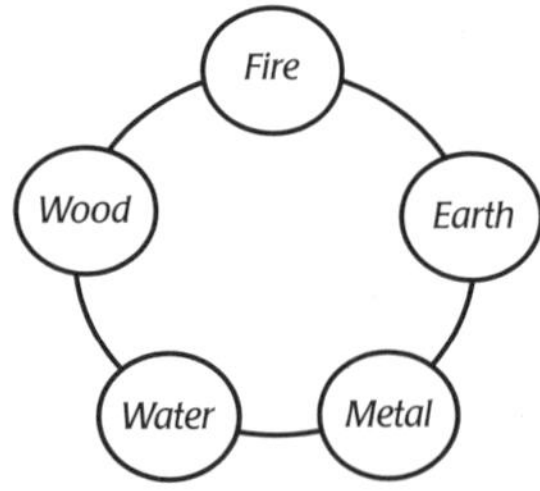

April 16

Soft Eyes Exercise

Close your eyes and stand easily for several minutes until you are relaxed and centered. With the pads of the fingers of both hands, very gently massage both eyes through the closed eyelids until the eyeballs seem to soften slightly. Let your hands drop to your sides, take 2 or 3 relaxed breaths, and then slowly let your eyes open and let the world come in. Do not stare or focus. Blink often. Do not reach out with your eyes to focus on any object or any point in the visual field. This is not a matter of throwing your eyes out of focus; it's merely that they are focused on nothing in particular. Become aware of the entire visual field, giving no part of it any more importance than any other part. Slowly turn your head from side to side. Let any movement, shape or color be an integral part of the whole field, related to everything else within it. Notice any increase in depth of field or intensity of colors. Now, try to walk around with soft eyes. Notice your sensations and your relationship to people and objects in the room.

Record your visions . . .

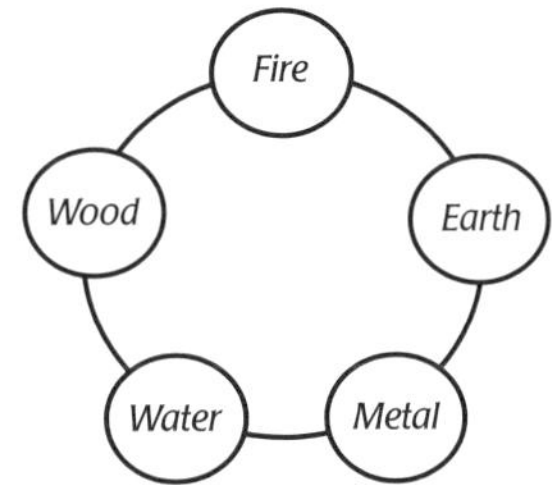

April 17

"...in regard to the liver the secretions become tears..."

- Nei Jing

Tears are a natural secretion of the body, which are associated with the Wood energy. There are two types of tears: one lubricates the eye, and the other pours out in response to an emotional or physically irritating stimulus. Tears are usually a sign that one has been "moved" in some way, or is experiencing an intense emotion. Tears are an expression of that emotion, and are often experienced as a release of built-up emotional tension. One patient said, "I always like how tears clear my sight—how decisions come clear after a cry."

Exercise

Think of the last time you really cried about something. Then cut an onion; compare the experiences.

Record your visions . . .

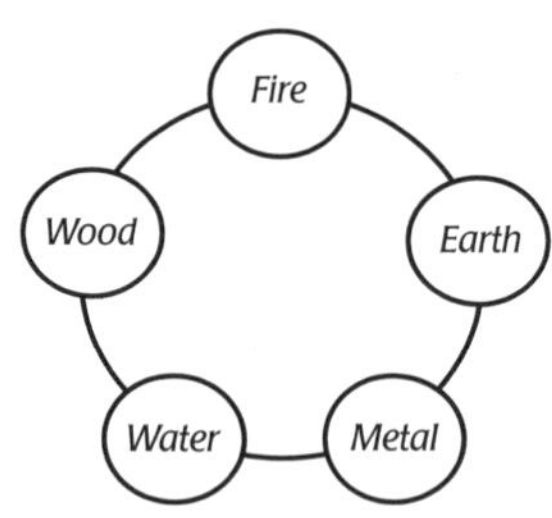

Visions

April 18

Tears actually express many emotions, not just grief. We can weep for joy, or cry tears of rage or frustration. Moments of great beauty or poignancy can call forth tears, as can gratitude, sympathy, or fear. People often experience tears as a relief, and often speak of them as "cleansing." There is often a calm mental clarity after tears that was absent before—as if a lot of static was cleared away. In a way, tears are like Nature's emotional safety valve.

Ideally, we don't even notice the tears that lubricate our eyes, and the ability to cry easily and spontaneously at appropriate moments is a sign of emotional health. When someone has dry eyes, with not enough tears to lubricate them, or has difficulty crying, or conversely, if someone's eyes are watery or they cry at the drop of a hat, we need to look at the Liver and the Wood Element to find the imbalance.

Exercise

Watch a movie that you know has brought you to tears in the past. Let yourself indulge in the emotions that the movie calls forth.

Record your visions . . .

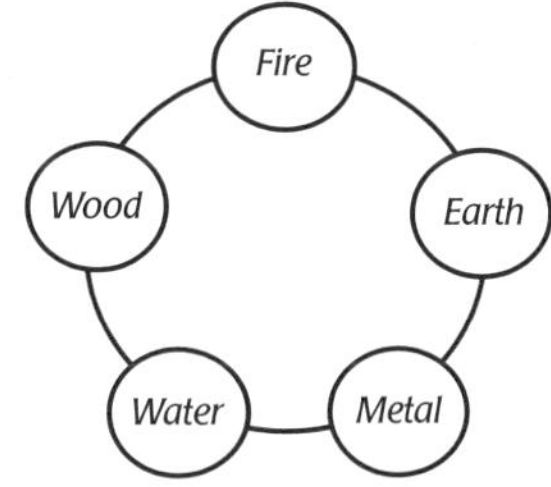

Visions

April 19

"...of the flavors they create the sour flavor,..."

- Nei Jing

The taste associated with the Wood element is sour. Vinegary foods, pickled foods, grapefruit, and lemon juices are the typical things you might crave if you have an imbalance in Wood. A certain amount of the sour taste supports and stimulates the Liver and Gall Bladder. But too much of the sour taste can begin to be "injurious." In the classics it says: "If too much sour flavor is used in food, the flesh hardens and wrinkles and the lips become slack."

You have probably been eating too much sour-flavored food if your muscles have begun to be affected. A small amount of the sour taste, however, such as a glass of grapefruit juice in the morning, can promote better digestion.

Exercise

Before breakfast, drink a glass of unsweetened grapefruit juice. The sour taste will stimulate your digestion and also encourage bile production in the liver.

Record your visions . . .

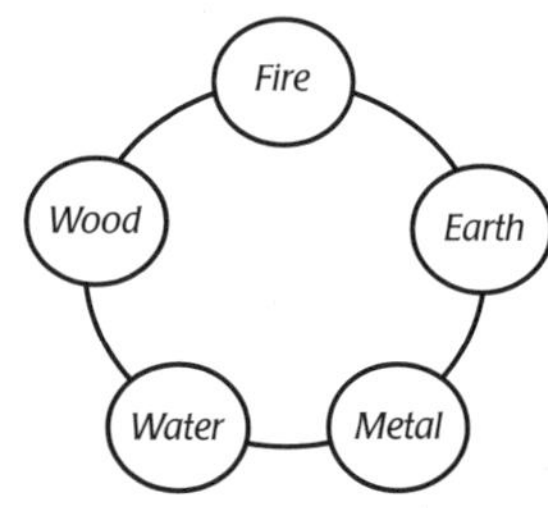

April 20

"The sour flavor is injurious to the muscles, but the pungent flavor counteracts the sour flavor."

- Nei Jing

Elsewhere in the classics it says: "The pungent flavor has a dispersing effect; the sour flavor has a gathering and binding effect... When the liver (is sick) it has the tendency to disintegrate. Then one should quickly eat pungent food which dispels this tendency. One uses pungent food in connection with the liver in order to supplement its function and to stop leaks, and one uses sour food to drain and expel."

The importance of the proper balance of the five flavors can be seen in the following passage from the *Nei Jing*: "Man receives the five atmospheric influences as food from Heaven and the five flavors as food from Earth...The five flavors enter the mouth and are stored by the stomach. The flavors which are stored nourish the five atmospheric influences, and when these influences are well-blended they produce saliva. Together all these influences help to perfect the mind, which then begins to function spontaneously."

Exercise

Make a dandelion salad: 1/2 pound dandelion greens, with a dressing made of 1 clove of garlic, 2 teaspoons lemon juice, and 1 teaspoon olive oil.

Record your visions . . .

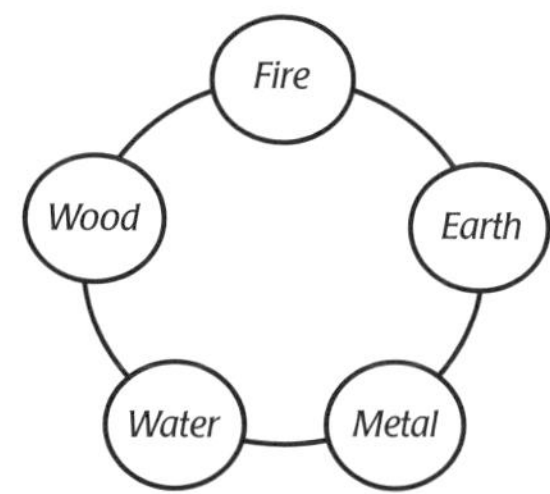

April 21

"Therefore if people pay attention to the five flavors and mix them well, their bones will remain straight, their muscles will remain tender and young, their breath and blood will circulate freely, their pores will be fine in texture, and consequently, their breath and bones will be filled with the essence of life."

- Nei Jing

All people use food to heal sickness. In the *Nei Jing* it says, "The first method [of getting well from diseases] cures the spirit; the second gives knowledge of how to nourish the body;..." Only after these methods have been tried does it suggest "poisons and medicines" or acupuncture. Of course, the Chinese don't separate "food," "herbs" and "medicine" as strictly as we do.

The specific element associations for foods as given in the *Nei Jing* can often seem quite arbitrary, yet the knowledge of these associations can be very clinically useful. For example, wheat is often associated with the Wood phase, and many people with Wood imbalances have a wheat intolerance.

Exercise

Saute dandelion greens, or steam some asparagus—they will stimulate your digestion after a winter of rich food.

Record your visions . . .

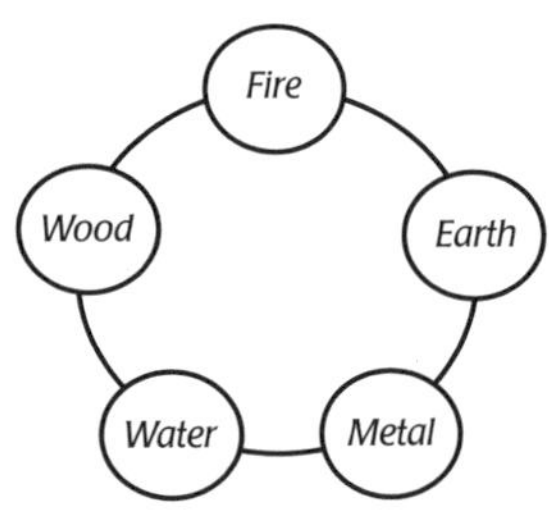

Visions

April 22

Correspondences between food and the seasons is more complicated than the other classical associations. Foods associated with Spring and with Wood energy are connected because of the sour flavor. But the effect of the food upon the organ itself is also considered.

The classical correspondences for Wood are: grain—wheat; fruit—peach; meat—chicken; vegetable—mallow. Sour foods are: lemon, plum, grapefruit, crab apple, grapes, mango, olive, peach, raspberry, adzuki beans, tomatoes, and vinegar.

The important thing in the Spring is to eat less, and even to fast, in order to cleanse the body of the fats and heavy foods of the winter. Young plants, fresh greens, sprouts, and immature wheat or other cereal grasses all have the expansive, rising qualities associated with Wood energy. Pungent foods are also used for their strengthening effect on the Liver, such as garlic and raw onions, and pungent cooking herbs—basil, fennel, marjoram, rosemary, caraway, dill, bay leaf—are desirable in the Spring.

Exercise

Try spring cleaning your body with a short fast. Use Elson Haas' book, *Staying Healthy with the Seasons*, to guide you on this.

Record your visions . . .

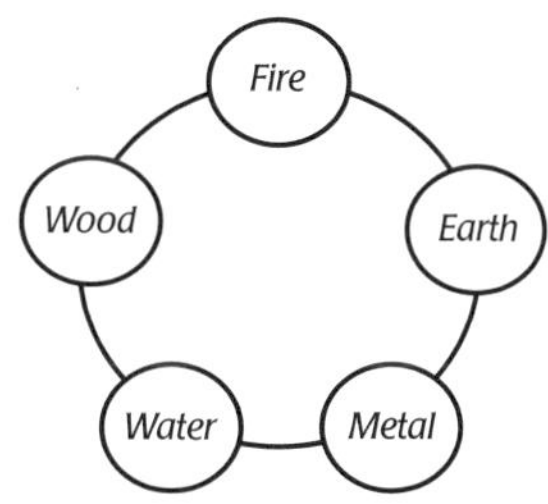

Visions

April 23

"...its smell is offensive and fetid."

- Nei Jing

As with the Water element, the Wood element has an odor associated with it, which manifests in the human body during times of imbalance. This odor is usually called "rancid" in the modern texts, but in the *Nei Jing* it is translated as "offensive and fetid." It is sometimes described as smelling like rotten leaf mold on the forest floor, or alternatively like stale cooking oil or bacon grease hanging in the air. It is the most aggressive of the 5 odors, often seeming to attack the nose. It is, therefore, one of the easiest to recognize, once it is labeled.

For most of us in America, daily showers, mouthwash, deodorants, and perfumes make it difficult to detect any odor in a reasonably healthy person. Thus, when we do smell one of the 5 odors, it is a clear diagnostic clue. This state of imbalance may be only temporary —for example, if someone becomes extremely angry, he or she may emit a strong whiff of rancid but have no long-standing imbalance in the Wood element.

Exercise

Save your bacon grease and other leftover fats and oils from cooking. Keep them in a jar for a week or so, then open the jar and smell. This gives you some idea of the odor of rancid.

Record your visions . . .

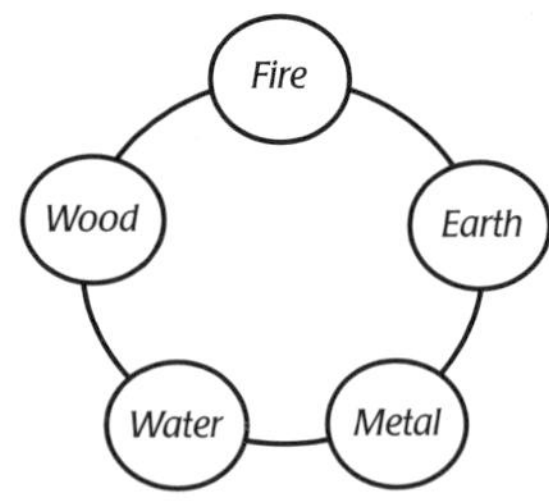

Visions

April 24

"The three months of spring are called the period of the beginning and development (of life). The breaths of Heaven and Earth are prepared to give birth; thus everything is developing and flourishing."

- Nei Jing

Spring is the time of year associated with birth. It is certainly the time of year when the process of birth is most noticeable in Nature —everywhere, animals are having babies and new green plants are coming out of the ground. The capacity to grow a bud, or a new plant—the power to give birth to something—the Chinese ascribed to the energy of Wood. Thus, no matter what time of year someone gives birth to something, whether a baby, an idea, or a creative project, the Wood energy fuels it.

Exercise

Paint a picture, dance, write a poem—express your birthing energy!

Record your visions . . .

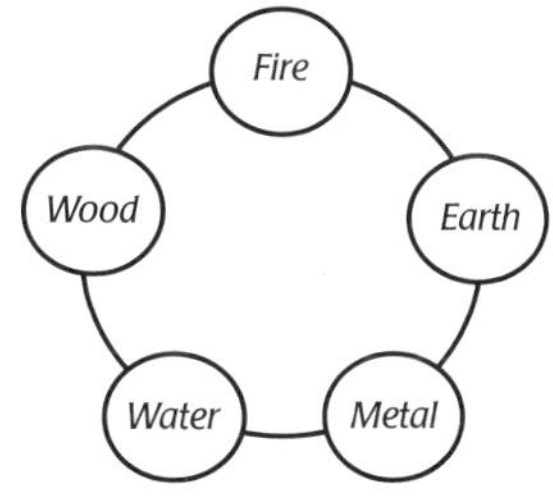

Visions

April 25

Although we tend to think of birth as an event, a single moment in time, it is actually a process that has its own phases and seasons. In human birth, we speak of the stages of pregnancy and of labor—each stage having its own characteristics, sensations, and purposes. A bud does not unfold in a single moment, nor does a flower bloom from nothing in a single instant. With time-lapse photography, we can watch this process happening, but only with a microscope can the remarkable cellular changes be seen. Even creative ideas, although they may seem to come in a blinding flash of inspiration, usually follow a period of germination; seeds of ideas planted long ago in the fertile ground of the unconscious mind. All creation is a process of birth, the moment of physical manifestation being only the climax.

Even though this human birth process can now be documented scientifically, there is still much mystery that surrounds birth. The impetus, the initiating spark that propels new life into being, is still unknown. Here in the West we link this power to God. In ancient China, they ascribed it to the Supernatural Powers of Heaven, manifesting in the Spring as Wood energy.

Exercise

Ask your mother, or another relative, about your own birth. Get as many details as possible—was it easy, or hard? How easy is it for you to give birth to things in your life now?

Record your visions . . .

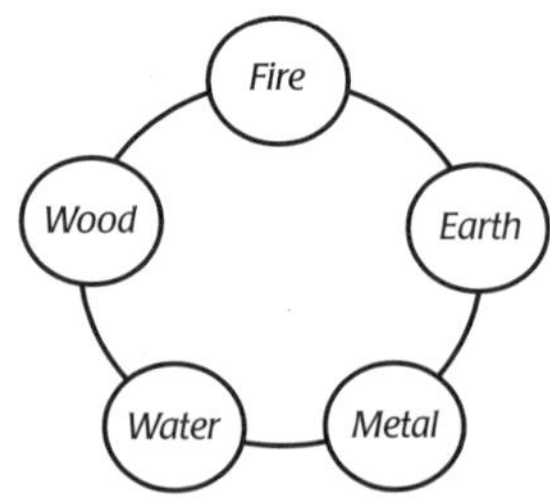

April 26

The Story of a Sperm and Egg: Yin/Yang Seeds of a Lifetime

He enters looking for her—searching past his brothers as she waits expectantly in the antechamber knowing that he is on his way. He finds her. She embraces him. They meet and are perfect for one another. The union destroys an old boundary and creates a new one. Neither knows where the other starts and stops. They become something they were not. They are a mystery—a completion of one another—a passionate mitosis as they travel together to a safe place —their lodging—a home. They grow together helping each other form structures and internal powers—purposeful and detailed in their journey. Corded to their dwelling, they are safely nourished and connected, wandering freely within bounds of their anchor.

And so they grow—fluid within fluid—a paradise of intimate communion and vast weaving—until they grow as big as their dwelling will allow. In the urgency of a greater call wistful echoes of their first meeting are heard.

It is time now—the next part of the Journey beckons to them —where they are they can go no further—and so on the threshold of new life their old home holds them tight—hugs and squeezes and moves them lovingly and laboriously out of her with a power equal to their own. They are afraid. They are angry and excited—expectant and joyous. They are sad. They feel for one another—comforting and consoling. They find their route and in noble majesty they exit and enter in union. They crown as one.

"All the Universe resounds with the Joyful cry 'I am."

Dianne M. Connelly, Ph.D., M.Ac.

Record your visions . . .

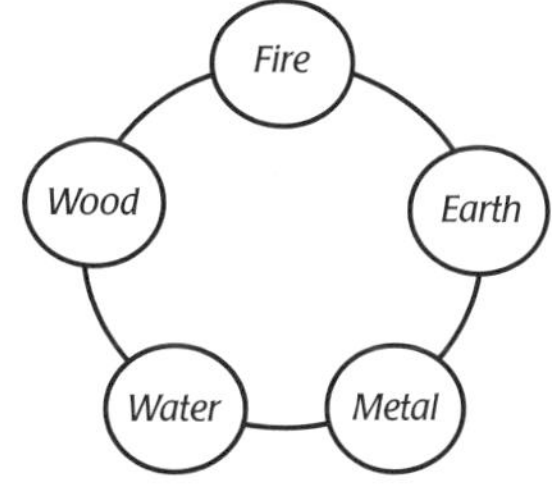

Visions

April 27

"After a night of sleep people should get up early (in the morning); they should walk briskly around the yard; they should loosen their hair and slow down their movements (body); by these means they can (fulfill) their wish to live healthfully."

- Nei Jing

The Spring is a time when, after the long hibernation of winter, we once again feel the urge to get out and exercise, to move our bodies and stretch our muscles. As the weather gets warmer, it feels easier to be active outside—blood and energy flow more easily when not coagulated from cold! Hence, the advice to "walk briskly" around the yard.

In the quotation above, the suggestion that people should "slow down their movements" is probably a reference to doing Tai Chi, the slow-moving exercise form and martial art done by many Chinese in the early morning. The slowness of the movements helps to counteract the frenetic energy of Spring.

Exercise

Start an exercise program. Or sign up for a class in Tai Chi.

Record your visions . . .

Visions

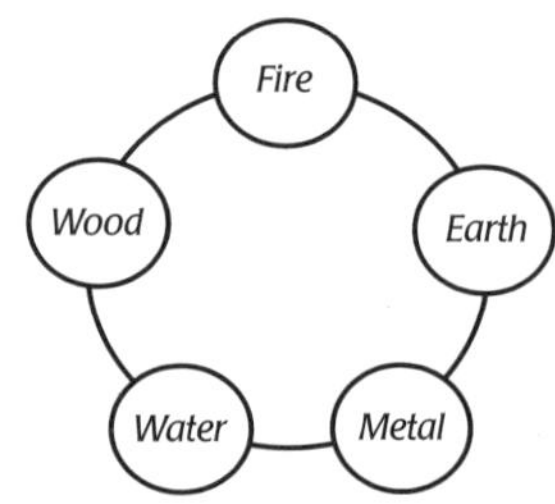

April 28

People who are strong in Wood energy need to move more than others. They find it almost impossible to sit still, and would prefer to be in motion—doing, achieving, and accomplishing. Other people can find it hard to keep up with them, as they seldom rest but move quickly from one project to another. They thrive on lots of physical exercise, and when movement is thwarted can become frustrated, antsy, and depressed.

Moving your body freely and getting adequate exercise helps keep Wood energies in balance. Long periods of enforced inactivity (i.e., sitting at a desk all day), can lead to a tremendous build-up of these energies, with resulting health problems such as high blood pressure; muscles locked in spasm; headaches; insomnia; emotional agitation; and fatigue. Many people in America today find little time to exercise; it's probably not a coincidence that we're seeing a lot of fibromyalgia, multiple sclerosis and chronic fatigue syndrome these days, all of which affect movement.

Exercise

Learn a new sport, or join a volleyball team.

Record your visions . . .

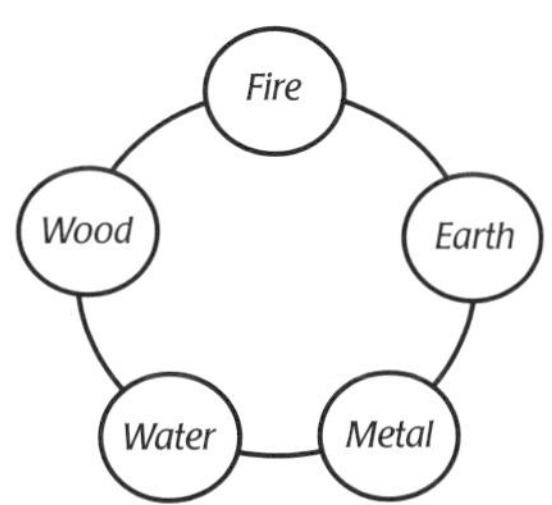

April 29

"In terms of overall morphology, the hand is well proportioned..."

- Yves Requena
Morphotypological Hand Diagnosis in Acupuncture

The Wood hand is well-proportioned, neither too long, too short, too wide, or too narrow, but it is knotty, like the branches of a tree. The palm of the hand and the inside surfaces of the fingers are grooved by many small lines. These grooves criss-cross the palm, and show as a series of parallel lines on the fingers. The dorsal or backside of the hand has a hard appearance with little flesh, looking exactly like knotty wood. The finger joints are often swollen and sometime deformed, creating again the appearance of gnarled tree trunks.

The fingernails can also reflect the quality of a person's Wood energy. Normally, the Wood fingernail is as well-proportioned as the rest of the hand, being neither too long or too short, and it is usually oblong and convex. However, in someone with strong Yang Wood, the nails can be hard and strong, with a large white area. Someone whose Wood is weak will have brittle and fragile nails, easily broken or peeling. High energy Wood types will frequently bite their nails, as well.

Exercise

Examine your hands for signs of Wood traits. Make handprints with poster paints, and compare them to others in your family.

Record your visions . . .

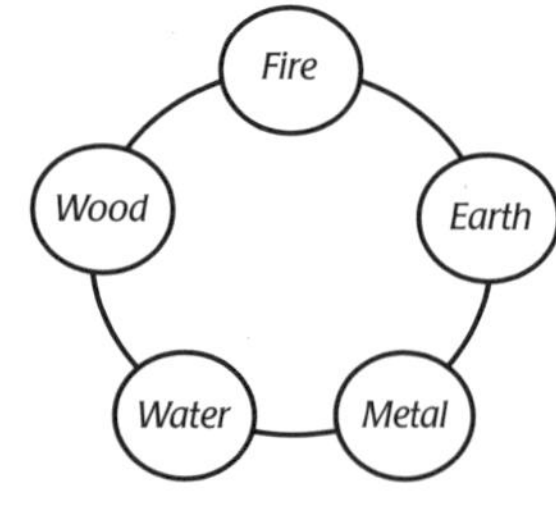

April 30

"The supernatural powers create wind in Heaven and they create wood upon earth....In times of excitement and change they grant the capacity for control."

- Nei Jing

The energy of Wood gives us the capacity to take control of a situation, whether it needs control or not! We see this as healthy in someone who takes control of his life and makes positive plans and decisions to move his own life forward. We also see it as a healthy response in someone who is placed in an emergency situation—we all respect and admire the person who can step in and "take control" when things are threatening, dangerous, or chaotic. Emergency Medical Technicians are good examples of this.

When out of balance, however, this tendency to take control can become overbearing. Someone whose Wood is imbalanced might need to be in control of every situation, and control everyone else's life, as well as his or her own. A good example of this is the woman who won't let her husband or children into the kitchen because they might mess it up.

Exercise

How much control do you feel you have in your life? Can you take control in an emergency, or do you look to someone else to do it?

Record your visions . . .

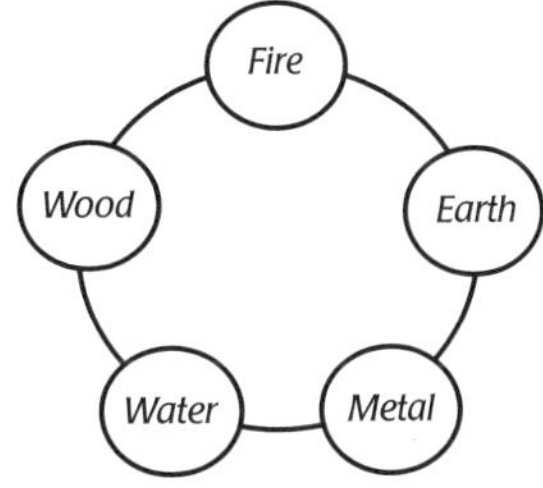

Visions

May 1

In Springtime, activities and projects that have languished all winter suddenly seem urgently in need of shaping up. We often have a burst of energy to get organized and clean up these loose threads. "Spring cleaning" is all about taking control, throwing out the old, planting the new, letting in fresh air.

We all have dealt with someone whose organizing impulses have become overriding. This is the "We've always done it this way" person, who relies on set plans and traditions, rather than creativity or current needs. In Spring we have the impulse to change things, reorganize office space and schedules, as well as the energy to "buck the system" and overcome the resistance of our co-workers.

Exercise

Open all your windows and air out your house from the winter. Set up a "Suggestion Box" at work to generate new ideas for the way to do things.

Record your visions . . .

Visions

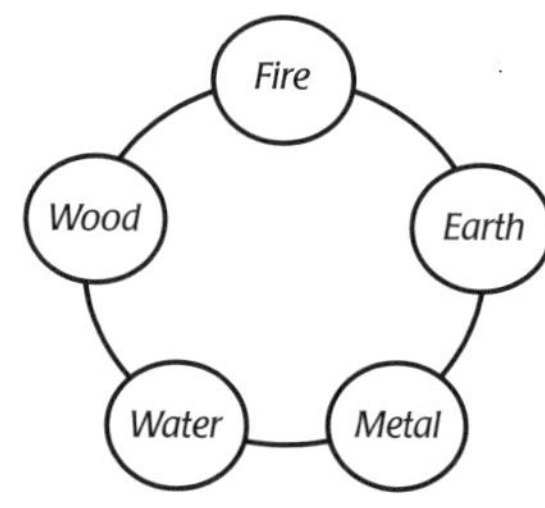

May 2

tale of the new ones

Having done our penance
as worms we spun ourselves
golden shells and hung
dreaming in the wind's cradle–
in the turbulent sleep of chrysalis
we were transfigured

the first heat of spring found us
fighting our cocoon, pushing out
dragging our crumpled wings
behind us–
we spread fragile membranes
to both sides and watched
as they dried to
dusty iridescence
in the sun

with the first
scent of flowers
we began to make
love to the garden

- Janice MacKenzie

Exercise

Plant a windowsill garden. Include flowers that will attract butterflies.

Record your visions . . .

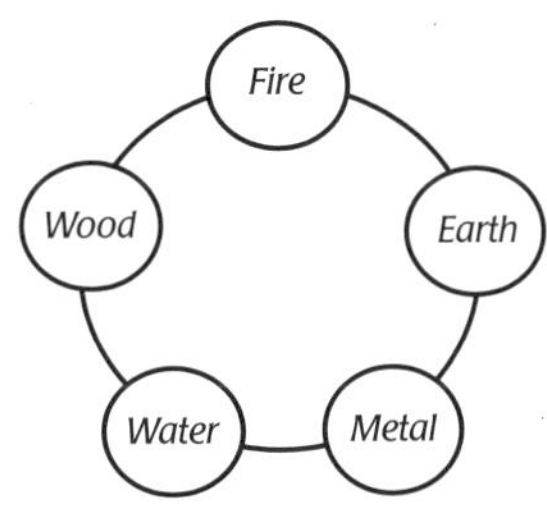

Visions

May 3

"It all began with the tiny acorn that fell from mother oak one windy autumn day. How did she teach the young one so much about being true to the self? What did she say in her own way as she bid it adieu? An abundance of starch, proteins, fats, and vitamins had been stored in the two plump seed leaves surrounding the tiny embryo. Everything was ready for its decision to burst out of its protective shell. But the embryo was in no hurry. It slept through the first winter under a blanket of twigs and leaves. Perhaps mother oak had cautioned it against peeping out too soon, lest angry winter nip its fragile shoot. Perhaps she related the tragic experience of the wayward acorns, which did not heed this wise advice during the Cretaceous period a hundred million years ago.

The embryo awakens with the coming of spring. The chemical reactivity of the enzymes and hormones is accelerated by the warm temperatures. The reserve food-stuff is solubilized and transported to the tips of the shoot and root, where the most feverish activity is occurring. The dextrose sugar, twenty or so amino acids, and other compounds are rearranged and joined in new configurations. These are incorporated into the enlarging tissues, as the growing points burgeon through the softened wall of the acorn. The tap root sinks into the soil with firm commitment. There, at that precise spot, the oak will make its life for several hundred years."

- R.G.H. Sui, *Ch'i*

Exercise

Plant a tree for a loved one. Plant another one for the environment.

Record your visions . . .

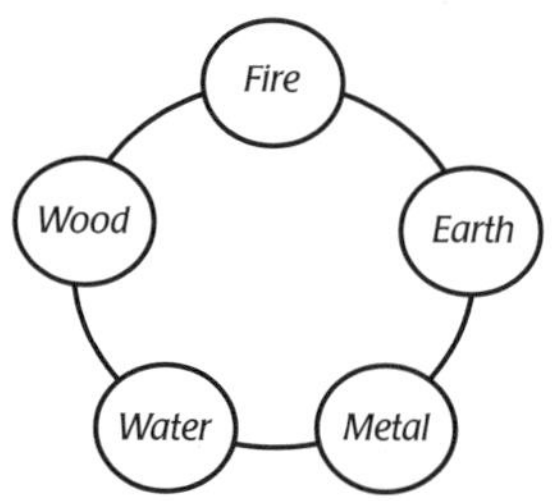

Visions

May 4

"A child said, What is the grass?..."

- Walt Whitman, *Leaves of Grass*

Shrubs, trees, grass, vines, and flowers are all expressions of the energetic phase called "Wood." They root in the earth, and have stems, branches, and leaves that grow upward into the sky. This capacity to be rooted and to grow is a key aspect of Wood Energy.

A new blade of grass needs strength in order to break through the ground's surface in the first place, and determination to stay alive and grow even in the uncertain weather of Spring. Yet a blade of grass is so soft and pliable, so easily crushed. It can be trampled, yet spring back and keep on growing. This is a good metaphor for the Wood energy of a child, and for the energy of our "child within"—vulnerable yet determined and tough. Our assertive will-to-grow must yield without ever giving up.

Exercise

Take your shoes off and walk in the greenest grass you can find.

Record your visions . . .

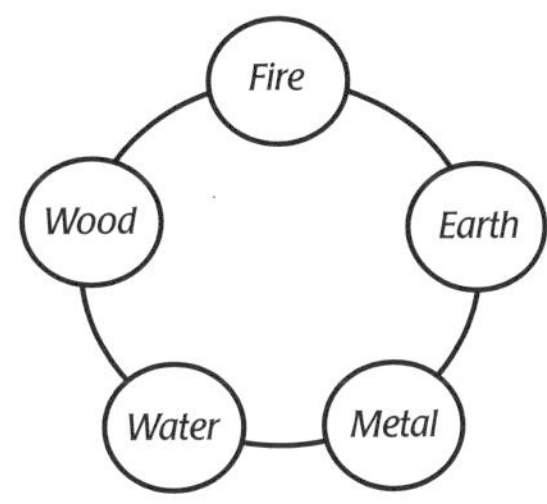

May 5

"I saw in Louisiana a live oak growing.
All alone stood it, and the moss hung down from the
branches;
Without any companion it grew there, uttering
joyous leaves of dark green,
And its look, rude, unbending, lusty, made me think
of myself..."

- Walt Whitman

Trees, with their longer life-cycle, which is closer to a human's, offer other images of growth. They not only grow upward and downward, but also outward, in expansive rings. These layers of organized growth reflect the Wood's organic organization of life—patterned, yet adapting to seasons and weather and micro-climates. The endless variety of trees make apt metaphors for the types of Wood energy we encounter in the human realm—graceful and flexible like the weeping cherry, strong and durable like the oak, and dry and brittle like the dead trunk of a poplar.

Exercise

What kind of tree are you?

Record your visions . . .

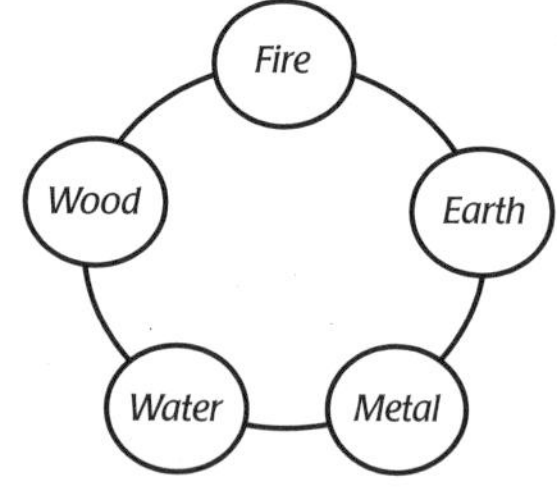

May 6

"Green...pervades the liver and lays open the eyes and retains the essential substances within the liver."

- Nei Jing

The Chinese view of the organs is a foreign, difficult concept to those of us raised with American medicine and biology. Although they use the same names that we do, the functions they ascribe to the various organs are very different from those that a Western doctor or scientist would outline. Seeing the Liver as a "military leader who excels in his strategic planning" is a far cry from our general view of the liver as a site of metabolic and chemical transformations. Chinese medicine sees the organs as body-wide systems of energy, whereas American medicine sees an organ as a way-station within a system.

Yet, there is some overlap. For example, a Western scientist sees liver function as storing excess glucose in the body in the form of glycogen and then releasing it when necessary into the bloodstream, as a short-term calorie reserve for muscular activity. Thus, the Liver "plans" for a rainy day, when the body may need more glucose than is available. As in the quote above, the Liver "retains the essential substances"—like a field marshall who arranges alternate supplies for his troops.

Exercise

Go sugar-free for a week and notice how you feel.

Record your visions . . .

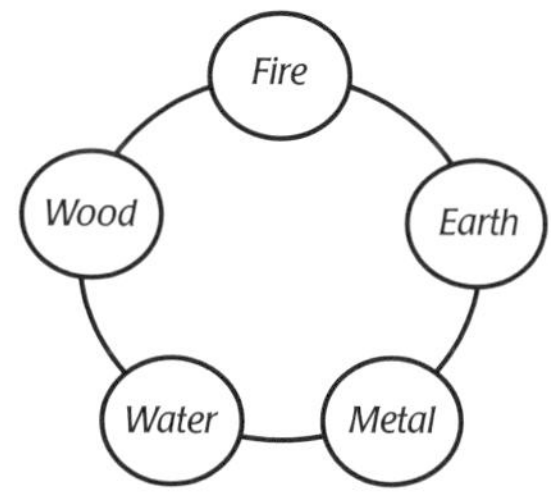

May 7

Traditional functions of the Liver, according to the Chinese, include: maintaining the smooth flow of energy, blood and emotions; storing the blood when the body is at rest and restoring it to the Heart upon exertion; ruling the sinews (muscles and tendons); and nourishing the eyes and nails. According to Simon Mills, British herbalist and author, the Liver is "Essentially a *Function* of *circulation*, of distribution, operating particularly to marshal the body's energies for the rigors of change, helping to maintain calm equilibrium of internal movement in flux and stress (it is only when it is disturbed that the system becomes sensitive to wind, the meteorological metaphor for changeable stresses)...It is particularly linked with *muscular exertion* and *emotional arousal*." Thus, the Liver both provides the energy for muscular exertion, and benefits from that exertion because of the increased circulation.

Exercise

An hour of gardening can burn as many calories as a three-and -a-half mile brisk walk, according to Barbara Pearlman, author of *Gardener's Fitness: Weeding out the Aches and Pains.*

Record your visions . . .

Visions

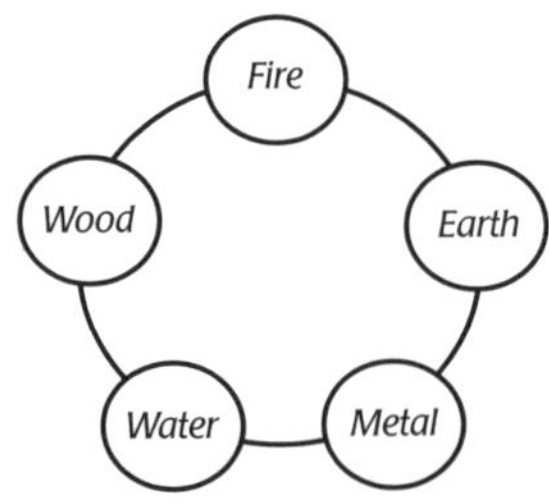

May 8

The Gall Bladder, as one of the Yang organs, does not have as many traditional functions as the Liver. However, it is perceived as special among Yang organs because it is the only one that doesn't deal directly with food, drink, or their waste products or have direct communication to the exterior, as do all the other Yang organs (via the mouth, rectum or urethra). In fact, because it stores the bile, a "clean" and refined substance, it more closely resembles a Yin organ.

The primary functions of the Gall Bladder are: to store and excrete bile; to control judgment and decision-making; to energize the sinews; and to assist the Liver. The first of these, of course, is the same as the Western understanding of the gall bladder, which is to store and concentrate the bile from the liver and then to excrete it into the small intestine to aid in the digestion of fats. In a sense, the Gall Bladder must "decide" the appropriate moment to release some bile, and the correct amount. Therefore, the whole digestive function depends upon the Gall Bladder's appropriate judgment. If a disturbance in the Liver or Gall Bladder obstructs the smooth flow of bile, then the Stomach and Spleen's functions may be impaired as well, with symptoms of nausea and belching.

Exercise

Observe how much and which kinds of fats are in your diet.

Record your visions . . .

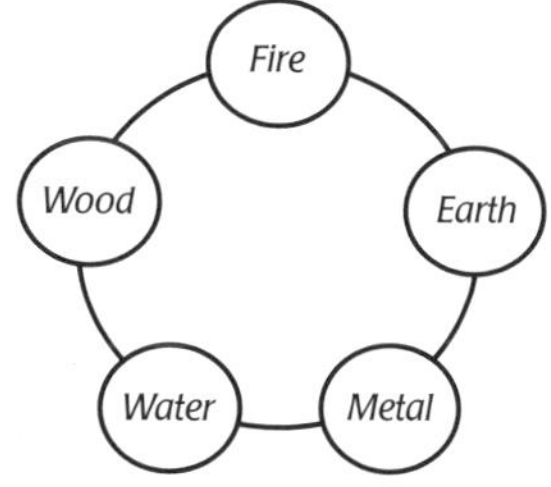

May 9

When the anger from the Liver is concentrated in the Gall Bladder, it condenses into a bitter, resentful, lingering anger that in English we sometimes call "bile." Indeed, the anger coming from the Gall Bladder is much more vitriolic than the everyday anger from the Liver—we speak of flaming, disrespectful behavior as being "galling," and say that we are "really galled" by certain people or events. Sometimes, these resentments become as hard and inflexible as a "stone." The *Nei Jing* says, "The gall bladder causes fits of anger." Thus, when the concentrated resentments finally are released, they can squirt out in particularly nasty ways.

Exercise

Give yourself a 5-minute scalp massage the next time you shampoo, concentrating on the sides of your head and behind your ears. This stimulates the Gall Bladder meridian.

Record your visions . . .

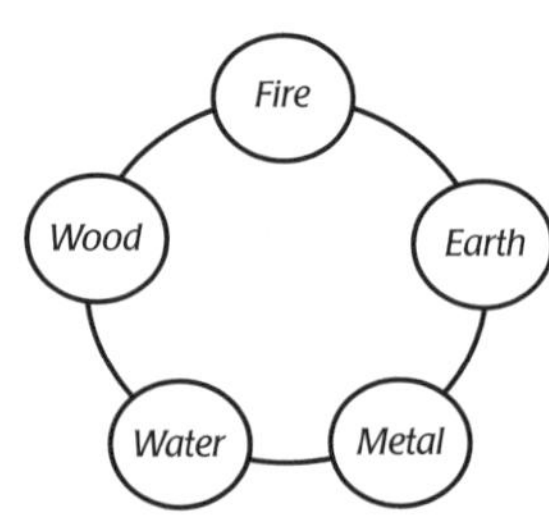

May 10

Besides controlling decision-making, the Gall Bladder is also said to give an individual courage and initiative. For this reason, in Chinese, there are several expressions, such as "big gall bladder," meaning "courageous," and "small gall bladder," meaning "timid or fearful."

This is an important function of the Gall Bladder on a psychological level. It controls the spirit of initiative, the "drive," and the courage to make decisions and make changes. Although, as we have seen, the Kidneys also control the "drive" and vitality, the Gall Bladder gives us the capacity to turn this drive and vitality into positive and decisive action. Thus, a deficient Gall Bladder will cause indecision and timidity and the affected person will be easily discouraged at the slightest adversity.

- Giovanni Maciocia,
The Foundations of Chinese Medicine

Exercise

Listen to some wild, angry rock 'n' roll music to get "psyched" to do a task that you have been avoiding.

Record your visions . . .

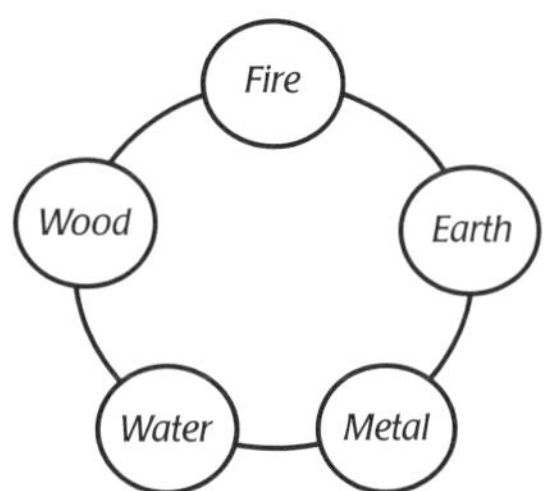

Visions

May 11

"...and of the musical notes they create the note chio (角);"

- Nei Jing

The sound *Chio* corresponds to the sound of violent winds. In the ancient practice of war divination used to ascertain the morale of armies before battle, the diviner blew his qi or "vital energy" through a pipe and set up a disturbance, causing his *qi* to act on the army's collective *qi*. Therefore, if he played a strong note, the army's morale was strong. A five-fold division was made according to certain timbres or qualities of sound. In the Chinese *Book of War,* these five qualities of sound were interpreted according to the assessment of a group *qi* : "If it is *chio,* the army is troubled; many vacillate, and lose their martial courage."

The sound of a raging wind can be unsettling—witness the well-known effects of the Santa Ana winds in California. Strong winds can make the mind feel buffeted, confused, and indecisive—the description of Wood out of balance.

Exercise

Tape a calming line from a favorite song on the dashboard of your car—something like "Let it be," or "I've got a peaceful, easy feeling." Sing it aloud as needed in traffic.

Record your visions . . .

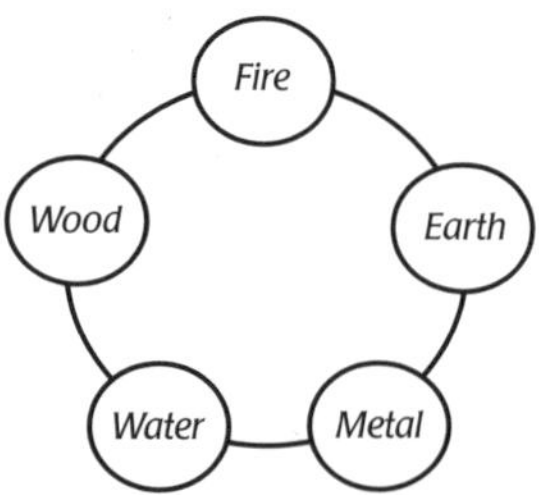

Visions

May 12

Spring musical instruments were made of bamboo—a plant that remains green, even in winter. From the *Book of War*: "The sound of bamboo flutes is a gurgling like flood waters. Flood waters entail levies. Levies involve gathering the people (for their tasks). When the man of breeding listens to the sound of the bamboo pipes *yu, sheng, hsiao,* and *kuan,* he thinks of officials who have been the shepherds of the people."

And from the ancient text *Tz'u Hai* : "'What's called *chio* is orderly,' as the people in an ordered state. This sound is both circular and elongated, clear and muddy." (Clear and muddy refer to high and low vibrational frequencies.) The idea that certain tones can produce certain associations and moods appears in many musical traditions, from Hindu chants to Western principles of harmony to New Age synthesized music. The healing power of music, first mentioned in these ancient medical and political texts, is being investigated and used by practitioners today.

Exercise

While working at home, put on a tape of Japanese bamboo flute music. How does it make you feel?

Record your visions . . .

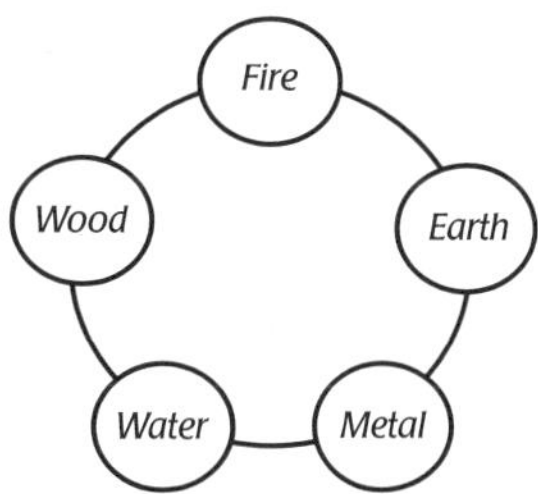

Visions

May 13

"Very early in the morning of today, I did get out of my bed and I did get dressed in a quick way. Then I climbed out the window of the house we live in. The sun was up, and the birds were singing. I went my way. As I did go, I did have hearing of many voices—they were the voices of earth, glad for the spring. They did say what they had to say in the growing grass, and in the leaves growing out from tips of branches. The birds did have knowing, and sang what the grasses and leaves did say of the gladness of living. I too did feel glad feels, from my toes to my curls."

- Opal Whitely (aged 6 or so), from her childhood diary

Exercise

What is your earliest childhood memory? Is it a happy one?

Record your visions . . .

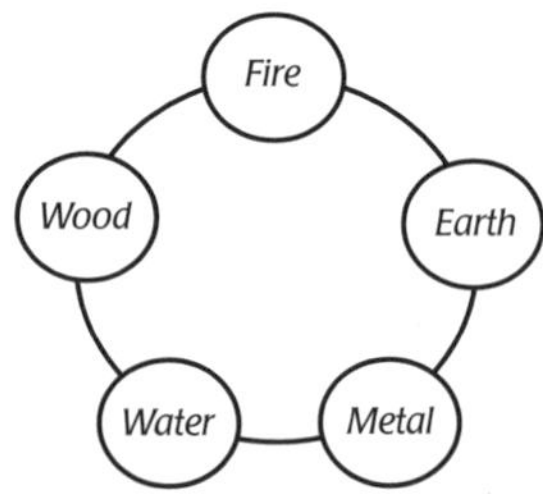

May 14

Here is a tree older than the
forest itself
The years of its life defy reckoning.
Its roots have seen the upheavals
of hill and valley,
Its leaves have known the changes
of wind and frost.
The world laughs at its shoddy
exterior
And cares nothing for the fine grain
of the wood inside.
Stripped free of flesh and hide,
All the remains is the core of
truth.

- Han-shan
T'ang Dynasty poet

Exercise

Study carpentry or woodworking; feel the different textures of wood as you saw, hammer, turn on a lathe, sand, stain, paint, and varnish it.

Record your visions . . .

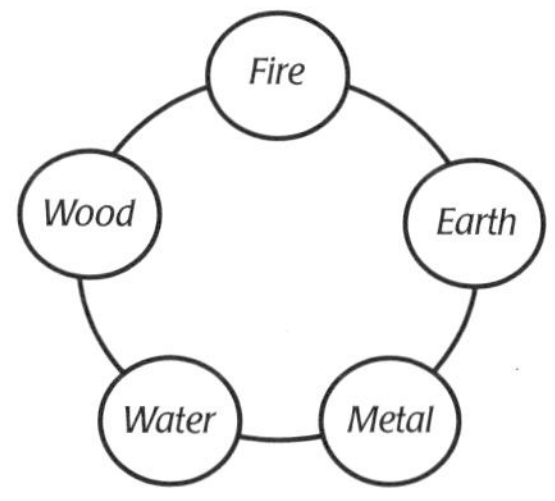

May 15

What distinguishes a garden from a meadow? Someone has sown the seeds of certain plants in it, and then has weeded out any other plants that happen to grow there. This weeding, as any gardener will tell you, can be a very satisfying activity—when you are done, the vegetables are in neat rows, and the flowers stand out in orderly and eye-pleasing patterns. Out of Nature's boggling profusion, the gardener has chosen to focus all of her attention on just a few plants, and to eliminate all others.

Inside of us as human beings, the Wood energy is also constantly proliferating—new ideas, new projects, new visions are constantly sending forth fresh shoots. If we spend our energy trying to develop all of them, or jumping from one to another, our lives may become a mess of tangled vegetation—the kind of strong plants that take over from those that require more careful nurture. Weeding is an important function of Wood energy, as we decide what we can uproot, ignore, or throw away. We can then water, fertilize, and nurture the ideas and plans that mean the most to us. Our life gardens will then be orderly, pleasing, and productive.

Exercise

Reorganize your desk; start with one drawer, and keep at it until you finish the task over time. Throw out everything for which you no longer have a use.

Record your visions . . .

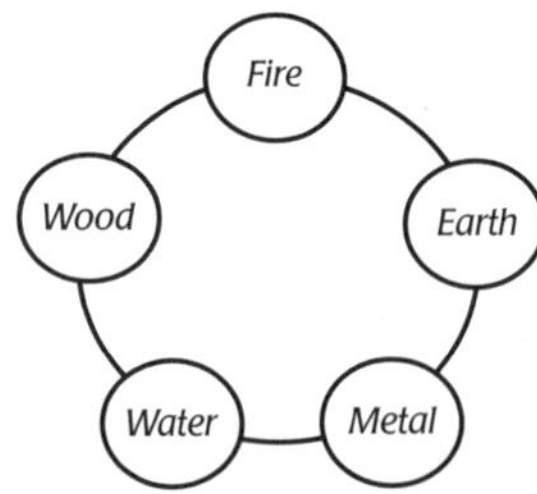

Visions

May 16

"During an acupuncture treatment for the Spring season last year, my practitioner asked quite casually, 'What are you doing that's new this Spring'? I was taken aback—in fact, I was just doing the same old routine of seeing patients, working for the acupuncture society, and handling social obligations. Although I was enjoying my life, there was nothing that I could really call *new* about it. My life already felt too full of work and other activities; something new would require letting go of something already there. My practitioner's question dramatically brought home that all was not well in my Wood energies —I was not in harmony with the season. Perhaps I needed to 'weed my garden' or do some pruning so that some new things could grow there. I clearly had to get rid of some of the dead branches, so that I could be revitalized by the season. Now, in the Spring, I make sure to ask myself (and my patients), 'What's new?'"

– From a practitioner's journal

Exercise

Take a course in something you've always wanted to learn.

Record your visions . . .

Visions

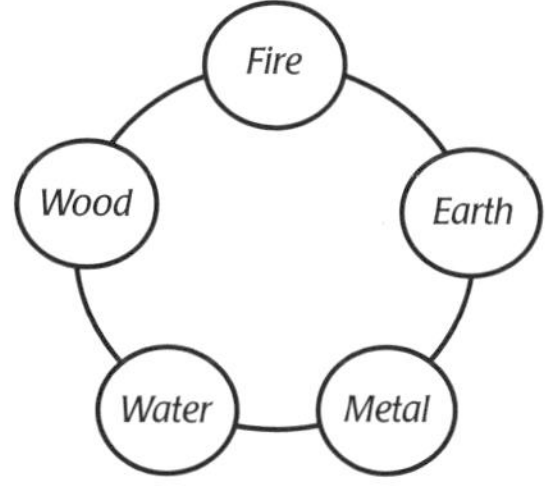

May 17

The power of Wood to step forward and try new things is the birthright of every child. By the plans and decisions we make (or others make for us), we begin to shape our personality in the world. The task of childhood is to grow and to learn, so any time we experience growth or learn something new, it is our Wood energy that is being expressed.

Every spring we have an opportunity to experience again the giddy, headlong rush of enthusiasm for life we experienced as a child. We call this feeling "Spring Fever." In fact, every day we can access this feeling if we are in balance with our Wood energies. Much has been made lately of getting in touch with the often-buried feelings and energies of the "inner" child. These techniques strengthen the Wood energy within us.

Exercise

Just for today, go for a walk with no destination and let your feet take you where they will. Remember the childhood art of doing nothing.

Record your visions . . .

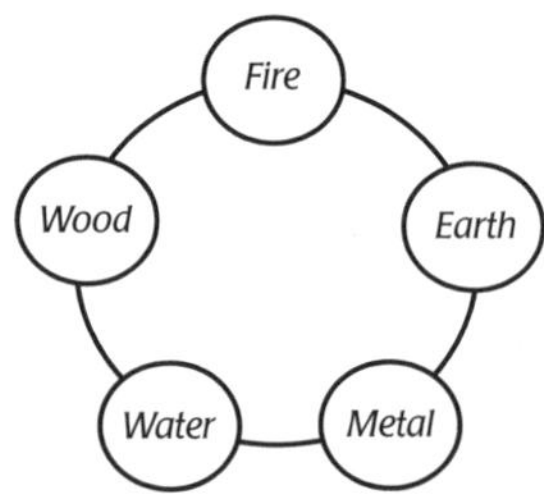

May 18

First Spring

This has been the first spring
That I haven't experienced
That sad-regretful feeling
Of having missed something irrevocable
Other years the spring came unawares
Without my noticing
The little buds unseen until they were fully grown
From green to reds and yellows
Forsythia and dogwood
The first wave of flowers
Harbingers of things to come
Were here and gone
Before I noticed them
So narcoticized was I
That I didn't see the birth of spring
Nor feel the pain
As boughs bear down with buds again
This has been a different kind of spring for me
As I sit in the park under my favorite tree
I've learned the meaning of reciprocity
I have helped give birth to spring
And spring in turn is mothering me

- Judith S. Field

Exercise

If it's a warm, sunny day, sit in a garden and see if you can watch things grow before your eyes. Listen to the sounds and smell the smells of Spring.

Record your visions . . .

Visions

May 19

"I merely took the energy it takes to pout and wrote some blues."

- Duke Ellington

"Anger is fuel," says Julia Cameron in *The Artist's Way*. It propels us into action, and points and shoves us in a direction. It empowers us to act on our ideas and creative impulses, rather than stuffing them.

The act of creation seems to move the Wood energy so that negative feelings transform. Julia Cameron again: " I have come to believe that creativity is our true nature, that blocks are an unnatural thwarting of a process at once as normal and as miraculous as the blossoming of a flower at the end of a slender green stem." As in the above quote, creativity can transform a pout into a song.

Exercise

Visualize something you'd like in your life, and make a collage of it, using cut paper, magic markers, pictures cut from magazines, glitter, and paint.

Record your visions . . .

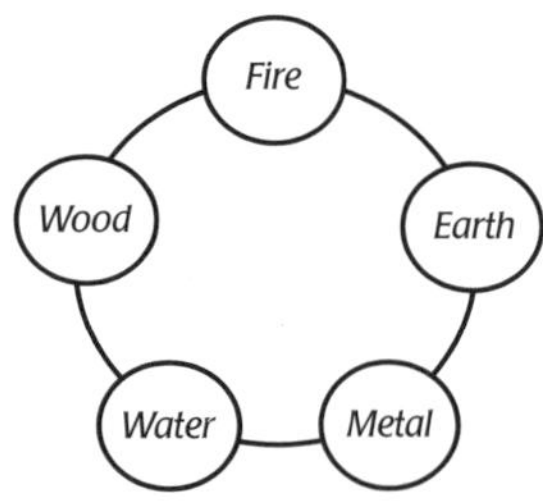

May 20

How shall the mighty river
reach the tiny seed?
See it rise silently
to the sun's yearning,
sail from a winter's cloud
flake after silent flake
piling up layer upon layer
until the thaw of spring
to meet the seedling's need.

- Antoinette Adam,
Weavings

Exercise

Buy a plant for every room in your house. Check to see how often each should be watered, and make up a schedule for yourself to water them.

Record your visions . . .

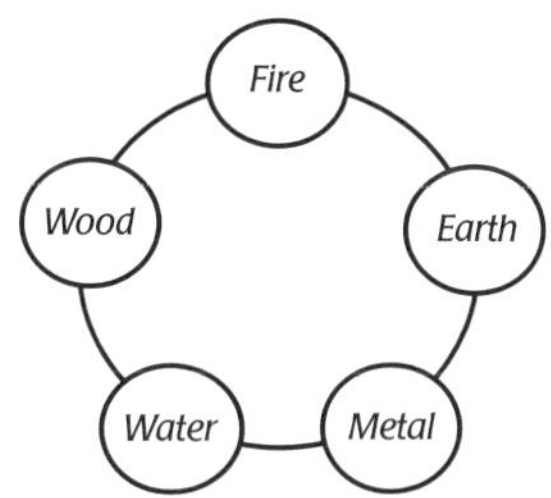

May 21

"The creation of something new is not accomplished by the intellect but by the play instinct acting from inner necessity. The creative mind plays with the objects it loves."

- Carl G. Jung

Like the new plants growing out of Winter's mud, creative ideas seem to pop out of the unconscious into the light of day. Wood's capacity for planning and organization can then help to shape the idea into reality.

Creativity is aligned with the playful, spontaneous energies of childhood. This "playing" is not done in a linear, rational way, and cannot be rigidly structured or scheduled. Author Brenda Ueland said, "Imagination needs noodling—long, inefficient happy idling, dawdling and puttering." Making the creation manifest, however, may need the organizing and structuring aspects of Wood.

Exercise

Waste an entire afternoon playing in the park.

Record your visions . . .

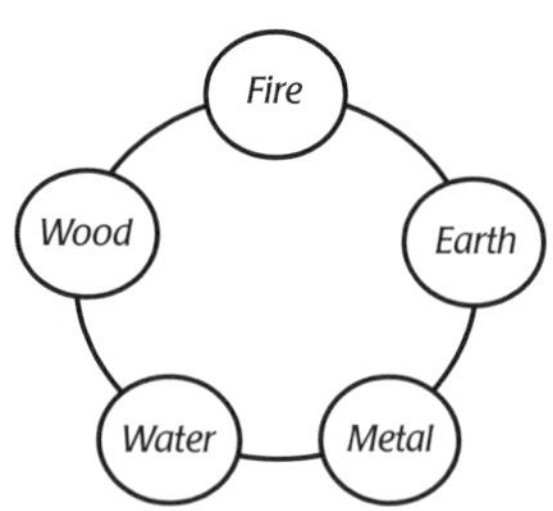

May 22

Behold, my brothers, the spring has come;
The earth has received the embraces of the sun
And we shall soon see the results of that love!

Every seed is awakened and so has all animal life.
It is through this mysterious power that we too have
our being
And we therefore yield to our neighbors,
Even our animal neighbors,
The same right as ourselves, to inhabit this land.

- Sitting Bull

Exercise

Explore seed catalogs for interesting varieties of flowers or herbs to plant in your garden this year.

Record your visions . . .

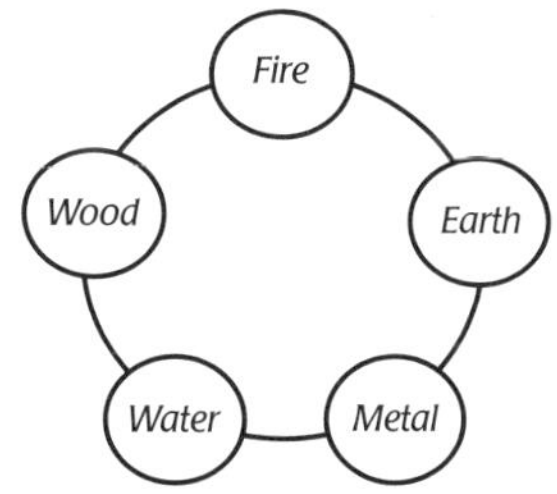

May 23

The clear vision and determination of Wood gives us the capacity to stand up for ourselves, to put ourselves forward, and to claim what is ours. We say that people with balanced Wood energy are self-confident, "go-getters," with initiative and gumption.

When this energy is excessive, assertiveness can be seen as aggressiveness, pushiness, or egomania. Because the Wood energy is bound up with the ego, we say that someone with excessive Wood energy is "full of himself," "self-important," or just "has a big ego."

The opposite of this is the person who has a weak ego, and is seen as timid, lacking in "fiber," weak-willed, and passive. This person is said to have low self-esteem. There is an acupuncture point on the Liver meridian named "Great Esteem," which might be used in these cases.

Exercise

Listen to the way you talk to yourself. Replace negative words with encouraging ones.

Record your visions . . .

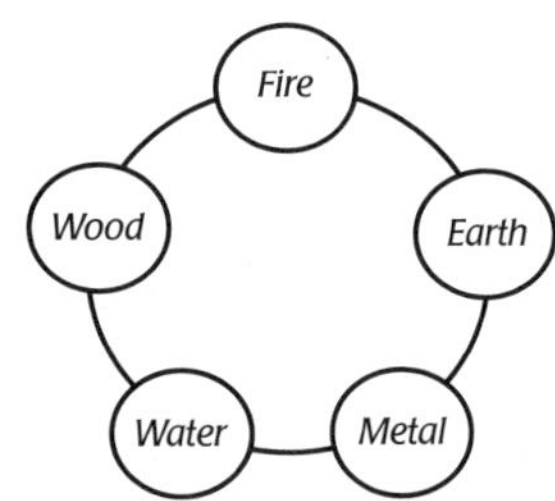

May 24

An aspect of Wood energy linked with assertiveness is boundaries. With a healthy ego, we have an appropriate sense of our own boundaries—what is me and what is not-me. We can defend ourselves from unwanted invasion or attack. On the body level, Wood energy has a role to play in the immune system.

On the psychological level, healthy Wood enables you to say "no" to someone. It gives you the power to maintain your boundaries so your time, your energy, and your life aren't leaked away to others. This is an important issue for people in the helping professions, as well as for women with children, whose lives are devoted to giving energy to others. Is it any wonder that many mothers of young children develop gall bladder disease?

Exercise

Practice saying "No."

Record your visions . . .

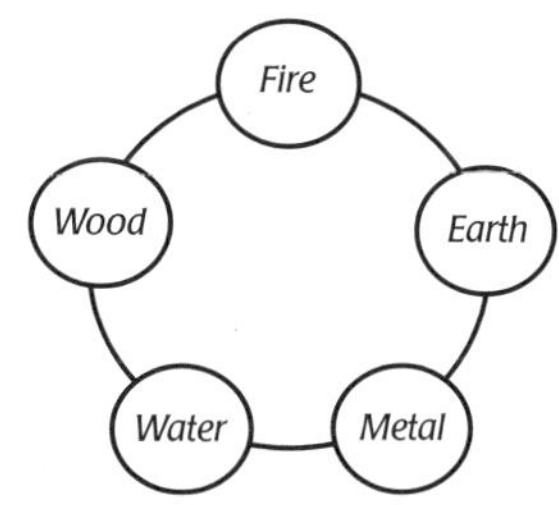

May 25

"When the shaman-poet and warrior Fionn macCumhail imbibed knowledge and understanding from consuming part of the Salmon of Wisdom, he at once burst into ecstatic song, celebrating the glory of the natural world:

May: fair aspected,
perfect season;
blackbirds sing
where the sun glows,

The hardy cuckoo calls
a welcome to noble summer;
ends the bitter storms
that strip the trees of the wood.

Summer cuts the streams;
swift horses seek water;
the heather grows tall;
fair foliage flourishes..."

- John Matthews
The Celtic Shaman

Exercise

Travel someplace you've never been to see new vistas.

Record your visions . . .

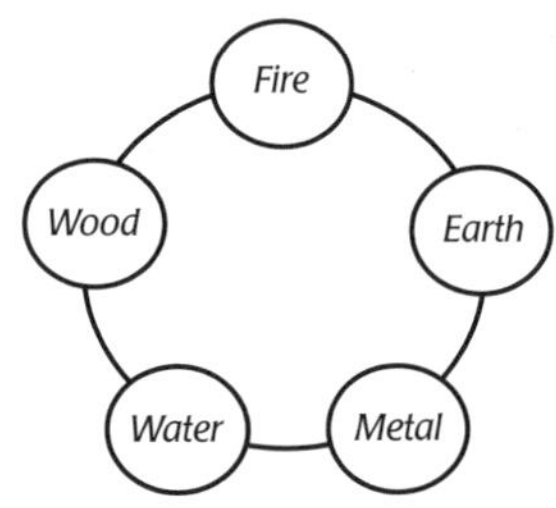

Visions

Sunflowers, watercolor

SUMMER

火

Summer/Fire

"The south wind arises in Summer..."

"The three months of summer are called the period of luxurious growth. The breaths of Heaven and Earth intermingle and are beneficial. Everything is in bloom and begins to bear fruit."

"The supernatural [powers] of summer create heat in Heaven and fire upon Earth. They create the pulse within the body and the heat within the viscera. Of the colors they create the red color...and they give to the human voice the ability to express joy."

- Nei Jing

The energy of the Summertime is Fire. Fire as a metaphor contains all of the qualities of this season—warmth, light, expansiveness, and transformation. The sun's heat and light now bring the plants that sprouted in the Spring to full maturity and flowering. In our own lives, we experience this flowering during early adulthood, as our bodies reach full growth and sexual maturity. This time of life concerns the fiery, passionate energy of sexuality, romance, relationships, and partnering. We seek connection, communication, and expression, and if our Fire energies are healthy, we experience love and the joys of friendship and intimacy.

Weak Fire energy may leave us cold, joyless, lonely, and unhappy. Our relationships may be unfulfilling, chaotic, or destructive. Or, we may experience real problems in communication, in letting others know our thoughts and feelings. Without Fire, life would lose much of its savor and meaning. In the words of the old song: "The greatest thing/ you will ever learn/ is just to love/ and be loved in return."

The Fire energy in our bodies governs our physical warmth and the circulation of blood. The ability to maintain an even body temperature and to be adequately warmed from within is governed by Fire. Problems with circulation, such as arteriosclerosis, varicose veins, and chronically cold hands and feet could point to an imbalance in the Fire energy.

The organs associated with the Fire element are the Heart and Small Intestine. The Heart is both the pump that circulates our blood, and the place in the body where we feel love and joy. The Chinese classics say that the Heart stores the Shen, or spirit. Thus, it is really the center or master coordinator for the whole body-mind-spirit.

The Small Intestine is seen as the Sorter of the Pure from the Impure. This process is alchemical, sorting physical substances into pure and impure in the digestive tract, as well as sorting on the mental and emotional levels. It assists the Heart by making sure that only pure substances, thoughts, and feelings pass through to the Heart.

Two functions associated with Fire are not connected to specific organs. They are the Heart Protector and the Triple Heater. The Heart Protector protects the Heart physically through the circulatory system, by regulating the amount of blood that flows into the heart, and also emotionally, by absorbing blows and traumas so that the Heart itself is never touched. The *Nei Jing* says the Heart Protector "guides the subjects in their joys and pleasures"—and so is equated with love, sexuality, and the ability to enjoy oneself.

The Triple Heater maintains an even temperature in the organs and in the rest of the body. It links all of the organs and functions together, making sure there is coordination and harmony. It also governs the social temperature, the warmth between people, and in the environment, allowing for harmony in the social milieu.

Mentally, the Fire energies have to do with the clarity of thought — with insight and understanding, and the wisdom of the Heart. The Small Intestine helps to sort out ideas, and to separate out the waste from the essentials.

As in the West, the Chinese strongly associate the Heart with happiness—but they also link it to sadness. The capacity for sadness is a power granted by Fire, since only a strong Heart can bear to truly feel the sadness and poignancy of life. Again, we look for appropriate balance—excess joy in the form of ceaseless pursuit of pleasure or a manic drive can be as injurious as constant sadness.

Spiritually, the Fire energy has to do with the qualities of insight, understanding, compassion, and love. The classics say: "The Heart stores and harbors the divine spirit." When our connection to divine spirit is strong, we experience harmony and balance of all the elements within us, an integrity of life, and a spark of divine consciousness. You could almost say that the Fire element represents consciousness itself—the capacity for self-knowledge, insight, and compassion. In the words of Teilhard de Chardin: "Someday, after mastering the wind, the waves, the tides and gravity, we shall harness for God the energies of Love, and then, for the second time in the history of the world, we will discover fire."

May 26

"The supernatural [powers] of Summer create heat in Heaven and fire upon Earth."

- Nei Jing

Summer is the season connected to the Fire element, which makes good intuitive sense since it is the season with the hottest temperatures and the most hours of daylight. The sun, which is the purest emblem of Fire, is closest to the earth in summer, bringing its dynamic qualities of warmth and light to bear upon the earth and its creatures. In the Summer, all of the new growth that began in the Spring flourishes and reaches its maximum height—the Chinese would say it reaches a state of maturity. In human life, this would be the time of young adulthood—when our bodies and minds mature, and we become capable of functioning in society on our own.

Exercise

Sit in the sun and feel its warmth on your skin.

Share your expressions . . .

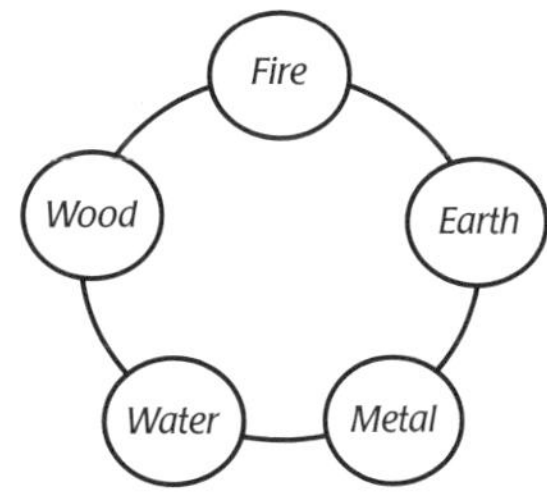

May 27

Summer is an expansive time—the trees and plants grow continuously and steadily, although not as rapidly as in the Spring. Spring's quick spark gives way to the steady flame of Summer. Just so, our human activity evens out in adulthood and we move at a slower but steadier pace. In nature, this part of the cycle is necessary to reach a point where the plants can reproduce themselves and bear fruit. In human life also, this flourishing is what we naturally grow toward if allowed to mature without interference. For some people, too much inhibition in the Spring of childhood could lead to an inability to expand and flourish in adulthood, resulting in a cramped and immature personality—one who can spark an idea but not carry it through to completion.

Exercise

Finish one task today that has been hanging over you for a long time. Use your Fire energy to steadily make progress toward your goal.

Share your expressions . . .

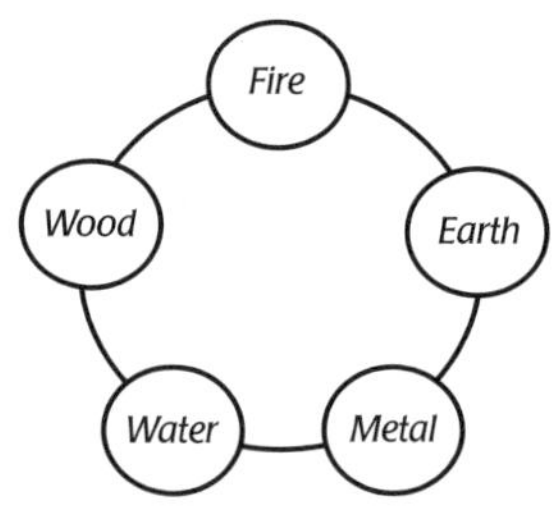

May 28

Heat is the climate associated with the season of Summer. According to Chinese thinking, "heat" goes beyond the matter of simple temperature. "Heat" is associated with expansion, activity, dynamism, rising up, boiling, and melting. By observation, the Chinese saw that when heat was applied to water, it caused the water to boil, become active, expand, and rise up in the form of steam. They extrapolated this principle to other natural phenomena—including human life.

Thus, the summer was seen as a time for maximum human activity. In the *Nei Jing*, in the chapter on the appropriate activities for Summer, it says "After a night of sleep people should get up early (in the morning). They should not weary during daytime..." With more hours of daylight, we can accomplish more during the summer than any other time of year, and since the energy of summer is expansive, it is appropriate to do so.

Exercise

Get up at sunrise at least one day this week. See how much more you can accomplish with your longer day.

Share your expressions . . .

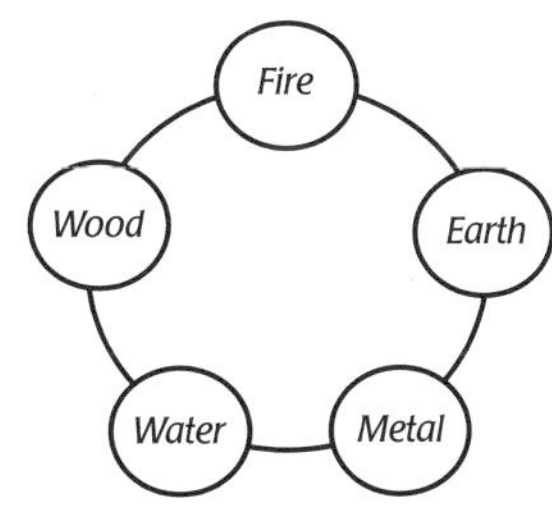

Expressions

May 29

In the Summer, our bodies expand and become energized, in contrast to Winter's contraction and stillness. We can move more freely and work more energetically. This is correct conduct for the Summer time—however, some people become so "overheated" that they carry this Fire energy into other seasons, where it is less appropriate. These people often feel irritable, agitated, and uncomfortable. Physically, they may experience insomnia, hot flashes, inflamed joints and muscles, feverishness, palpitations, or high blood pressure. Mentally, they have trouble concentrating because their thoughts race too fast and become confused. Emotionally, they can experience a manic exuberance but be incapable of committing to anyone or anything. This "excess heat" tends to be exacerbated in the Summer.

When we are in balance with the "heat" climate of Summer, we feel warm and expanded, relaxed but energized, and capable of a sustained effort that brings our projects to completion. We enjoy the heat of the Summer, and can adapt our activities to be in harmony with it.

Exercise

List three activities that are easier for you to do in Summer than any other time of year.

Share your expressions . . .

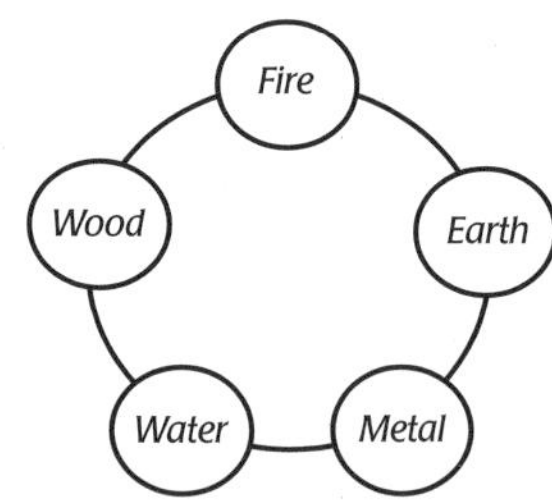

Expressions

May 30

"Red is the color of the South..."

- Nei Jing

In the *Nei Jing*, Summer is associated with the color red. Again, the tie-in with Fire is obvious here—red is the color of Fire just as blue is the color of Water. The color red inspires a sense of heat, liveliness, excitement, warmth—the essence of Fire energy. We only have to watch the sun setting on a hot summer's day as a fiery red ball to see where the Chinese got this connection.

In English, we have phrases that also illustrate this connection —"red-hot coals," "red in the face," "red with exertion," "rosy-red complexion," "red as blood," etc. Most of our connections with the color red embody life, love, warmth, and excitement.

Exercise

Watch the sun setting and see how it reddens as it nears the horizon. Go inside and light a red candle.

Share your expressions . . .

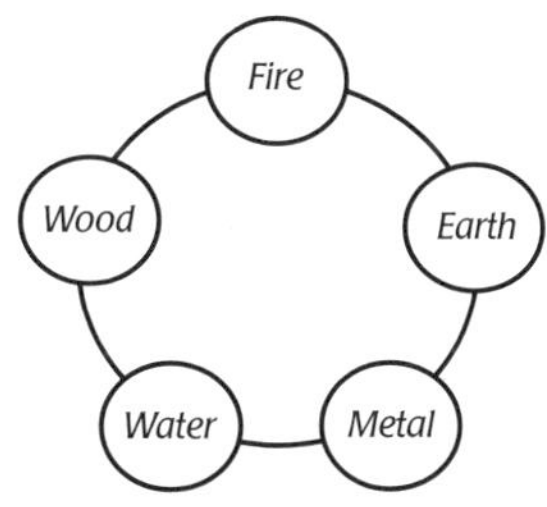

May 31

"O, my luve is like a red, red rose.."

- Robert Burns

The connection of red with Fire energy shows up in many ways in our human lives. Someone with a Fire imbalance can show a predominantly red hue emanating from the face, or a strong preference for red clothing. Conversely, the face could show an ashen, "lack-of-red" color—an absence of red—and the person could declare a strong dislike of red clothing.

We can use the color red to enhance the Fire energy in ourselves. If we are feeling a bit cold or low in energy, wearing the color red can actually make us feel warmer and livelier. However, if we are feeling overheated or scattered, then the color red will tend to make us feel worse. Red is a good counterbalancing "warm" color to wear in the Winter or when we feel cold or drawn in.

Exercise

Wear something red today; put red satin sheets on your bed.

Share your expressions . . .

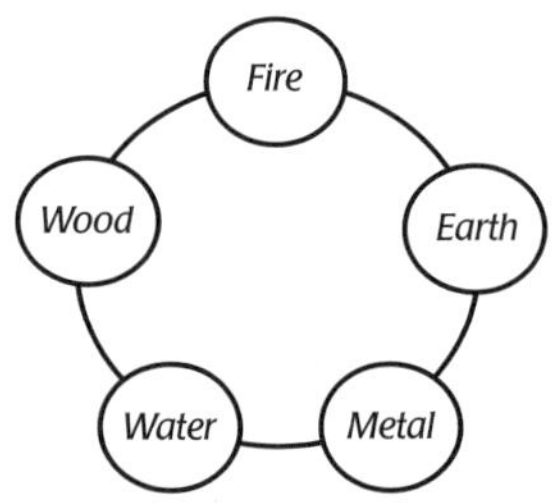

June 1

"Nourishment and growth come from the South. The Sun makes the life of those who live in the regions of the South plentiful and nourishing."

- Nei Jing

South is the direction of the compass associated with the Fire element and the season of Summer. For those of us in the Northern hemisphere, this connection makes a lot of intuitive sense—the further South one goes, the warmer it gets! Also, windows facing South get more sunlight all year round. Many other philosophic systems from Northern hemisphere climates have correlated the direction of South with the energy of Fire, including some Native American traditions and the Celtic or Wiccan practices. Sun Bear, a Chippewa sacred teacher, said in his book, Dancing with the Wheel, "The South is the time of summer, of the years of our fruitfulness, and of our most rapid growth."

Exercise

Lie on a sunny, grassy hillside facing South and watch clouds pass overhead.

Share your expressions . . .

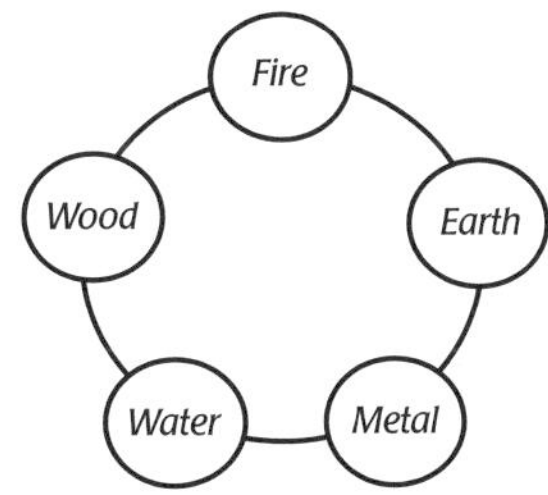

Expressions

June 2

The *Nei Jing* states that acupuncture originated in the Southern regions of China: "The people who live in the regions of the South crave sour food and curd. They are secretive and soft in their ways and attached to the red color. Their diseases are bent and contracted muscles and numbness. These diseases are most fittingly treated with acupuncture with fine needles. Hence the treatment with the nine needles comes from the South."

The Chinese character for South combines characters for luxuriance and for creeping vegetation, or vines. In one Chinese dictionary, the character for South is defined as "the country of lianas" [a type of tropical vine]. Thus, we can see the ancient classical connection between the direction of South and the season of Summer, as stated in the *Nei Jing*: "The three months of Summer are called the period of luxurious growth."

Exercise

Walk in a flower garden and admire the flowers. Notice how lush the vegetation is now as compared to Spring.

Share your expressions . . .

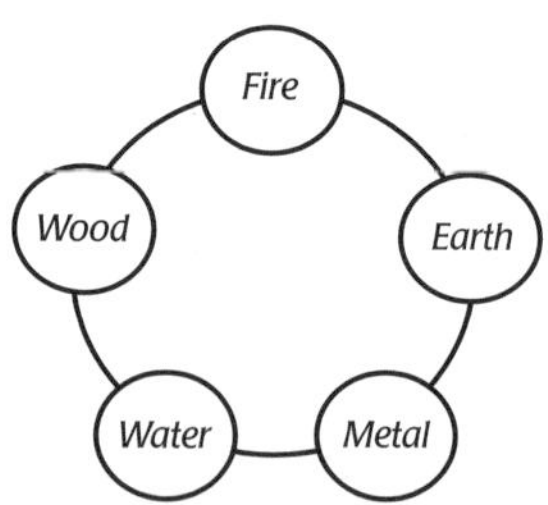

June 3

"Red is the color of the South, it pervades the heart...."

- Nei Jing

The Heart is one of the organs associated with the Fire element, along with its sister organ, the Small Intestine. The *Nei Jing* says, "The heart is like the minister of the monarch who excels through insight and understanding." Professor J. R. Worsley calls the Heart "The Supreme Controller"—the one official who oversees all of the activities of the other officials of the Kingdom. As such, the Heart coordinates and unites all aspects of the body-mind-spirit. Thus, when the Heart is balanced, all is well in the Kingdom; however, if the monarch falls sick, there is panic and chaos in the land, a terrifying sense that all is out of control. When we feel this loss of control inside of us, the Chinese would call it an imbalance of the Heart.

Exercise

Close your eyes, place your hands over your heart and repeat this affirmation: "I am in the center and in control of my life at every moment."

Share your expressions . . .

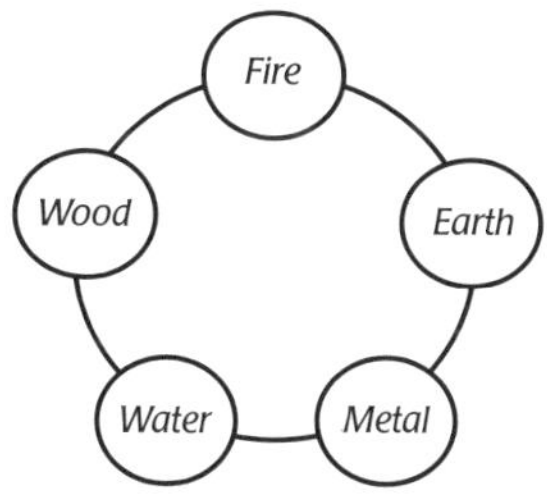

June 4

The Heart as an organ is a muscular pump that regulates the circulation of the blood. Its astonishingly strong, enduring pumping action is regulated by an electrical system that keeps the beat steady, as the electrical impulse causes the heart muscle to contract. The rate and rhythm of the heartbeat are also determined by our breathing and our mental and emotional states.

The centrality of this organ and its connections to the emotions are captured in many popular expressions: "the heart of the matter;" "speaking from the heart;" "a blow to the heart;" "whole-hearted;" "heartland;" etc. Thus, the Heart represents the deepest part of ourselves—our "home," and the place from which we relate to others. It is the seat of deep connections, of love and compassion, of sharing and communication. In Chinese medicine, we say that the "*Shen* spirits," which are the intermediaries between Heaven and the individual, have their abode in the Heart. Thus, it is a place that is considered sacred, the place in us that connects us to the Divine.

Exercise

Do the following Buddhist meditation on loving-kindness to open your heart:

"My heart fills with loving-kindness. I love myself. May I be happy. May I be peaceful. May I be liberated.

"May all beings in this vicinity be happy. May they be peaceful. May they be liberated.

"May all beings on the planet be happy. May they be peaceful. May they be liberated.

"May all beings everywhere, whether near or far, whether known to me or unknown to me, be happy. May they be peaceful. May they be liberated."

Share your expressions . . .

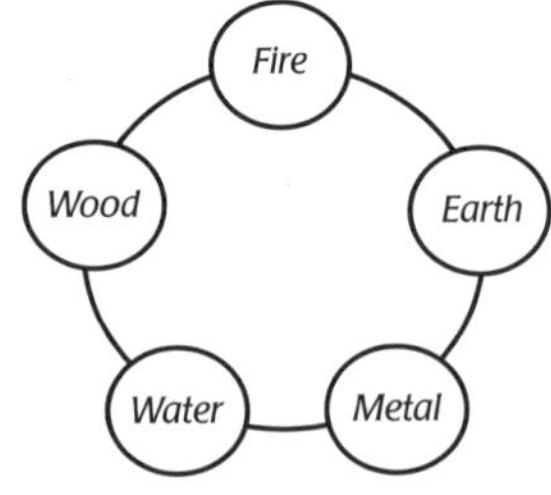

Expressions

June 5

"...the small intestines are like the officials who are trusted with riches, and they create changes of the physical substance;..."

- Nei Jing

The Small Intestine is the "sister" organ of the Heart, and although this pairing seems odd from a Western scientific standpoint, it makes perfect sense from a Chinese medical point of view. Since the Small Intestine receives and assimilates the bulk of our food, its job is to separate out what is of nutritional value from what is to be passed out as waste. Professor J.R. Worsley calls the Small Intestine the "Sorter of the Pure from the Impure." This sorting process is happening on all levels of body, mind, and spirit, so that there is a continuous sorting of our emotions and thoughts, as well as what we ingest in the form of food, sounds, ideas, pictures, feelings, etc. Thus, the Small Intestine sorts out the rubbish and brings only the "pure" material to the Heart.

Exercise

Sort your mail, or sort out the top of your desk.

Share your expressions . . .

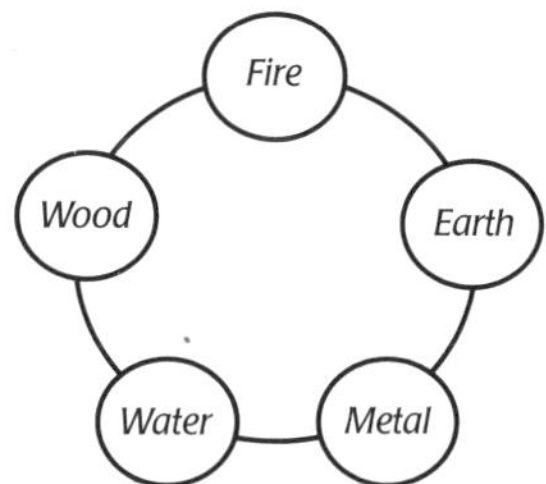

June 6

If the sorting function of the Small Intestine is not working well, then the body-mind-spirit becomes confused. On the physical level, this could mean poor digestion and assimilation of food because of poor sorting, or a hearing problem because of the inability to sort out voices from background noise. If the sorting problem is on the mental level, it could mean an inability to "think straight," to prioritize, or to figure out what is really important to focus on. On the emotional level, it could mean the tendency to associate with people who are not good for us, since we cannot discriminate "pure" from "impure."

One powerful example of this emotional confusion is the long-term effect of child abuse, where someone is beaten, raped, or teased by a parent or relative who is supposed to "love" them. When "love" is equated with pain, that person may be unable to sort out what "love" means, or to differentiate between love and abuse. Often these people find themselves in abusive relationships as adults—perpetuating the confusion.

Exercise

Before you get out of bed in the morning, spend a few minutes organizing your priorities. Notice whether work tasks or relationships are higher on the list.

Share your expressions . . .

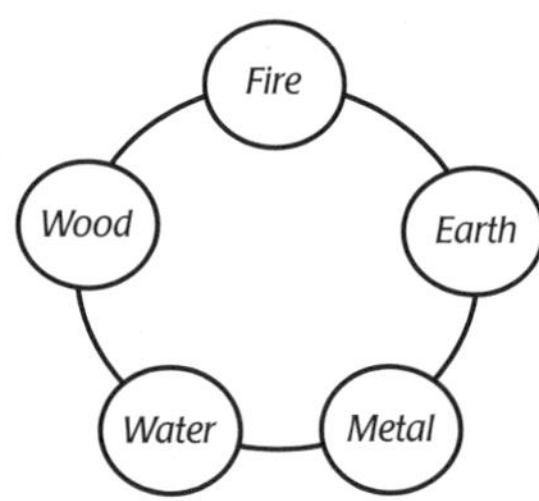

Expressions

June 7

"...the middle of the thorax (the part between the breasts) is like the official of the center who guides the subjects in their joys and pleasures.."

- Nei Jing

In addition to the Heart official, there is another aspect of our Fire energy, which has to do with the balancing of joy and pleasure in our lives. This official has several names, including Heart Protector and Circulation/Sex, and has no organ structure to which it belongs. It is a system-wide function, which, among other things, protects the heart from emotional blows and trauma. By absorbing the shocks otherwise destined for the Heart, the Heart Protector or Circulation/Sex official allows the Heart to function uninterruptedly. It enables us to face rejection, insult, or loss without damage to the Heart itself. In addition, it enables us to experience enjoyment and pleasure.

Exercise

Think of something that gives you joy and figure out how to get more of it into your life.

Share your expressions . . .

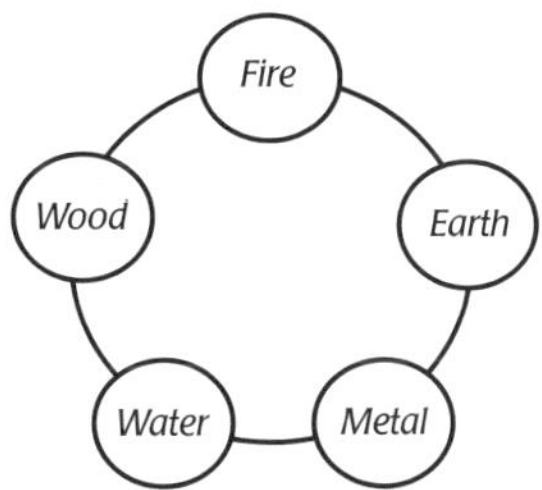

Expressions

June 8

The name Circulation/Sex points to one physiological explanation for how the Heart Protector protects the Heart: according to the Frank Starling Law of the Heart, taught in college physiology classes, the heart can only pump the amount of venous blood that is returned to the right atrium. Thus, the blood vessels of the circulatory system can protect the heart by dilating or constricting appropriately to limit how much blood flows back into the heart. That way, the heart is not overwhelmed by sudden floods or drops in blood volume.

Sexual "heat" is another function of the Circulation/Sex official, which regulates changes in blood flow, body temperature, and lubrication during sex. Sometimes we even speak of an "electricity" between two people, and what could that be but the Fire at a particularly high and crackling intensity?

Exercise

Spend some loving time with your partner. "Build a fire" in your partner and have some great sex.

Share your expressions . . .

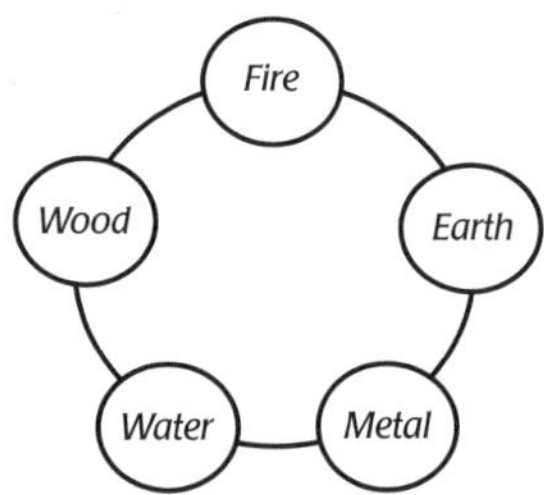

Expressions

June 9

The Heart Protector official, as part of the Fire element, shares Fire's connotations of warmth, love, joy, and happiness. We speak of someone as being a "warm" person, caring, compassionate, even "fiery." Since relationships of all kinds are governed by the Heart Protector, it affects our very ability to love, to share with others, and to enjoy the sexual act.

If the Heart Protector does not do its job, then there is no warmth, no love, no joy. Not only that, but the Heart official itself, not being adequately protected, is in danger of being injured. Lack of Fire means relationships with others are cold and lacking in vitality. If the Fire sputters, there could be impotence, frigidity, rejection of others, and emotional coldness. Many cardiac diseases have as their root cause this lack of Fire.

Exercise

Write a letter to someone you love—even if you live with them! Speak from your heart.

Share your expressions . . .

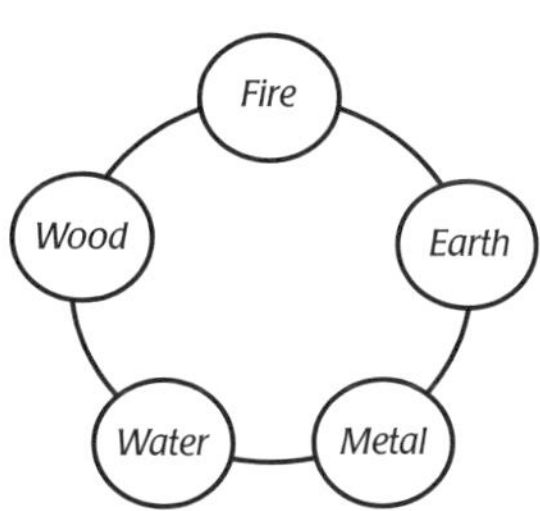

June 10

"...the burning spaces are like the officials who plan the construction of ditches and sluices, and they create waterways;..."

- Nei Jing

The Three Heater, also called the Triple Warmer or Triple Burner, is the "sister" function of the Heart Protector, and works closely with it. As with the Heart Protector, there is no anatomical organ connected with the Three Heater—it is a system-wide function having to do with the heat of the body and its circulation. In a sense, you could say that the Three Heater is the heating (and cooling) system of the body-mind-spirit, and the "ditches and sluices" and "waterways" are the heating ducts carrying heat to all parts of the body-mind-spirit. They connect all of the organs and maintain temperatures at optimum levels for the whole system to function in comfort, harmony, and balance.

Exercise

Walk from an air-conditioned room to the out-of-doors on a hot day and notice how your body adjusts.

Share your expressions . . .

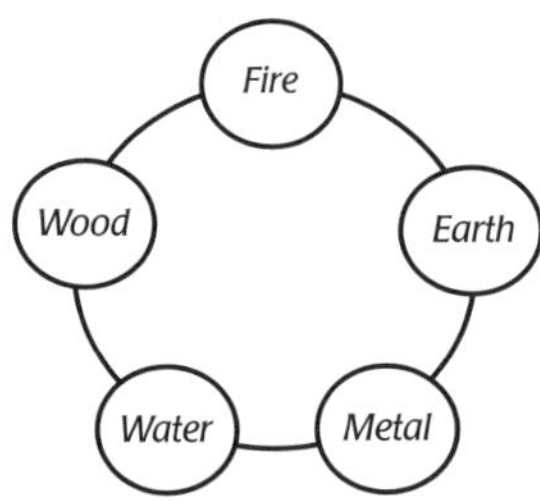

June 11

The three "burning spaces" mentioned in the quote earlier are called the Three Jiao and they divide the torso into three areas, the Upper, Middle, and Lower Jiao. The Upper Jiao (the chest area) corresponds to the Heart and Lungs, the Middle Jiao (between the navel and the rib cage) to the Stomach, Spleen, Liver, Gall Bladder, and Small Intestine, and the Lower Jiao (below the navel) to the Large Intestine, the Urinary Bladder, and the Kidneys. Thus, the functions of respiration, digestion, and elimination are all affected by the temperature of the three zones. All three Jiao must be in harmony with one another in order for the organ systems to function in a coordinated way.

If the Middle Jiao is too hot and the Lower Jiao too cold, it could result in symptoms such as ulcers combined with chronic constipation. This unevenness could also cause the emotions to "blow hot and cold" or for all of the body's energies to be up and down like a yo-yo. In general, the Three Heater governs our state of internal and external harmony.

Exercise

Feel the three zones on your own torso—notice any temperature differences.

Share your expressions . . .

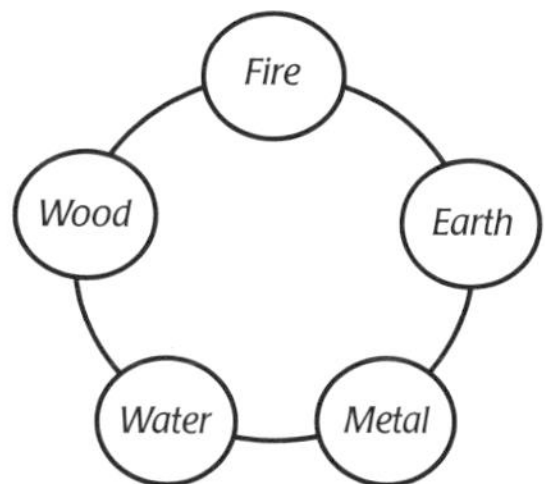

June 12

"...of the emotions they create happiness and joy."

- Nei Jing

Joy, like fire, is ephemeral and expansive, warming us and bringing us light and laughter. The ancient Chinese believed that for true joy to exist, the Heart official had to be healthy. As the classic texts say: "The heart is like the minister of the monarch who excels through insight and understanding...When the monarch is intelligent and enlightened, there is peace and contentment among his subjects; they can thus beget offspring, bring up their children, earn a living and lead a long and happy life." These ancient words capture the Chinese ideal of a balanced joy—contentment within the steady warmth and intimacy of family and village.

Exercise

Throw a party. Feel the joy of your connections to a community of friends.

Share your expressions . . .

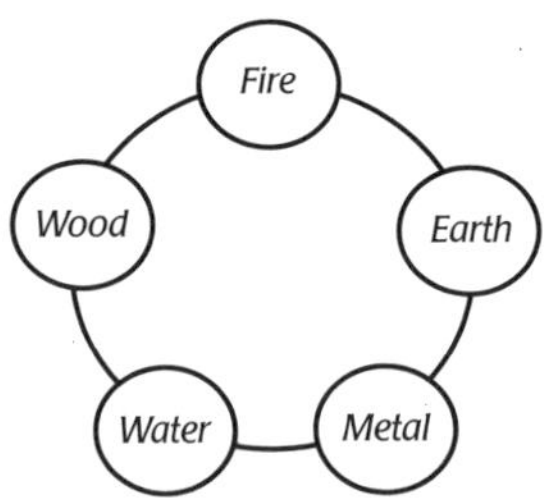

June 13

"Extravagant joy is injurious to the heart...."

- Nei Jing

To the Chinese, too much joy is just as out of balance as too little. In the West, our ceaseless striving for excitement and pleasure could be one reason we experience so much heart dis-ease—the stress of striving for constant joy leading to high blood pressure, heart attacks, and cardiovascular problems.

The advice from the Chinese on how to obtain true joy comes from a chapter of the *Nei Jing* devoted to staying in balance with the seasons. Here is the advice for Summer: "After a night of sleep people should get up early (in the morning). They should not weary during daytime and they should not allow their minds to become angry. They should enable the best parts (of their body and spirit) to develop; they should enable their breath to communicate with the outside world; and they should act as though they loved everything outside."

Exercise

Get up with the sun and go to a local park. Spend some joyful time playing with your child or pet.

Share your expressions . . .

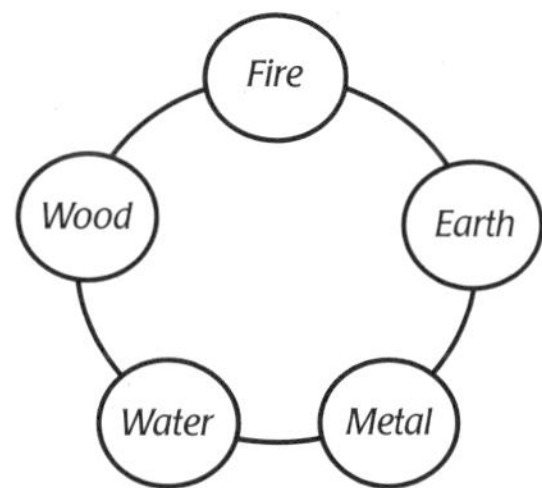

Expressions

June 14

The times of day associated with the Fire element are divided into two blocks: from 11 a.m. to 3 p.m. is associated with the functioning of the Heart and Small Intestine; the other block, from 7 p.m. to 11 p.m., is associated with the Heart Protector and Triple Heater. During both blocks of time, the Fire energy will be emphasized, but it will manifest differently, depending on the specific organ.

When the Heart function is at its peak (from 11 a.m. to 1 p.m.), the qualities of compassion, universal love, and fellowship will be emphasized. Lunch can therefore be an especially harmonious time for meetings and group endeavors—whether a "power lunch" or a break from work. It is a time for warmth and sharing, and for connecting all of us together in the human family. If someone always eats lunch alone, it could point to a lack of energy in the Heart official.

Exercise

Invite a new friend to lunch.

Share your expressions . . .

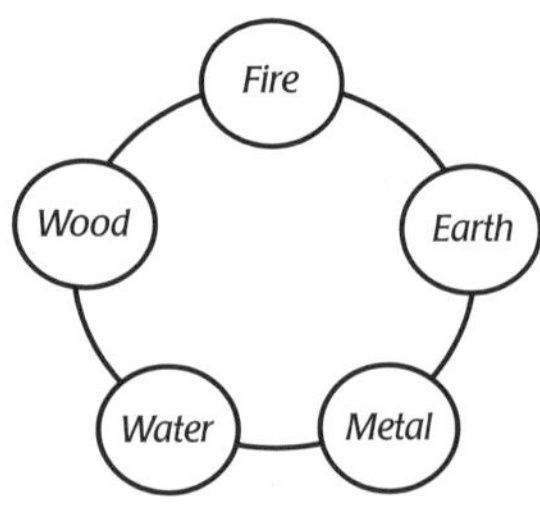

Expressions

June 15

Sometimes we need to look not only at the 2-hour block of time associated with a particular organ or meridian, but also at the 2-hour block of time opposite to it on the 24-hour cycle. So, for example, the hours from 11 p.m. to 1 a.m. are the direct opposite of Heart time, and a symptom or problem that occurs then could also be related to an imbalance in the Heart. It is well-known lore in hospitals that most heart attacks occur around midnight, when the Heart official is at its nadir.

The hours from 1 p.m. to 3 p.m. are when the Small Intestine, the official in charge of sorting out the pure from the impure, is functioning at its peak—right after lunch! This explains why we are sometime sleepy right after lunch and find it difficult to concentrate on our work, especially if our work involves any mental "sorting." If this official is weak or overtaxed, then those hours will be especially difficult. Again, the hours directly opposite, from 1 a.m. to 3 a.m., can also show some strain in this official.

Exercise

Leave your watch behind today and see if you can tell the time by how your feel.

Share your expressions . . .

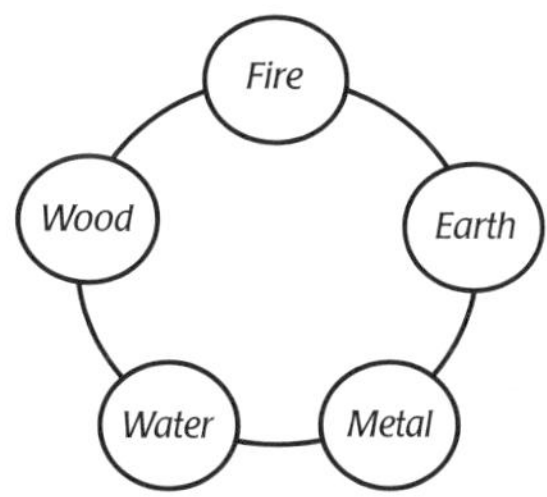

Expressions

June 16

The time of day associated with the Heart Protector is from 7 p.m. to 9 p.m. This means that the energy of the Heart Protector, which has to do with fun, enjoyment, communication, and love, is at its peak during the early evening. In our culture, these hours are often used for getting together with family and friends for social time or entertainment. For most people, the work day is over, so now is the time for relaxation, communication, and connection.

If someone is usually alone in the evenings, then it could indicate an imbalance in the Heart Protector official. Perhaps the desire to connect, to be with people, is why most households have the TV on in the evening—it substitutes for real company or gives the family a reason to sit down together. Someone who drags around all day but feels more energized during these hours could be indicating that he needs the energy of the cosmos at this time to support him. People who are grieving or ill can feel particularly lonely at this time.

Exercise

Ask a friend to go for a long, easy walk through a picturesque place at sunset.

Share your expressions . . .

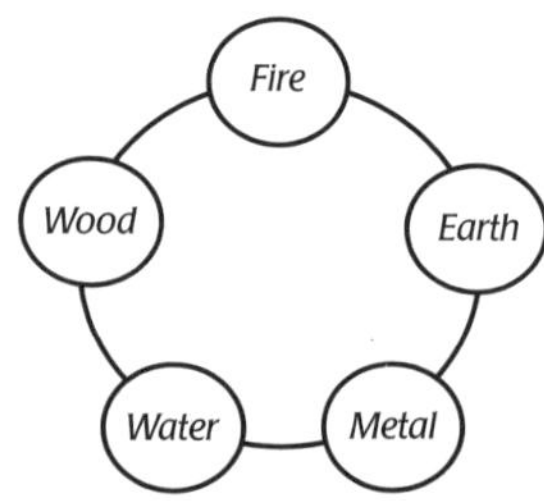

Expressions

June 17

The Triple Heater is at its peak from 9 p.m. to 11 p.m., and since it is a Fire official, these hours are also concerned with Fire activities, such as social gatherings, entertainment, and relaxation. Since the Triple Heater also has the specific task of keeping the body at a uniformly warm temperature, imbalances in the Triple Heater can show up as getting either very hot or very cold during these hours. Someone whose Fire element is really deficient might even choose to go to bed by 9 p.m., in order to be snuggled under the covers by Triple Heater time.

Trouble during the opposite hours of Fire, from 7 a.m. to 11 a.m., can also indicate an imbalance in Fire. People who have a hard time getting out of bed, or who find it hard to get moving in the morning, could be pointing to a Fire deficiency that is especially pronounced during Fire's low time.

Exercise

What is your usual bedtime? If it's between 9 and 11 p.m., notice what your body temperature feels like then.

Share your expressions . . .

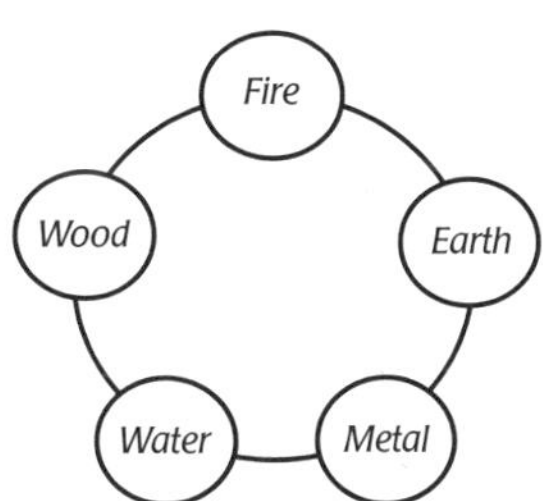

Expressions

June 18

"Shall I compare thee to a Summer's day?"

- William Shakespeare

Just as the Spring was correlated to childhood in the life cycle, so Summer is correlated with early adulthood. The Wood energy of budding and rapid growth is now given over to the slower energy of maturation and blossoming. Our focus shifts from self-development to relationships; from learning to expressing; from latency to sexual maturity; from Wood to Fire.

Although we manifest all of the elements during all seasons and during all stages of life, each life stage is connected to a particular element and to particular life tasks, which must be fulfilled before moving on to the next stage. In early adulthood, the tasks of Fire include: finding one's sexual identity; making friends and forming committed relationships based on trust and sharing; assuming adult responsibilities; making a household; and doing one's duty for the community.

Exercise

According to this definition of maturity, how is your Fire energy in terms of your life cycle?

Share your expressions . . .

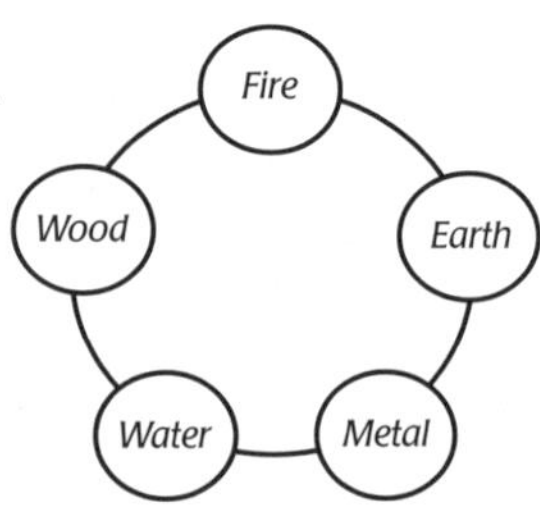

Expressions

June 19

Like a flower in full bloom, we come into the peak of our physical functioning during the Fire season of our lives. Our bodies become sexually mature, and our emotions deepen and push us to find lifelong intimate partners. The need to make friends and connections is paramount, and the quality of our relationships is a major preoccupation. The time of preparing for adult life is pretty much over—now we move fully into life, finding work that is satisfying, and beginning to master some field of endeavor. We are now at our most expansive, ready to reach for the stars in a way we may never be again. Like the flower, we show our beauty to the world.

Exercise

You can bloom at any age. Wear a bow in your hair, or a colorful tie. Smile! Let your own warmth and charisma shine through.

Share your expressions . . .

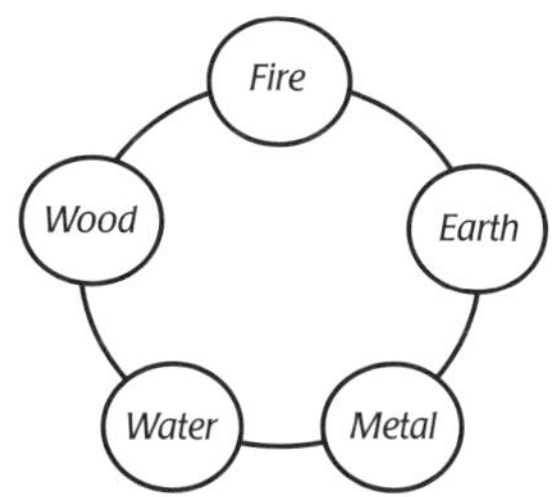

June 20

"The three months of Summer are called the period of luxurious growth... Everything is in bloom...."

- Nei Jing

In Summer, the plants reach a certain level of maturity and flower as their means of expression and reproduction. Up till then, the plants have channeled all resources towards growing leaves, extending the root structure, and thickening stems. Now the plant's energy is diverted from this expanding growth and put toward blossoming. This flowering signals that the plant is mature, since it can now reproduce itself.

This is very similar to how it is with humans. We also grow in a single-minded way for a number of years —then we suddenly need to express and communicate who we are. This act of expression is a sign of increasing maturity; it is one step in beginning to relate to others.

Exercise

What expression flowered early in your life? What kinds of buds and blooms are appearing now?

Share your expressions . . .

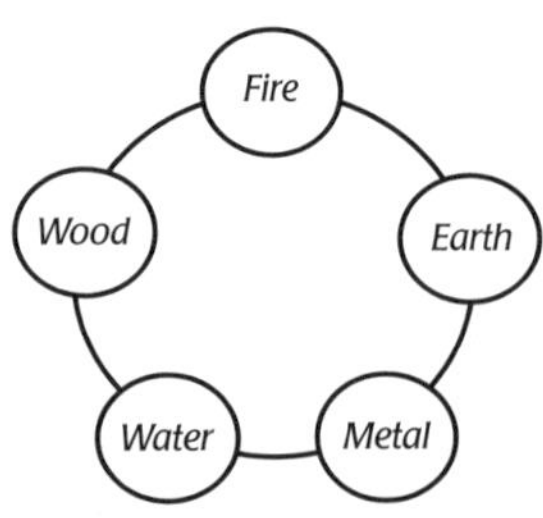

Expressions

June 21

There are many different kinds of flowering. Some plants only have one bloom, which dies quickly. Others put forth bloom after bloom, sometimes for an entire season. What kind of plant are you? Did you bloom early or were you a late bloomer? Are you an annual or a perennial? Did you put forth one bloom or many?

Botanists often identify plants by their flowers. Many leaves, root structures, or seeds look similar, but flowers are distinctly individual, saying clearly, "I am a day lily" or "I am an aster."

In our truest expressions, we each have a unique flowering. The expressions could be anything—poems, pictures, quilts, gardens, meals, furniture—even just the way we walk and talk can be an expression of ourselves.

Exercise

Draw a picture of the kind of flower you think you are—what color, size, shape, and sturdiness?

Share your expressions . . .

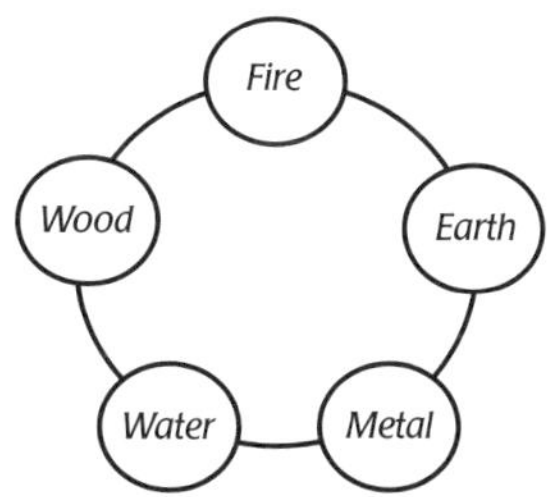

Expressions

June 22

"The viscera are in thorough communication and bound by circulation with the heart, and the blood that is stored by the heart, and thus the blood fills the pulse with the force of life(breath)."

- Nei Jing

The Fire element governs the blood vessels. These complex networks communicate with every aspect of the body, and bring nourishment and oxygen to every cell via the blood. The Fire energy controls the circulation of blood through these vessels, as well as the health of the vessels themselves. Weak tone of the blood vessel walls can lead to low blood pressure and varicose veins, while hardening of the vessels can lead to high blood pressure and heart disease. Any symptom of the blood vessels from poor circulation in the extremities to thrombosis can indicate an imbalance in the Fire element.

Exercise

End your next shower with a 30-second blast of cold water. Feel your blood vessels constrict.

Share your expressions . . .

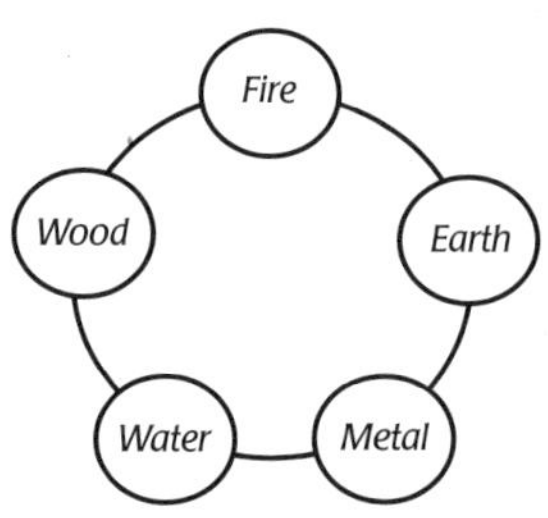

Expressions

June 23

"The heart rules over the tongue."

- Nei Jing

There are two reasons for the connection between the heart and the tongue. One is that the tongue is a good indicator of the general health of the heart. If the tongue is too red or swollen, it means the heart energy is strong or excessive, and the person may be unable to relax or slow down; if the tongue is pale or dry, it could mean that the heart is weak, or that the blood is deficient in some way.

The other connection has to do with the tongue's role in speech. Because the Fire element is associated with communication and relationship, the tongue's importance to speech gives it a clear link with the heart. Speech impediments such as stuttering and slurring can be symptoms of a Fire imbalance. Through speech, we express who we are to the world around us, and our tongue's ability to speak clearly is a sign of the clarity of our Fire energy and our ability to be in relationship.

Exercise

Look at your own tongue. What color is it? Does it look hot or cold?

Share your expressions . . .

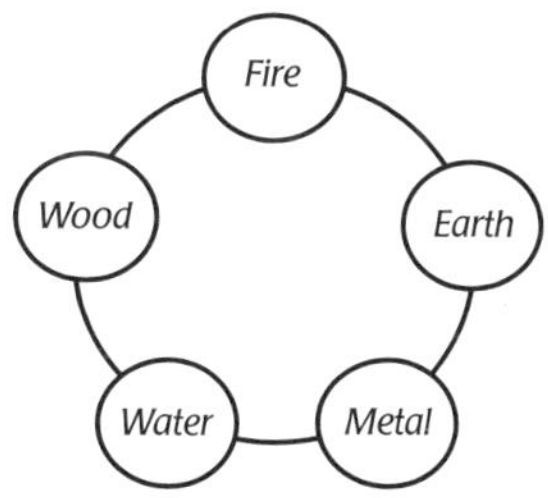

Expressions

June 24

"Red is the color of the South, it pervades the heart and lays open the ears....."

- Nei Jing

The ears are the orifice of the Fire element. This makes sense because one of the primary functions of the Fire element is communication, and being able to hear is as important as speaking for communication to happen. The "ears" refers not only to the physical ability to perceive sound, but also to the discriminating power of the mind in sorting the sounds into recognizable words. The Small Intestine pathway, one of the four Fire meridians, governs the function of Sorting in the body-mind-spirit, and its trajectory on the body goes right to the ears. The last point on the pathway is called "Listening Palace." The Triple Heater pathway also wraps around the ears, and has points with names such as "Ear Gate" and "Harmony Bone."

Exercise

Go to a busy restaurant, and listen to the many voices talking at once. See if you can pick out certain voices against the noisy background.

Share your expressions . . .

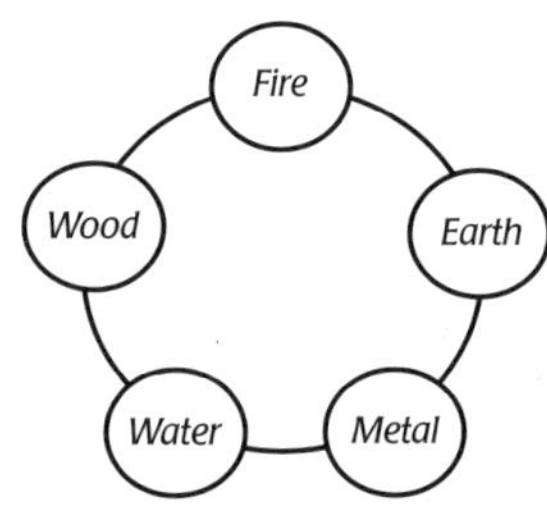

Expressions

June 25

"now the ears of my ears awake...."

- e.e. cummings

Hearing presumes relationship and communication, and the Fire officials are all about relationship. As Dianne Connelly says, "Via speech we express who we are to the world around us, and by hearing we discover through sound who the world around us is."

The capacity to listen to another is a power that is granted by the Fire element within us. Dianne Connelly again: "Give me your listening and together we bring forth the world. I give you my listening, and you speak your life." When we are truly listened to, then we can speak truly. Chuang Tzu, one of the great Taoist masters, pointed the way: "Cease listening with the mind and listen with the vital spirit..." When we listen in this deep way, the Fire element in one person touches the Fire in another, and the result is the heart connection of true communication.

Exercise

Truly listen to the next person who speaks to you.

Share your expressions . . .

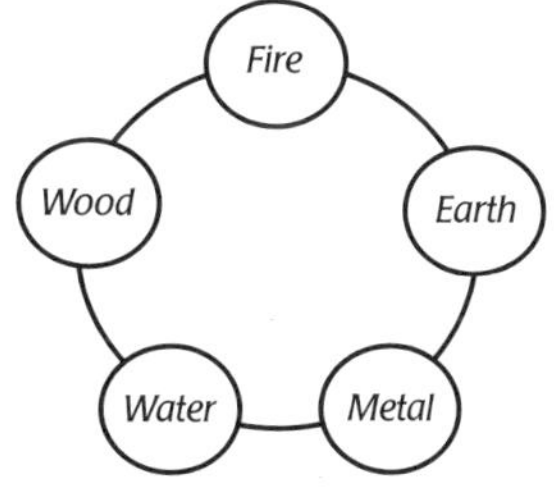

Expressions

June 26

"The complexion of a person shows when the heart is in a splendid condition."

- Nei Jing

One of the external manifestations of the Fire element is the complexion. As the complexion is one of the most visible aspects of a person, it is a quick way to check out the health of the Fire element and specifically, the Heart energies. The complexion is different from the colors that emanate from the face; it is more a description of the skin quality, texture, and clarity.

The Fire element's manifestation in the complexion is shown in the smoothness or roughness, the ruddiness or the paleness, the dullness or the radiance of the skin. When we say that someone has a beautiful complexion, we are really talking about the way the spirit of that person shines through the skin.

Exercise

Treat yourself to a luxurious facial, complete with mud pack and salt scrub.

Share your expressions . . .

Expressions

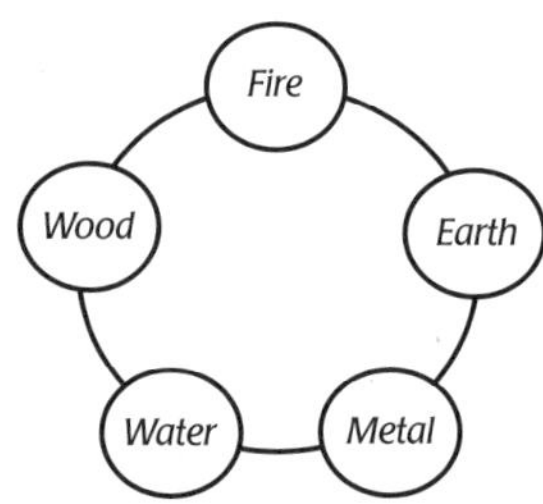

June 27

"...and they give to the human voice the ability to express joy."

- Nei Jing

The sound of voice associated with the Fire element is laughing. This sound can be a sprinkling of actual laughter in someone's speech, or it can be an undercurrent of amusement and warmth in the voice, which implies that the speaker is ready to laugh at any moment. Usually the laughing voice is rapid and somewhat explosive—the speaker constantly interrupts himself to tell something even funnier or more interesting. There is excitement in the voice, and infectious enthusiasm. Sometimes, just hearing this voice will make you smile.

In someone whose Fire energies are out of balance, the laughter will be omnipresent, even if the person is angry or sad. At times, the voice quality can border on manic, and be so rapid-fire and chaotic as to be confusing to listen to. These Fire types are often being told to "Slow down!"

Exercise

Tell the same joke to three different people.

Share your expressions . . .

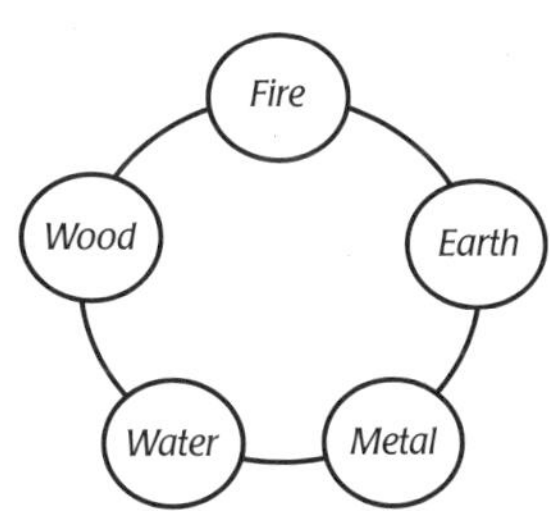

June 28

"The supernatural [powers] of Summer create heat in Heaven and fire upon Earth....In times of excitement and change they grant the capacity for sadness and grief."

- Nei Jing

Although Fire energies are connected to joy, the classics say that Fire also grants the capacity for sadness and grief. Although this may seem at first contradictory, in fact, the capacity to feel both joy and sadness depends on healthy Fire energies. When someone's Fire energy is really low, there is a protective numbing in which the person feels neither joy nor sadness. This often happens when there is a sudden shock or great loss—the person concerned seems so calm and detached. Only when the shock has worn off and the person's Fire energies are somewhat restored, do the grief and sadness flood in.

Exercise

If you feel sad, know that it is a strength in you that allows you to feel this sadness. Cheer yourself up by reading a book that makes you laugh out loud.

Share your expressions . . .

Expressions

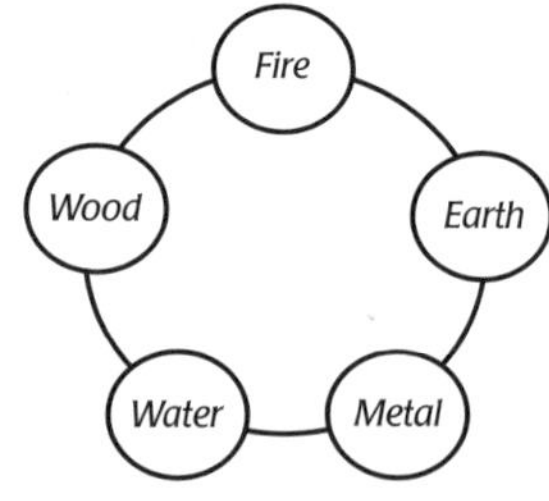

June 29

"...there ain't no cure for the summertime blues!"

- Eddie Cochran and Jerry Capeheart

The energy of Summer is all about happiness, enjoyment, good times, vacations, getting together with people, sharing, laughing, talking, etc. But what happens when the summer season rolls around and you find yourself alone? When people can't participate in Fire activities, they can become intensely lonely. It may seem that everyone else is off having a wonderful time somewhere, and that only you are out of step, uninvited, out of harmony with the universe.

We've all felt this at one time or another, usually (and thankfully) for short periods of time. But there are people for whom this state of loneliness becomes chronic—a constant feeling of isolation that pervades everything, leading to depression and despair. If you've ever been in this state, you know how hard it is sometimes to pull out of it —yet, how a phone call from a friend,or a brief kindness from a stranger, can completely transform your mood.

Exercise

Practice random acts of kindness—pay the next person's toll at the toll booth, or hold the door for the next person at the office.

Share your expressions . . .

Expressions

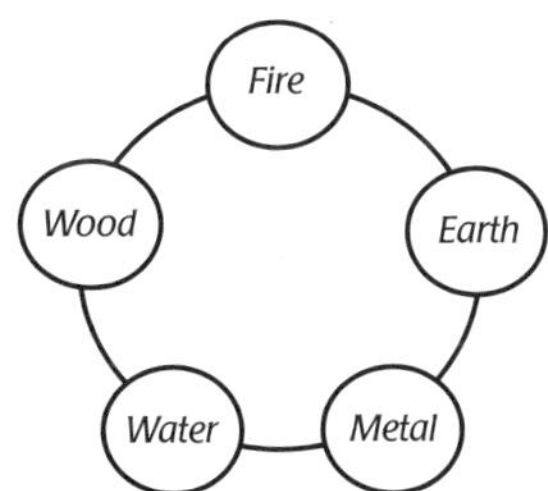

June 30

Many people are surprised to hear that you can have too much Fire energy. "If Fire has to do with love and joy and communication," they say, "how can you have too much of it?" Well, if you substitute the words "sexual attraction" for "love," and "manic behavior" for "joy," and "compulsive talking" for "communication," you can see how it is possible to have too much Fire!

Lack of Fire can make one lonely, joyless, and uncommunicative; too much Fire creates the same results with a different face. Someone who "sleeps around" and is very promiscuous may not be experiencing more love in his/her life—only more sexual partners. People who are manic only seem to be having a good time; in reality, they may be speeding around, talking a mile a minute, to cover up a basic loneliness and emptiness. Someone who seems to be the life of the party may in fact be generating all that laughter in order to make up for a lack of genuine love and connection the rest of the time.

Exercise

Think of someone who loves you unconditionally, and send them a card.

Share your expressions . . .

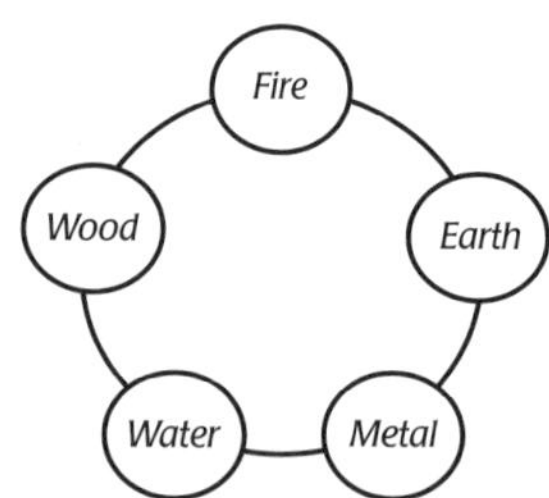

July 1

"Red is the color of the South....its smell is scorched."

- Nei Jing

When the Fire energies are out of balance, the body gives off a scorched odor. This odor is different from body odor caused by exertion, sweating, or not bathing. It is (usually) fainter but unmistakable and is easiest to smell on the back of the neck or on the abdomen. A Chinese doctor will rely on smelling this odor to complete a diagnosis.

In the U.S., it is not polite to notice body odors, much less actively sniff someone out, so we do not train ourselves to distinguish them. Nor does English have many specific smell words. We have to use analogies instead—that is, we can say that a certain odor is "like" something else whose odor is familiar. In the case of scorched, we can say that it is "like" clothes just taken out of the dryer. It has also been described as like something burning, like smoke, and like bread in the toaster.

Exercise

The next time you give someone a hug, sniff the back of his neck. Does he smell scorched?

Share your expressions . . .

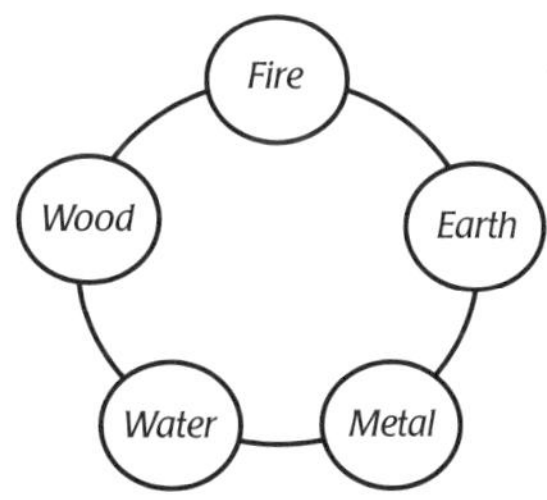

July 2

"Heat produces fire and fire produces the bitter flavor."

- Nei Jing

The flavor connected to the Fire element is bitter. Bitter greens, coffee, beer, and dark chocolate are some of the foods that give Summer's bitter taste. A temperate amount of the bitter flavor is stimulating to the Fire energies, but too much of the bitter flavor can be unhealthy. The *Nei Jing* says: "...the bitter flavor is injurious to the spirit..."

When you feel low, you might be tempted to drink a cup of coffee or a bottle of beer. People who feel lonely might crave dark chocolate (especially since it contains a substance which mimics a hormone that your body produces when you are in love). The number of "chocoholics" in our culture is an interesting commentary on our need for Fire energy!

Exercise

Drink a cup of decaf coffee slowly, savoring the bitter taste. Or eat a small piece of dark bitter chocolate.

Share your expressions . . .

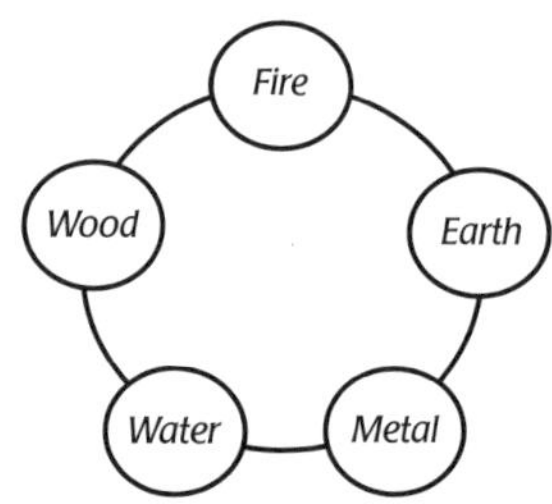

Expressions

July 3

"the bitter flavor has a strengthening effect..."

- Nei Jing

The specific foods that the *Nei Jing* associated with the bitter flavor and the Fire element are: "wheat, mutton, almonds, (apricots), and scallions." In other texts, the grain associated with Fire is corn, or sometimes glutinous millet, and the fruit is the plum. Although different texts associate different foods with each element, the general principle remains that each season has its own preferred taste and its own foods that support the body in that season.

The bitter flavor of early and mid-summer greens is probably the easiest healthy example to find in our Western diet. Generous helpings of these green leafy vegetables would definitely have a strengthening effect, due to their high concentrations of iron and other nutrients.

Exercise

Eat some bitter greens in a salad, such as chicory, endive, or escarole.

Share your expressions . . .

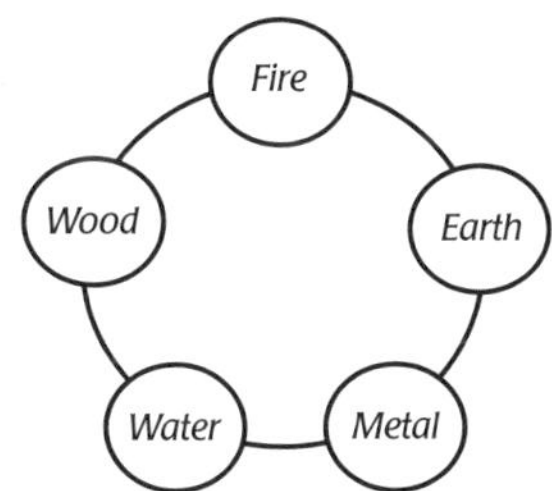

July 4

The general rule for Summer cooking is to eat a variety of summer fruits and vegetables, cooked lightly, and to regularly add a little spicy or pungent flavor. Even though the heat tempts you to eat cold food, try to avoid iced drinks and ice cream as these cause contraction and interfere with digestion.

Some suggestions for the hottest days are: salads, sprouts (especially mung, soy, and alfalfa), cucumber, tofu, and flower and leaf teas, including mint and chamomile. Some fruits for the summer are apples, watermelon, lemons, and limes. Avoid heavy foods on hot days as they will cause sluggishness. Such foods include: meats; eggs; nuts; seeds; and grains.

One of the dietary recommendations that seems counter-intuitive is to add hot-flavored spices to your food in the Summer. The rationale for this is that, even though at first they increase warmth, they ultimately bring body heat out to the surface and cause sweat, which cools the skin. With heat on the surface, your body mirrors the summer climate and will be less affected by it.

Exercise

Get some friends together and go to see the fireworks on July 4th. Share a watermelon.

Share your expressions . . .

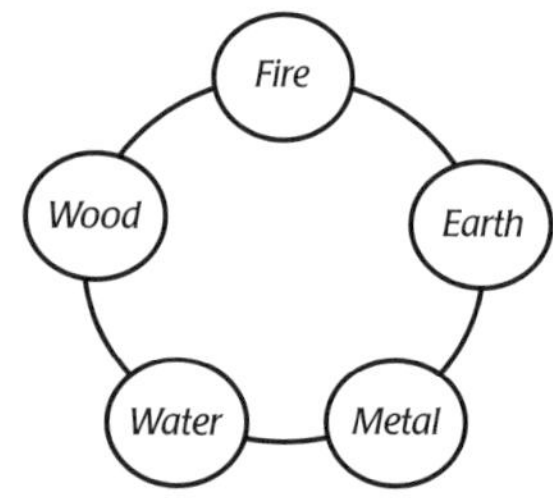

Expressions

July 5

"...in regard to the heart the
secretions become perspiration...
[...it leaks out through the pores of the skin.]"

- Nei Jing

Perspiration is a bodily secretion linked to the Fire element, and is a vital, if sometimes overlooked aspect of physical functioning. The Chinese recognize that the lack of or overabundance of perspiration could point to a serious imbalance or disease: "...if people do not perspire freely in the heat of summer, they will get intermittent fever in fall." Many treatments are devised specifically to either promote or inhibit perspiration. In some illnesses, the stimulation of perspiration is thought to bring about a cure of the illness. Western/allopathic medicine sees perspiration as a sign that a fever has "broken." Many herbalists believe that promoting a sweat will drive out the illness.

The Chinese understood that perspiration was an "unclogging" or cleansing of the body. Many other cultures have this idea, including many Native American tribes who use "sweat lodges" as rituals of purification, and Scandinavian countries who use saunas. However, it is also recognized in China that profuse sweating without exertion can be an unhealthy sign.

Exercise

Go to a "sweat lodge" ceremony.

Share your expressions . . .

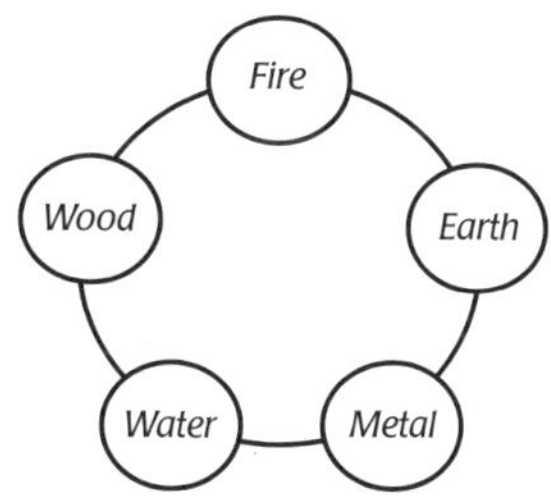

Expressions

July 6

Although the Heart is the primary organ connected to perspiration, all of the body's energetic systems have some relationship to it. The Chinese even classify different types of perspiration coming from different organs: "After heavy eating and drinking, perspiration is produced by the stomach. When man is shocked and startled he does violence to his spirit and vitality, and perspiration is produced by the heart. When man carries a heavy burden while taking a long journey, perspiration is produced by the kidneys. When man, during rapid marching, is apprehensive and full of fear, perspiration is produced by the liver. When the body is shaken in hard toil, perspiration is produced by the spleen." Here in the West, we also recognize that there is a difference between the sweat from vigorous exercise, the sweat from an intensely hot day, and the nervous "cold sweat" brought about by fear or anticipation.

Exercise

Exercise enough to break into a light perspiration.

Share your expressions . . .

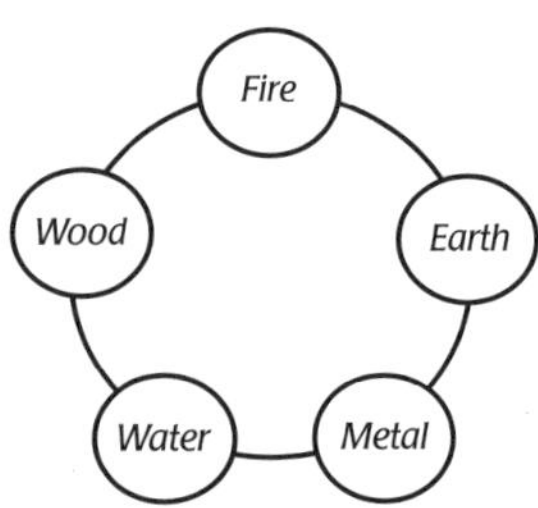

Expressions

July 7

"The extended use of the eyes hurts the blood [affects the heart]..."

- Nei Jing

The *Nei Jing* talks about the "five exertions" that are hurtful to the body. These are five common activities which, if done to excess, can cause imbalances in the five "organs" or energetic spheres of the body. In the case of the Fire element, it is the extended use of the eyes, which hurts the Heart. This means that reading to excess, or sewing or doing any close work for too long a period of time will create a problem in the Heart official. The eyes need to be open to the Spirit —not always closely focused.

This makes sense if you think of the Heart as the abode of the Shen spirit, and the eyes as the "windows of the soul." The connection of the eyes to the Spirit is made in other chapters of the *Nei Jing*: "The spirit cannot be heard with the ear. The eye must be brilliant of perception and the heart must be open and attentive, and then the spirit is suddenly revealed through one's own consciousness...."

Exercise

Watch at least one sunset this week.

Share your expressions . . .

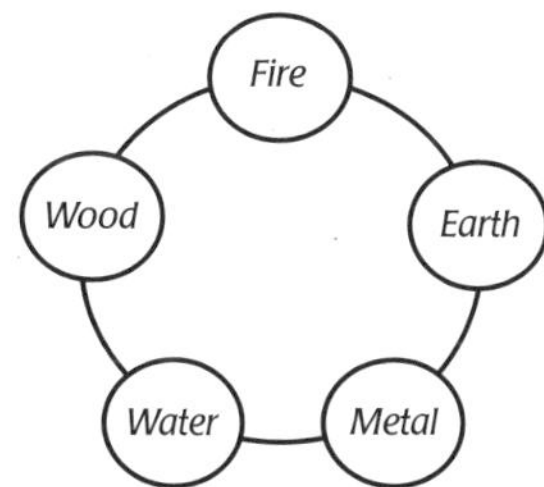

Expressions

July 8

"A man is only half himself; the other half is his expression."

- Ralph Waldo Emerson

In the Summer, the cosmic energies are in alignment for the expression of the creative ideas we had in the Spring. To put it another way, Wood is ready to burn! Humans must express their thoughts and feelings in an outward way, so that the energy can continue to flow around the cycle. The expression can be verbal, physical, or artistic, but must proceed from the level of mere thoughts and feelings to active manifestations in the outer world. This movement from idea to manifestation, from inner to outer, is like the movement from a bud to a flower—it is an unfolding and expanding into form of what was a small seed.

Exercise

Write a poem. Paint a picture. Or learn to draw cartoons, and make up funny sayings to put in the bubbles.

Share your expressions . . .

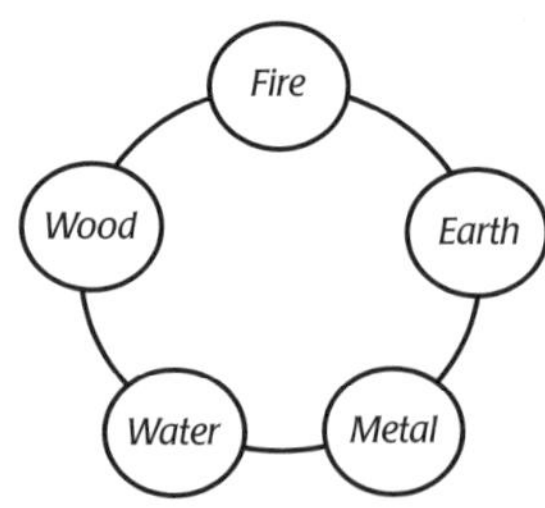

July 9

When our Fire energy is weak, we have difficulty expressing ourselves, and this difficulty can take many forms. We can be shy and hesitant, cold and withholding, or frustrated and inarticulate. Stuttering is a symptom often associated with Fire, because the tongue obeys the Heart, and the stutterer has such difficulty with clear expression. Also, many people with difficulties in expressing themselves can experience a constriction of the throat, leading to hoarseness, chronic sore throats, and laryngitis.

People who are afraid to express themselves physically might move stiffly, feel inhibited sexually, or be unable to dance. Painters might freeze in front of a blank canvas, writers might have writer's block, musicians might be unable to compose. The importance of expression for health and happiness is aptly summed up by poet e.e. cummings: "I'd rather learn from one bird how to sing / than teach ten thousand stars how not to dance."

Exercise

Go dancing with a friend. Work up a sweat. Keep at it until you feel looser.

Share your expressions . . .

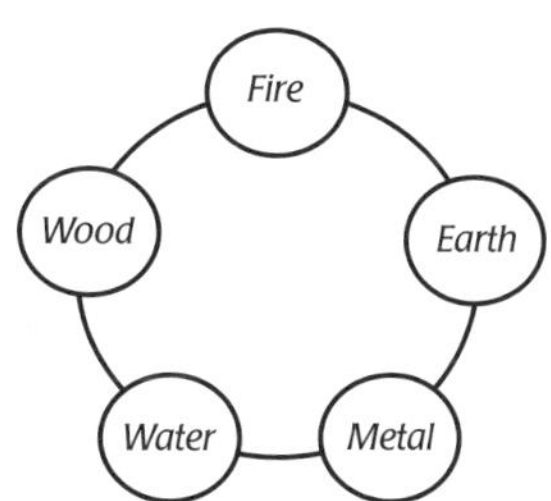

July 10

Opal Whitely's diary expresses the free outpouring of a child's heart onto the page. Without grown-up inhibitions to her language, she writes poetry in every line. In this passage, she writes of the joy of dancing and movement in nature:

"Most every day, I do dance. I dance with the leaves and the grass. I feel thrills from my toes to my curls. I feel like a bird, sometimes. Then I spread my arms for wings, and I go my way from stump to stump, and on down the hill. Sometimes I am a demoiselle, flitting near unto the water. Then I nod unto the willows, and they nod unto me. They wave their arms, and I wave mine. They wiggle their toes in the water a bit, and I do so, too. And every time we wiggle our toes, we do drink into our souls the song of the brook —the glad song it is always singing. And the joy-song does sing on in our hearts. So did it today."

- Opal Whitely (1899-1991),
from her childhood diary

Exercise

Put on some salsa music and dance while you do your chores.

Share your expressions . . .

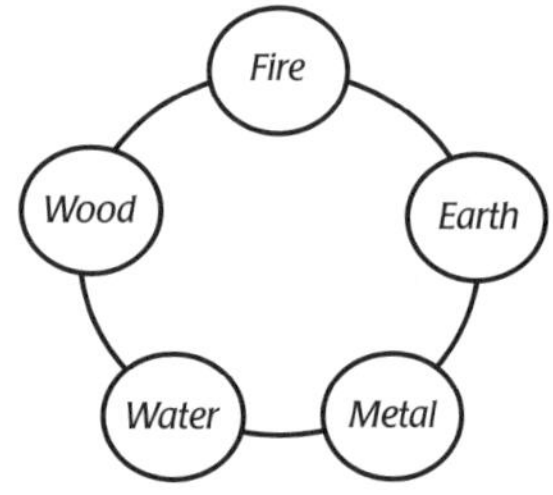

Expressions

July 11

"The word disease means "not having your elbows in a relaxed position." "Ease" comes from the Latin *ansatus*, "having handles," or "elbows akimbo"—a relaxed posture, or at least not at work. Dis-ease means no elbows, no elbow room. Ease is a form of pleasure, disease a loss of pleasure. A specialist in disease should begin his questions for diagnosis with issues of pleasure. Are you enjoying life? Where is it not pleasurable? Are you fighting pleasure somewhere or in some part of your body that is seeking pleasure?"

- Thomas Moore,
Care of the Soul

Pleasure is an experience in life that the Chinese linked with the Fire element and with the Heart Protector official in particular. In the *Nei Jing* it says, "the middle of the thorax (the part between the breasts) is like the official of the center who guides the subjects in their joys and pleasures.." Thus, it was recognized as an important function of the body-mind-spirit to feel pleasure, and the capacity to feel pleasure was seen as a sign of health.

Exercise

If you can, spend a day at the beach; lie in the sun, splash in the waves, and listen to the sounds of summer.

Share your expressions . . .

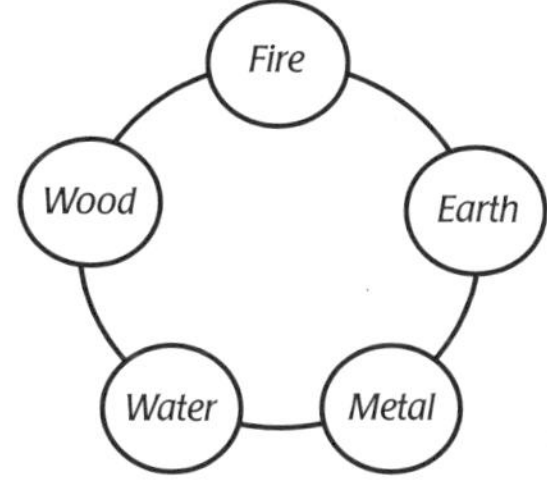

Expressions

July 12

The Chinese attitude toward pleasure contrasts with the Puritan work ethic, which places the predominant value on work and accomplishment, and allows pleasure only after the work is done. Many of us are so indoctrinated with this ethic that we become workaholics who find it difficult to relax and enjoy life! We look down on "pleasure-seekers" and fear that we are being "self-indulgent" if we allow some pleasure in our lives.

If your life has been lacking in pleasure lately, take some time and list several things that would really give you pleasure—even if you know you "shouldn't" or "couldn't." For some, it might be a foot massage, or some time in the sauna, or simply going to a good concert. Let your heart imagine as many pleasurable possibilities as you can. Leave the list in a drawer for several days. Come back and read it again. Notice which ones you could do right now. Experiencing pleasure is a way of staying in balance and being healthy, in Summer and every day.

Exercise

Enjoy just doing nothing.

Share your expressions . . .

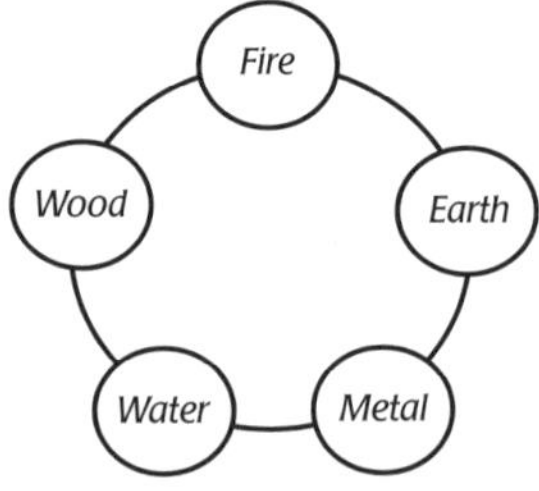

July 13

"The three months of Summer are called the period of luxurious growth.... After a night of sleep people should get up early (in the morning). They should not weary during daytime and they should not allow their minds to become angry. They should enable the best parts (of their body and spirit) to develop; they should enable their breath to communicate with the outside world; and they should act as though they loved everything outside."

- Nei Jing

"If I speak in the tongues of men and of angels, but have not love, I am a noisy gong or a clanging cymbal. And if I have prophetic powers, and understand all mysteries and all knowledge, and if I have all faith, so as to remove mountains, but have not love, I am nothing."

- First Corinthians 13, 1-3

Exercise

Think of three people who love you, and three people who you love.

Share your expressions . . .

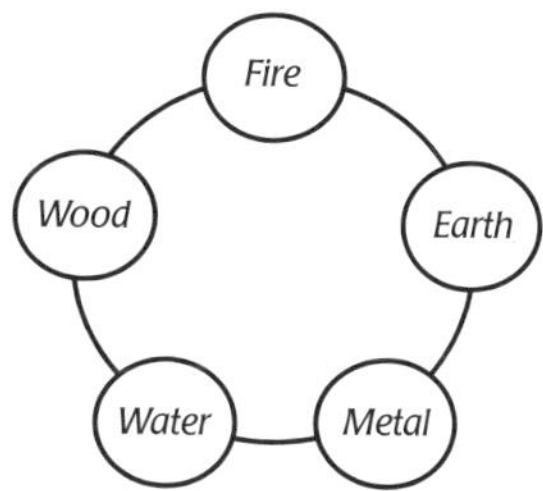

Expressions

July 14

Love is a word that encompasses so many shades of meaning that we really should have at least 15 words to cover all of them. It encompasses everything from the tender caring of a parent to the passion of lovers to the exalted union that a mystic feels with God. The poets say it best—on the following page, Elizabeth Barrett Browning expresses the mature love that one adult feels for another. It is an evocation of an idealistic and complete love, which resonates with anyone who has ever, however briefly, felt that deeply about another human being.

The Fire element grants us the strength to feel love. When our Fire is low, we may feel unloved and unloving, unable to summon feelings of affection that we know we are capable of at other times. Yet, the primacy of love, the importance of it in human life, was understood by the ancient Chinese no less than our own poets and prophets.

Exercise

Have loving compassion for yourself and extend it to others today.

Share your expressions . . .

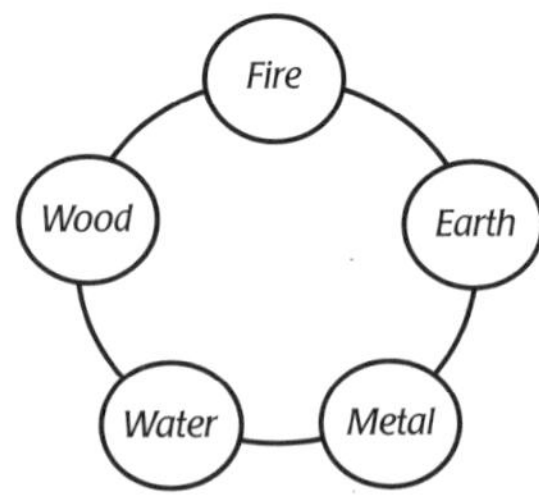

July 15

"How do I love thee? Let me count the ways.
I love thee to the depth and breadth and height
My soul can reach, when feeling out of sight
For the ends of Being and ideal Grace.
I love thee to the level of every day's
Most quiet need, by sun and candle-light.
I love thee freely, as men strive for right;
I love thee purely, as they turn from praise.
I love thee with the passion put to use
In my old griefs, and with my childhood's faith.
I love thee with a love I seemed to lose
With my lost saints—I love thee with the breath,
Smiles, tears, of all my life!—and, if God choose,
I shall but love thee better after death."

- Elizabeth Barrett Browning

Exercise

Is there anyone in your life who you feel this way about? If not, why not?

Share your expressions . . .

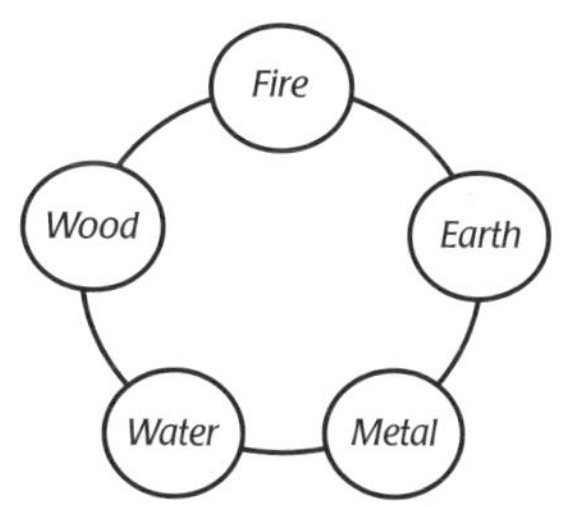

July 16

"There are just some things no one can do alone: conspire, be a mob, or a choir, or a regiment. Or elope."

- Renata Adler

The ability to relate to other people arises from Fire energy and is essential to our development. The quality, depth, and variety of our relationships are dependent on the strength of our Fire energies within.

When our Fire is strong and balanced, we are capable of committed intimate relationships with love partners, enduring friendships, warm and fulfilling connections to family members, strong ties to our communities, and an easy flow between ourselves and casual acquaintances, strangers, and the family of man. We can feel intact and protected as we open our hearts appropriately in these different situations, allowing for easy communication and interchange of feelings and ideas with these different circles. We feel warmed, nourished, and enlivened by this interconnected web of relationships.

Exercise

Call or write a friend you haven't been in touch with for a long time.

Share your expressions . . .

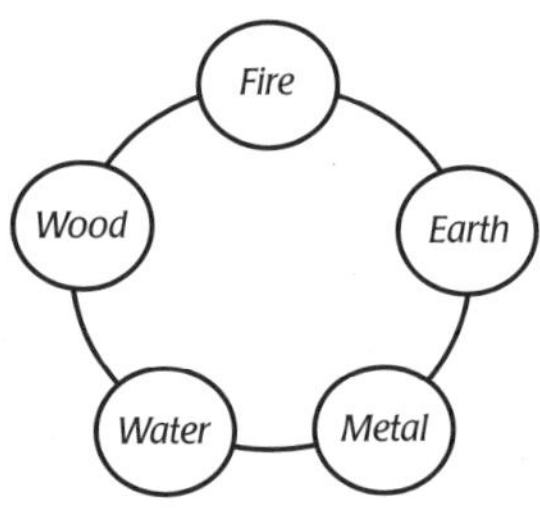

Expressions

July 17

When our Fire energy is too low or too high, we may experience difficulties in relating to others. Low Fire may lead to the chill of loneliness or alienation, as if "nobody loves me." Fire pulsing out of control may emerge as anger and resentment, rather than warmth and support. Perhaps there are many superficial relationships, but nobody who is allowed to get too close. Reluctant to connect at a deep level, we cling tightly to a few trusted people, and "freeze out" everybody else. In all cases, this lack in our relationships is a sign of a Fire imbalance.

During the Summer is a good time to attune to these issues. With the clarity that Fire brings in this season, we may have a moment of "illumination," which helps us to make necessary changes in our relationships.

Exercise

Invite some friends for a cookout. Notice why you included certain people and not others.

Share your expressions . . .

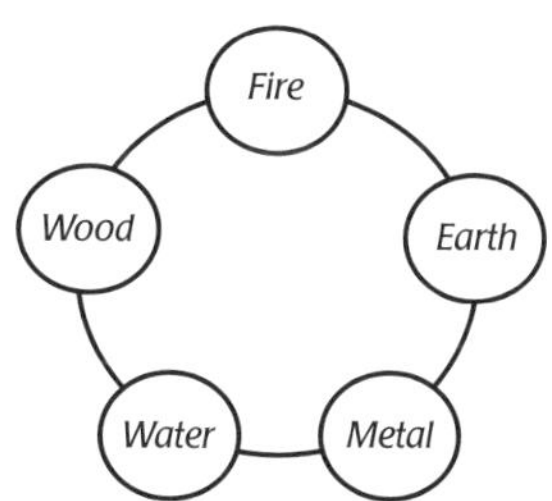

Expressions

July 18

Let me not to the marriage of true minds
Admit impediments. Love is not love
Which alters when it alteration finds,
Or bends with the remover to remove:
O, no! it is an ever-fixed mark
That looks on tempests and is never shaken;
It is the star to every wand'ring bark,
Whose worth's unknown, although his height be taken.
Love's not Time's fool, though rosy lips and cheeks
Within his bending sickle's compass come;
Love alters not with his brief hours and weeks,
But bears it out even to the edge of doom.
If this be error and upon me proved,
I never writ, nor no man ever loved.

- William Shakespeare

Exercise

Send this poem, or another one that expresses how you feel, to the one you love.

Share your expressions . . .

Expressions

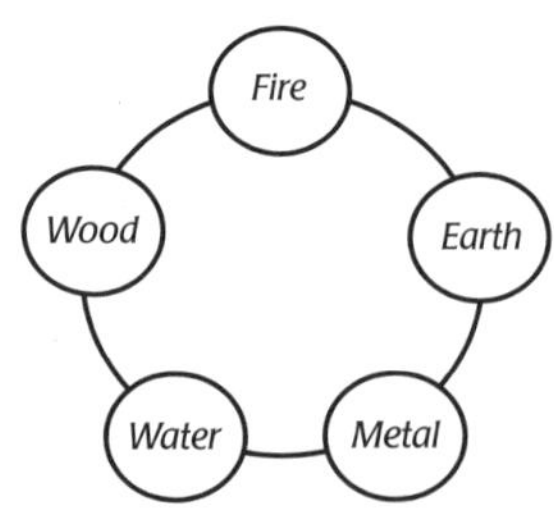

July 19

"one's not half two. It's two are halves of one:"

- e.e. cummings

One of the primary preoccupations of someone in the Fire phase of life is romantic connection and merging. This phase is usually strongest in early adulthood, but can occur anytime someone feels a need to connect heart to heart. The poets down through the ages have spoken of "two hearts becoming one" and "the merging of two souls." Someone whose Fire energy is out of balance may desire an intimate relationship acutely, but may be unable to sustain a satisfying relationship over time and ends up trying again and again with multiple partners. Sometimes the thrills of romance and sexual experiences become addictive, and the person doesn't move on to the next phase of creating a home and nurturing the next generation (Earth). Of course, some may direct their Fire energies towards non-romantic relationships, such as with friends, children, projects, causes, or gurus.

Exercise

Play some music that was popular when you were 18, and remember the feelings you had then about someone you had a crush on.

Share your expressions . . .

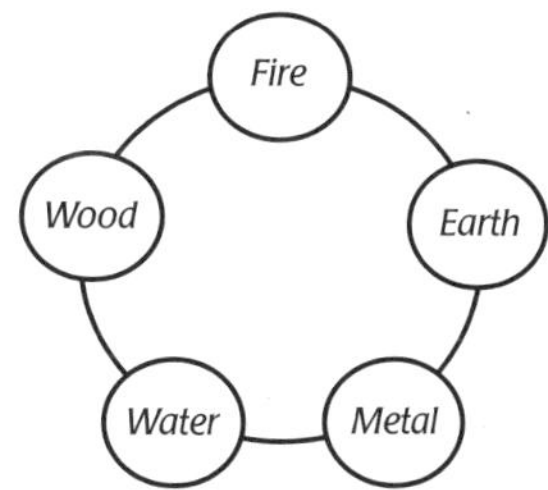

July 20

you burn like a solar furnace
but I do not wilt
beneath you –
like a spring/green plant
I unfold my soft new leaves,
open my petals to your light
strong, white as a knife,
till your sun/heat makes me
burst
into blossom, veined and bulging
radiating with the life
you give me, crimson flower
throbbing with it, waving
in the wind, ecstatic –
dancing on the sharp tip
of your flame

- Janice MacKenzie

Exercise

Think about your most powerful sexual experience.

Share your expressions . . .

Expressions

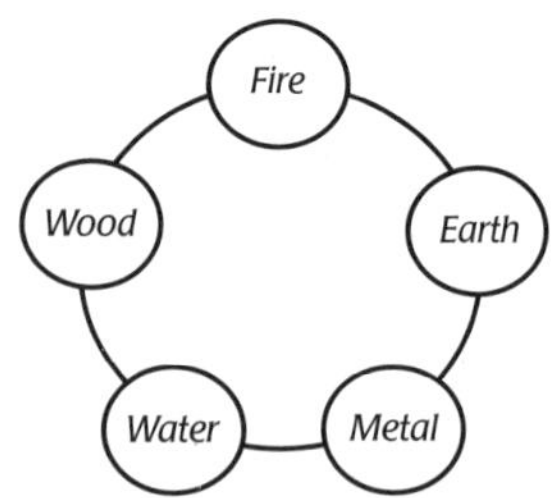

July 21

"Camerado, I give you my hand!
I give you my love more precious than money,
I give you myself before preaching or law;
Will you give me yourself? will you come travel with me?
Shall we stick by each other as long as we live?"

- Walt Whitman

Since the Heart Protector acts as a kind of gatekeeper to your innermost sanctuary, you need trust and caution to selectively open it and allow those you love inside. Children can be naively open-hearted and trusting. They can also be wary of everyone who isn't their mother. They are inexperienced and can't judge people yet, so they are sometimes open-hearted and sometimes close-hearted in ways that frustrate and worry adults. Parents have to serve as the child's Heart Protector, making sure that no hurtful people or dangerous situations harm the child, teaching them who is safe to let into their hearts and lives.

Exercise

List three people you trust completely.

Share your expressions . . .

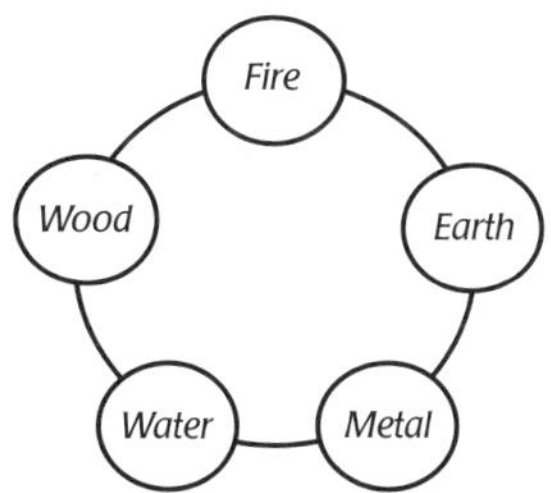

Expressions

July 22

As a child extends out from the sphere of the parents into the school and community, the Heart Protector also develops, enabling the child to begin to evaluate people outside the family. It is almost like a muscle that develops with use—the more you practice interacting with new people, the stronger your Heart Protector becomes.

At a certain point, the young adult risks new levels of intimacy in the sexual connection. The ability to have this be more than simply a physical act, to have it be truly a meeting of hearts and a "communion of souls," requires trust both of oneself and of one's partner. When the Heart Protector is strong and healthy, there is a sense of trust that, no matter what happens, you will be okay. There is truly a sense of inner protection, of deep security within the self, when you can open your heart and body to another person. When there is no trust, the door remains closed, the inner sanctuary sealed.

Exercise

Repeat this affirmation: "I am safe and protected in my very core."

Share your expressions . . ."

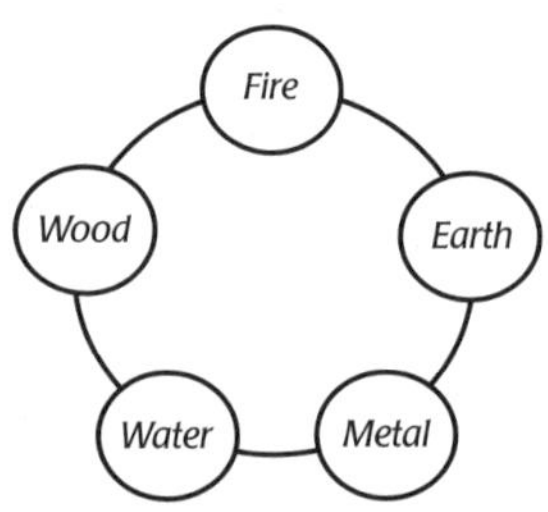

Expressions

July 23

"..the heart is like the minister of the monarch
who excels through insight and understanding;"

- Nei Jing

Compassion is one of the spiritual qualities of the Fire element. The Heart is the abode of the *shen* spirits—the *shen* being the presence of Heaven in a human being. The *Nei Jing* says: "Let me discuss *shen,* the spirit....The spirit cannot be heard with the ear. The eye must be brilliant of perception and the heart must be open and attentive, and then the spirit is suddenly revealed through one's own consciousness. It cannot be expressed through the mouth; only the heart can express all that can be looked upon." Compassion flows from the heart's insight.

Compassion is the ability to love and care about others in an unconditional, ego-less way—to see other people as no different from oneself. It is agape—the love that Jesus talked about in the New Testament: "You shall love your neighbor as yourself."

Exercise

Babysit for friends so they can go out. Mow your neighbors' lawn one day when they're not at home.

Share your expressions . . .

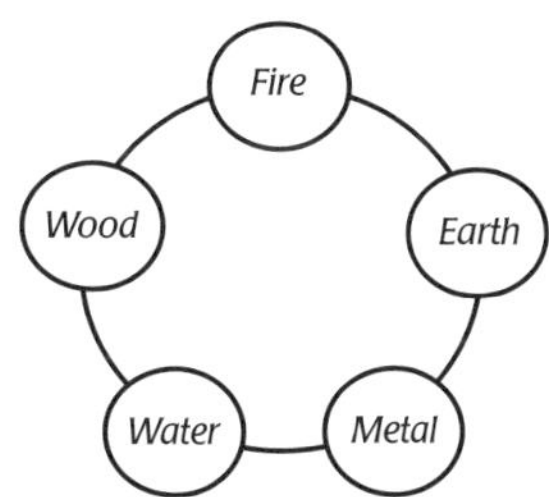

Expressions

July 24

In simple terms, compassion is the ability to put yourself in another's place, and to put that person's welfare before your own. It is in some ways like the love a parent has for a child, but with less expectation of return. I think of it like the love of a grandmother for her grandchild—whole-hearted, and yet with a certain detachment.

One of the people most exemplifying the path of compassion is Yeshi Donden, the Tibetan physician for the Dalai Lama. Every day he recites this Buddhist prayer: "May all living beings be free of suffering and the cause of suffering....May everything I do go to ensure that they be free of suffering and the cause of suffering...May all living beings have joy and the cause of joy....May I be the one to ensure, to remind them they are in fact living in joy and have the causes of joy. May all living beings interrelate fully, lovingly, compassionately and joyously with one another, without any discrimination or partiality of near and far, of like or dislike. May I be the one that does everything in my power to see that they do this. May I be the one to make sure that this takes place."

Exercise

Repeat this prayer to yourself every morning for a week.

Share your expressions . . .

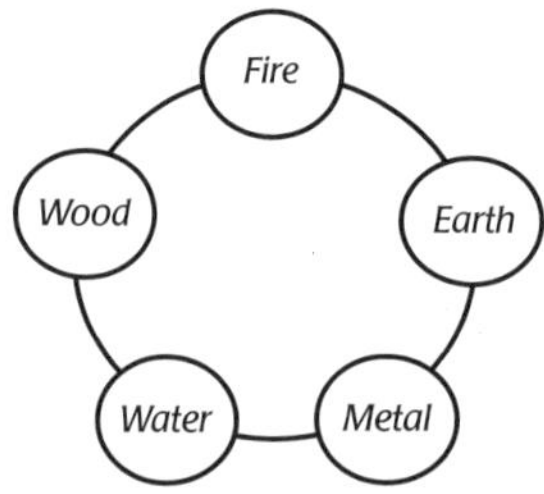

July 25

"...the current trend to imagine the heart as a mechanical pump or as a muscle is extremely narrow and may be implicated in the widespread occurrence of heart trouble. When we talk this way, we lose sight of soulful images of the heart as the seat of courage and love. Thinking of the heart as an object, we take it for a walk or run it for exercise, but it loses all its metaphoric power and is reduced to a function...we are attacking the heart when we treat as a mere physical organ what poetry and song for centuries have treated as the seat of affection. It isn't easy for us, so imbued with modern categories of thought, to remember our own biases in this matter. Of course the heart is a pump. That's a fact. Our problem is that we can't see through the thought structures that give value to fact and at the same time treat poetic reflection as nonessential. In a sense, that point of view is itself a failure of heart. We think with our heads and no longer with our hearts."

- Thomas Moore,
Care of the Soul

Exercise

What thoughts are in your heart today? Give them expression, in words or in pictures.

Share your expressions . . .

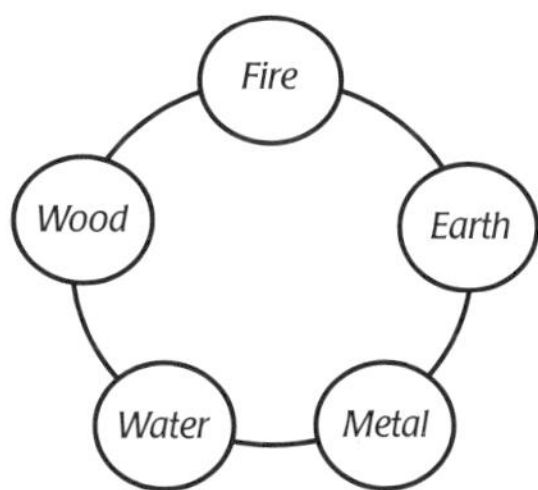

July 26

"On Memorial Day weekend of 1988, the heart and lungs of Tim L., an eighteen-year-old victim of a motorcycle accident, were removed and rushed to Yale-New Haven Hospital. There, Clair Sylvia's own heart and lungs, which doctors estimated could not have lasted more than another month, were detached, removed, and replaced.

"After the transplant, Sylvia experienced unsettling changes. While she initially downplayed her sudden new interest in beer, chicken nuggets, and green peppers, she was unable to ignore her new need—indeed compulsion—to be on the go. It was as if some outside force was propelling her into constant motion. Although medical professionals had insisted that the heart was merely a pump, a muscle, she wondered if there was another explanation.

"Sylvia eventually met with Tim L.'s family. In the course of their conversation, Mrs. L. remarked that Tim had had "tremendous energy." Everyone said that he loved green peppers. And one of Tim's sisters mentioned that Tim had "loved chicken nuggets."

- *Natural Health*, March/April 1995

Exercise

If your heart were transplanted, what traits would you pass on?

Share your expressions . . .

Expressions

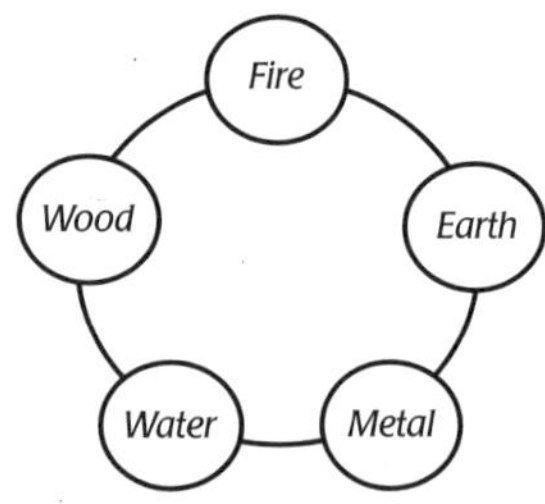

July 27

"Laughter is the best medicine."

- Anonymous

Humor is a special part of life that is associated with the Fire element. We all like to laugh, and people who can make us laugh are people we like to have around us. Although love makes the world go round, it's humor that greases the wheels. Just being in a "good humor"can make one's day go faster, can lighten many a dark and difficult situation.

"Humor" is a word that comes from the Latin word "humere," meaning "to be moist." In medieval physiology it referred to one of four fluids believed to circulate in the human body and determine someone's temperament. In a sense, humor helps lubricate social interactions and makes our relationships "juicy.

Exercise

Play with a child. Remember what it was like to just act silly and giggle?

Share your expressions . . .

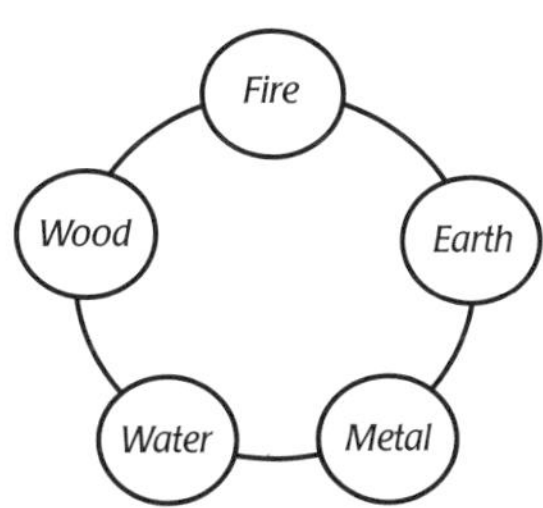

July 28

"The Fire hand is long....and this is especially true of the fingers, which are slender and agile, capable of resembling the flickering flames in their movements."

- Yves Requena,
Morphotypological Hand Diagnosis in Acupuncture

In examining the body, one of the things that a Chinese doctor looks at is the shape of the hand. The Fire hand is long with tapering fingers, like a flame. Someone with a Fire hand is capable of spreading his fingers very wide apart, like the rays of the sun. In addition, the Fire hand is very graceful and flexible, and the little finger bends easily and naturally, resembling a hook. The fingernails are long, narrow and pointed, and convex from base to tip. Sometimes, the nail is so pointed that the hand resembles a chicken claw!

Exercise

Examine your hands and those of your family. Does anyone have a Fire hand?

Share your expressions . . .

Expressions

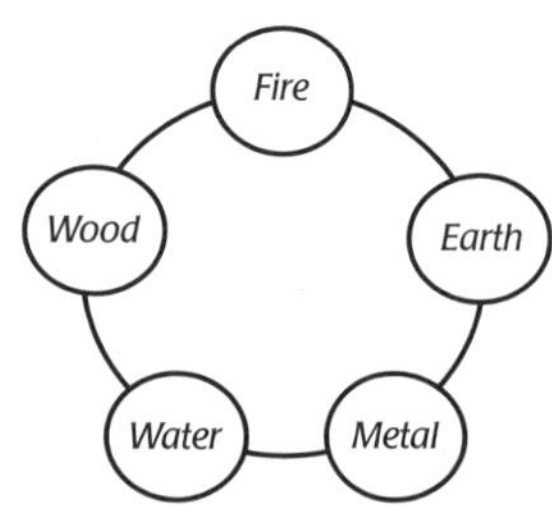

July 29

"To treat and to cure disease means to examine the body, the breath, the complexion, its glossiness or degree of moisture and the pulse....

Nei Jing

Each of us is always expressing, at every moment, the elements within us, and we manifest through our bodies the strengths and weaknesses of those elements. Looking at someone's hand and seeing that it is mostly a Fire hand simply gives us one more piece of information about that person. It helps us see constitutional tendencies, and may be a clue to someone's energetic preferences.

People often connect by shaking or holding hands. We find certain hands pleasing and others ugly. We read a lot of character in a person's hands, in their gestures and animation. Add the knowledge of hand shapes and it amplifies our ability to understand and diagnose illness.

Exercise

In this Summer season, notice the hands of the people you meet and the people you know well. See if what you know about them correlates with their hand type.

Share your expressions . . .

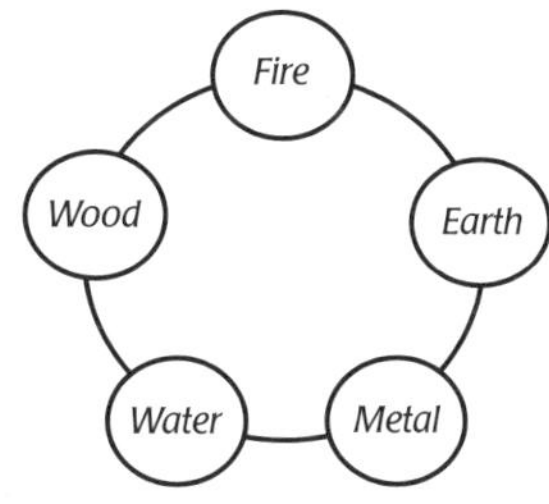

Expressions

July 30

"If the sound is <u>chih</u> there is restlessness and much irritation; the soldiers are tired."

- *Book of War*

The musical note corresponding to the Summer season and the Fire energy is *chih*. A musical sound is difficult to explain in words, so one way is to link it with other qualities of sound in nature. *Chih* was said to correspond with lightning flashes.

Since lightning doesn't really have a sound, we need to think about sounds and reverberations that we associate with lightning, flame, something expanding or exploding with heat, or irritability. These give us the flavor of the sound *chih* as it relates to the Fire energy.

Exercise

Watch a summer thunderstorm, and think of the lightning flashes as musical notes. How does this "music" affect you?

Share your expressions . . .

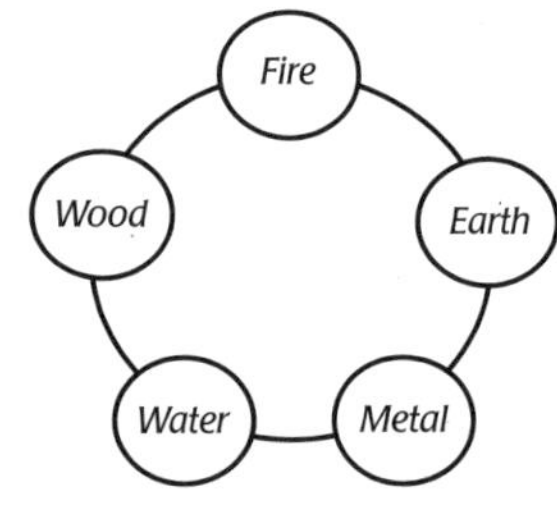

E x p r e s s i o n s

July 31

In ancient China, the materials used to make musical instruments corresponded to the the seasons. In Summer, the silk-stringed zither was played during the season when silk worms were spinning their cocoons. The tones this instrument produced were thought to correspond to certain emotional effects: "The sound of silken strings is a wailing. Wailing stimulates integrity. Integrity establishes resolution. When the man of breeding listens to the sound of the (silk-stringed) zithers *chih* and *se*, he thinks of resolute and righteous ministers." And from the ancient text *Tz'u Hai*: "What's called *chih* is varying and changing, it alternates, attacks, with repeated variations. *Chih* is happy..."

Resonance is one of the central ideas in Chinese philosophy. There is some evidence that even in ancient China, different tones and rhythms were used in healing to cause different emotional effects.

Exercise

Listen to some Chinese zither music. Let yourself be open to the emotions that are evoked.

Share your expressions . . .

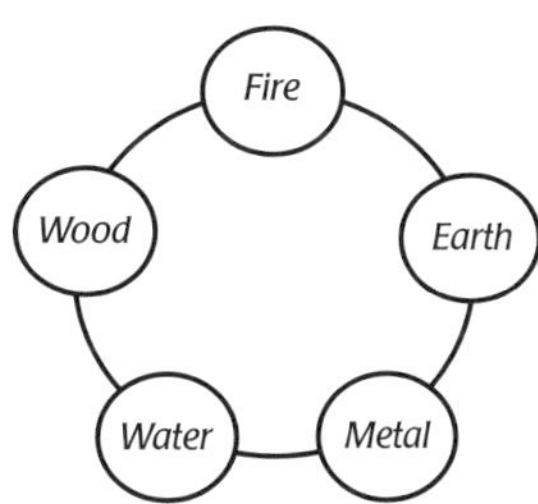

August 1

Thank you Father for your free gift of fire.
Because it is through fire that you draw near to us
every day.
It is with fire that you constantly bless us.
Our Father, bless this fire today.
With your power enter into it.
Make this fire a worthy thing.
A thing that carries your blessing.
Let it become a reminder of your love.
A reminder of life without end.
Make the life of these people to be baptized like
this fire.
A thing that shines for the sake of people.
A thing that shines for your sake.

- Masai Prayer

Exercise

List 5 things that fire has given you today, either directly or indirectly.

Share your expressions . . .

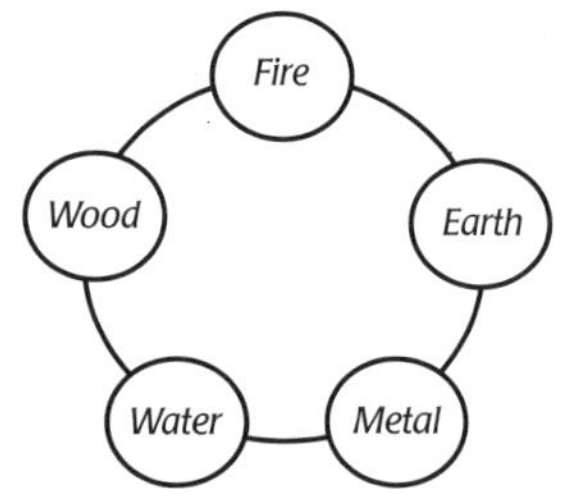

Expressions

August 2

People have always recognized the necessity of fire—for warmth in the winter, for cooking food, for light in the moonless night, for forging metals, clearing fields, and as a protection against wild animals. Many people reverenced fire and the sun. The Masai prayer goes beyond the literal, practical value of fire to the connection between fire and divine love, the spark of life itself.

Although Americans today may not cook or light their homes with open flames, the electricity that we use is also a manifestation of Fire. Indeed, we are even more dependent on Fire today, though we release the stored heat in many forms —fossil fuels, microwaves, electricity, nuclear power—and hide open flames deep within engines and boilers.

And the Fire-element part of us still enjoys the ritual use of actual fire in the form of fireplaces, barbecue pits, hibachis, bonfires, fireworks, candles, kerosene lanterns, cigarettes, and pipes! As we gaze into the flames of a fire under a star-filled sky, we experience again this ancient connection, the gift that warms and illuminates our bodies and hearts.

Exercise

Build a bonfire and create a ritual to celebrate fire.

Share your expressions . . .

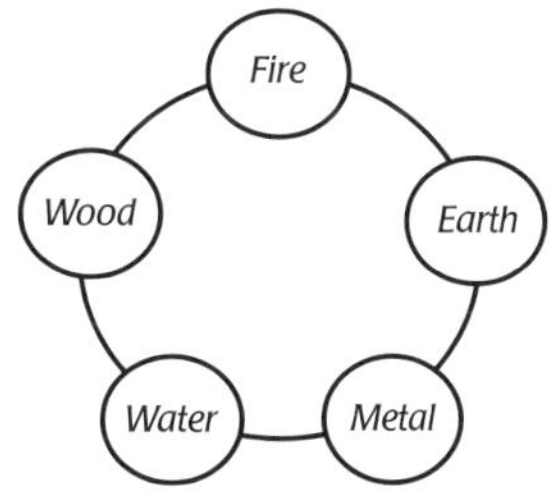

August 3

"The problem is—most girls are looking for Mr. Right, and most guys are looking for Ms. Right Now."

- Saying on a greeting card

We can think of the true maturation of a relationship as the point when the people involved can sustain a commitment to each other over time. It is a commitment to transmute the excitement and discovery of the Wood phase of a relationship, which can be likened to the initiating spark, into the steady glow of a long-burning hearth fire. The capacity to carry through this commitment is a measure of the strength of the Fire element in us.

How and why people make long-term commitments to be together, to care for one another, may be very different depending on age and cultural background. Many humans in most societies and time periods married as teenagers, at the will of their parents. However, the desire and capacity to make this kind of commitment comes from a well-balanced and mature Fire energy.

Exercise

Who or what are you committed to in your life?

Share your expressions . . .

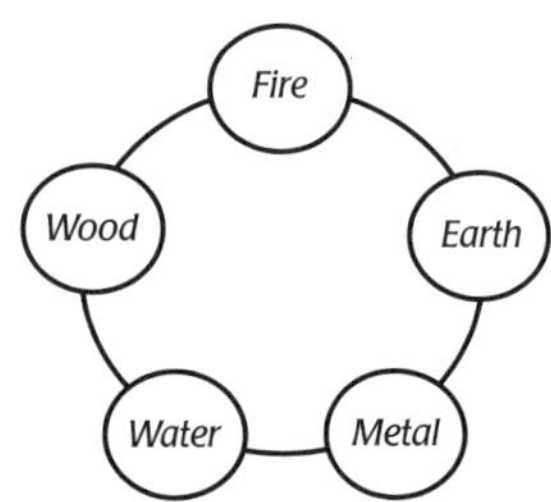

Expressions

August 4

The Triple Heater regulates more than the physical temperature of the body—it also regulates our social temperature, how we interact in the world with other people, the atmosphere or ambiance we create around us. Some people are naturally "warm" and seem to flow easily in social situations, while others tend to "freeze up" when confronted with people they don't know. Being able to regulate our social temperature to feel comfortable, no matter where we are, is a strength of the Triple Heater official.

A sensitive Triple Heater person will make sure that the ambiance of a space is conducive to good interaction at a meeting or party, monitoring the room temperature, closing off drafts or ventilation, providing good light, comfortable seats, and space to move around easily. This is the person who will make sure that everyone is introduced, and that no one is left standing in a corner. The Triple Heater wants to make sure that group relations are harmonious and balanced.

Exercise

The next time you are in a party or meeting, pay attention to the group "temperature"—is there anything you could do to make it more comfortable for everyone?

Share your expressions . . .

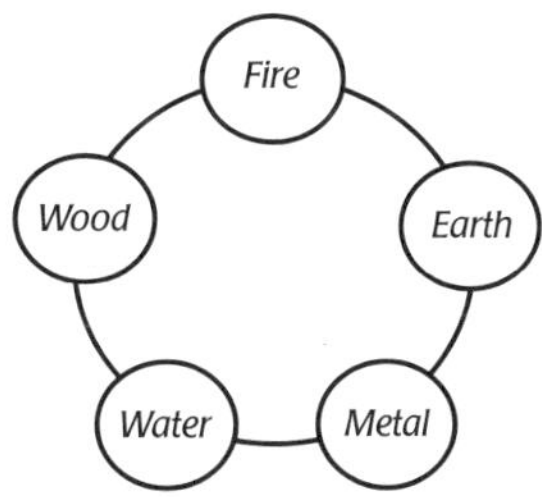

August 5

"I loaf and invite my soul,
I lean and loaf at my ease observing
a spear of summer grass."

- Walt Whitman
Song of Myself

These lines by Walt Whitman epitomize the difference between Fire and Wood energies, between Summer and Spring. The energy of Summer is more relaxed, more about "loafing" and enjoying life in a leisurely way, without the goal-oriented push of the Spring. Wood energy is much more directed, needing a goal and a sense of looking forward to the future. The energy of Fire is more timeless, concerned with the Now, the present moment of awareness and enjoyment. To continue to strive, plan, and focus on the future during the Summer pushes against the seasonal vibration, which says, "Slow down; stop and smell the flowers."

Exercise

Pack a sandwich and spend an afternoon just riding a bike or rowing a boat, stopping when you feel like it, to eat a leisurely lunch under some trees.

Share your expressions . . .

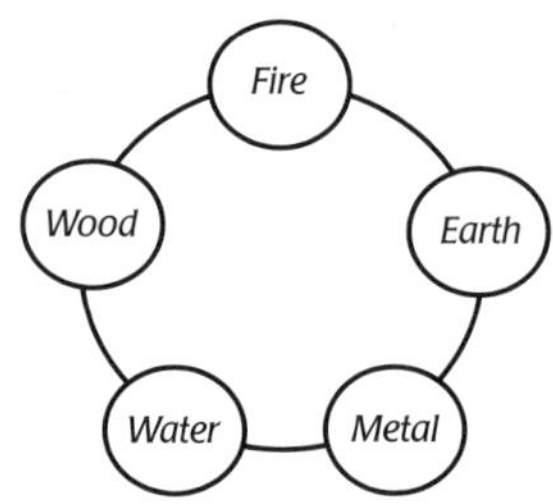

Expressions

August 6

"...the heart is like the minister of the monarch... When the monarch is intelligent and enlightened, there is peace and contentment among his subjects; they can thus beget offspring, bring up their children, earn a living and lead a long and happy life..."

- Nei Jing

Ted Kaptchuk, author of *The Web That Has No Weaver*, speaks of the spiritual virtue of the Heart as being "propriety," the ability to be appropriate to the situation, to be at the right place at the right time. Propriety refers to the sacred duties of the emperor, who was the center of the kingdom in the same way the Heart is the center of the body-mind-spirit. Among the important duties of the emperor was conducting sacred rituals, for example, to face the South on the summer solstice and say the appropriate ritual words. Thus, the emperor demonstrated "propriety," and because he did these things, his subjects had "peace and contentment."

Exercise

Every day this week, show up for every appointment exactly on time.

Share your expressions . . .

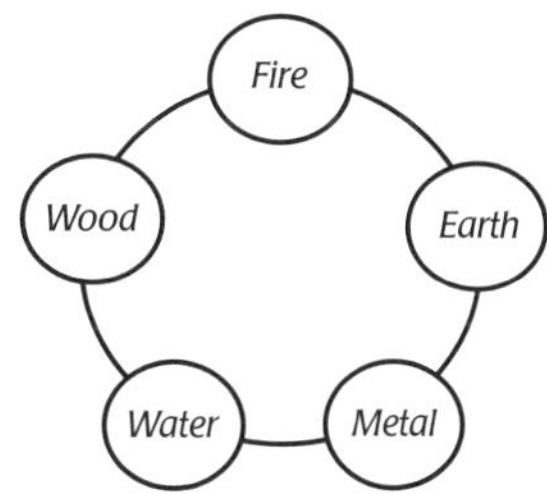

Expressions

August 7

"...the heart stores and harbors the divine spirit;..."

- Nei Jing

The Heart as the monarch of our own body-mind-spirit kingdom must have the virtue of propriety so that we can behave appropriately. Showing up at the opera in a bathing suit, or wearing an expensive evening gown to the beach, would be an exaggerated example of lacking propriety. We have all met people whose behavior and conversation were not appropriate to the context. We often find these people disturbing because we sense that they don't realize how inappropriate they are. In Chinese medical thought, we say that these people have "disturbed *shen*," and diagnose it as a symptom of the Heart. The *shen* refers to the spirits that have their abode in the Heart, and these *shen* spirits are the intermediaries between Heaven and the individual. Of course, some people who seem not to "fit" come from a different cultural or spiritual context, and fit a larger or different truth.

Exercise

Go to the theater or a big concert—dress up for the occasion.

Share your expressions . . .

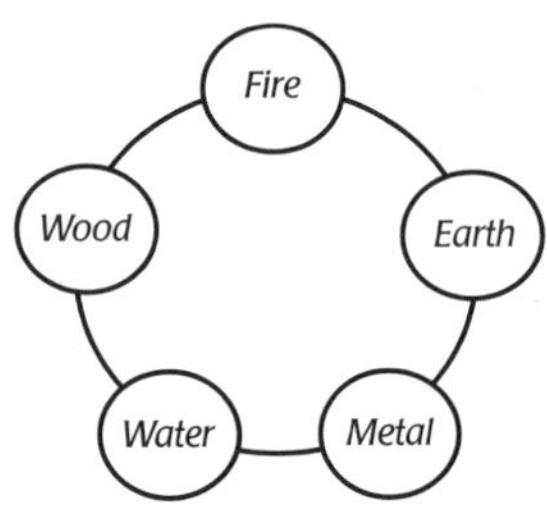

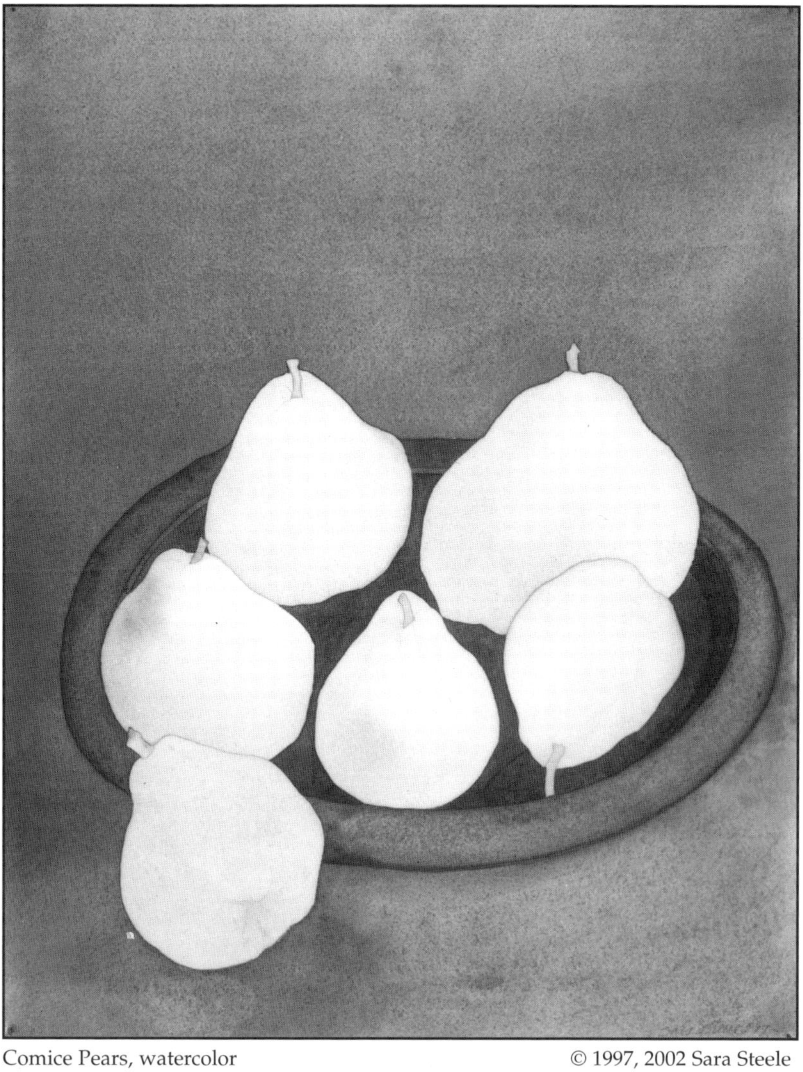

Comice Pears, watercolor

LATE SUMMER

土

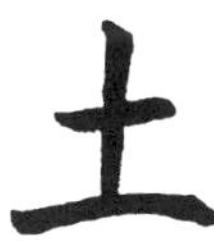

Late Summer/Earth

"Nature has four seasons and five elements."

"The [mysterious] powers of the earth create humidity in Heaven and fertile soil upon earth. They create the flesh within the body, and of the viscera they create the stomach."

"The region of the center, the Earth, is level and moist. Everything that is created by the Universe meets in the center and is absorbed by the Earth."

- Nei Jing

Earth is the name the Chinese give to the energy of Late Summer. This special season was added to the four traditional seasons to create numerical consistency with the five elements. In the yearly cycle, it is the transitional season between Summer and Fall, although some ancient texts correlate it to the transition times between each of the other four seasons.

Late Summer is the season of the harvest, the gathering in of all that has been produced the rest of the year. As such, it is correlated with nourishment and abundance, a time when grains are reaped and fruits are picked in preparation for Winter. It is a golden time of contentment and security, of basking in the glow of achievement and satisfaction. The energy of Earth is that of rich, ripe stillness.

We experience this energy at mid-life, when we raise families, create a body of work, or are productive in our jobs. It is a time of stability, when we settle down and create a home for ourselves. After the hard work of youth and early adulthood, we begin to reap the rewards of our labors. Our thoughts turn to nurturing the next generation, and the tasks of parenting, mentoring, and solidifying what we've created. This season is associated with "Mother" earth—the primary nurturer—and so we need to "mother" something at this phase of our lives.

Late Summer can be a time of great fulfillment, if we've planted our seeds well and tended them carefully as they grew. It can also be a time of great unhappiness and insecurity if, like the grasshopper in the tale of the grasshopper and the ant, we've put nothing away for the Winter. Those who have no harvest within feel needy, desperate, disconnected, and uncentered—"like a motherless child."

The Earth energy in our bodies governs our ability to nourish ourselves through the foods we eat, how we "harvest" our daily bread. It also governs all the cycles and rhythms of life—the menstrual cycle, our sleeping, eating, and breathing cycles. Any disruption of a natural cycle, or any difficulty with eating or digestion could point to an imbalance in the Earth.

The organs associated with the Earth are the Stomach and Spleen/Pancreas. They are essential for digestion and the nourishment of the whole body-mind-spirit. The Stomach in the classics is called "the official of the public granaries"—it receives the food we eat and must transform it into something that the body can use. The Spleen/Pancreas, in the Chinese model, is in charge of distributing the nourishment throughout the body.

On the mental level, Earth energy enables us to "digest" ideas, to process our experiences, and to form thoughts. An imbalance in Earth could lead to obsession, thinking the same thoughts over and over again in a futile attempt to digest something mentally. This going around in circles could also become a kind of obstinacy or stubbornness, the inability to accept any new ideas while we "chew" on the old ones.

The emotion connected to Earth is sympathy. Again, this can be seen as a kind of "motherly" feeling, of being empathic toward others in need, and wanting to care for them. In the best sense, it is a compassion for all of life, a generous giving of oneself when the need arises.

The negative side of this is worry—when the sympathy turns obsessive. As with all the emotions, the important thing is the ability to flow between them. Someone who is always asking for sympathy, or someone who is always sympathetic to others but refuses to receive any sympathy, is pointing to an imbalance in Earth energy.

Spiritually, Earth energy grants us the capacity to be grounded in reality, to be balanced and stable in the world. As Dianne Connelly says, "We are balanced and centered within, interacting and connected without." Ultimately, it is being at home in oneself. Then, out of this calm and nourished center, we can feel sympathy and compassion for all life, and a desire to care for all of creation.

August 8

"Yellow is the color of the center; it pervades the spleen...its kind (element) is the earth...The spleen rules over the long Summer."

- Nei Jing

The season connected to Earth energy is the Late Summer, or Long Summer, as it's called in the *Nei Jing*. Although not seen as a separate season in our culture, we feel it as a climate change that begins, in the American Northeast, during mid-August or early September, when the days are warm but the nights are cool—before the leaves actually start turning colors and falling, but well after summer is really over. We sometimes call this time "Indian Summer." It is a particularly golden time of year—many of the crops are ripe, the fruit trees and vegetable gardens are heavy with fruit. A feeling of peace and plenty prevails.

Exercise

At sunset, sit by an open window, turn off the lights and close your eyes. Listen to the night song of the crickets and other insects, and feel the slight tang in the air as the heat of the day cools toward dark.

Make your connections . . .

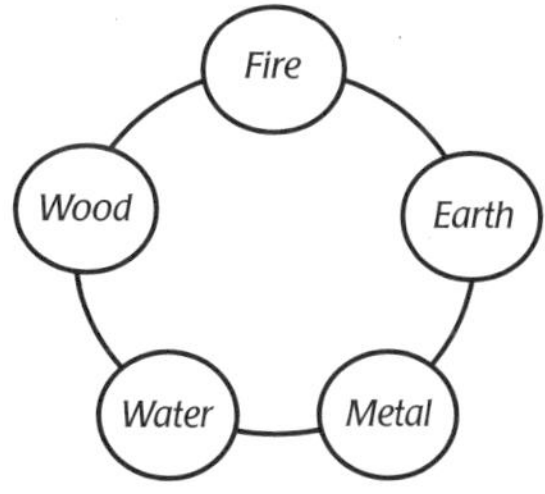

Connections

August 9

In Late Summer, the Earth holds us like a mother holds a baby in her arms. As Mother Nature, she is ever present, loving, and compassionate, and we can always turn to her for reassurance and security. She feeds us and serves us on all levels of body, mind, and spirit. In the season of Late Summer we are particularly aware of her nourishing and nurturing qualities, as full harvests provide us with abundant food for the Winter.

If we are in balance with this season, we feel secure, grounded, and connected to life at all levels. We are firmly rooted, have our "feet on the ground," and we feel nurtured in body, mind, and spirit. Feeling safe in our center, we are able to join in the dance around us. To be "earthy" is to be in touch with our fleshly bodies and the world of the senses. In Late Summer, we bask in the golden glow of the harvest, feeling ripe and complete, nurtured and capable of nurturing others from our bounty.

Exercise

After every meal, take five minutes to sit with your hands on your belly. Feel the soft roundness, and allow yourself to feel the contentment that comes from a full stomach after a good meal.

Make your connections . . .

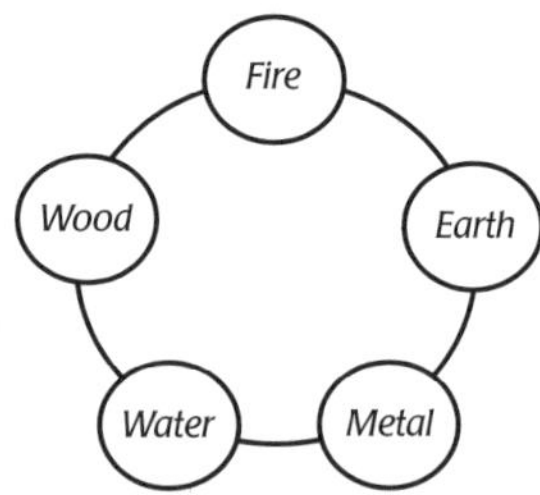

Connections

August 10

At the still point of the turning
world. Neither
flesh nor fleshless;
Neither from nor towards; at
the still point,
there the dance is,
But neither arrest nor
movement. And do not
call it fixity,
Where past and future are
gathered. Neither movement
from nor towards,
Neither ascent nor decline.
Except for the point,
the still point,
There would be no dance, and
there is
only the dance.

- T. S. Eliot

Exercise

Sit in the sun and feel as if you were soaking in this warmth to last you through the winter. Become the still point.

Make your connections . . .

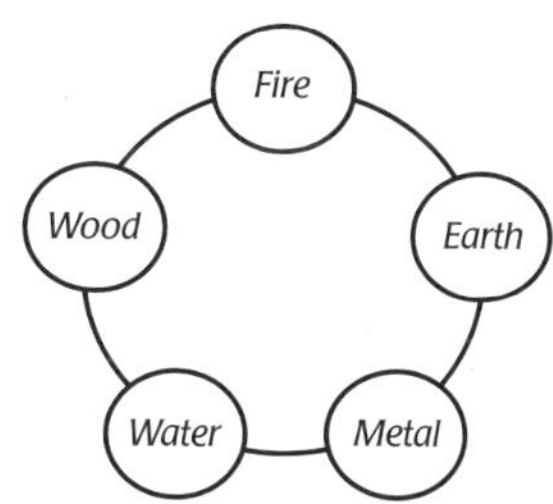

Connections

August 11

The previous lines from T.S. Eliot capture the essence of Earth as the center. It does not move in any direction, yet serves as the hub of the wheel, around which everything else turns. Earth is, therefore, the "ground of our being," that from which everything else arises. Earth generates, supports, and nourishes the other four elements. It is the stability of the ground under our feet, as well as the loving nourishment the Earth gives us, which provides us with a strong center for health.

In the cycle of the seasons, this "still point" comes in Late Summer, after the spurt of Spring and the luxurious flourishing of the Summer. All Nature pauses to soak in the completion of the growth cycle. The rising energies of Yang as expressed in Spring and Summer, and the sinking energies of Yin as expressed by Autumn and Winter, reach a momentary balancing point. Here is a time that is neither Yin nor Yang, but a perfectly balanced time of peace, plenty, and abundance.

Exercise

Go to a favorite nature area, and find a place to lie down, directly on the ground. Relax and close your eyes. Feel the stillness of the Earth under you. Feel its steady pulse.

Make your connections . . .

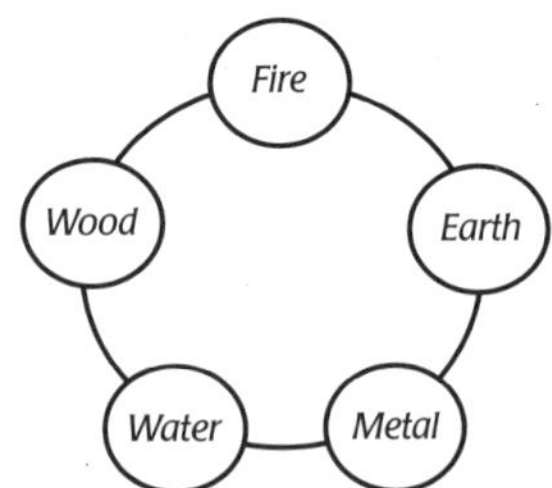

Connections

August 12

"Yellow is the color of the center...."

- Nei Jing

Yellow is the color associated with the Earth element and the season of Late Summer. The Chinese word for yellow, *huang*, includes oranges and browns, especially the color of soil or earth. (There is no separate word for "brown.") Hence, its logical use as the color for the Earth element.

In many parts of the world, this color seems to be more prevalent in nature in Late Summer. Leaves begin to turn a bit yellow, wild sunflowers and black-eyed susans line the roadsides and the fields, the grain begins to turn yellow and brown, and even the sun seems more golden-yellow in the late afternoons. Many fruits and vegetables that ripen now are yellow: corn; squash; pumpkins; and melons. Nature herself seems to emphasize the "golden" harvest.

Exercise

Pick a bouquet of wild sunflowers and black-eyed susans and put them in your bathroom.

Make your connections . . .

August 13

Many American homes use yellow walls, woodwork, and furniture in their "comfort and activity" rooms—we often have "cheerful" yellow kitchens (rooms for nourishment) and comfortable and comforting family rooms done in "earth tones." "Buttery" conjures up something that is yellow, rich, and nourishing. This color, like the steady warmth of Late Summer, gives us the feeling of being surrounded by the arms of Mother Earth.

Of the yellow hue surrounding the face when there is an imbalance in the Earth energies, the *Nei Jing* says, "...when their color is yellow like that of oranges they are without life."

Yellow is also a color we can use to support our own Earth energy. If our Earth energy is weak, we can wear yellow or surround ourselves with it in our homes or workplaces to foster feelings of security and comfort.

Exercise

Wear something yellow or brown today to support your Earth.

Make your connections . . .

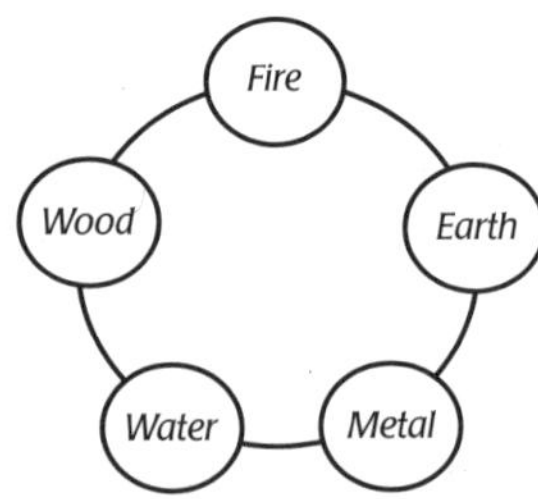

Connections

August 14

"Humidity is created by the center. Humidity nourishes the earth..."

- Nei Jing

Humidity is the climatic condition connected to the Earth element and to the season of Late Summer. Certainly for many people, Late Summer is a time of year associated with very hot and humid weather. The air sometimes feels thick with moisture, and there can be a sticky, oppressive atmosphere that sometimes culminates in a thunderstorm. Late Summer is a season of morning mists and evening fogs, when distances look blue because of the moisture in the air, when the mists in the trees look like smoke from Indian campfires (hence the name "Indian Summer").

When we experience internal "humidity," our body retains "dampness," which can lead to many physical ailments that resemble the properties of dampness in the natural environment—such as heaviness, swelling, and edema.

Exercise

Go out at dawn on a humid day and look for spider webs covered in dewdrops.

Make your connections . . .

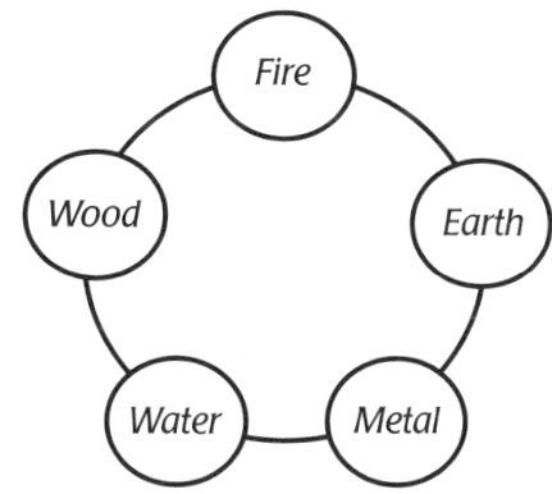

Connections

August 15

"The central region produces dampness
Dampness produces Earth...."

- Claude Larre and Elisabeth de la Vallee

Since dampness is wet, heavy, slow, and lingering, when we are Damp our own internal energy feels sticky, heavy, and stagnant, with sore and heavy limbs, dull headaches, sluggish digestion, excess mucous, and obstructions that can lead to lumps, nodules, and tumors.

It goes without saying that someone with a "damp" internal climate will have difficulty when the weather outside is humid or damp. These people will also dislike humid and damp weather, and will want to avoid damp surroundings where they live or work. To be in harmony with this climate, it is necessary to slow down your movements and activities, to avoid foods (such as sugar and dairy products) that cause your internal environment to be damp, to try to stay as dry as possible, and to cultivate patience and contentment with what is.

Exercise

Curl up with a blanket and watch the rain.

Make your connections . . .

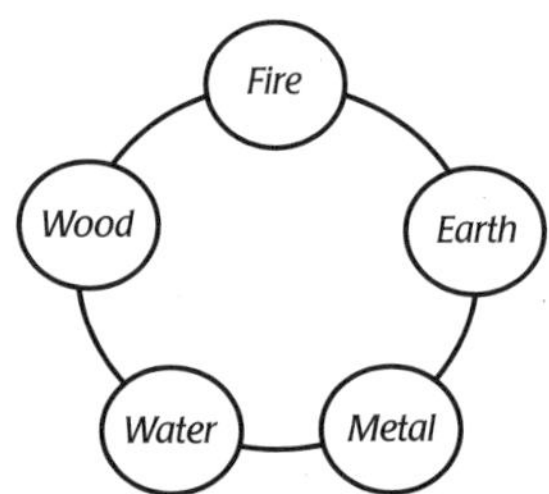

Connections

August 16

"...the stomach acts as the official of the public granaries and grants the five tastes;..."

- Nei Jing

The Earth energy within us produces what we need for existence. The Official of the Stomach, also called the Official of Rotting and Ripening, takes in the food we eat, and transforms it into substances that can be used by the cells of our bodies. This chemical process is akin to fermentation, and is a crucial step in the process of digestion. The *Nei Jing* says, "The stomach acts as a place of accumulation for water and grain and as a source of supply for the six bowels... The five flavors enter the mouth and are stored by the stomach in order to bring nourishment to the five viscera and to the breath of life... Thus all force of life and all the flavors go towards the stomach, where they are digested..." Elsewhere, it says that the Stomach has "...the power of transforming the dregs and the sediment." Thus, the Stomach is a place of storage and a place for the transformation of energy.

Exercise

Eat a healthy breakfast. Don't skip the most important meal of the day.

Make your connections . . .

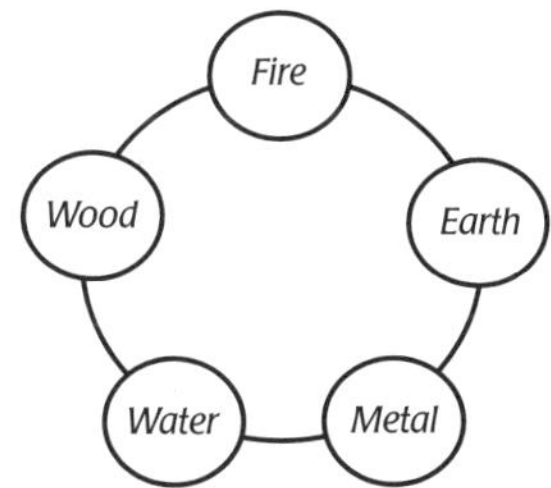

Connections

August 17

In Western physiology, the Stomach mixes food with gastric secretions, which prepare it for further digestion and absorption in the Small Intestine. This is the "rotting and ripening" function—by mixing the food with hydrochloric acid, pepsin, and mucus, the Stomach creates chyme, a milky, murky semi-fluid and acidic paste, which contains the partially digested food in a form that can be handled by the rest of the digestive system.

The Official of Rotting and Ripening operates on the emotional, mental, and spiritual levels, as well. The mind and emotions must be fed as surely as the body—"Man does not live by bread alone." For many who live in food-rich, industrialized nations, our real hunger is an emotional and spiritual one. Many people are "starved" for affection. Others feel a real spiritual hunger, which goes unfulfilled. If the Stomach Official is not working properly, we cannot transform our experiences and emotions so that they nourish us.

Exercise

Serve yourself your morning coffee or tea in a beautiful cup, one that you had put away because it was too "good" for everyday use. Linger over it in bed or in a patch of sunlight.

Make your connections . . .

Connections

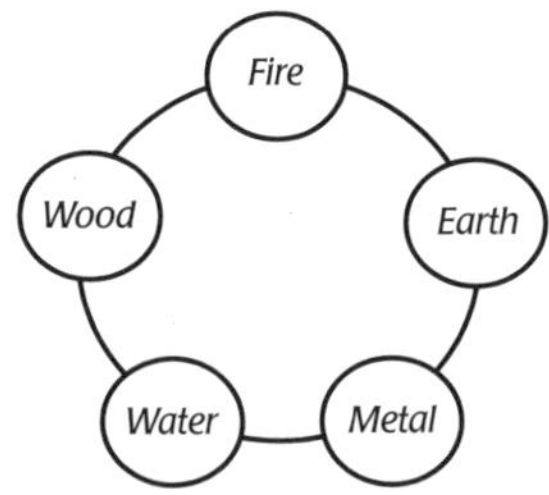

August 18

"...the five viscera all desire their breath of life from the Spleen; it is the Spleen that is the foundation of existence of the five viscera."

- Nei Jing

The Spleen/Pancreas is the Yin organ associated with Earth energy. (The "Pancreas" was tacked on to "Spleen" in later texts because of the pancreas' role in digestion.)Professor Worsley calls the Spleen the Official in Charge of Distribution and the Transporter of Energy, which distributes nourishing energy to other organs and to all parts of the body-mind-spirit. Chinese thought extends the metaphor far beyond the anatomical structure of the physical spleen. The Official can be likened to an urban transportation network, which distributes goods all over the world. In just this way, the Spleen official carries nourishment to all parts of the body-mind-spirit. One interesting fact: insulin, which is produced by the pancreas, is necessary for sugar metabolism because it transports the sucrose molecule through the cell wall.

Exercise

Go to a farm stand and buy lots of seasonal fruit for snacks instead of candy bars.

Make your connections . . .

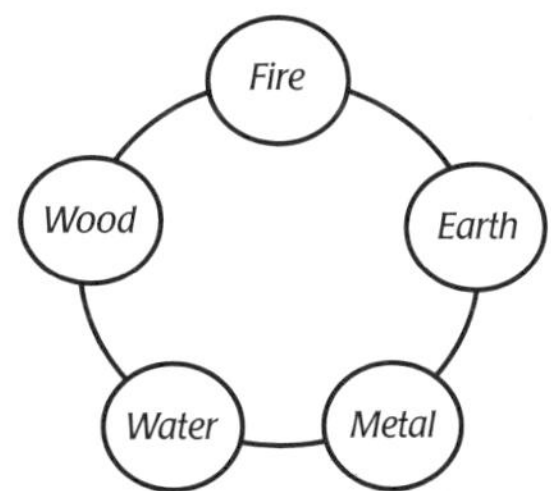

Connections

August 19

We notice the Spleen function most when it is <u>not</u> working well. As the *Nei Jing* says, "When the Spleen is in an excellent condition there is nothing that can be perceived, but when it is in an evil condition it can be easily seen." Thus, numbness or paralysis of areas of the body, obstructions and areas of stagnation in the body-mind-spirit could point to a Spleen official malfunctioning. Sluggishness and lethargy could mean that the system is malnourished. Thinking may be cloudy because the system is clogged up and not circulating. Working hand in hand with the Stomach, the Spleen is in charge of all aspects of digestion and assimilation, so any problems in digestion, of either food, ideas, or emotions, can be attributed to an imbalance in the Spleen official.

Exercise

For one week, eat a different grain for breakfast every morning. Try oatmeal, cream of wheat, buckwheat, yellow millet, or sweet rice. Compare your energy on the different grains.

Make your connections . . .

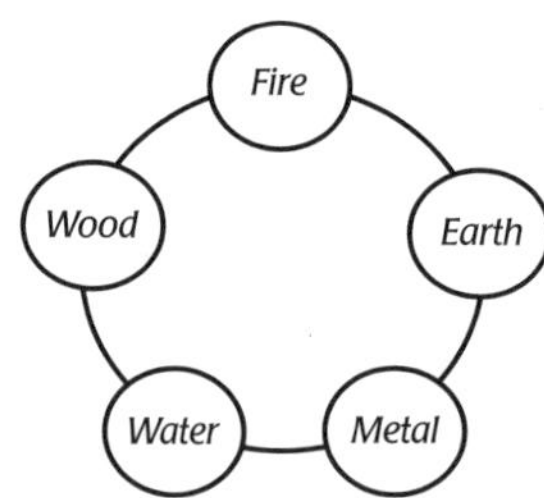

August 20

"...of the emotions they create consideration and sympathy."

- Nei Jing

Sympathy is the emotion connected to the energy of Earth. This is like the feeling of empathy, compassion, and thoughtfulness, which a mother has for her child. Like a mother with a child, sympathy flows best when we have plenty of nourishment to offer. If we ourselves feel nourished, supported, and cared for, then it is easy to extend sympathy, compassion, and consideration to others.

Mother Earth cares for and provides for all creatures equally, good and bad. She is giving and for-giving. The *I Ching* (another Chinese classic text) says, "The earth in its devotion carries all things, good and evil, without exception." She is sympathetic and compassionate to all.

Exercise

Do you feel supported by the people in your life? Do you support others?

Make your connections . . .

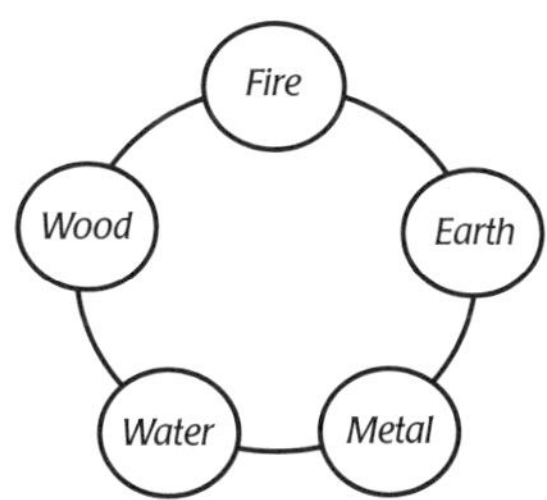

August 21

It is the essence of healthy Earth to be sympathetic, generous, and giving of support in an even-handed and unconditional way. When sympathy is excessive, however, it can turn into anxious worry, a kindred but less positive emotion connected with Earth. Imbalance can manifest as too much sympathy or worry about others, without paying enough attention to the self. Earth imbalance can also manifest as a bottomless need for sympathy and love—a neediness that can never be filled. This type of person can be very draining to be around, especially for the Earth types who give too much! Parents of young children, healthcare givers, teachers, therapists, and social workers are especially at risk. Their sympathies are constantly being called upon by the young, old, needy, and troubled, who need care and support, and they can exhaust their own store of nourishment.

Exercise

Who took care of you when you were a child? How do you take care of your body now?

Make your connections . . .

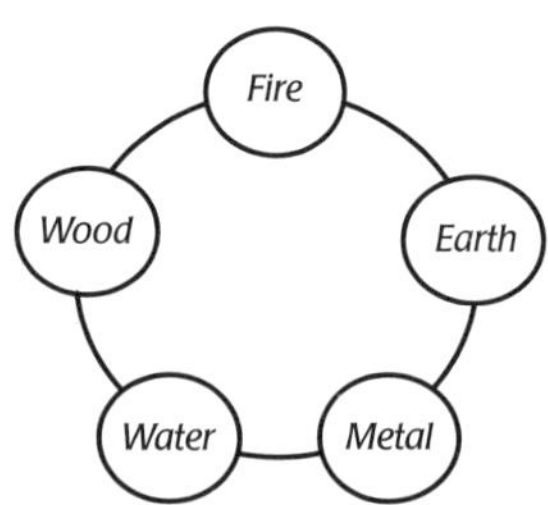

August 22

Earth energy functions at its peak from 7 to 11 in the morning. Specifically, the Stomach peaks during breakfast hours from 7 to 9 a.m., and the Spleen from 9 to 11 a.m. The Chinese believe that breakfast is definitely the most important meal of the day, since it is during Stomach time that your body has maximum energy for receiving the food and for digesting it. How foolish are those who eat little during this time of the Stomach's maximum efficiency! These same people will then eat a large and heavy meal from 7 to 9 p.m., straining the Stomach official during its low time of the day.

The Stomach Official is also at its peak, receiving mental and emotional nourishment at this time, so reading something inspirational over breakfast and repeating positive affirmations will be more effective then.

Exercise

Between 7 and 9 a.m., eat a hearty breakfast and notice how your energy feels the rest of the day.

Make your connections . . .

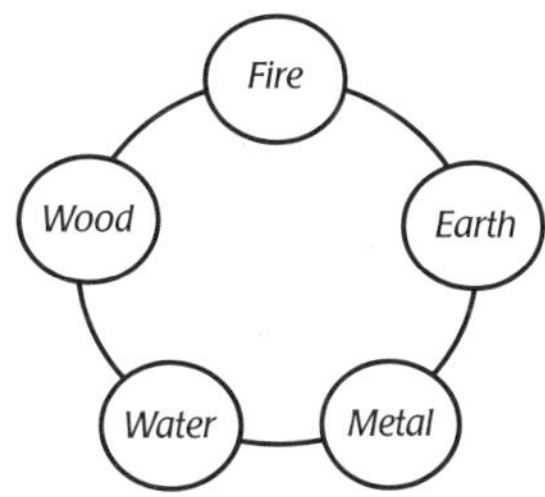

August 23

The hours from 9 to 11 a.m. feature the Spleen transporting the breakfast energy to every part of the body, and providing energy for the day's work. Many people feel that these hours are their most productive at work, and that they accomplish more in the morning than the entire rest of the day.

Those who are "morning people" are often referring to the state of energy in their Earth element. Conversely, those who have little energy in the morning will often tell you that they "sort of 'wake up' around 11 a.m."

Either a lot of energy or no energy during these times is an indication of the health of your Earth element, as is any symptom that gets markedly better or worse between 9 and 11 a.m.

Exercise

Between 9 and 11 a.m., take a walk. Be aware of nature and your connection to it, and notice the differences between how you feel at this time and at other times throughout the day.

Make your connections . . .

Connections

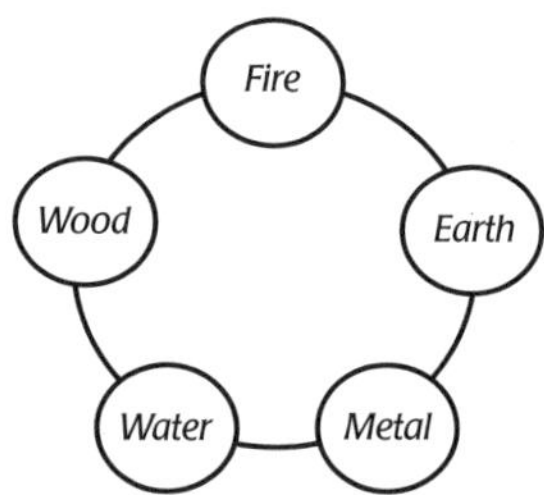

August 24

August goldenrod
and dark green pines
against the brilliant blue -
the hill behind me climbed,
the hill before me yet to go -
I stop under the shade of
white birches
a stray breeze lifting
my hair,
and drink a toast
to late summer's
sweetness,
rich in my mouth
as mulled wine

- Janice MacKenzie

Exercise

Go to a farm and watch hay being harvested and baled. Smell the sweet smell of new-mown hay.

Make your connections . . ..

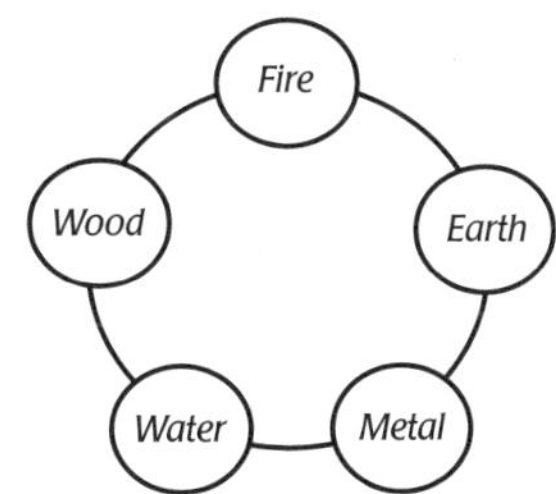

Connections

August 25

It is not enough that life be created—it must be continually sustained and nurtured. Although this aspect must be present during all seasons, it is especially noticeable during the Late Summer harvest, when fields and orchards teem with fruits and vegetables. In this season of plenty, we are fed by the Great Mother in full measure.

On the personal level, when Earth energy is strong, we can care for others physically and emotionally in tangible ways—we can cook meals for each other, do favors, run errands, give each other a shoulder to cry on, etc. When this energy is weak, we find it difficult to cook meals even for ourselves, and feel too overwhelmed and burdened to take on anyone else's troubles.

Exercise

If your mother is a nurturing person, call or visit her. Or, pay a visit to the most nurturing person you know.

Make your connections . . .

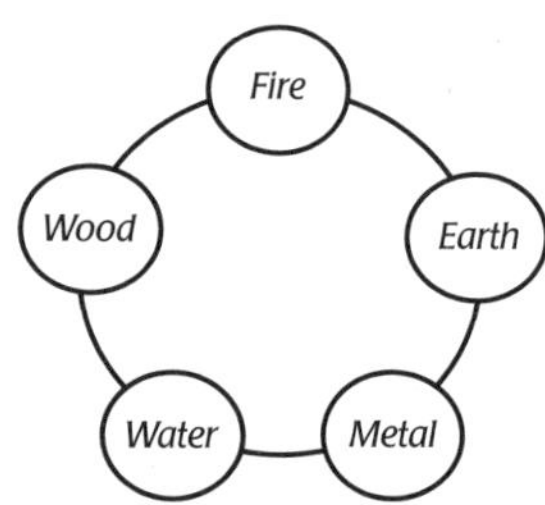

August 26

August.
The opposing
of peach and sugar,
and the sun inside the afternoon
like the stone in the fruit.

The ear of corn keeps
its laughter intact, yellow and firm.

August.
The little boys eat
brown bread and delicious moon.

- Federico Garcia Lorca

Exercise

Eat every meal as if you were tasting these foods for the last time. Realize that you won't be able to taste these red ripe tomatoes and sweet white corn in December.

Make your connections . . .

Connections

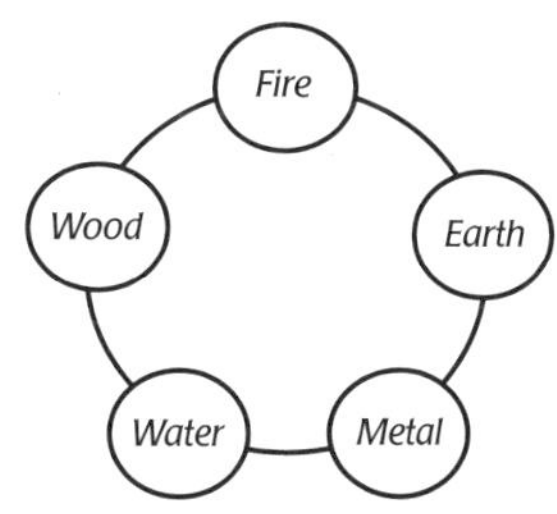

August 27

A common pattern for people whose Earth energy is out of balance is to nurture everyone around except themselves. These people will only cook meals for others, but not when they're home alone. They will loan money to others but not have enough for their own needs. They will listen to everyone else's troubles, but have nobody to listen to theirs. This constant nurturing without receiving any back is just as out of balance as being unable to nurture others. It may make us feel loved or valuable but eventually depletes our own energy.

It is a troubling sign of our times that many households eat breakfast on the road, lunch at their desks, and "eat-'n-run" dinners out of the microwave. Skipped meals, constant grazing, "fast food," and eating disorders are commonplace. Our collective Earth energy is too weak to feed the hungry of our own society, even as our fields produce record harvests.

Exercise

What was your relationship with your mother like? What is your relationship to food today?

Make your connections . . .

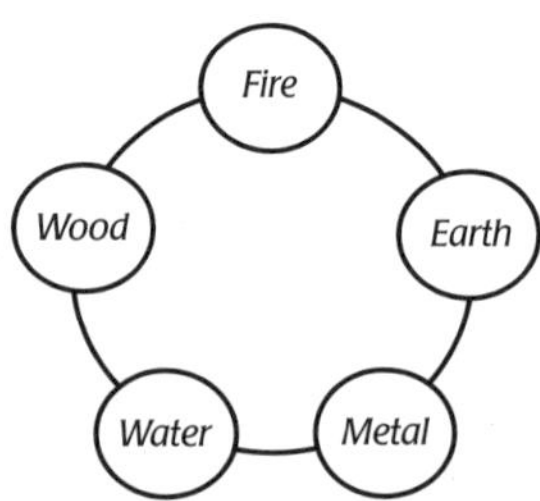

August 28

"As human beings functioning as potters, we center ourselves and our clay. And we all know how necessary it is to be 'on center' ourselves if we wish to bring our clay 'into center' and not merely to agitate it or bully it. As organisms in the natural rhythm of birth, growth, and death, we experience metamorphosis throughout our lives, as our bodies grow and change from infancy to ripeness, as our capacities for inner experience enlarge and strengthen. As potters, we have an especially immediate and concrete daily experience of both these more-than-physical processes. For as potters we handle our medium in the full range of its transformations. We dig our clay out of its earth bed; or if we do not always dig it ourselves, we do know the experience of digging and preparing it. We experience the mud, we experience the forces of time and destiny that have transmuted rock into plastic dust. We experience the raw ware, the sudden spell of a mobile act brought into stillness."

- M.C. Richards,
Centering

Exercise

Stand barefoot with your feet shoulder-width apart, knees slightly bent, back straight and arms hanging relaxed by your sides. Close your eyes, and shift your weight slightly from side to side and heel to toe to balance evenly. Experience being centered.

Make your connections . . .

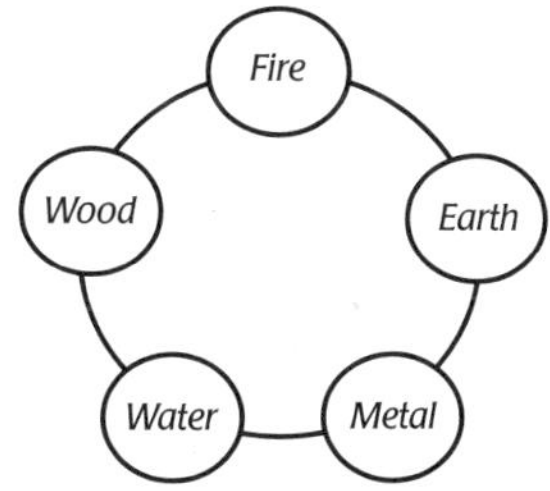

Connections

August 29

If Wood energy concerns individuality, and Fire energy is about intimate relationships, then Earth energy concerns family and community, the web of relationships within which we live. Earth energy enables us to belong, to feel "at home" somewhere and with a group of others who accept us. We survive together by mutually supporting each other, trading goods and services to get our needs met. The web of affection and obligation ties us together, holds us in and holds us up.

When our Earth energy is strong, we are able to create and maintain that family or community around us. If Earth energy is weak, however, we may feel alone, unconnected, or alienated from the human race. This lack of connection can make us feel unsupported and afraid, leading to symptoms such as agoraphobia and panic attacks. Schools, churches, clubs, and workplaces are all examples of communities that can give us a sense of belonging.

Exercise

Write your name in the center of a large piece of paper and write the names of everyone you know around you, with the closest friends near your name and the more distant ones far away. Draw lines between the names of those who know each other. Notice the web of connections that forms your community.

Make your connections . . .

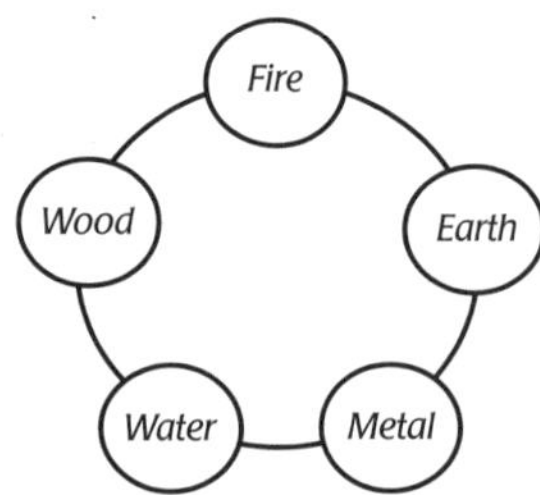

August 30

"Sharing a family meal wasn't something that happened a lot around my house. The daily dinner time routine when I was growing up in Richmond was to come home and find no one around but me.

"Now, after five years of living apart, I'm spending my senior year of high school living in Gary, Indiana, with my father and sister. The thing I value most is the supper we share.

"Every night, around 6:30, all of us—me, my father, my father's girlfriend, her two daughters, and my sister—sit down to dinner together. Last night we had pork chops, mashed potatoes, cabbage, and greens. We all trade off cooking different nights. If someone can't be there, we always save him some food. We look out for each other like that.

"Maybe this doesn't sound like such a big deal, but it's something I've never experienced before. In Richmond the family motto was "do for yourself." My motto was "eat what you can, when you can." I used to eat alone all the time, and so did everyone else. I ate a lot of fast food."

(Continued next page)

Exercise

Make a fruit salad with all the fruits that are in season in your area; share the salad with family or friends.

Make your connections . . .

Connections

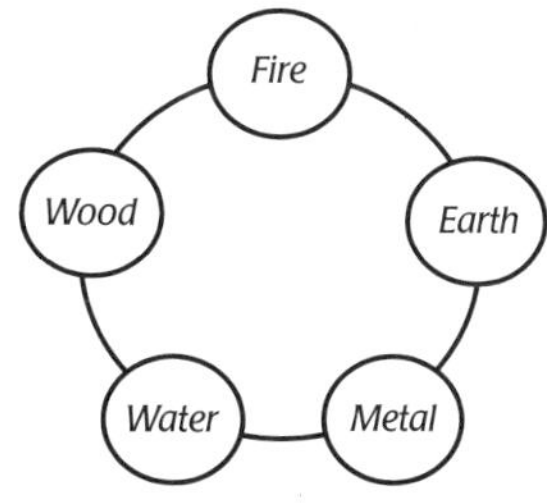

August 31

"The only time my family would sit down at a meal together was when we'd go to Grandma's house. Grandma's generation knew how it should be. They were raised to eat with the family.

"But my parents were young and struggling. When they got home they were either so tired they'd go right to bed, or else they'd want to go out and party. If they did eat at home, they'd eat by themselves in their bedroom...

"Holidays were the best part of the year because we'd eat with the whole family. We enjoyed the different kinds of food and the warm atmosphere in the house, and we hated for those days to end.

"For a long time I pretended to myself that I didn't care whether I ate alone. Now I know how good it feels to sit down every night and share a meal with my family. It means we're taking care of each other."

- by Ron Fox, 17,
reprinted from *YO! magazine*, Fall 1993.

Exercise

Visit a grandmother, your own or someone else's. Notice the different quality of nurturing that she gives.

Make your connections . . .

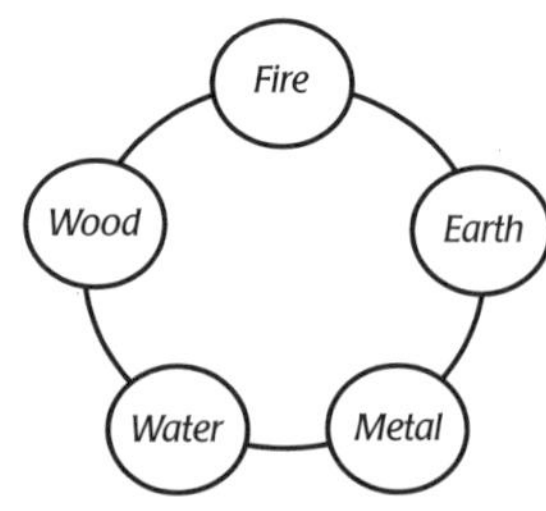

Connections

September 1

"The [mysterious] powers of the earth create humidity in Heaven and fertile soil upon earth ...of the flavors they create the sweet flavor...."

- Nei Jing

The taste associated with the Late Summer season and with the Earth energies is sweet. China scholar Joseph Needham described this association as "due to the finding of honey in bees' nests in the earth and to the general sweet taste of cereals." Actually, this harvest season is full of sweet-tasting foods, from the ripened grains to the fruits of trees and vines. It is a time when Mother Earth, at her most abundant, pours her sweetness out over the land. Mother's milk is slightly sweet; no wonder sweet is the taste most craved by children and by those in need of comfort.

Exercise

If you have a craving for sweets, the next time you want a candy bar, try a piece of watermelon instead.

Make your connections . . .

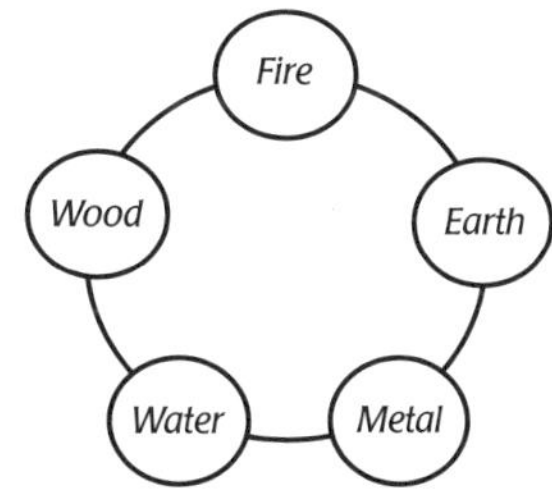

September 2

"At the tip of the tongue, we taste sweet things; bitter things at the back; sour things at the sides; and salty things spread over the surface, but mainly up front. The tongue is like a kingdom divided into principalities according to sensory talent...If we lick an ice cream cone, a lollipop, or a cake-batter-covered finger, we touch the food with the tip of the tongue, where the taste buds for sweetness are, and it gives us an extra jolt of pleasure. A cube of sugar under the tongue won't taste as sweet as one placed on the tongue."

- Diane Ackerman,
A Natural History of the Senses

The Spleen, one of the organs associated with Earth, is also called in some texts "Spleen/Pancreas"—pointing to another link between this energy and the sweet taste. In Western medicine, the pancreas is associated with diseases such as diabetes, hypoglycemia, and hyperglycemia, all of which have to do with sugar metabolism in the body. The strong desire to taste sweet is a clue, guiding you to look further at the state of balance of the Earth element.

Exercise

Eat a ripe peach very slowly, savoring the sweet juiciness of every mouthful. Lick your fingers when you're done.

Make your connections . . .

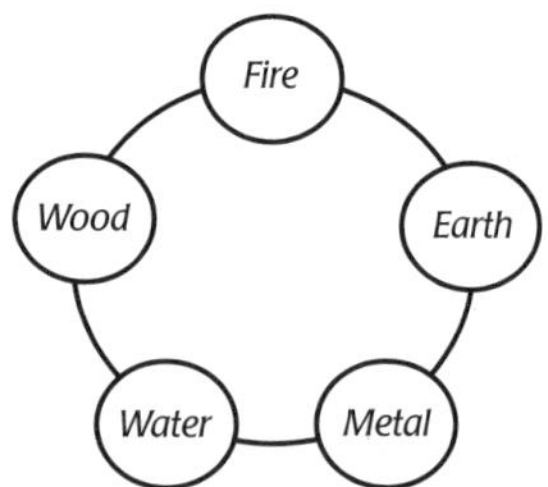

September 3

"...the earth produces sweet flavors."

"A (sick) spleen has the tendency to work tardily and lazily; then one should quickly eat sweet food to set it at ease. One uses bitter food to drain the spleen and one uses sweet food to supplement and to strengthen it."

- Nei Jing

There are certain foods that were traditionally associated with the Earth element, according to the Chinese classics: "Non-glutinous rice, beef meat, dates and mallows are all sweet." These foods, when eaten in combination with foods that support the other elements, will provide a healthy diet. Chinese dietary laws emphasize a balance of foods and flavors, rather than a strict adherence to any particular foods, to maintain health.

Exercise

Buy some organic dates at the health food store, and eat them, knowing that they have been associated with this season for thousands of years.

Make your connections . . .

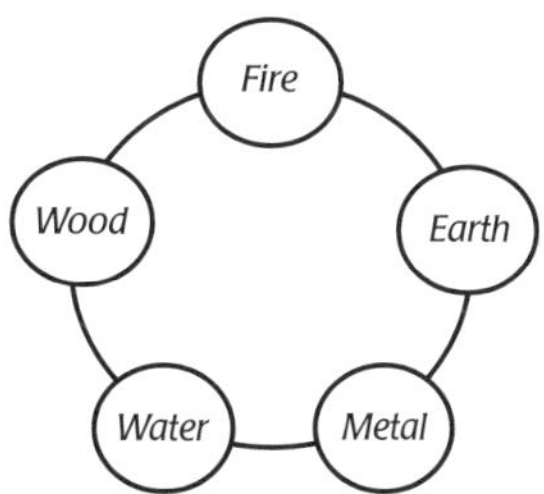

Connections

September 4

"...the sweet flavor has a retarding effect..."

- Nei Jing

Each of the flavors has a specific effect on the energy of the body. Henry C. Lu, in *Chinese System of Food Cures*, says that the sweet taste can slow down acute symptoms and neutralize the toxic effects of other foods. He also says that sweet foods improve the digestive functions, which is why they are recommended for people with weak digestion. Of all the foods that he lists under each flavor, the list for sweet foods is the longest: apples; apricots; bananas; barley; beef; brown sugar; cabbage; carrots; cinnamon; corn; dates; eggplant; figs; grapes; honey; kidney beans; lettuce; licorice; mangos; milk; olives; peaches; pears; plums; pork; rice bran; shrimp; squash; stringbeans; sugar cane; sweet potatoes; tomatoes; walnuts; watermelon; white sugar; and yellow soybeans are just some of the foods considered sweet.

Exercise

It's tomato season. Eat a juicy tomato with salt, or make home-made salsa with cilantro, onions, lime juice, and chili peppers.

Make your connections . . .

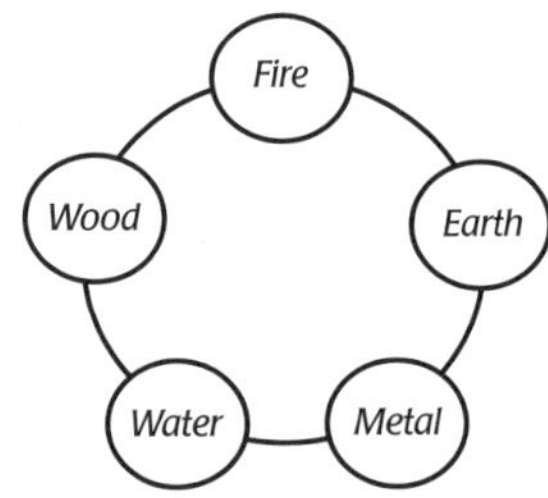

September 5

One of the primary functions of the Earth officials is that of nourishing the body-mind-spirit. The food that we ingest must first be transformed into something usable by the body, and then distributed to every cell, to nourish that cell. The health of our Earth energy determines whether that nourishment happens. We all know people who eat all the right foods and yet who don't seem to be nourished by them—people who seem perpetually hungry and dissatisfied at the same time. This could mean that their Earth energy is unable to "harvest" the good food that they eat, and/or that the nourishment doesn't reach the cells. It takes more than nourishing food to nourish our bodies—it also takes an appropriate balance internally to make the most of that nourishment.

Likewise, our minds and spirits must take in and assimilate nourishment. Many people are on an insatiable quest for information and spiritual knowledge, yet remain dissatisfied and spiritually impoverished.

Exercise

Give yourself a view first thing in the morning: either a vase of fresh flowers, a framed print or painting of a beautiful scene, or a photograph of a favorite place.

Make your connections . . .

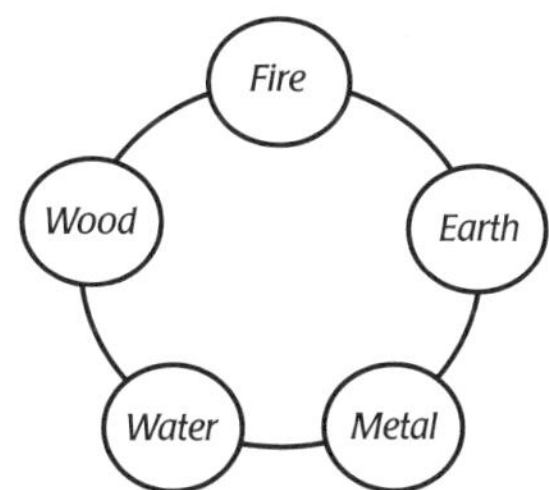

September 6

"In the Wise Woman tradition, health/wholeness/holiness comes through adding on to, that is, through nourishment. Problems, pains, diseases, and illnesses are not fixed, or cured, or even brought into balance, in the Wise Woman tradition, but honored, supported, respected for their truth, nourished, and added on to the truth of the whole being."

- Susun Weed

The capacity to nourish something is such a fundamental and yet almost forgotten art in our modern world. We tend to look for more dramatic solutions to problems, to force growth and healing on passive individuals. Nourishment, as Susun Weed talks about it in her *Wise Woman Herbal: Healing Wise,* has more to do with an attitude of humility and respect for the individual, of gently feeding and supporting someone so that their own strengths begin to take over and manifest. The one doing the nourishing becomes invisible. It is such a simple and yet profound thing to just nourish another human being —yet the source of nourishment is sometimes taken for granted.

Exercise

Get involved in feeding the homeless or working in a soup kitchen. Know that you are being of service to others and completing the circle of nourishment.

Make your connections . . .

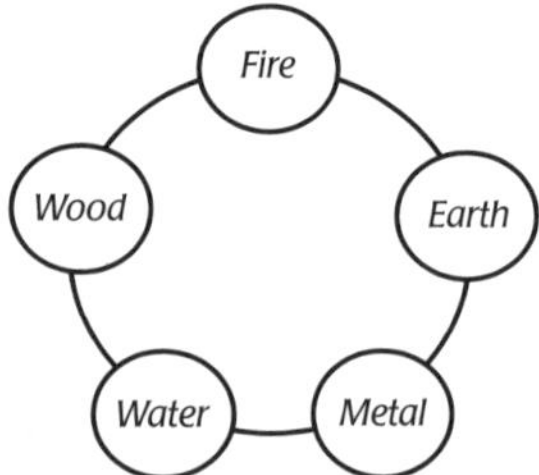

Connections

September 7

"The stomach rules over the mouth."

- Nei Jing

The mouth is associated with the Earth element because it is the orifice through which food nourishment comes into the body. Food and drink enter through our mouths, where the process of digestion begins, and then go to the Stomach, where many chemical transformations happen. Later, the Spleen distributes the energy from the food to all parts of the body. Thus, the mouth is essential to this process and is a completely interconnected part of it.

The health of the mouth—the lips, the gums and the mouth lining—is a reflection of the health of the Earth energy within us. Any swelling, cracking, or peeling of the lips could indicate an imbalance in the Earth, as could sore and bleeding gums. Mouth ulcers, chancre sores, or sore spots anywhere inside the mouth could indicate a problem in the digestion. Many diseases related to the mouth could be due to a poor diet and lack of proper nourishment.

Exercise

Make yourself a cup of chamomile tea and sip it slowly, allowing the herbs to cleanse your mouth and gums.

Make your connections . . .

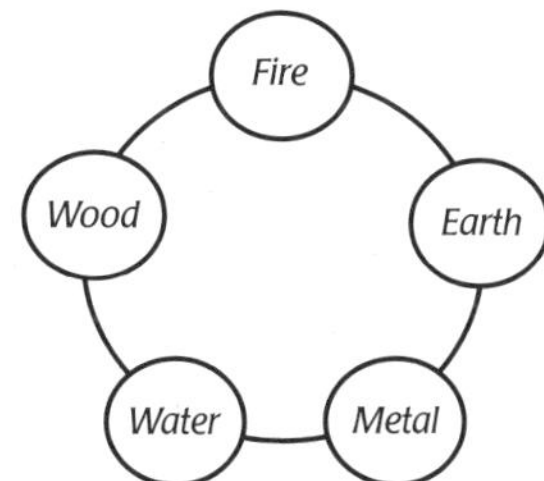

Connections

September 8

"By the mouth all kinds of Tastes penetrate the body, and what are Tastes or cereals or any food but the form or shape of Earthly Breaths? .... This opening at the mouth is specially linked with Earth, and the sweet taste of the Earth, and the assimilation, penetration and digestion of the Breaths of Earth in the shape of nutriment and food."

- Claude Larre and Elisabeth Rochat de la Vallee

What we take in through our mouths becomes us through the process of transformation and assimilation. The mouth is another portal, like the eyes, nose, and ears, for connecting to, and interpenetrating with, the outside world. It is the primary way that young babies have of experiencing the world, and if there is some deprivation of nourishment or suckling in infancy, it can lead to what psychotherapists call an "oral fixation." A Chinese doctor might call this the beginning of an Earth imbalance!

Exercise

Make a list today of everything that you put into your mouth.

Make your connections . . .

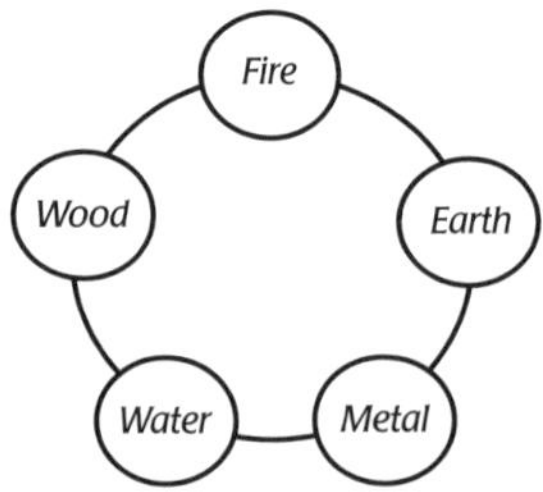

Connections

September 9

"The color and appearance of the lips show when the stomach is in a splendid and flourishing condition."

- Nei Jing

The Earth element has a superficial manifestation that can tell you at a glance the condition of the Spleen and Stomach energies in an individual. The lips, which circle the mouth, are visible clues to the balance within. If the lips are full, soft and pink, then the condition of the Stomach is probably "splendid and flourishing." If, however, they are thin, dry and cracked, or discolored, then probably there is an imbalance in the Earth.

The texture of the lips reveals the condition of the stomach. A sore on the right side of the mouth indicates excess acidity or the beginnings of an ulcer on the left side of the stomach. A sore on the left side of the mouth points to a problem on the right side of the stomach. Chapped lips may also indicate stomach problems.

Exercise

If your lips are dry or cracked, buy some flavored chapstick as a treat!

Make your connections . . .

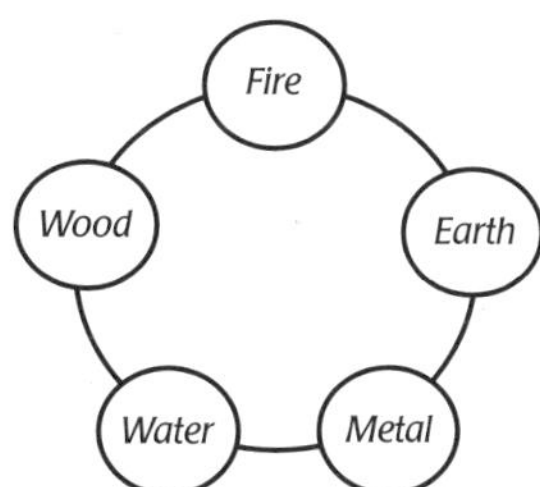

September 10

"These organs influence the lips and cause the flesh around them to be light color."

- Nei Jing

The lips should be of about equal thickness. If the upper lip is enlarged or swollen, it could indicate a problem in the upper digestive tract, possibly a problem with overeating. If the lower lip is swollen, it could indicate a weakness in the intestines, with consequent constipation. Our current cultural obsession with extra-thick lips, and movie stars having plastic surgery to "enhance" their lips, seems very bizarre to those trained in Oriental diagnosis!

The color of the lips is especially important. They should be a rich pink color—not too pale and not too dark. If too pale, they could indicate a nutritional deficiency, or even anemia. If too dark, they could indicate a stagnancy in the blood circulation. In both cases, the Earth element, as responsible for digestion and for the production of blood, would be saying "I need help."

Exercise

How is the health of your lips? Do you need to make changes in your diet?

Make your connections . . .

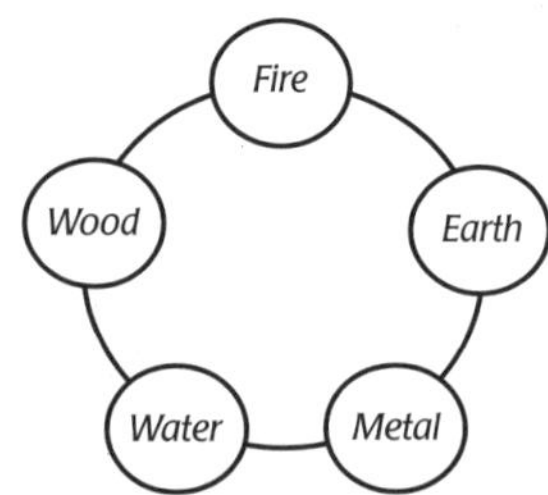

September 11

"They create the flesh within the body...."

"Thus the spleen harbors the force of life of the flesh."

- Nei Jing

The part of the body governed by the Earth element is the flesh. The flesh is distinct from the skin and the muscles that enable us to move; it is the solid matter that covers the bones and gives us our shape. The tone, texture, and temperature of the flesh are indicators of the health of the Earth element within us. It can be firm or flabby, slack or taut, doughy or stringy, cold or warm. The flesh shows the quality of the nutrition in a person, and illnesses that involve the wasting away of flesh are often due to imbalances in the Earth. There are some conditions in which people experience pain in the flesh, and it is clearly not in the muscles, bones, or joints. Fibrositis and fibromyalgia are two medical names for diseases of pain in the flesh.

Exercise

Get a massage. Wallow in the pleasure of this attention to your flesh.

Make your connections . . .

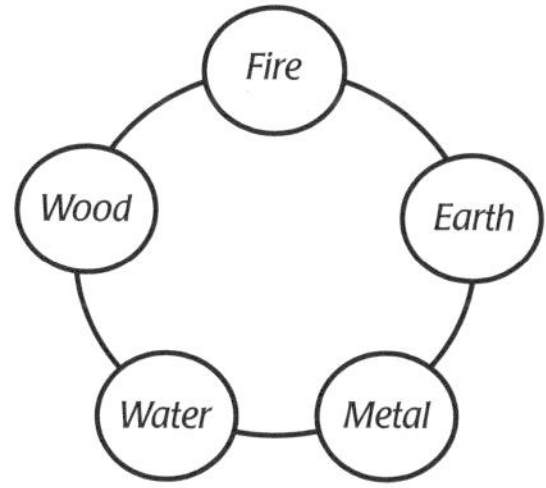

Connections

September 12

A synonym for flesh might be "connective tissue." Anatomy books describe connective tissue as "cells and fibers enmeshed in a ground substance or matrix." The viscous matrix contains many cells of several varieties, including macrophages, fat cells, plasma cells, and other white blood cells, and a loose, irregular arrangement of fibers. From this description, it is easy to see how improper nutrition would show up in the flesh—the fluids, fats, and proteins necessary for healthy connective tissue would be deficient.

"Flesh" is a word that has many connotations in our culture—from the vaguely salacious (porno films named "Flesh City" and "In the Flesh"), to the sinful ("The way of the flesh is an abomination to the Lord") to the unflattering ("fleshy"). The quote from Shakespeare that goes "That this too, too solid flesh should melt /and resolve itself into a dew" has been parodied endlessly in diet commercials. It is interesting that we are so uneasy with this aspect of ourselves that most closely mirrors our state of balance in the Earth element.

Exercise

Are you comfortable with your body now? How do you feel about your flesh?

Make your connections . . .

Connections

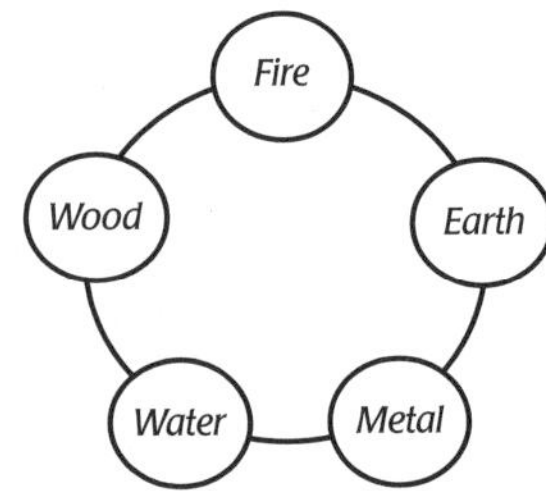

September 13

"The Goddess is first of all earth, the dark, nurturing mother who brings forth all life. She is the power of fertility and generation; the womb, and also the receptive tomb, the power of death. All proceeds from Her; all returns to Her. As earth, She is also plant life; trees, the herbs and grains that sustain life. She is the body, and the body is sacred. Womb, breast, belly, mouth, vagina, penis, bone, and blood - no part of the body is unclean, no aspect of the life processes is stained by any concept of sin. Birth, death, and decay are equally sacred parts of the cycle. Whether we are eating, sleeping, making love, or eliminating body wastes, we are manifesting the Goddess."

- Starhawk,
The Spiral Dance

Exercise

Every day for a week, say this affirmation: "I like my body and feel totally comfortable in it now. Every cell in my body is bursting with beauty and health."

Make your connections . . .

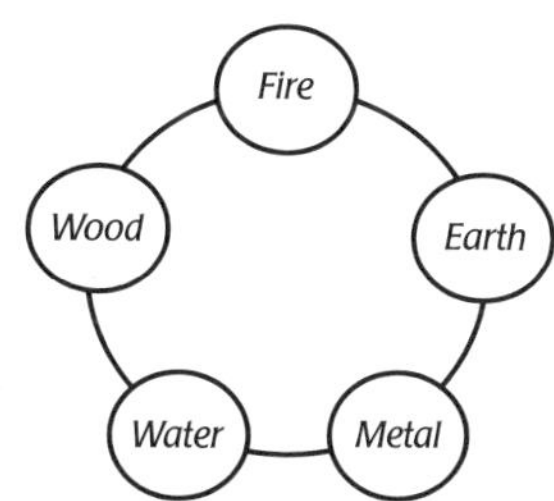

Connections

September 14

"Holding the stem of the pipe toward the heavens, she said, "With this sacred pipe you will walk upon the Earth; for the Earth is your Grandmother and Mother, and She is sacred. Every step that is taken upon Her should be as a prayer. The bowl of this pipe is of red stone; it is the Earth. Carved in the stone bowl and facing the center is this buffalo calf who represents all the four-leggeds who live upon your Mother. The stem of the pipe is of wood, and this represents all that grows upon the Earth. And these twelve feathers, which hang here where the stem fits into the bowl, are from Wanbli Galeshka, the Spotted Eagle, and they represent the eagle and all the wingeds of the air. All these peoples, all the things of the universe, are joined to you who smoke the pipe. All send their voices to Wakan Tanka, the Great Spirit. When you pray with this pipe, you pray for and with everything."

- The Legend of White Buffalo Woman,
as told by Black Elk in *The Sacred Pipe*

Exercise

Read *Black Elk Speaks* or *The Sacred Pipe* to appreciate how another culture lived in harmony with the earth.

Make your connections . . .

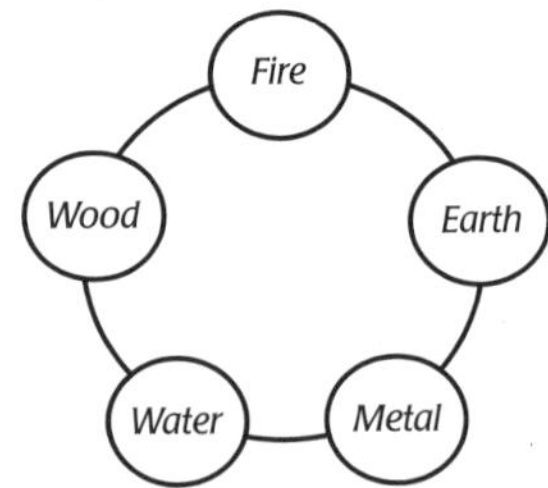

Connections

September 15

Late Summer is the season when plants begin to bear fruit. The plants put their energy into the nurturing of future life in the seeds. To provide nourishment for the seeds and to keep them alive until Spring, the plant grows a thick pulpy layer of starches and sugars around the seeds—the fruit. When the fruit falls to the ground, it will protect the seeds inside throughout the winter and provide the food needed by the seeds to begin growth in the Spring.

Fruiting is a part of the natural growth cycle that also happens in humans. After the Springtime of our youth and the Summertime of our early adult years, the Late Summer comes with its task of nurturing new life. We as humans fulfill this task in many ways—the most biological of which is to have children and care for them. Childbearing and rearing is the most direct expression of this Earth energy of Late Summer—the children are the fruit we bear, carrying the seeds of future life within them.

Exercise

How do you nurture new life, in yourself or in others?

Make your connections . . .

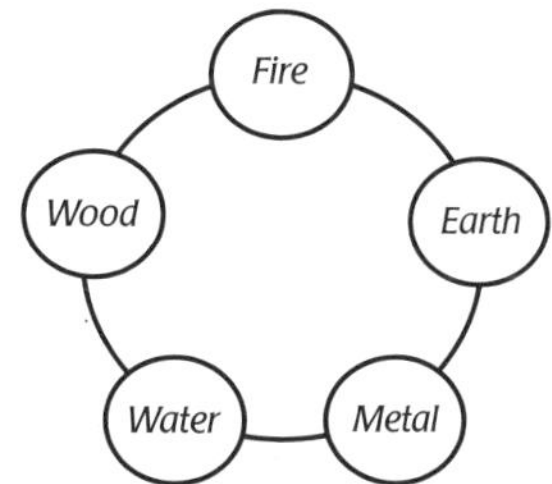

September 16

late summer
the days sleep in
haze and hollyhocks
blue air full of
golden cricket whine
we move slowly
savoring the sweet
affluence of
season's end
a profusion of
black-eyed susans
yellowing the fields–
soon cooler winds
will swirl the wild
grasses sorrel to
white on the hills–
we sense the
subtle clearing
of the air
as we face the
surrender to
winter

- Janice MacKenzie

Exercise

Sit outside for ten minutes and listen to the insects.

Make your connections . . .

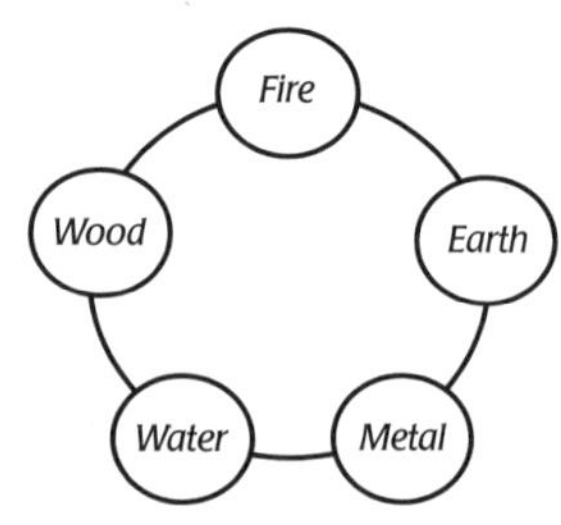

Connections

September 17

"Yellow is the color of the center... and its smell is fragrant..."

- Nei Jing

When the Earth energies are out of balance, a person's body will give off a fragrant odor, which is easily perceptible to the trained nose. Although we have positive associations with the word "fragrant," the true fragrant odor is a cloying and sickly sweet smell, which is not necessarily pleasant. It is akin to the odor of heavy perfume hanging in the air, and it is to avoid confusion that I ask patients not to wear perfume on the days of their treatments.

Fragrant is one of the easiest of the odors to detect when you are beginning to learn how to smell for diagnostic purposes. Perhaps it is because we have learned to "tune out" unpleasant odors, but find it acceptable to notice and even comment on someone smelling "good" (usually this means sweet and fragrant). It is important to remember that a strong fragrant odor is still a sign of imbalance.

Exercise

Wear your favorite fragrance today, whether perfume, lotion, or essential oil.

Make your connections . . .

Connections

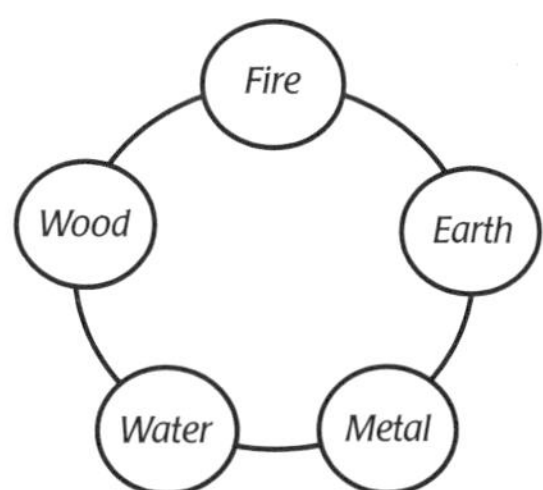

September 18

"In times of excitement and change they cause the emission of belching."

- Nei Jing

The Earth element has a special power or capacity that appears during times of excitement and change. This power has been translated as belching, although the Chinese character for "to belch" can also be translated as "to be obstinate." This is a wonderful example of the way the Chinese language layers together two concepts that both happen to apply!

In the case of belching, the Earth organs of the Stomach and Spleen are in charge of digestion, and belching is a natural part of this process of "rotting and ripening."

The other meaning of "obstinacy" also links with the Earth in the sense of sticking to one idea, or of obsessively circling around one thought or concept, which is the hallmark of Earth-style thinking. When we imagine someone who is obstinate, we picture someone "digging in his heels," or "standing firm," which definitely conjures up someone well connected to the Earth!

Exercise

Instead of driving to do your errands today, walk. Feel your pace slow down to Earth's rhythm.

Make your connections . . .

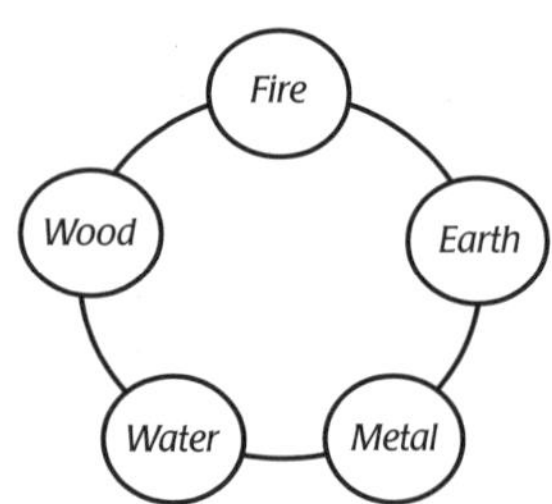

Connections

September 19

"We are nourished by our Mother the Earth from whom all life springs. We must understand her dependence, and protect her with our love, respect and ceremonies.

"The faces of our future generations are looking up to us from the earth, and we step with great care not to disturb our grandchildren.

"We are a part of the great cycle of life with four seasons and endless renewal as long as we abide by this absolute law.

"When we disturb this cycle by interfering with elements, changing or destroying species of life, the effects may be immediate or may fall upon our children who will suffer and pay for our ignorance and greed."

**- The Traditional Circle of Elders,
Navajo-Hopi Joint Council,
from their 1982 letter to the
United Nations General Assembly**

Exercise

Go outside and take your socks and shoes off. Walk barefoot in the grass, letting your feet really make contact with the earth. Feel the grass, pebbles, twigs and dirt with your toes.

Make your connections . . .

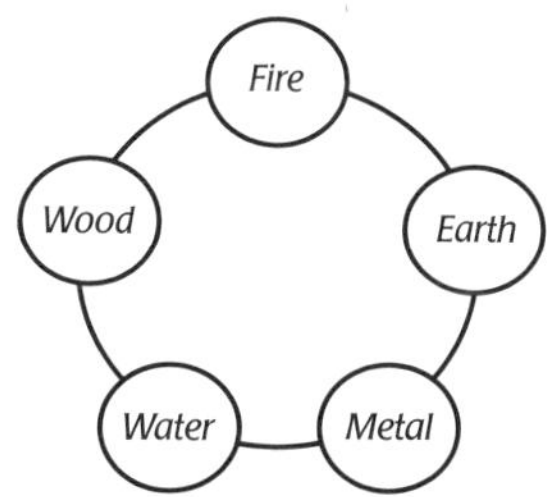

September 20

"'Medicine wheel' is the name given to large circles of stones found on the ground in many places in North America. These circles had been used in ceremonial ways by early Native peoples. As well as representing the whole Wheel of Life on Earth, they were often aligned with certain other stones or geographic features to indicate solstices and other planetary and astrological events.

"The term 'medicine wheel' also refers simply to the full Circle of Life as represented on the stone wheel. Different tribes and cultures have varied ways of dividing the Wheel of Life into its various aspects. However, in the medicine wheel I use, Earthly life and its aspects are divided into the four quadrants of the cardinal directions.

"The east represents the dawning and illumination of morning light, and thus our awakenings, awareness, and "aha's!" In the circle of the year, the east denotes Spring and green shoots of plants showing above the ground. Birth and childhood are here...

(Continued on next page)

Exercise

On the night of a full moon, try sleeping in the moonlight on your roof, in your backyard, in an open field, or on top of a mountain. Make sure you bring a warm sleeping bag and an insulating mat.

Make your connections . . .

Connections

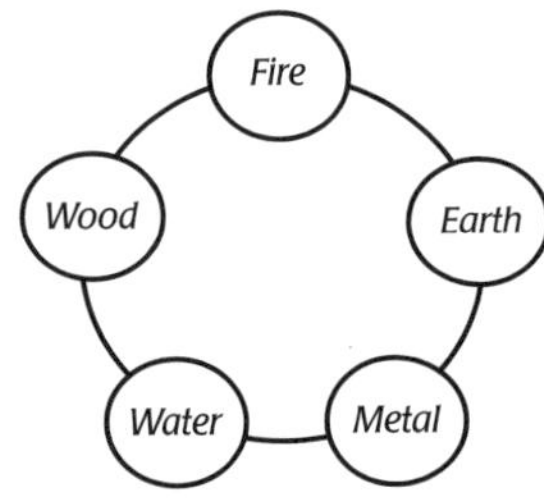

September 21

"...The south then holds the place midday in the twenty-four-hour cycle, and represents midsummer in the yearly cycle—the times of most intense heat and active growing... It is a place not only of external warmth, but of the warmth of our hearts; the openness to learning and growth of youth; the laughter that warms our lives and opens our minds... In the west we find twilight and autumn. We call this the Looks Within Place, for the sun is going down, and we stop our active work to come to a more contemplative time—a time to go within... Autumn brings the time of harvest, when we gather not only the external fruits, but the internal fruits or lessons of our experience... The white of snow and winter lie in the north. It is a time of seeds lying still within the ground in germination, and thus a deeply internal time of beingness rather than one of doing. ... As in the west we harvest the facts and information of the cycle, in the north we distill those facts into wisdom; here sit the law and truth underlying all things."

- Brooke Medicine Eagle,
Buffalo Woman Comes Singing

Exercise

Attend a Native American Pow-Wow. Listen to the drums and (if invited) join in the dance.

Make your connections . . .

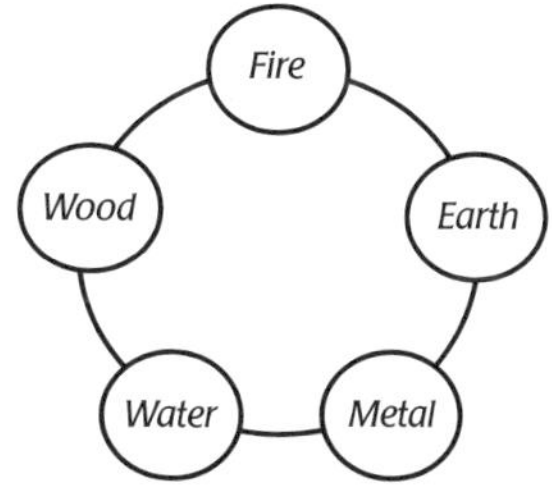

Connections

September 22

"In terms of overall morphology, the Earth hand is short."

- Yves Requena,
Morphotypological Hand Diagnosis in Acupuncture

The Earth hand has a thickness and solidity quite different from the Fire hand. The palm of the Hand is square, and the fingers are short and sausage-like; in comparison to other hand types, the Earth hand itself is usually short. The lines of the finger-joints, on the palmar side of the hand, form a single fold. The base of the palm and the area under the thumb are particularly thick and meaty; when the fingers are drawn together, the entire hand takes on the general shape of a short, rounded pear.

Often, Earth hands will have the appearance of having been used for hard work; they will be calloused, blistered, and have dirt worn into the cracks from gardening or working with tools. The Earth hand is often as practical as the person to whom it belongs.

Exercise

Garden, either outside or indoors. Put your hands in the soil.

Make your connections . . .

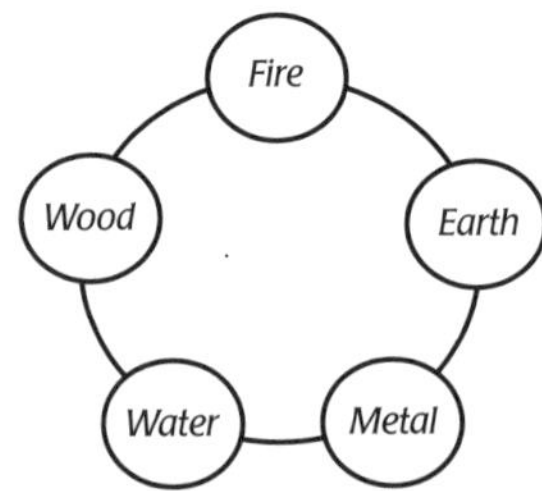

Connections

September 23

I think I could turn and live with animals, they're so
placid and self-contain'd,
I stand and look at them, long and long.

They do not sweat and whine about their condition,
They do not lie awake in the dark and weep for their sins,
They do not make me sick discussing their duty to God,
Not one is dissatisfied, not one is demented with the mania
of owning things,
Not one kneels to another, nor to his kind that lived
thousands of years ago,
Not one is respectable or unhappy over the whole earth.

- Walt Whitman,
Song of Myself

Exercise

Lie down and hug a pet you care for. Stroke its fur, and talk to it. Imagine that some of the unconditional love you are feeling for this animal is traveling through your fingers, back through your hand and arm to your heart, connecting your heart to your pet's.

Make your connections . . .

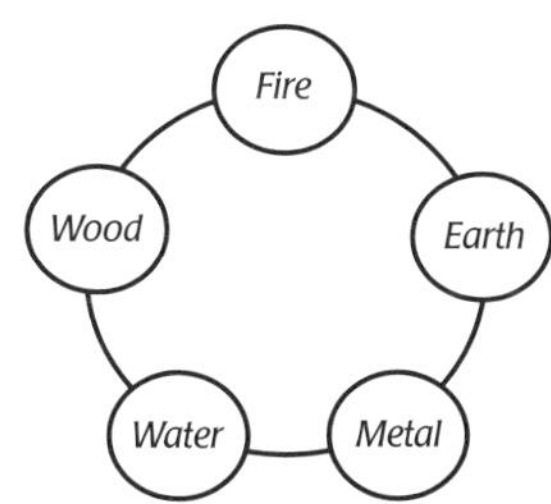

Connections

September 24

The Sevenfold Path of Peace

- When we are at peace within our own hearts we shall be at peace with everyone and with our Mother the Earth.
- When we recognize that our planet itself is a living organism co-evolving with humankind we shall become worthy of stewardship.
- When we see ourselves as stewards of our planet and not as owners and masters of it there shall be lasting satisfaction from our labors.
- When we accept the concept of Right Livelihood as the basic right of all we shall have respect for one another.
- When we respect the sacredness of all life we shall be truly free.
- When we free ourselves from our attachment to our ego-personalities we shall be able to experience our Oneness.
- When we experience our Oneness—our total connectedness with all beings—we shall be at peace within our own hearts.

- Danann Parry
The Earthstewards' Handbook

Exercise

How far are you along this path?

Make your connections . . .

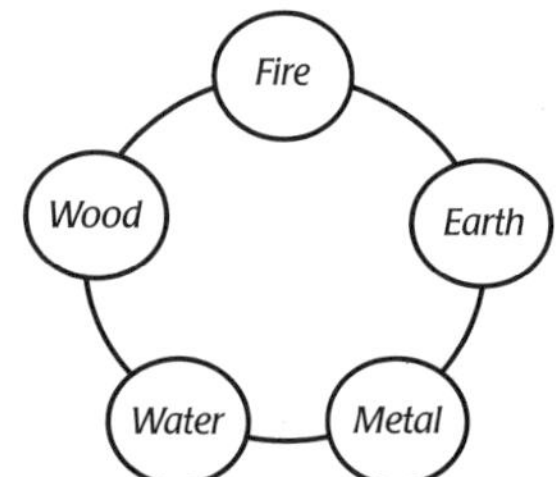

Connections

September 25

"...to be in a sitting position for too long a time is hurtful to the flesh...."

- Nei Jing

Of the five exertions that hurt the body, sitting is the one related to the Earth element and to Late Summer. Too much sitting can obviously mean a lack of exercise, and lack of exercise can lead to atrophied muscles, poor circulation, and, consequently, lots of aches and pains. We know that a sedentary lifestyle can lead to being overweight and to having poor cardiovascular health. This is the problem of the "couch potato," someone who would rather watch TV than do something active. The number of patients with fibromyalgia is increasing every year. (Fibromyalgia is a poorly understood syndrome in which the patient suffers debilitating pain in the muscles and flesh of the body.) People whose jobs require them to be in a sitting position for many hours need to counterbalance this with active exercise in order to balance their Earth energies.

Exercise

Keep track today of the number of hours you spend sitting. Make sure you also take a long walk to counterbalance them.

Make your connections . . .

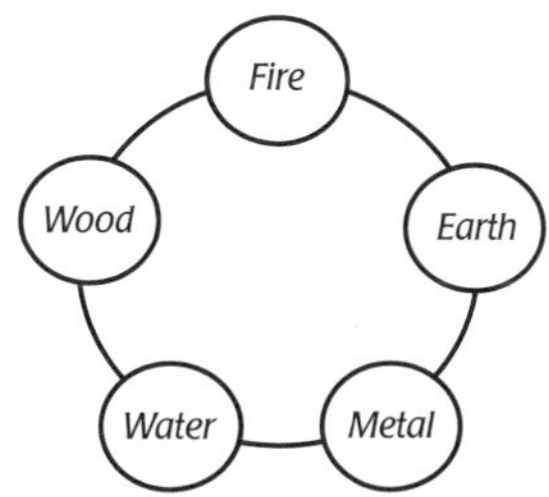

Connections

September 26

Behold! Our Mother Earth is lying here.
Behold! She gives of her fruitfulness.
Truly, her power she gives us.
Give thanks to Mother Earth who lies here.

Behold! On Mother Earth the growing fields!
Behold the promise of her fruitfulness!
Truly her power she gives us.
Give thanks to Mother Earth who lies here.

Behold on Mother Earth the spreading trees!
Behold the promise of her fruitfulness!
Truly her power she gives us.
Give thanks to Mother Earth who lies here.

– Pawnee Hako Ceremony

Exercise

If you don't have a garden, nurture your "green" needs by visiting a flower shop. Linger over the flowers, sniffing them, asking their names. Buy a single exquisite bloom to take home with you.

Make your connections . . .

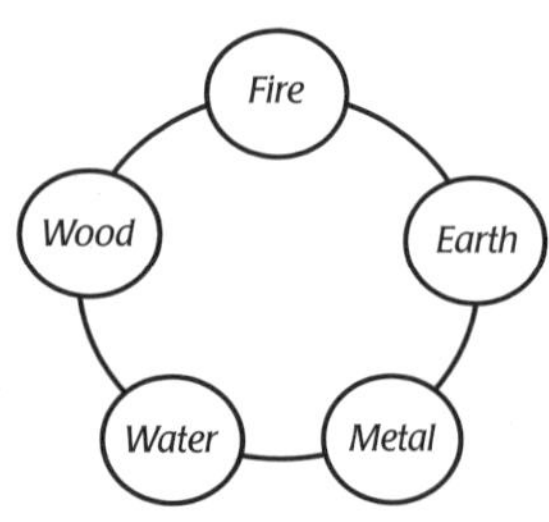

Connections

September 27

"...of the musical notes they create the note kung (宫).."

- Nei Jing

The musical note connected to the Earth energies and to the season of Late Summer is *kung*. In some ancient texts, the names of the notes refer to the positions of the instruments in a ceremonial ritual. In the Western musical tradition, the scale goes from high to low, but the Chinese scale had the *kung* note always listed in the middle, an arrangement that suggests that at one time there were five stations around a central dancing floor. *Kung* means "acts like a prince," and has been translated as a house or a palace. Joseph Needham, a Chinese scholar, suggests that the *kung* was the instrument placed in the central position. Its sound is described in another ancient text as "heavy and thick as the virtue of the nobleman is also serious and heavy."

Exercise

Listen to your favorite music and hum it as you go about your day.

Make your connections . . .

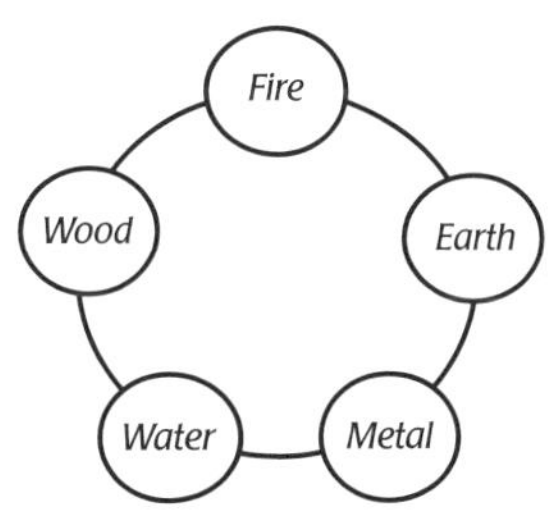

September 28

The actual instrument that played the note *kung* is never mentioned directly in the texts, but was probably either a drum or a large gong or bell. The sound is also described as corresponding to "rumbling thunder," so either of these ideas would fit. The primary link to Earth, however, is in the idea of centrality, of this instrument and this note being in the middle. The direction for the Earth energy is the center, and, therefore, by the Chinese system of correspondences, the note corresponding to Earth must be in the center, as well. In the classic *Tz'u Hai*, it says: "*Kung* is central, as is the high noble; it is a net for the far sounds...The image is one of the superior man, the palace (the hub of the wheel)." Certainly a large drum or a gong provides a "heavy" sound which radiates out from itself as the center, providing a hub for other musical notes around it.

Exercise

Buy an inexpensive drum and learn how to play it.

Make your connections . . .

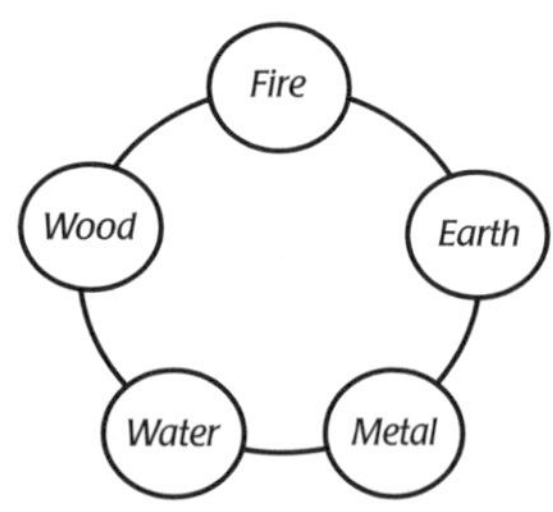

Connections

September 29

Traditional "Charge of the Star Goddess"

I who am the beauty of the green earth
and the white moon among the stars
and the mysteries of the waters,
I call upon your soul to arise and come unto me.
For I am the soul of nature that gives life to the universe.
From Me all things proceed and unto Me they must return.
Let My worship be in the heart that rejoices, for behold–
all acts of love and pleasure are My rituals.
Let there be beauty and strength, power and compassion,
honor and humility, mirth and reverence within you.
And you who seek to know Me, know that your
seeking and yearning will avail you not, unless
you know the Mystery:
for if that which you seek, you find not within yourself,
you will never find it without.
For behold, I have been with you from the beginning,
and I am that which is attained at the end of desire.

– Poem version by Starhawk

Exercise

Look for the harvest moon this month. It will be unusually big and with an orange hue. The full moon at harvest time enables farmers to keep working long after the sun goes down.

Make your connections . . .

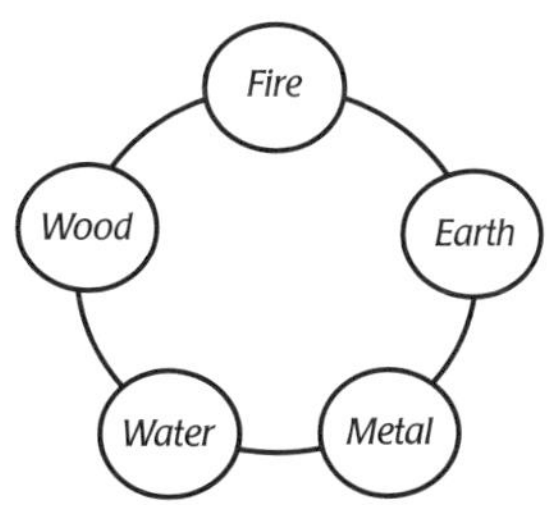

Connections

September 30

"...and they give to the human voice the ability to sing."

- Nei Jing

The sound of voice asociated with the Earth element is singing. This sound is closely connected to the ideas of mother and sympathy —just think about how a mother talks to her child! The voice will have a lilting, sing-song quality, very soothing and reassuring, often repeating phrases like a refrain in a song. We all instinctively fall into this voice quality when we are with a young child or with anyone who is afraid and in need of reassurance.

In someone whose Earth energies are imbalanced, the voice will continually sing no matter what is going on. Even if the person is angry, the voice will sing and sing. Usually, the person is completely unaware of this voice quality, and would be surprised if it were pointed out. Unlike the groaning and shouting voice qualities, singing is usually considered a pleasant voice quality by others, and does not lead to the same boredom or irritation. In fact, people may be drawn to someone who has a singing voice because of the implied sympathy they will receive there!

As with other voice qualities, there is also a variation of singing which is the total lack of singing. This quality is an extremely flat monotone, no colorings or shadings, no highs or lows. This lack of singing is also a sign of an Earth imbalance, but it is not necessarily a sign that the person is unsympathetic—in fact, quite the reverse could be true. The voice quality gives an indication of the element which is out of balance, but it does not tell you whether that element is excessive or deficient.

Exercise

Feed the birds. Listen to the songs they sing you in return.

Make your connections . . .

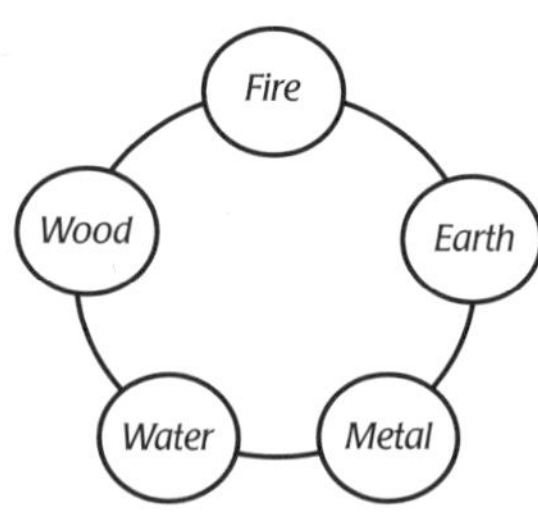

Connections

October 1

Try this exercise for getting in touch with your own inner Earth:

Lie down in a comfortable position, close your eyes, and take a few deep breaths. Now imagine that your awareness is a tiny point of light. At first, it will seem as if this point of light is in your head. Now imagine that this point of light can move, and begin to consciously move this point of light around inside your body. As you move it from your head down into your torso, imagine that you can see your organs, your heart pumping, your stomach gurgling, etc. Notice what colors you see, and if you feel any particular emotions when your awareness is in certain parts of your body. If any part of your body seems dark or in pain, imagine that the point of light radiates healing energy to that area. Spend as long as you want to, moving around, then bring the point of light back to your head, take a deep breath, and open your eyes.

Exercise

Rub your back with a back brush, sponge, or back scratcher. Try lying on the floor and rolling your back over a ball to massage your back muscles.

Make your connections . . .

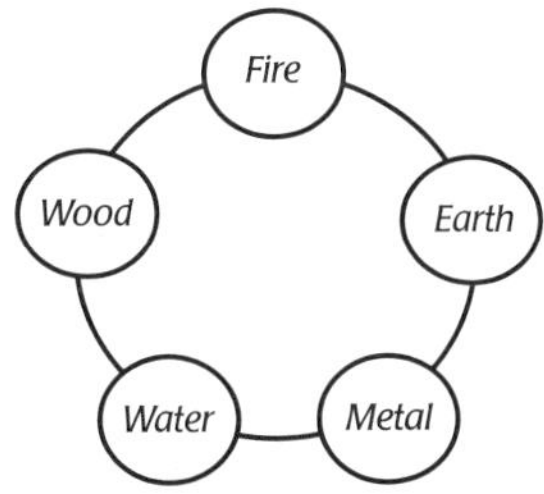

Connections

October 2

A little too abstract, a little too wise,
It is time for us to kiss the earth again,
It is time to let the leaves rain from the skies,
Let the rich life run to the roots again.
I will go down to the lovely Sur Rivers
And dip my arms in them up to the shoulders.
I will find my accounting where the alder leaf quivers,
In the ocean wind over the river boulders.
I will touch things and things and no more thoughts,
That breed like mouthless May-flies darkening the sky,
The insect clouds that blind our passionate hawks
So that they cannot strike, hardly can fly.
Things are the hawk's food and noble is the mountain,
Oh noble
Pico Blanco, steep sea-wave of marble.

- Robinson Jeffers

Exercise

Try this with a friend: take turns blindfolding each other and leading each other through a garden, feeling the texture of leaves, rocks, and grass with your fingers, hands, cheeks and feet.

Make your connections . . .

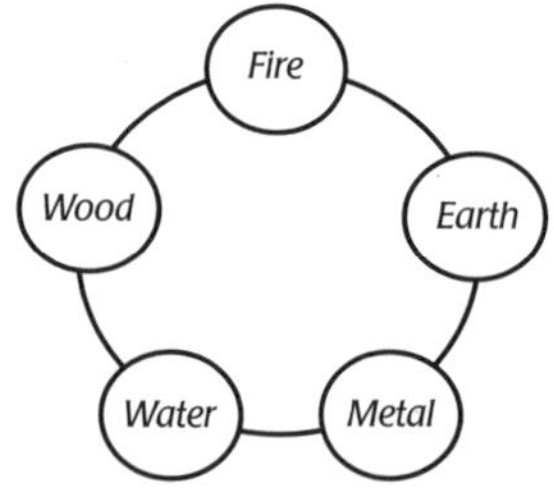

October 3

"...To the tribal and traditional peoples of the world the whole of creation was holy, they lived in a sacred land, and maintained it by honouring it and by invoking the help of the gods of the land...The relationship of the shaman with the earth is all-important; it is the expression of a bond, an exchange of energies between man and earth. In fact, when a shaman or shamanka tells of 'relating to the earth' they are talking of a form of partnership. The earth is whole, a living being in whose complex ecosystem a thousand different kinds of lives exist in harmony. Those who take from the earth must somehow give back to it. We can draw upon the vast resource of energies beneath our feet at any time of the day or night, but we must always remember to give back what we have taken. We only borrow what we take, and what is given is ours, but not to keep."

- John Matthews,
The Celtic Shaman

Exercise

Put a hummingbird feeder outside your kitchen or bedroom window.

Make your connections . . .

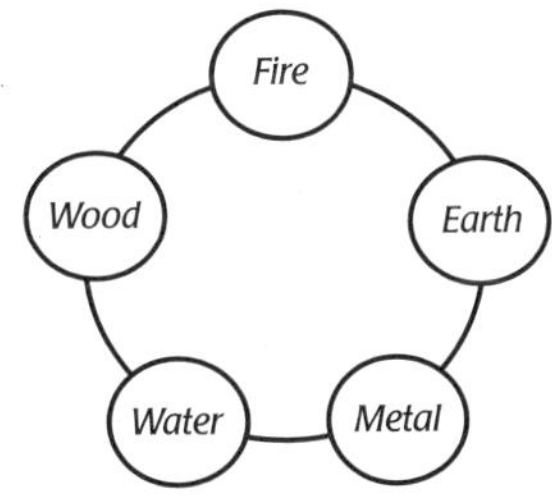

October 4

"...the spleen harbors ideas and opinions..."

- Nei Jing

Each of the five energetic phases "harbors" a spiritual quality that is unique. For the Earth energy, it is *Yi*, which translates as "thought," or, as above, "ideas and opinions." Ted Kaptchuk, who is my source for this material, calls this a virtue, and says it is the ability to consider all the possibilities of a situation. This capacity should lead to the best way of realizing something, as the Spleen "digests" the possibilities, and then transforms them into an opinion. When your Earth energy is strong and healthy, then your "thought" is clear and coherent.

When there are problems with your Earth energy, however, thought can become muddled, obsessive, or scattered. As Kaptchuk says, someone with a Spleen imbalance can think about things a lot, but not select an option. They accumulate possibilities but can't transform them. The accumulated material then presses down on them and keeps them from moving, so that the very possibilities of change become a burden.

Exercise

Is there a "thoughtful" or obsessive person in your life? Can you see them as an Earth person?

Make your connections . . .

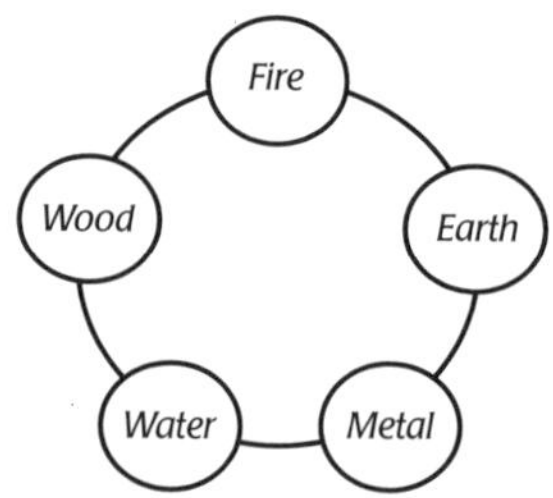

October 5

Elisabeth Rochat de la Vallee says about thought: "...after the becoming of thoughts there is the ability for them to spread out far and wide very powerfully. Afterwards, as a result, you have *lu*, reflection, meditation, planning and projection. We can find in this spreading out far and powerfully the expression of what we, rather later, call the yang of the Spleen, the ability to distribute and transport and so on. You can understand now why, when in pathological terms we say the yang of the Spleen is not enough, thought and reflection are disturbed and weak. It's exactly the contrary of being able to go far and powerfully. If the yin of the Spleen Essences are not enough then thinking is poor and you lose your memory..."

Thus, someone whose Earth energy is strong is capable of being "thoughtful," of projecting out to others in a way that someone whose Earth is deficient is unable to do. Some people, while bright enough, are muddled, forgetful, and "spacey"—we often say these people "don't have their feet on the ground!"

Exercise

How is your thinking—clear or muddled?

Make your connections . . .

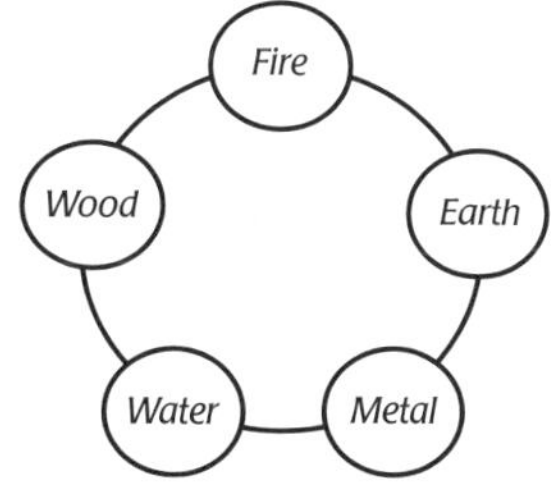

Connections

October 6

I believe a leaf of grass is no less perfect than the journey-work of the stars,

And the pismire is equally perfect, and a grain of sand, and the egg of the wren,

And the tree-toad is a chef-d'oeuvre for the highest,

And the running blackberry would adorn the parlors of heaven,

And the narrowest hinge in my hand puts to scorn all machinery,

And the cow crunching with depress'd head surpasses any statue,

And a mouse is miracle enough to stagger sextillions of infidels.

- Walt Whitman,
Song of Myself

Exercise

Visit a lake or the ocean and just breathe deeply for twenty minutes, lying on the shore.

Make your connections . . .

Connections

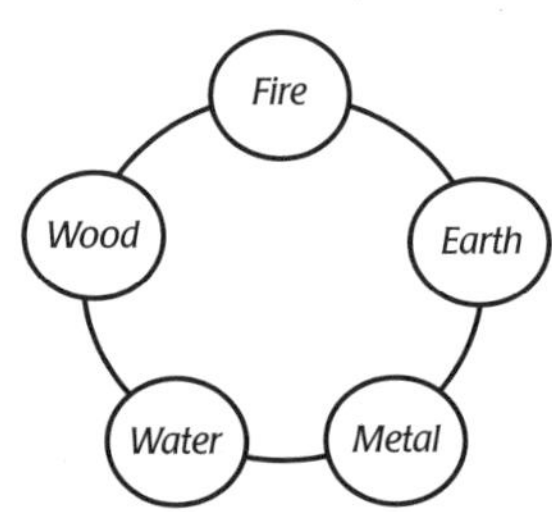

October 7

Anytime we carry something through to its completion, to the point where it leaves us and goes out to nurture new life in its turn, we are expressing "fruiting" energy. Writing a book, painting a picture, making something with our hands, teaching someone a skill, and finishing a project are all activities that produce a "fruit," which then goes out into the world to nourish new life elsewhere.

In mid-life, both men and women have this need to bear fruit —to be "productive." The nurturing of new life happens not only on the biological level, but on the mental and emotional levels, as well. Teaching, mentoring, and coaching are other ways of nurturing new life. Many men who resisted the idea of children in their twenties and thirties, suddenly develop a strong interest in having kids in their forties and fifties. In general, there is a strong need to have something to show for your labors at this time of life—if not a tangible product, then at least the gratitude of those you've nurtured along the way.

Exercise

What fruit have you harvested from this year's efforts?

Make your connections . . .

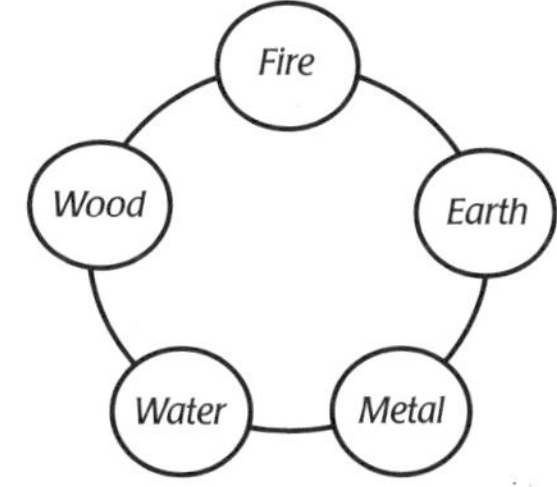

Connections

October 8

Grandfather,
Look at our brokenness.

We know that in all creation
Only the human family
Has strayed from the Sacred Way

We know that we are the ones
Who are divided
And we are the ones
Who must come back together
To walk in the Sacred Way

Grandfather,
Sacred One,
Teach us love, compassion, and honor
That we may heal the earth
And heal each other.

- Ojibway Prayer

Exercise

Research the gardens or parks open to the public in your area. Volunteer at the one closest to you.

Make your connections . . .

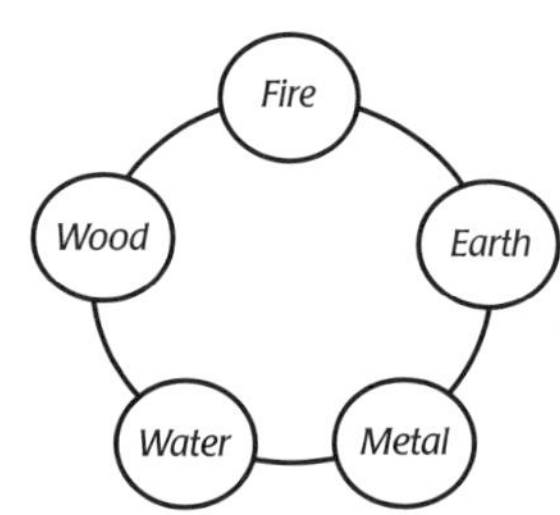

Connections

October 9

"Sometimes I feel like a motherless child,
Sometimes I feel like a motherless child,
Sometimes I feel like a motherless child,
A long way from home,
A long way from home."

- Traditional Black Spiritual

"All sickness is homesickness, homesick for ourselves and for each other. All our daily events, events born of the day, are our journey manifest, our call to come home. All healing is a coming home. The journey is a cycle, a circle of movement..."

- Dianne Connelly

"The best thing we can do is make wherever we're lost look as much like home as we can."

- Roger Fry

Exercise

Are you "at home" in your home? Is there any way you could make it feel more like home?

Make your connections . . .

Connections

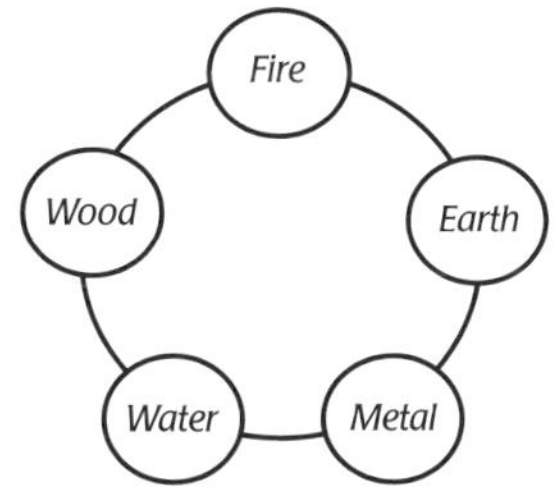

October 10

One of the qualities associated with healthy Earth energy is groundedness. When we meet someone who is grounded, we feel that they are firmly rooted in the world, unshakable and centered, with a strong sense of themselves. We feel that they are solid, and that we can depend upon them—they are often described by others as "reliable," "dependable," and "steady." When you are "grounded," you are in touch with your body and its needs, and also with the immediate practical considerations of your life and the lives of those around you. You are rooted in the physical realities of life, and know how to take care of yourself, both financially and emotionally. Grounded people are generally very secure.

There are some activities that we commonly do that can unground us—the most predominant one being travel. Flying, or driving at high speeds for many miles, means that we literally leave the ground, and it seems that our bodies and our psyches do not like this. We can feel physically sick, experience jet lag, and feel anxious, insecure, and cranky when we travel.

Exercise

Create a "comfort kit" for traveling—a small bag of goodies to carry with you. Include a small teddy bear, some snacks, some hand lotion with a scent you like, and some objects that bring back pleasant memories.

Make your connections . . .

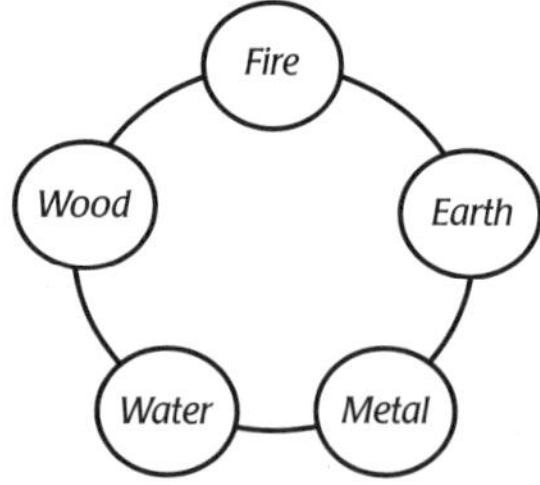

October 11

"We know ourselves to be made from this earth. We know this earth is made from our bodies. For we see ourselves. And we are nature. We are nature seeing nature. We are nature with a concept of nature. Nature weeping. Nature speaking of nature to nature.

"The red-winged blackbird flies in us, in our inner sight. We see the arc of her flight. We measure the ellipse. We predict its climax. We are amazed. We are moved. We fly. We watch her wings negotiate the wind, the substance of the air, its elements and the elements of those elements, and count those elements found in other beings, the sea urchin's sting, ink, this paper, our bones, the flesh of our tongues with which we make the sound "blackbird," the ear with which we hear, the eye which travels the arc of her flight. And yet the blackbird does not fly in us but in somewhere else free of our minds, and now even free of our sight, flying in the path of her own will."

- Susan Griffin

Exercise

Go to a nature preserve and spend an afternoon watching the birds and animals.

Make your connections . . .

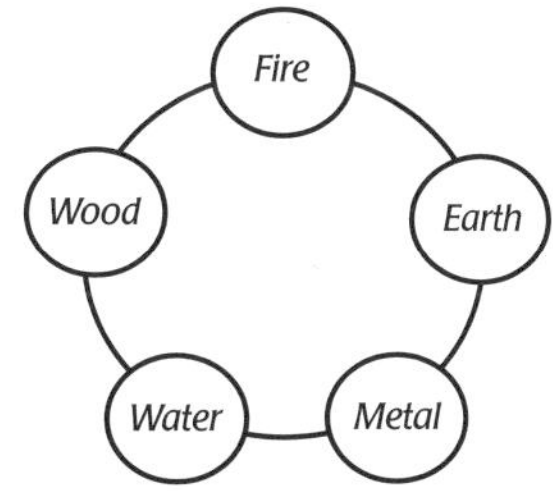

October 12

"At the center of the earth there is a mother."

- Susan Griffin,
Our Mother

The most basic association with Earth energy is Mother. When we are babies, our mother is our Earth, the ground of our being. Mother gives us life, feeds us, sustains us, comforts us, promotes our growth and development, protects us, and loves us. Without her, we would die—quite literally, in some cases. From her, we get our sense of security, of the world as a friendly, caring, and nurturing place. From our relationship with her, we form our relationship to the world and to our own body and its needs. Those who have a good relationship to Mother (and it needn't be the biological mother), are secure individuals who can nurture and care for themselves and others.

Exercise

Do you provide your own financial and material support? What would happen if you could not do that?

Make your connections . . .

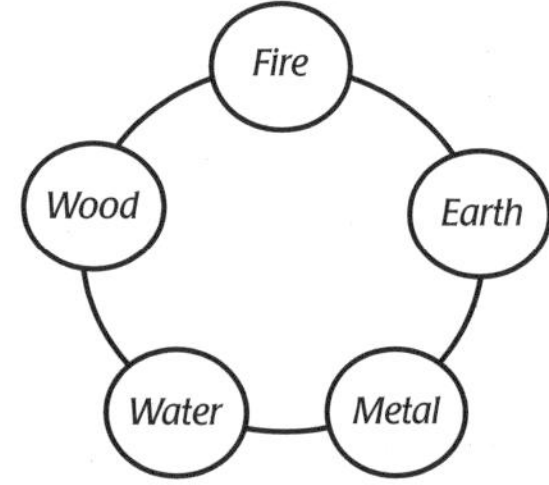

Connections

October 13

Many poplars and many elms shook overhead,
and close by, holy water swashed down noisily
from a cave of the nymphs. Brown grasshoppers
whistled busily through the dark foliage. Far
treetoads gobbled in the heavy thornbrake.

Larks and goldfinch sang, turtledoves were moaning,
and bumblebees whizzed over the splashing brook.

The earth smelled of rich summer and autumn fruit:
we were ankle-deep in pears, and apples rolled
all about our toes. With dark damson plums
the young sapling branches trailed on the ground.

- Theokritos,
Sappho and the Greek Lyric Poets

Exercise

Go to an orchard and pick your own fruit.

Make your connections . . .

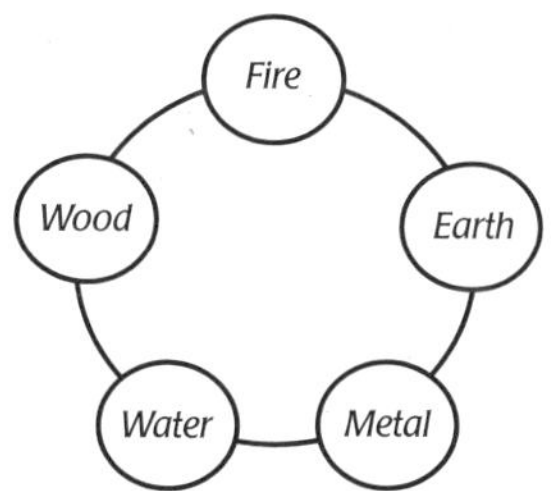

Connections

October 14

Wild Geese

You do not have to be good.
You do not have to walk on your knees
for a hundred miles through the desert, repenting.
You only have to let the soft animal of your body
love what it loves.
Tell me about despair, yours, and I will tell you mine.
Meanwhile the world goes on.
Meanwhile the sun and the clear pebbles of the rain
are moving across the landscapes,
over the prairies and the deep trees,
the mountains and the rivers.
Meanwhile the wild geese, high in the clear blue air,
are heading home again.
Whoever you are, no matter how lonely,
the world offers itself to your imagination,
calls to you like the wild geese, harsh and exciting–
over and over announcing your place
in the family of things.

- Mary Oliver

Exercise

Go for a hayride. Listen for wild geese migrating.

Make your connections . . .

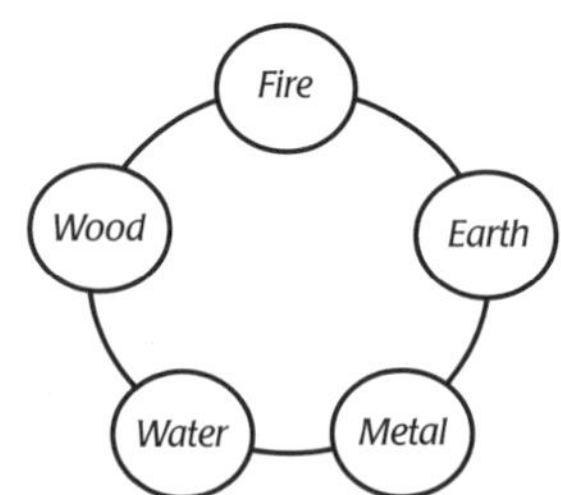

Connections

October 15

"Sons and daughters of the earth, steep yourself in the sea of matter, bathe in its fiery waters, for it is the source of your life and your youthfulness.

"You thought you could do without it because the power of thought has been kindled in you? You hoped that the more thoroughly you rejected the tangible, the closer you would be to spirit: that you would be more divine if you lived in the world of pure thought, or at least more angelic if you fled the corporeal? Well, you were like to have perished of hunger.

"You must have oil for your limbs, blood for your veins, water for your soul, the world of reality for your intellect: do you not see that the very law of your own nature makes these a necessity for you?"

- Pierre Teilhard de Chardin

Exercise

Place a scented geranium in a sunny bathroom, where it will release its scent while you take a luxurious bubble bath.

Make your connections . . .

Connections

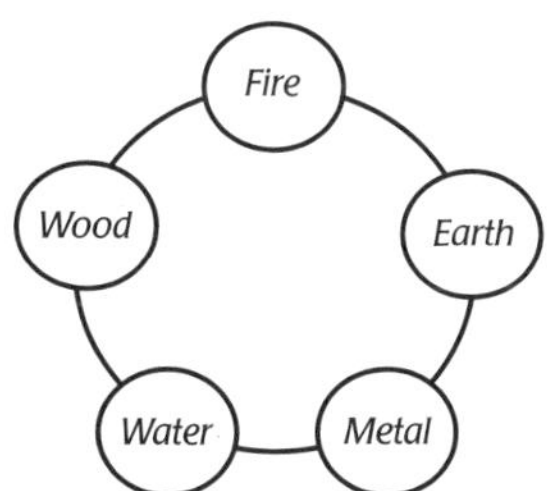

Staghorn Fern, watercolor

FALL

金

Fall/Metal

"The west wind arises in Fall."

"The three months of Fall are called the period of tranquility of one's conduct. The atmosphere of Heaven is quick and the atmosphere of Earth is clear."

"The [mysterious] powers of Fall create dryness in Heaven and they create metal upon Earth. Upon the body they create skin and hair, and of the viscera they create the lungs. Of the colors they create the white color...and they give to the human voice the ability to weep and to wail."

- Nei Jing

The energy of Fall is called Metal. Metal in nature consists of the metallic ores, minerals, and gems of the earth. Iron, copper, and zinc provide strength and conductivity, while gold, silver, and gemstones represent quality and value. In addition, the minerals in the soil provide the richness that nourishes living things.

Another aspect of Metal energy is more closely akin to Air. The Chinese do not include the element Air in their Five Element system, but Metal has many associations that are similar to those ascribed to Air in Western systems. For example, both Air and Metal energies concern mental and spiritual activities, including the workings of the mind, the intellect, and communication. Metal has a further connection to Air through the breath, since the Lungs are organs associated with Metal.

In our human lives, Metal energy is about receiving and letting go. As the trees shed their leaves every year, so must we pare down in preparation for Winter. We also turn inward, pause and take stock of how far we've come in the year's growth. Sometimes there is a sense of loss or melancholy at this time. If it's been a good harvest, there is a feeling of completion and perfection, a solid sense of our own value and worth. Often, we are inspired with new ideas, which will stay in seed form until next Spring.

We experience this energy primarily at mid-life, when the children are grown, or when career goals have been achieved. It's then that we begin to look back and evaluate the quality of our lives, when we measure our worth and look for meaning. This leads to a spiritual or philosophical focus, and many at this time begin to follow a spiritual path. Some people will go off to Tibet, join a monastery, or begin following a guru. This spiritual focus is a very important and essential part of the life cycle, since without it, life can begin to seem very flat, a repetitious round of duties and obligations without meaning or flavor. In the words of Plato, "The unexamined life is not worth living."

The Metal energy in our bodies governs our basic rhythms of receiving and letting go through the breath and through our bodily eliminations. The rhythm of our breath also governs other cycles in the body, including the heart rhythm and the blood circulation. Breathing is one of the principal ways we replenish our energy, and is thus essential to every life process. To breathe is to live, and from a baby's first breath to the last dying gasp, we are in a rhythm of give and take with the Universe. Elimination is just as important as breathing—without it, our energy backs up, becoming polluted and stagnant, and we become increasingly inert and lifeless.

From this, it is not surprising that the organs associated with the Metal element are the Lungs and Large Intestine. Professor Worsley says the Lungs "receive the pure qi from the Heavens." Thus, we receive air (qi) into our lungs, and also into every cell of our bodies. The Large Intestine, says the *Nei Jing*, are "like the officials who propagate the Right Way of Living, and they generate evolution and change." This is certainly a more lofty vision of the Large Intestine than we have here in the West! But truly, if our Large Intestine is not working properly, then our whole life process begins to slow down, becoming stagnant and stuck, so that change becomes impossible —we've lost the rhythm of taking in and letting go, which allows for change.

Since the skin is also an organ that breathes and eliminates, it is connected to the Metal element, as well. In fact, the Chinese call it the "third lung." Often, imbalances in the Metal element will show up on the skin in the form of psoriasis, eczema, acne, and boils. The mental aspects of Metal have to do with inspiration, and the ability to "take in" information, on one hand, and the ability to "let go" of old thoughts and ideas, on the other. The inability to be open to new ideas or the rigid holding onto old thoughts and useless information could both point to an imbalance in Metal.

The emotion connected to the Metal energy is grief. The ability to grieve and mourn a loss appropriately is a healthy aspect of Metal, but prolonged grieving, or the inability to grieve, both point to an imbalance here. It is not unusual for someone going through a period of grief to experience bowel problems and/or breathing difficulties for a while. If these symptoms persist beyond a reasonable time, it shows that the person is "stuck" in the grief and needs assistance completing the grieving process and moving on.

The Metal energies, because of their connection to breath and the Qi from the Heavens, are perhaps closest to the idea of spirituality of all the five elements. The spiritual aspects of Metal have to do with our connection to Spirit through the breath, and to the Divine Masculine Principle of the Universe. Just as Earth is associated with the Great Mother, so Metal is associated with the Heavenly Father. Metal relates to our sense of our place in the scheme of things, our essential worth or value, and our quest for meaning. We can feel this aspect of Metal as a longing or searching for connection to the Divine, a desire for perfection and purity, and the attraction toward enlightenment as a goal.

This important aspect of the natural cycle allows us to move from the fullness and ripeness of the Late Summer season into our Winter's rest, by first taking stock of what we've accomplished, then eliminating the inessential, and storing the rest away for the depths of the Winter ahead. As with each other phase, this Metal stage of the year and of our lives can be skipped only at great peril—for in the Metal phase, we connect to the meaning of our lives, and become re-inspired for another cycle to begin after a Winter's rest.

October 16

"The [mysterious] powers of Fall create dryness in Heaven and they create metal upon Earth."

- Nei Jing

Fall is the season connected to the Metal element. The energy of the year, which has been rising through Spring into Summer and has reached a "still point" in Late Summer, is now beginning its descent into Winter. The movement is one of concentration and condensation, like the heavy white frosts of autumn, which are a condensation of vapors out of the cold air onto the still-warm earth. This creates dryness in the air.

Fall is the time of the harvest, when all of the grain, fruits, and vegetables are completely ripe and ready to be cut. In China, Fall was considered the time of punishment because it was the time when you harvested the cereal crops and cut off the heads of criminals!

Exercise

Walk through the woods and be aware of all of the smells of autumn—the fragrance of new-mown hay, the dry smell of the just-fallen leaves, the hint of wood smoke in the air.

Note your distillations . . .

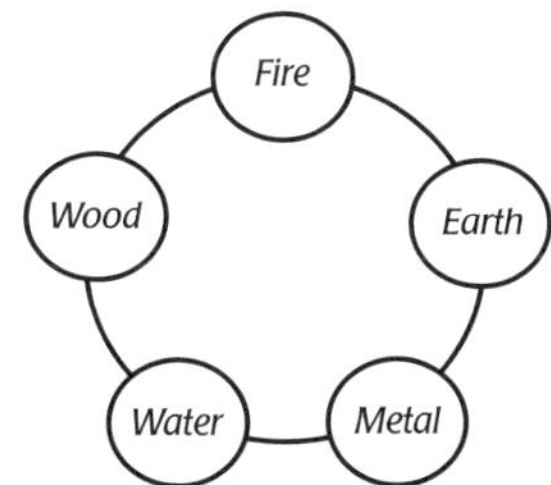

October 17

Autumn is a time of strict accounting, of weighing and measuring the value of things, so that everything is balanced. In the Chinese classics, it says that Autumn puts everything back in the balancing scales.

It is also the time when all vegetation begins to wither and shrivel, when the leaves fall off the trees, when the earth is stripped bare for the Winter. It is a time of cleaning out, letting go, and paring down to the bare essentials. This is necessary, in order to concentrate the energy inside, to withstand the rigors of Winter.

In our bodies also, we need to concentrate our vitality inside —for example, we shouldn't sweat in the Autumn the way we do in the Summer, because we are losing vitality to the outside. Just so, our emotions need to be concentrated inside, and we need to be tranquil and at peace throughout this season in order to be in harmony with the energy of Autumn.

Exercise

Take a walk and let your mind empty of all your plans and concerns of the day. Strive for tranquility.

Note your distillations . . .

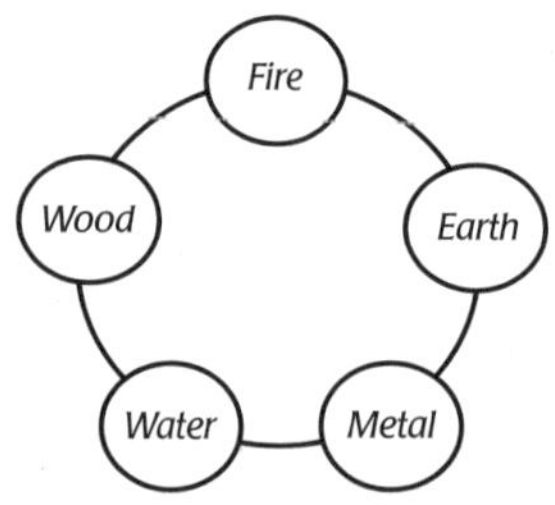

Distillations

October 18

"Precious metals and jade come from the regions of the West. The dwellings in the West are built of pebbles and sandstone. Nature (Heaven and Earth) exerts itself to bring a good harvest..."

- Nei Jing

Just as the East is correlated to the Spring, because it is the direction from which the sun rises and thus signals beginnings, so the West is correlated to Autumn, the setting of the sun, and endings.

The Chinese character for West is *xi* (西). It is based on the image of a bird resting on its nest. This follows from the character for East (*dong*), which is the image of the sun. The Chinese say that the sun transforms itself into a bird at the end of its course to the West. Thus, the West is the region of the sunset, and at sunset, birds go to roost.

Exercise

Watch the sunset today, appreciating how much earlier it gets dark now, and how time seems shorter with fewer daylight hours.

Note your distillations . . .

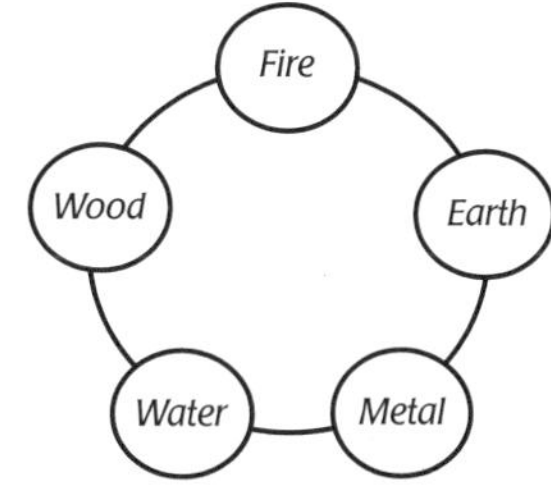

October 19

There are other connections linking the Autumn with the direction of the West. Elisabeth Rochat de la Vallee notes that the quality of the energy of the West has the same quality as the energy of Autumn: "something urgent, a concentration and a gathering." In the Autumn there is the abundance of the harvest as well as the threat of bareness, and this is seen as similar to the sunset in the West: "...at the moment of sunset there is an overflowing of light, but at the same time it's the beginning of night, of darkness and cold." It is the time of the balance between light and darkness.

In Chinese legends, the West was also the special region where the Spirits go after death. The traditional explanation is that the Spirits need a dwelling place where there is peace, balance, and equilibrium. In such a place, the Spirits can rest in serenity. Since the West is the region of the sunset and of balance between light and darkness, it is an appropriate place for the Spirits.

Exercise

Spend some time today thinking about and honoring those whom you've loved, who have died. Create a ritual to express your feelings, such as placing fresh flowers on an altar, or visiting grave sites.

Note your distillations . . .

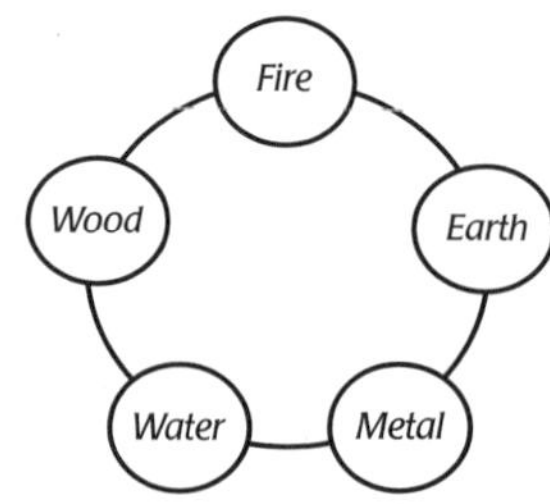

Distillations

October 20

"Scorched dryness is created by the West. Dryness creates metal...The [mysterious] powers of Fall create dryness in Heaven and they create metal upon Earth."

- Nei Jing

Dryness is the climate associated with the Fall season and the Metal element. For those of us who live in the Northeastern United States, this is an easy association to make: after the humidity of Late Summer, the air of Fall is very dry and clear. The Chinese classics talk about this as a function of the condensing aspects of Fall, in which the moisture in the air condenses in the form of heavy dews and frosts, and thus, leaves the air dry.

In addition, all of the vegetation begins to dry out, to wither, and fall to the ground. The leaves of the trees, which all summer were green and pliant, now turn yellow and brown and become thin and brittle like paper. Our own bodies feel the effects of Fall by becoming drier as well—many people complain of dry skin, dry hair, and dryness in the sinus passages at this time of year.

Exercise

Rake leaves, or walk through the woods and feel the leaves crinkling underfoot.

Note your distillations . . .

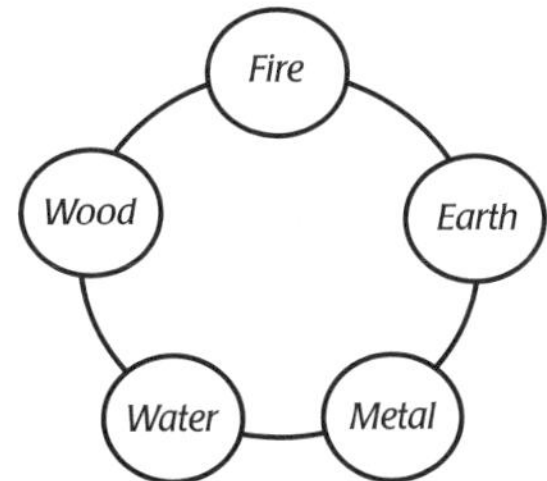

October 21

In the life cycle, Fall corresponds to retirement age, and it is at this age that many people experience more dryness physically. Not only skin and hair, but also internal secretions begin to dry up then, so that women cease their menses, men have less sperm, and many other bodily secretions and hormones are less. It is a compliment if we say that an older person is "still juicy," and not one to say that someone is "all dried up!"

When we are out of balance in the Metal element, then we may feel much better in the Fall, when the seasonal dryness supports us. On the other hand, someone who is already too dry may have a much more difficult time in the Fall. Asking someone if they prefer a dry climate can tell you a lot about the state of their Metal energy.

Exercise

Pamper yourself and buy an expensive herbal body lotion to keep your skin moisturized and supple through the Fall.

Note your distillations . . .

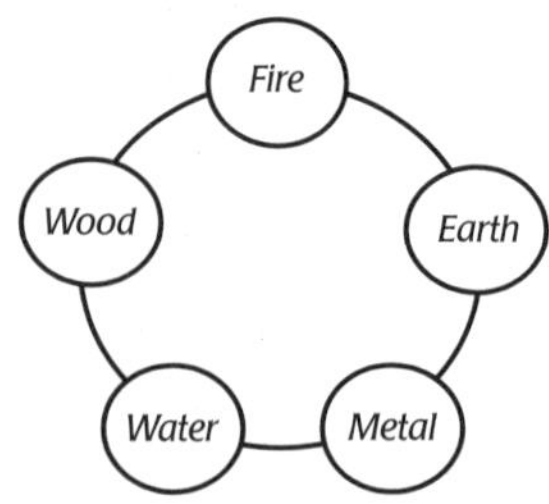

Distillations

October 22

"...Of the colors they create the white color..."

- Nei Jing

White is the color associated with the Metal element and the season of Fall. This connection is very easy to see if you know that white is the color for mourning in China, and that people there wear white for funerals. Thus, the season of mourning, loss, and grief is represented by the color white.

There are many other associations to this color that may help us to understand its connection to the season and the Metal element. For one thing, Fall is the season of heavy white dews and frosts. For another, Metal is shiny and brilliant, and is used to make weapons and swords, which are instruments of death. White is also the color of the light at sunset, just before the day dies into night, and it is the color of bones within the earth after a certain time, another connection to death.

Exercise

Today, dress entirely in white. Notice how it makes you feel.

Note your distillations . . .

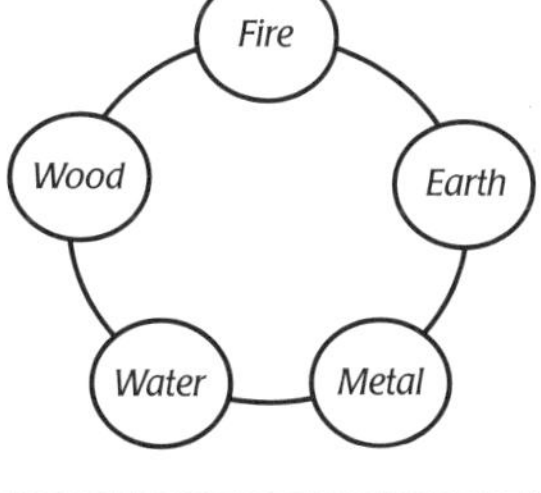

Fire
Wood
Earth
Water
Metal

Distillations

October 23

Here in the West, we seem to associate white with purity—hence, brides wear white at weddings, nurses and doctors wear white uniforms, and holy men are often depicted wearing white robes. Since the Metal element is often associated with a striving for perfection and a longing for spiritual enlightenment, we in the West also have good reasons for connecting the color white with the Metal element.

One final interesting connection is that every direction has a particular deity or genie (according to the Chinese), and the genie of the West has the face of a man, the claws of a tiger, and white body hair!

White can be used to support the energy of Metal within us. Someone who has a marked preference for white clothing and surroundings might be expressing an imbalance in the Metal element. Someone who can't stand white could be expressing an imbalance in the same element.

Exercise

Place a single white flower in a white vase on your desk or kitchen table today.

Note your distillations . . .

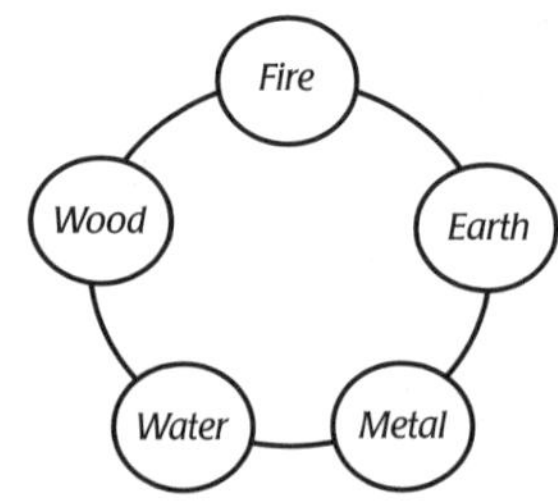

Distillations

October 24

". . . and of the viscera they create the lungs."

- Nei Jing

The Lungs are organs associated with the Metal element, along with their sister organ, the Large Intestine. They are considered the organs that "Receive the Qi Energy from the Heavens." The Chinese believe that there are two ways one can replenish the qi energy in the body—one is through food from the Earth, and the other is through breathing air from the Heavens. Therefore, the Lungs are important organs because through them, the body's vital qi energy is restored on a daily basis.

On a gross physical level, the Lung official grants the capacity to draw air in freely through the nose and to expand the chest, allowing oxygen to penetrate the alveolar walls in the lung tissue, and enabling the cells of the body to take in fresh oxygen through their membranes.

Exercise

Breathe deeply. Pay attention to your breath, imagining that with each breath you are receiving the qi energy of the Heavens.

Note your distillations . . .

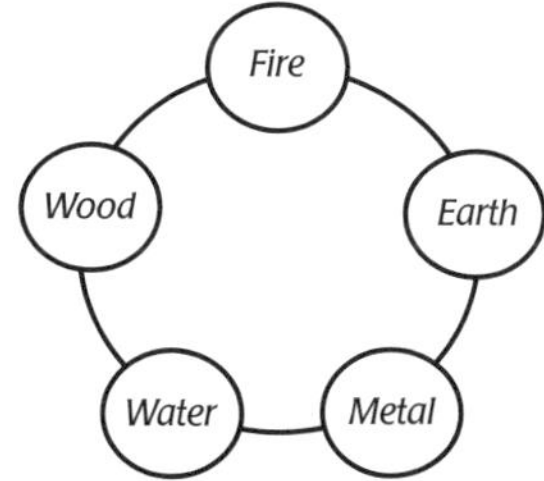

October 25

The ability to "take in" or receive operates from the level of the Lungs as organs, down to the level of each individual cell. Without this function, the cells cannot perform their work, metabolism slows down, and finally comes to a halt. An oxygen-deficient brain lapses into unconsciousness. Within a few minutes of being deprived of oxygen, the body dies.

This concept of "receiving the qi energy from the Heavens" goes beyond the simple matter of breathing oxygen, however. We must also be able to receive emotionally and spiritually, in order to be vitalized on those levels as well. If we cannot "breathe" emotionally, we can feel cut off, emotionally "starved," or dead inside. If we cannot breathe spiritually, we have no connection to the Heavens and feel uninspired, depressed, and without meaning in our lives.

Exercise

Learn or practice a breathing meditation, either from one of the many books on the market, or by listening to a tape. Do this every day for a week.

Note your distillations . . .

Distillations

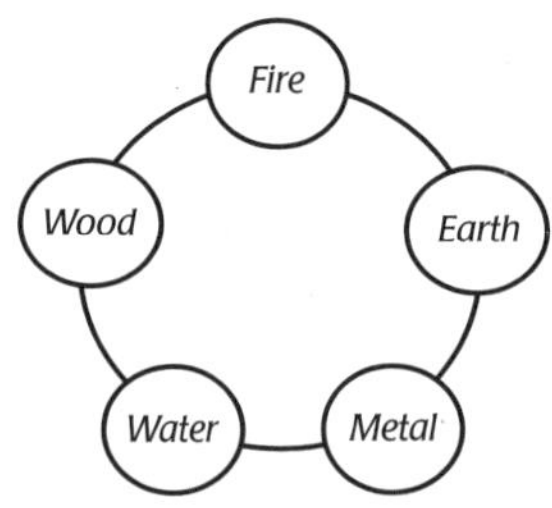

October 26

"...the lower intestines are like the officials who propagate the Right Way of Living, and they generate evolution and change..."

- Nei Jing

The Large Intestine is the other organ associated with the Metal element. Another name for it is the "Drainer of the Dregs." It is responsible for collecting the solid waste matter, absorbing the water back into the body, and expelling what is left. It can be likened to the garbage collector for the body-mind-spirit.

If this function is working well, then everything that is not needed by the body-mind-spirit is eliminated and there is room to take in something new. Thus, "evolution and change" are generated, and the complementary link with the Lungs is seen—only if something is eliminated can something new be received.

Exercise

To assist good elimination and keep the intestines well-toned, eat a diet high in natural foods—fresh fruits, raw or lightly steamed vegetables, and whole grains.

Note your distillations . . .

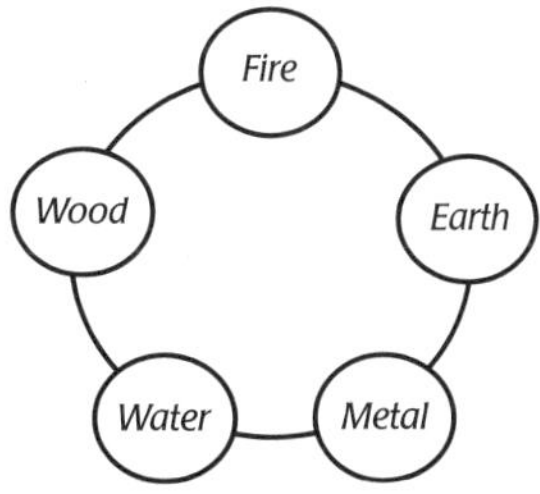

October 27

"These organs are called 'vessels,' and have the power of transforming the dregs and the sediment...."

- Nei Jing

The Large Intestine must do its part to transform and eliminate the "dregs and the sediment." If the Large Intestine official is not working well, then the garbage piles up and we feel bloated, constipated, toxic, and "stuck."

The ability to eliminate or "let go" of things is a necessary function on more than the physical level. Mentally, we must know when to hold onto a thought or idea and when to let it go so that our minds can flow freely with new thoughts. Emotionally, we must be able to release our feelings appropriately, so that we are not "uptight" or "all blocked up inside." Spiritually, the Large Intestine official helps us to eliminate everything that is inessential, so that we are refined down to our purest essence.

Exercise

While bathing, repeat this Zen prayer: "As I bathe this body, I vow with all sentient beings to wash from this body and mind all dust and confusion and feel healthy and clean within and without."

Note your distillations . . .

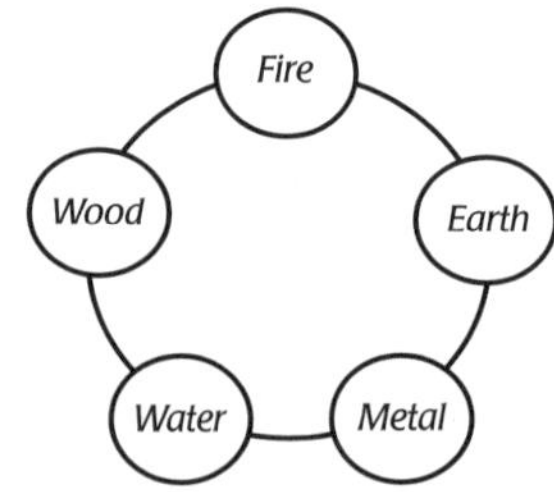

Distillations

October 28

room cleaning

my life is as tangled
as the tails of my Japanese kite
still hanging in the window
from two springs ago
the jars of colored stones
on the sill are dusty
when was the last time
I held them up to the light
in wonder
I feel tired with the weight
of these things, their dingy
disorder overwhelms me
now I just cut paths through
and leave large undifferentiated heaps
whole years of newspapers
and magazines, unsorted
letters banded in non-chronological packs
I am getting too old
to have a place for everything
I go desperate now
from day to day
trying to ignore the pandemonium
in my room
thinking: some day soon
I'll move back to the country
really sort through everything
straighten out my life
once and for all

- Janice MacKenzie

Note your distillations . . .

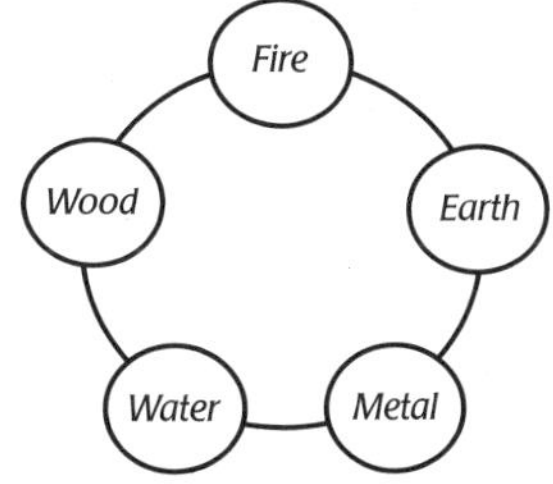

October 29

"Tears, idle tears, I know not what they mean,
Tears from the depths of some divine despair
Rise in the heart, and gather to the eyes,
In looking on the happy Autumn fields,
And thinking of the days that are no more."

- Alfred, Lord Tennyson

The emotion associated with the Fall season and the element Metal is grief. You may experience this as a deep melancholy or pervasive sadness as you watch the leaves fall and the days grow shorter. As the warmth of the sun withdraws and the energy of the plants is drawn down to the roots, so our energies turn inward, and we think about the past year and all our past years. Old regrets may surface, old losses become fresh and poignant again. If there is a loss for which you've never really grieved, each Fall presents an opportunity to get in touch with that grief again, to mourn and to let it go.

Exercise

Remember your losses, and take time to mourn them. Find the new beginning in every ending. Consciously let go of each day as it ends.

Note your distillations . . .

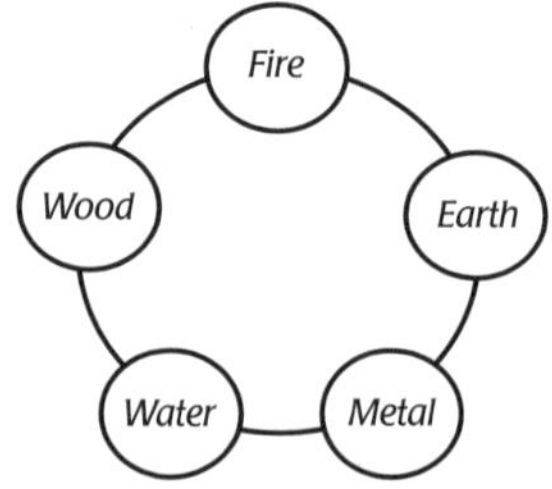

Distillations

October 30

After great pain, a formal feeling comes–
The Nerves sit ceremonious, like Tombs–
The stiff Heart questions was it He, that bore
And Yesterday, or Centuries before?

The Feet, mechanical, go round–
Of Ground, or Air, or Ought–
A Wooden way
Regardless grown,
A Quartz contentment, like stone–

This is the Hour of Lead–
Remembered, if outlived,
As Freezing persons, recollect the Snow–
First – Chill – the Stupor – then the letting go–

- Emily Dickinson

Someone who is carrying around a lot of unexpressed grief may feel the Fall to be an especially difficult time of year. The constant undertone of grief can become overwhelming in this season, leading to deep depression and despair. It is actually best, if you are feeling this way, to let yourself cry and release the emotion completely. Thus cleansed, you become aware of an intense beauty in this emotion, one that might inspire you, like Tennyson or Dickinson, to write poetry, or paint a picture. Thus, through the crucible of grief, something precious is created.

Exercise

Write your thoughts in a journal. Express any old grief in words.

Note your distillations . . .

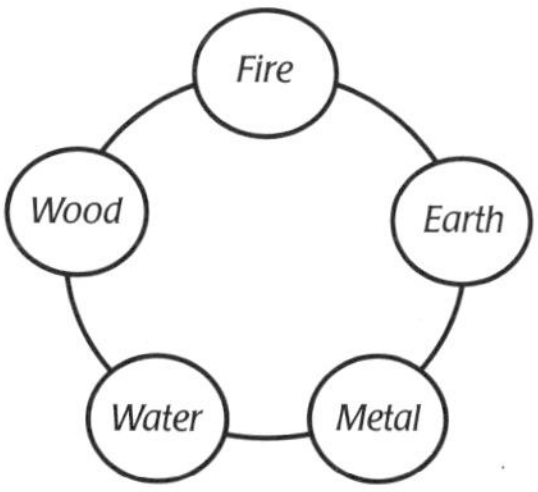

Fire
Wood
Earth
Water
Metal

Distillations

October 31

*"Grief is a physical process.
The body mourns as truly as the soul."*

- Clysta Kinstler,
The Moon Under Her Feet

When we are grieving, our bodies reflect this process as much as our emotions do. Strong emotions release powerful chemicals into our bloodstream, and we experience many unpleasant sensations and uncontrollable reactions. Sometimes, it is only the body that mourns, since the person seems to feel no emotion at the time.

Since we know that the two organs associated with the Metal element are the Lungs and the Large Intestine, it is primarily these two organs that reflect the grief physically. Some people may experience their grief with a cold, but for others it can manifest as pneumonia, bronchitis, or asthma. In addition, for some, the grief will come out as a skin condition such as a rash, hives, or eczema, since the skin is the "third lung" and also breathes.

Exercise

Dress up for Halloween and go trick-or-treating with children. Is your mask hiding another mask, which covers your grief?

Note your distillations . . .

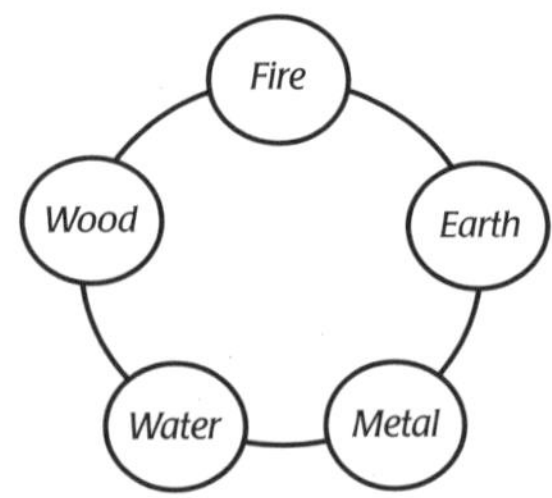

November 1

For some people, grief is accompanied by constipation or diarrhea, as the Large Intestine official registers its reaction. Thus, the body expresses in somatic form the intense emotion of grief, and as long as the grief is expressed fully, the symptoms in lungs, skin, and large intestine will disappear in due time.

For many people, however, the grief is not fully experienced or expressed on the emotional level, and the physical symptoms will remain, in chronic form, as a constant reminder of the unfinished emotional business. Unfortunately, instead of dealing with the grief, many people focus on clearing up the physical symptoms and forget that there ever was an emotional connection. Years later, they are still experiencing asthma, eczema, or colitis, going to doctor after doctor searching for a cure. A person trained in Chinese medicine may suspect a hidden emotional cause even when the patient does not remember it, because of the link between these organs and grief. Often, uncovering the root of the problem and dealing with the old buried feelings will bring about a healing of the physical symptoms, as well.

Exercise

Let go of one old grief today.

Note your distillations . . .

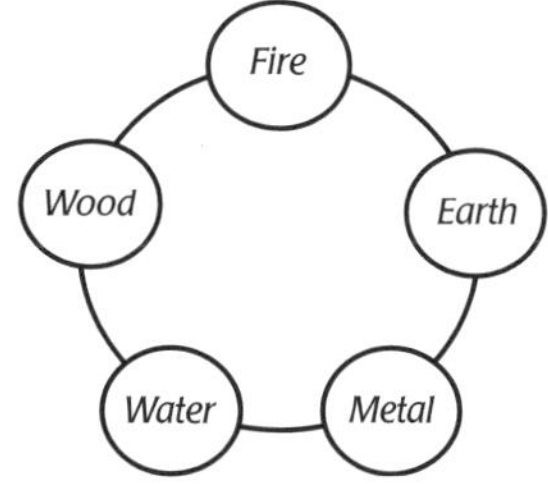

November 2

(Allen Ginsberg speaking about Jack Kerouac in an interview filmed by Richard Lerner in "What Happened to Kerouac?")

Allen Ginsberg: "...tears would come to his eyes very often in his later years in conversation when he talked about something that he felt sentiment about—his mother, his cat, his writing, his novels, the state of America—but particularly music, or Christ—particularly the crucifixion. Because he was going through a crucifixion, that is, the mortification of his body..."

Interviewer: "And yet this conference is about joy, and it seems like that's the Kerouac gift, more than the suffering..."

A.G.: "Well, yeah, it's about joy, but the kind of tears is... I mean it's one taste: joy and suffering at a certain point become one taste. Because it's existence itself—you're crying over existence, not inexistence [laugh]. Because the tears are appreciation of existence—the beauty and mortality and <u>sadness</u> of leaving existence. And the suffering <u>of</u> existence—which is so deep that it's joyful. To exist is joyful just by its very nature—even if it's suffering existence. Grief is not unadulterated pain—grief is also mixed with a sense of majesty and finality and realization of ultimate reality. It's why people weep—because they realize the ultimately real is ultimately real. Irrevocably so. There's only life and this is it."

Exercise

Howl at the moon.

Note your distillations . . .

Distillations

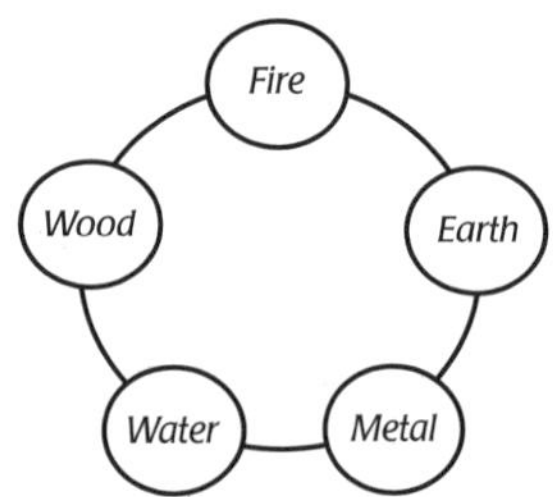

November 3

The time of day when the Metal element is functioning at its peak is from 3 a.m. to 7 a.m. The first block of time, from 3 a.m. to 5 a.m., is associated with the Lung official, and has to do with breathing and inspiration. In the ancient monasteries in China, the monks would rise at 4 a.m. in order to do their breathing meditations during this most auspicious time of the day. Most of us are sound asleep during those hours, but many are aware of a deeper, more restful sleep after 3 a.m., or conversely, of waking at that time and not being able to get back to sleep for a while.

In addition, anyone with lung problems can experience difficulty at this time. Many asthmatics wake up between 3 and 5 a.m. and need to use their inhalers. Because the lungs are associated with grief, anyone in a grieving process may experience a period of wakefulness at this time.

Exercise

If you find yourself awake at 4:00 a.m., try doing some deep breathing exercises instead of worrying.

Note your distillations . . .

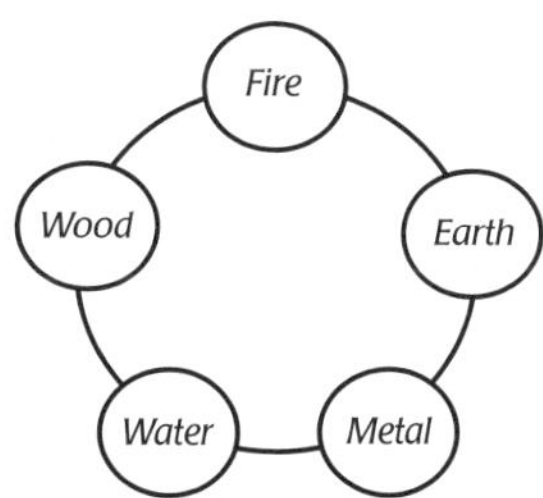

Distillations

November 4

The time from 5 a.m. to 7 a.m. is associated with the Large Intestine official, and is when that official is at its peak. This means that these hours are the best for elimination both of bodily waste and of unwanted thoughts and emotions.

If someone has a problem with "letting go"—either constipation or diarrhea, or an emotional holding onto old hurts and grievances—then waking during these hours may be beneficial as a way of utilizing the energy available then to correct the imbalance. Time spent in meditation or prayer then can help to purify the mind and emotions, even as moving our bowels and showering can purify our bodies. Cleansed both internally and externally, we can then face the new day, ready for fresh experiences.

Exercise

Arise at 5:00 a.m. every day for a week, meditate for 20 minutes, write in your journal, move your bowels, and shower before breakfast.

Note your distillations . . .

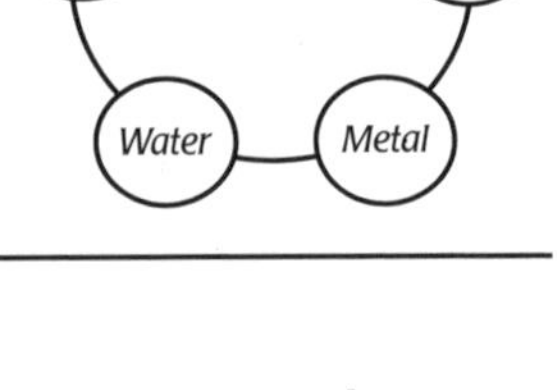

November 5

The time of life associated with Metal is roughly retirement age. Like the autumn season, it is about letting go—letting go of youth, of physical abilities, of all that we have accumulated—in order to flow into a new life stage.

For men, this stage of life often coincides with job retirement, but can happen earlier. I have known men who were laid off from their jobs in their late 40's or early 50's, and who then experienced a profound re-evaluation of their life goals and expectations. These men often went on to choose a new life course that was quite different from their previous occupation. For some men, this stage of life is accompanied by a strong attraction to spiritual disciplines of various kinds, like yoga, meditation, and tai chi. The old pursuits of money, cars, houses, and increased status lose their attraction and new longings come to the surface.

For women, this time often coincides with menopause and the time when all the children have left home. What used to be called the "empty nest" syndrome can now be seen as the time to turn inward and explore one's own spiritual development.

Exercise

Look at your high school yearbook. Think about what you thought you might do with your life then, and what you actually have done. Can you change your life to realign with your original purpose?

Note your distillations . . .

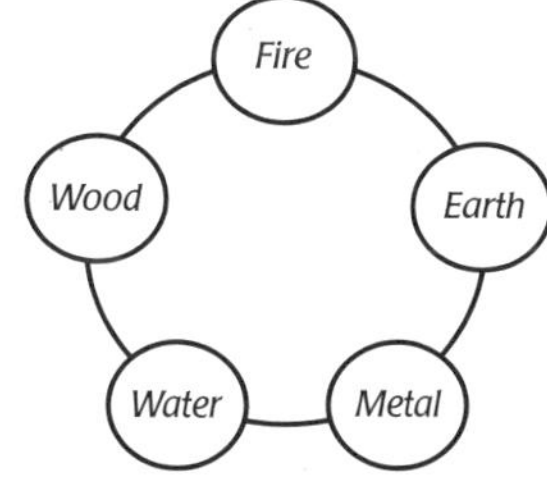

November 6

"...the lungs are the symbol of the interpretation and conduct of the official jurisdiction and regulation..."

"...the lungs harbor the animal spirits..."

- Nei Jing

The spiritual resource of the Metal element is identified in the *Nei Jing* as the "animal spirits." The Chinese name for these spirits is *po*, whose ideogram is made up of the character for white, *bai*, combined with the character *gui*, which means a Spirit of Earth. Thus, the *po* are linked with Earth, with a descending movement, and with essences. In human life, the *po* have authority over all vital and instinctive behavior. Certainly, breathing is an instinctive bodily function, and controls our most basic (animal) existence. Breathing is rhythmic —it puts things in order and keeps them in order. Metal energy helps us to have order in our lives.

Exercise

Create a regular schedule for your days and stick to it for one week.

Note your distillations . . .

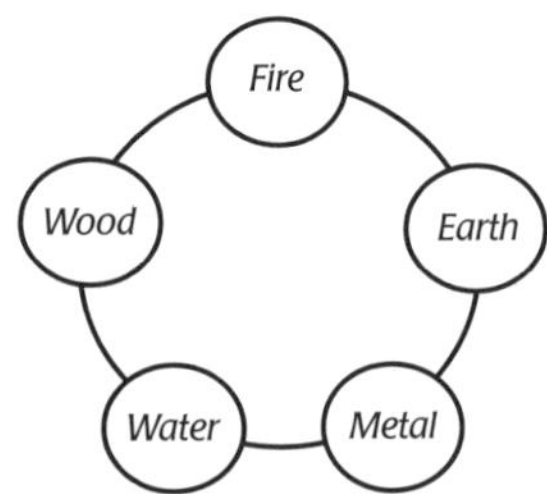

Distillations

November 7

"Wang Ping explains: The five spiritual resources are controlled by the five viscera...the lungs control the inferior, or animal spirits....

- Nei Jing

In the *Ling Shu*, another classic text, it is said that the *po* "go out and come in in association with the *jing*" (essences). This again points to the idea of the rhythm of life. As Elisabeth Rochat de la Vallee says, "The first going out is birth and the last coming in is death, it's just an appearance and disappearance with a form, a shape and a body in between forming individual life. Another possible meaning could be respiration, because in that process air is coming in and going out, and it's linked with the Lung. There is also the input of food and the expelling of waste. We can also have in mind the infinite number of coming ins and going outs through the pores, and all the interactions of Breaths."

Ted Kaptchuk says that the Virtue of the Lungs is Righteousness. When the rhythm of our "going out and coming in" is perfect, and our conduct is well-regulated, then we experience the perfection of spirit called Righteousness. Kaptchuk says that when this happens, we are aware of the beauty and preciousness of each moment of life.

Exercise

Create a ritual for yourself that you do every day.

Note your distillations . . .

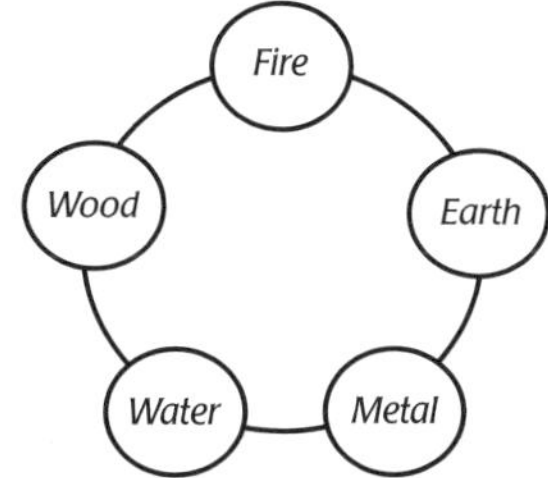

November 8

"The lungs are connected with the skin."

- Nei Jing

The Metal element fortifies the skin, and the healthiness of the skin often reflects the health of the Lungs and Large Intestine. Like the Lungs and Large Intestine, the organs associated with the Metal element, the skin must also receive and eliminate—in fact, it is sometimes called the third lung because it also breathes.

In both Chinese and Western medicine, lung and skin problems are seen as closely related. Someone who has eczema as a young child may later develop asthma, and skin rashes are commonly associated with colds and lung infections. Like the large intestine, the skin is important to the normal process of elimination, and can even help get rid of excess wastes.

Exercise

After your bath or shower today, brush your skin with a loofa sponge or skin brush to remove dead cells and stimulate the clearing of toxins.

Note your distillations . . .

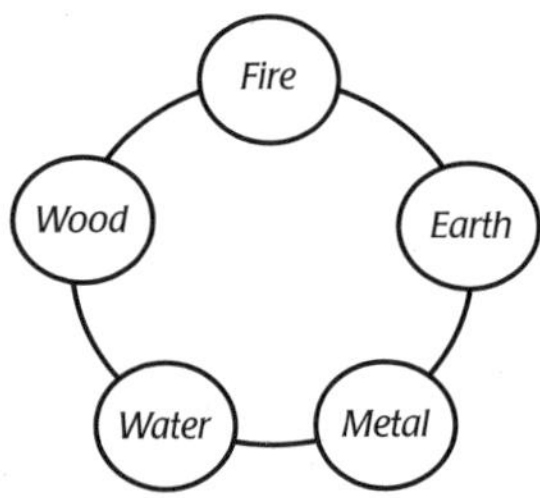

November 9

"Upon the body they create skin and hair..."

- Nei Jing

Acne and boils are common examples of elimination through the skin, and can occur more often when the internal organs of elimination are not working well. Natural remedies for acne and other skin outbreaks work to stimulate the kidneys, liver, and large intestine to function more efficiently.

In general, the overall vitality and health of the skin depends on the well-being of the Metal element. Dry skin, oily skin, or overly moist skin could point to an imbalance in Metal. If you have skin problems, then look to your lungs and large intestine to see why. Smokers and those who are chronically constipated are most at risk for skin problems, but anyone who has difficulty in breathing or eliminating may experience them. As far as the skin is concerned, breathing pure air and the proverbial "apple a day" are the ways to health and vitality!

Exercise

At the end of your bath or shower today, use cold water to close your skin pores and prevent heat loss and vulnerability to colds, as well as stimulate skin circulation.

Note your distillations . . .

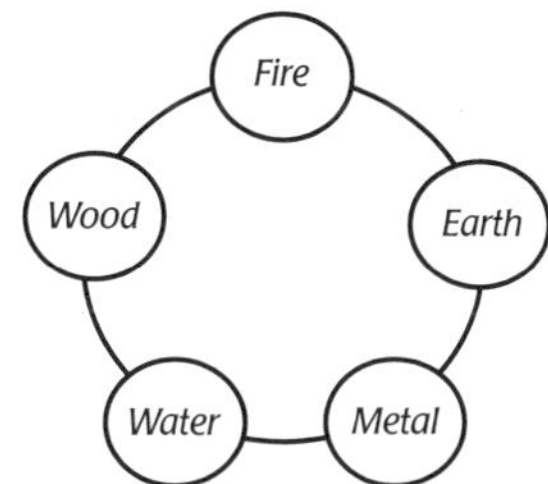

November 10

"The condition of the body hair shows when the lungs are in a splendid and flourishing condition."

- Nei Jing

In addition to the skin, the body hair also offers a clue to the state of balance of the Metal element within. Excessive body hair, loss of body hair, or the lack of body hair could all point to an imbalance in the Metal energies. Of course, cultural and genetic factors do come into play here, but within the norm of a given family or group, these signs can be important indicators of health or imbalance.

This is a clue that is often very difficult to see because body hair is often covered by clothing or, in the case of many women in Western culture, shaved off. Indeed, our cultural norms seem to favor the absence of body hair—if you are a man, it is generally better to have a "trimmed" beard if one at all, to be "clean-shaven" or "clean-cut," while to be "shaggy," "hairy," or "hirsute" is not generally a compliment. If you are a woman, of course, the only hair allowed is on your head!

Exercise

Do you have a lot of body hair? How do you feel about it?

Note your distillations . . .

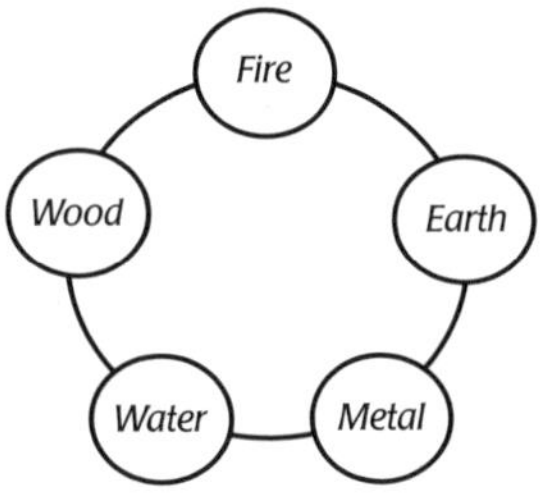

Fire
Wood
Earth
Water
Metal

Distillations

November 11

"The lungs govern the nose... Of the orifices they create the nose with its nostrils..."

- Nei Jing

The nose is both the orifice and the sense organ of the Metal element. Through the nose, fresh air is brought into the lungs and used air is released from the body. Thus, the nose has a role to play, both in nourishing the body with oxygen and in eliminating waste. The nose, like the eyes, ears, and mouth, is a portal through which we receive the world and interpenetrate with it. Problems that affect the nose, including blocked nostrils and growths in the mucus lining, could point to an imbalance in the Metal element.

As a sense organ, the nose provides a unique way of perceiving the world. The sense of smell is actually connected to the most primitive part of our brains, and has a lot to do with memory and instinctual responses. We have many expressions that show this connection: "to smell a rat;" "to smell something fishy;" "a nose for news;" "to sniff out the truth;" and "the nose knows." The loss of the sense of smell or a distortion in smell is usually indicative of an imbalance in the Metal element.

Exercise

Pay attention to your sense of smell. Try to smell as many different aromas as you can today.

Note your distillations . . .

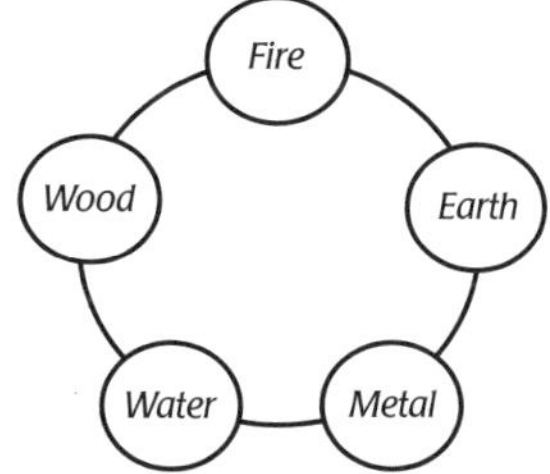

November 12

"....and its smell is foul and putrid."

- Nei Jing

The odor associated with the Metal element and the season of Autumn is rotten (called by the *Nei Jing* "foul and putrid"). This odor can be detected on someone who is out of balance in the Metal element, sometimes quite strongly. It is not body odor but a distinct smell having to do with the state of balance of the Colon and Lung energies. It is often subtle and easily disguised by perfumes and deodorants.

Of the five diagnostic odors, rotten is the easiest to pick out right away. It usually smells like human feces, but can also be described as "like a cesspool," "rotten meat," or "like something dead." The connection with death and corruption is very apt because the Autumn season is the season of death and the putrefaction of all vegetation for the year. Someone who smells "rotten" is indicating that they are having difficulty in the rhythm of life—the constant taking in and letting go of energy in the form of breath and food.

Exercise

Simmer a cinnamon stick, cloves, and an orange peel in some water to scent your home.

Note your distillations . . .

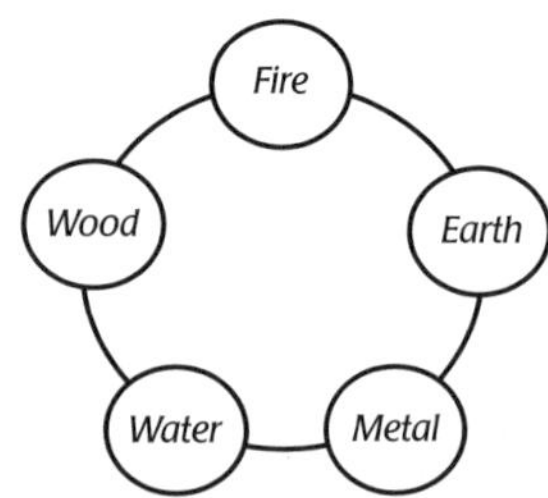

November 13

"...and they give to the human voice the ability to weep and to wail."

- Nei Jing

The sound of voice associated with the Metal element is weeping. This sound is naturally connected to the emotion of grief, which is the emotion of Metal. When someone is in an active grieving process, his voice will naturally tend to weep. This is not necessarily accompanied by tears, but is more a voice quality that sounds like tears. Sometimes a person's voice will weep incessantly, even when there is no cause for grief or when the occasion is happy. This continual weeping quality in the voice can be a sign of imbalance in the Metal element.

As with some of the other voice qualities, the sound of the weeping voice is usually completely unconscious on the part of the person who has it. It can elicit different reactions from people, ranging from sympathy to irritation.

Exercise

Listen to some old-time country music to hear the weeping voice —devotees of the genre call it a "cry" in the voice, and many of the songs are about lost love.

Note your distillations . . .

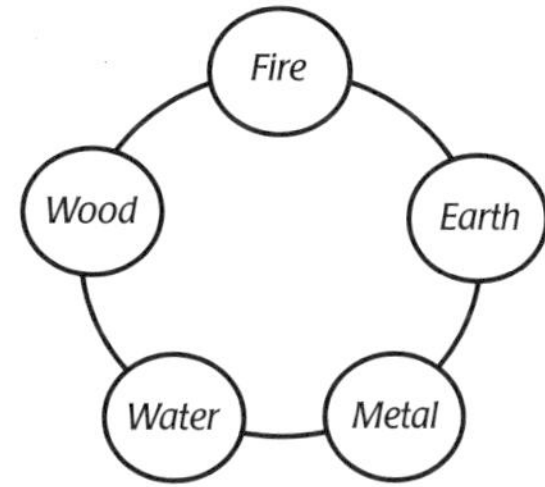

November 14

A good example of the weeping voice quality is Woody Allen's voice—along with his "sad-sack" character, his voice tells us he's a "loser" (i.e., loss = grief). When we hear this voice quality, we know that the person is grieving over a loss—although the loss may be 20 years old. Other examples of the weeping voice are George Jones and Tammy Wynette, country-western singers whose songs are replete with lost love, death and misery.

The other extreme is the absolute refusal to weep, with a voice that has a complete lack of weeping even when the occasion warrants it. This voice quality also speaks to an imbalance in Metal, in the energies of receiving and eliminating. A person who cannot weep, who cannot "let go" even in the sound of his voice, clearly needs help in the Metal element.

Exercise

Today listen to the voices of all of your friends and co-workers, and see if any of them weep. If so, does it correlate with anything else you know about their Metal?

Note your distillations . . .

Distillations

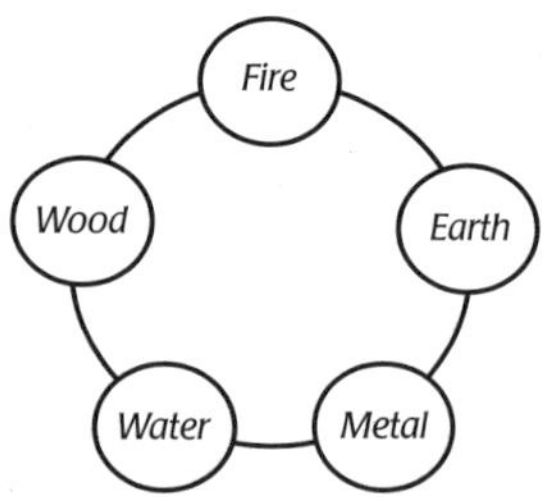

November 15

"...metal produces the pungent flavor..."

- Nei Jing

The taste associated with the Metal element and the season of Autumn is pungent. This taste, like other physical sensations, can only be described by example—the pungent flavor is spicy, like Indian curry or Szechuan food. It is acrid and slightly drying (another quality of Metal), and carries with it the connotation of constriction. Yet, its effect is the opposite: according to the *Nei Jing*, "The pungent flavor has a dispersing effect."

The ideogram for pungent or acrid is *xin* (辛). The composition of the character gives the idea of offending a superior, and also what happens after an offense has been committed, namely, punishment, pain and bitterness (what we might feel after a big bite of horseradish or chili peppers!). On the physical level, it can mean a wound or an injury, and on the psychological level, it can mean a painful constriction of the heart.

Exercise

Eat spicy foods that clean out your system: cayenne, ginger and curry are three common spices that promote good digestion and elimination.

Note your distillations . . .

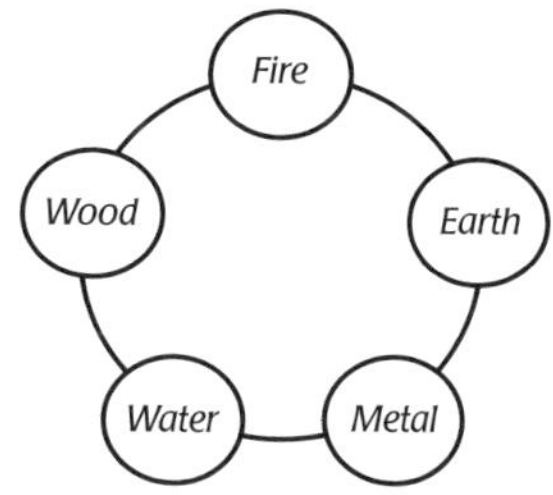

November 16

Each of the five tastes supports or influences a different major organ of the body. The *Nei Jing* says, "...the pungent flavor goes into the respiratory tract; when there is an illness in the respiratory tract one should not eat too much pungent food." As with the other tastes, a little of the taste is supportive and healthy, but too much is destructive of the related organs.

All of the tastes must be present in our diets to be healthy. Eating too much of the pungent flavor is as out of balance as never eating pungent food. Some particular pungent foods are: black pepper; chives; cinnamon; cloves; fennel; garlic; ginger; scallions; green pepper; leaf mustard; leek; marjoram; nutmeg; peppermint; radish; red pepper; rosemary; spearmint; star anise; sweet basil; tobacco; white pepper; and wine.

Exercise

Eat a clove of garlic today, either pressed into water or juice, or cooked with other vegetables. Garlic has been used through the centuries to treat coughs, sore throats, and lung ailments, and to prevent colds and flus.

Note your distillations . . .

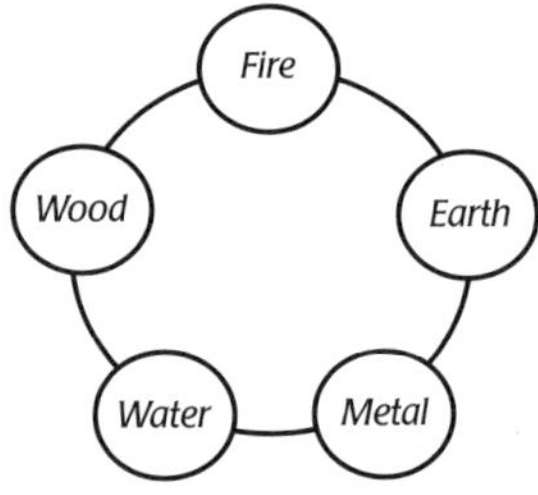

November 17

"Foods that move downwards are good in autumn, when things begin to fall..."

- Henry C. Lu,
Chinese System of Food Cures

When it comes to food and the seasons, there are many different schools of thought. Although pungent is the actual taste associated with Autumn and the metal energies, Henry Lu writes that foods with a downward movement are those that are good in autumn, and these have two flavors—sweet or sour. Sweet foods, such as honey, sugar, and watermelon, can slow down acute symptoms and neutralize the toxic effects of other foods. Sour foods, such as lemon and plum, can obstruct movement and are useful in checking diarrhea and excessive perspiration.

Exercise

Roast acorn squash halves with butter and brown sugar or maple syrup as a delicious Autumn dish.

Note your distillations . . .

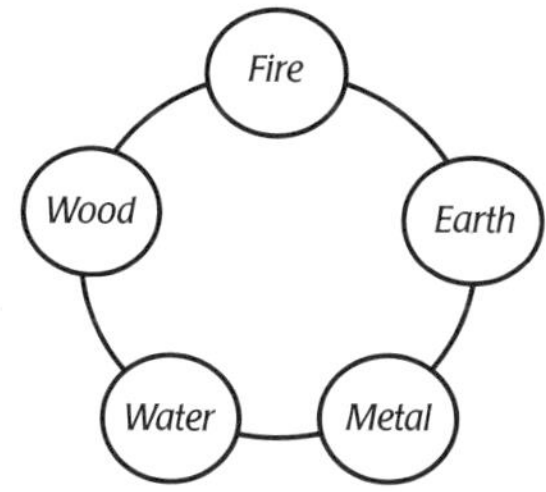

November 18

Foods with a downward movement are usually cold or cool in temperament. This means that they tend to generate cold or cool energy in your body, regardless of whether or not they are cold or cool when you eat them. Lettuce and watermelon are examples of cold foods; apples and cucumbers are examples of cool foods. In addition to these foods, the list of downward-moving foods includes: bamboo shoots; banana; barley; bean curd; chicken egg white; clams (freshwater); mushrooms; eggplant; grapefruit; muskmelon; peach; spinach; strawberries; tangerines; wheat; and wheat bran.

The foods traditionally associated with the Metal element are: rice; chestnuts; horsemeat (or chicken); and onions (according to the *Nei Jing*). Because the Autumn is also associated with dryness, foods that moisten may need to be added to the diet: tofu; tempeh; soy milk; millet; pears; apples; peanuts; sesame seeds; honey; rice syrup; milk and dairy products; crabs; oyster; mussels; and pork.

Exercise

Go apple picking. Eat a juicy apple right from the tree.

Note your distillations . . .

Distillations

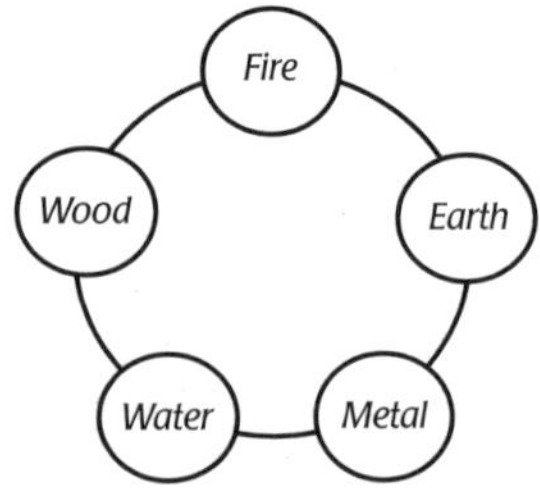

November 19

"The [mysterious] powers of Fall ... in times of excitement and change they create a cough."

- Nei Jing

It's no surprise that the Metal energies, associated with the Lungs, would have the power to create a cough in times of excitement and change. However, this cough is not one related to an upper respiratory tract infection, a cold, or a flu. This is a mysterious cough that seems to have no physical origin, which persists in spite of the best medical treatment and every variety of drug. We have to look at a more energetic reason for this cough, and often it has to do with an imbalance in the Metal energies.

Physically, a cough is the body's way of expelling mucus from the Lungs, or of expressing an irritation of the respiratory system. Thus, it is a rejection of something unwanted, and this echoes the Metal's function of eliminating waste and unwanted things—both physically and emotionally.

Exercise

Drink a tea made of coltsfoot leaf, licorice root, ginger root, and wild cherry bark for a tasty tonic for the lungs.

Note your distillations . . .

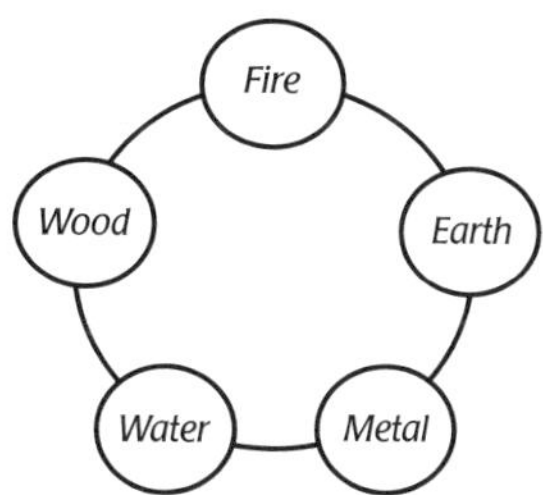

November 20

A cough can represent the body trying to expel something that it can't. I remember an example of a patient who developed a mysterious cough after an IUD was inserted.

Sometimes what is unwanted is simply too much change all at once. As an example of this, I once treated a woman who had a chronic cough for 2 years. It turned out that during that 2-year period, she changed jobs, moved offices, became engaged, got married, sold one house and bought another, became pregnant with her first child, and was put in charge of a big project at work that needed to be finished by the time of her maternity leave. In addition to all of this "excitement and change," it came out during our initial interview that when her beloved father died in 1981 of colon cancer, she had never grieved for him. The Lungs, of course, being the organ associated with the emotion of grief, were thus holding on to this "unwanted" feeling for all of those years.

Exercise

What three things do you need to eliminate from your life? What is stopping you from doing that?

Note your distillations . . .

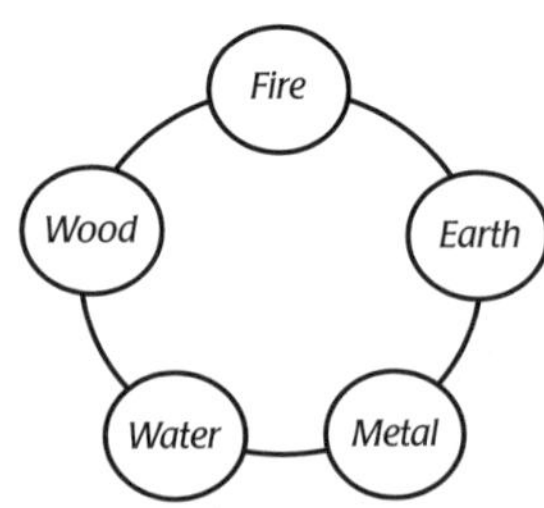

Distillations

November 21

The moon is full, the autumn nights grow longer,
In the north forests startled crows cry out.
Still high overhead, the star river stretches,
The Dipper's handle set to southwest.
The cold cricket grieves deep in the chambers,
Of the notes of sweet birds, none remain.
Then one evening gusts of autumn come,
One who sleeps alone thinks fondly of thick quilts.
Past loves are a thousand miles farther each day,
Blocked from my drifting and my sinking.
Man's life is not as the grass and trees;
Still the season's changes can stir the heart.

- Wei Ying Wu

Exercise

Go for a hayride. Enjoy the crisp air, the smell of hay, the slow swaying of the wagon, and the moonlight through the bare trees.

Note your distillations . . .

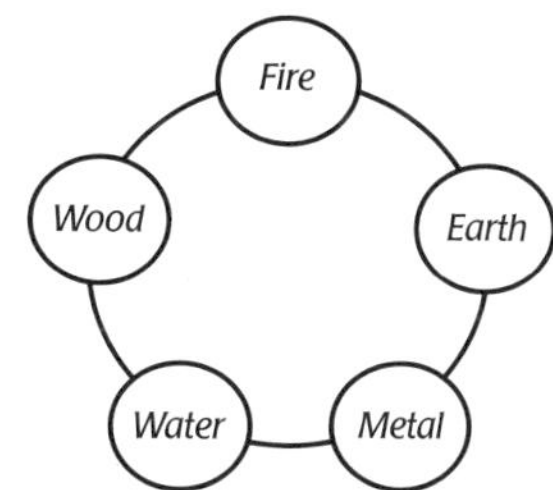

November 22

"...the lower intestines are like the officials who propagate the Right Way of Living, and they generate evolution and change..."

- Nei Jing

One of the primary activities connected to Autumn and Metal energy is elimination, or letting go. In nature, we see letting go in the pure surrender by the tree of every single leaf, the beautiful, as well as the shriveled. All are let go because the cycle is ended, and there is complete trust that next year a whole new crop of leaves will grow. Just so, we need to constantly empty ourselves in the complete trust that the universe will fill us up again.

When we let go, all kinds of new possibilities emerge. When we hold on, all movement stops and life is at a standstill; if the trees didn't shed their leaves, there would be no room for new growth in the Spring. If we do not let go of each breath, we cannot take the next one. Thus, each ending offers a new beginning.

Exercise

Clean out your drawers and closets, throwing away what is no longer useful to you. Be aware that you are creating room for something new to come in.

Note your distillations . . .

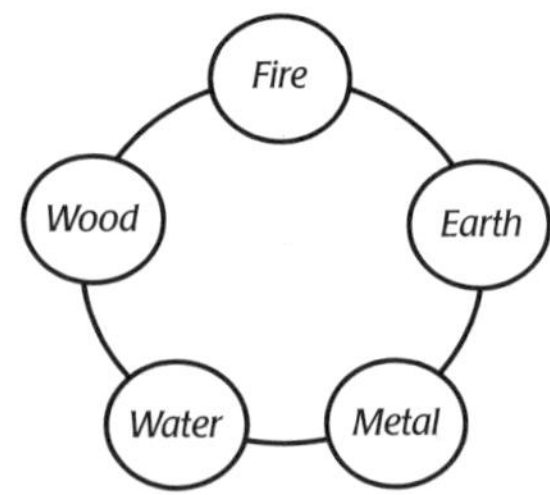

November 23

"My neighbor Howard says his mother saved everything. His mother made little cloth bags to hold pieces of string, each bag carefully labeled as to the length of the pieces. After her death they found one small bag of string labeled "too short to save."

- Helen Bevington

"Letting go" can take many forms, from letting go of things, such as old clothes, to letting go of old grudges. The process takes place on all levels of body, mind, and spirit, and is happening even on a cellular level. If you think about it, every cell in your body must take in nutrients and let go of waste products, so this process is automatic and continuous. When we consciously participate in this taking in and letting go, we experience the rhythm of the universe and its ceaseless changing.

Exercise

Go through your bookshelves and pull out books you no longer want. Give them away to friends, or take them to a second-hand book store or a library.

Note your distillations . . .

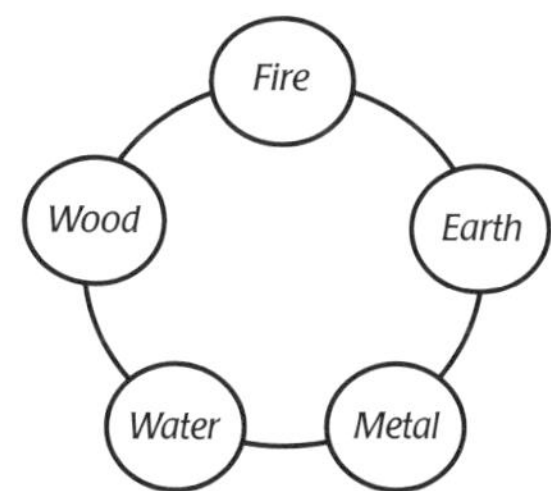

November 24

Mother of my birth, for how long were we together
in your love and my adoration of your self?
For the shadow of a moment, as I breathed your pain
and you breathed my suffering. As we knew
of shadows in lit rooms that would swallow the light.

Your face beneath the oxygen tent was alive
but your eyes closed, your breathing hoarse.
Your sleep was with death. I was alone
with you as when I was young
but now only alone, not with you,
to become alone forever, as I was learning
watching you become alone.
Earth now is your mother, as you were mine, my earth,
my sustenance and my strength,
and now without you I turn to your mother
and seek from her that I may meet you again
in rock and stone. Whisper to the stone
I love you. Whisper to the rock, I found you.
Whisper to the earth, Mother, I have found her,
and I am safe and always have been.

- David Ignatow,
New & Collected Poems,1970-1985

Exercise

Write to someone with whom you've lost touch.

Note your distillations . . .

Distillations

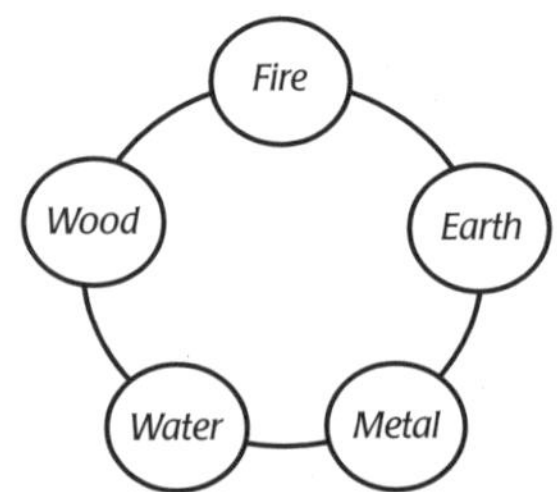

November 25

I will lie down in autumn
let birds be flying

Swept into a hollow
by the wind
I'll wait for dying

I will lie inert unseen
my hair same-colored
with grass and leaves

Gather me
for the autumn fires
with the withered sheaves

I will sleep face down
in the burnt meadow
not hearing the sound of water
over stones

Trail over me cloud
and shadow
Let snow
hide the whiteness of my bones

- May Swenson,
Nature: Poems Old and New

Exercise

Collect autumn leaves. Even in Florida and California, you can find leaves that change. Find as many different colors as you can, and place them on an altar.

Note your distillations . . .

Fire
Wood
Earth
Water
Metal

Distillations

November 26

"Precious metals and jade come from the regions of the West."

- Nei Jing

In Nature, the obvious associations with the Metal element are the metals found in the earth, such as iron, gold, and silver. These metallic ores are the richness of the earth, providing nutrients to plants and items of value to human beings. Metals provide the structure and strength for many of our buildings, and create the wires that connect us with sources of power and communication. The precious metals, because of their beauty and rarity, are seen as symbols of wealth and value. For example, wedding rings are made of gold because it is precious but lasts forever. I have noticed that people who have Metal imbalances, or those who feel a lack of value, will often wear a lot of gold or silver jewelry.

Exercise

Do you wear jewelry? If not, why not? If you do, are you drawn more to gold, silver, or gemstones? Is your watch an expensive one?

Note your distillations . . .

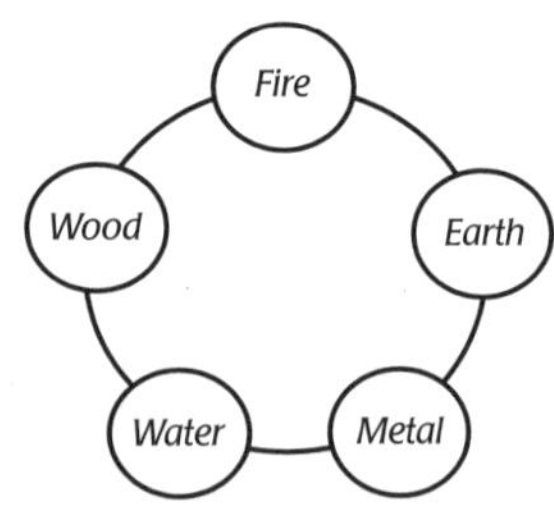

Distillations

November 27

Gems, precious stones, and crystals also fall under the category of Metal. Because of their beauty, perfection, and rarity, they have been prized down through the ages and seen as objects of great value. Diamonds, especially, have been linked with what is most precious, because of their clarity and endurance. They are used as an expression of the greatest love between a man and a woman, when he gives her a diamond engagement ring to symbolize eternal love.

With New Age devotees, crystals have further been linked with spirituality, so those seeking to feel value through their spirituality will often surround themselves with crystals. A strong attraction to gems and crystals could indicate that your Metal energies are strong, or that you are trying to bolster your sense of self-worth with these objects of outward value.

Exercise

Go to a shop that sells gems and crystals. Observe the different colors and facets, and the way the light sparkles on them. Buy one that particularly draws your eye, and place it where you can see it often in a sunny window.

Note your distillations . . .

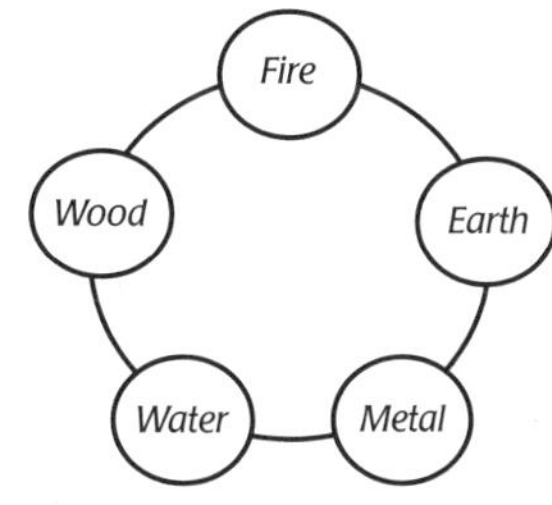

November 28

"The three months of Autumn are called overflowing and balancing."

- Claude Larre and Elisabeth Rochat de la Vallee

The season of Autumn has traditionally been seen in China as the time to measure everything exactly, in order that all trades and exchanges in the country could be done according to a true value. The value of gold and silver had to be verified at this time. The grain had to be weighed and measured so that a farmer could get a fair exchange for it. Thus, Autumn and its corresponding energy of Metal have come to be connected to the idea of value.

As the season turns colder and darkness comes earlier, we turn our energies inward and reflect on what is important to us. As we let go of what is no longer valuable to us (Large Intestine), we receive new inspiration and value from the Heavens (Lungs). As we slow down in preparation for Winter, we reflect on our own values, and see where they are not congruent with our actions.

Exercise

Think about what you most value in life. Looking back over the year, see where your actions were in accord with your values and where they were not.

Note your distillations . . .

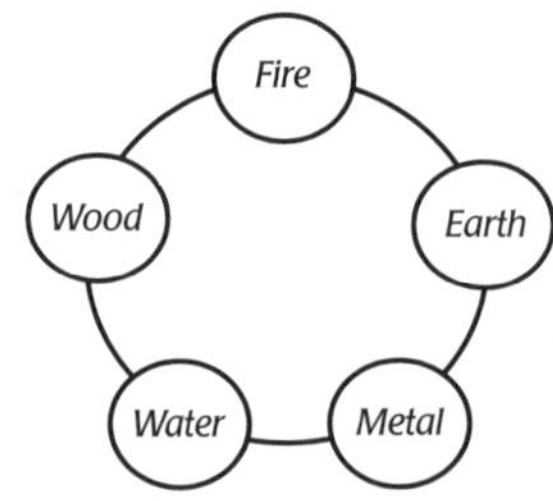

Distillations

November 29

"Autumn is the time of punishment when you cut the cereal crops or cut off the heads of criminals. In the Book of Rites, another of the Five Classics, it says that Autumn puts everything back in the balancing scales."

- Elisabeth Rochat de la Vallee

The slowed-down, more peaceful time of Autumn allows us to clarify who we really are and what we stand for in life, and to make the changes necessary. Our integrity demands that we strictly weigh everything in the balance, and "measure up!"

People whose Metal energies are weak or out of balance may not feel an intrinsic sense of value or self-worth. They will often focus on external symbols of value—for example, expensive clothes, jewelry, cars, and houses—to give them the sense of self-worth they are lacking. In more extreme cases, there may be a sense of total worthlessness, with a lack of regard for personal appearance.

Exercise

Do you like to wear expensive clothing? Or are you more comfortable in jeans and a teeshirt?

Note your distillations . . .

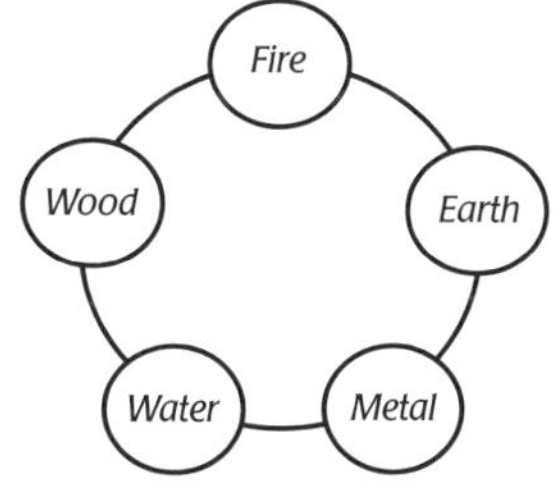

November 30

"I'm Nobody! Who are you?
Are you – Nobody – Too?
Then there's a pair of us!
Don't tell! they'd advertise – you know!

How dreary – to be – Somebody!
How public – like a Frog –
To tell one's name – the livelong June –
To an admiring Bog!"

- Emily Dickinson

Exercise

Do you consider yourself a worthy person? Do you feel you have to "make a name" for yourself, or are you content to be a "nobody?"

Note your distillations . . .

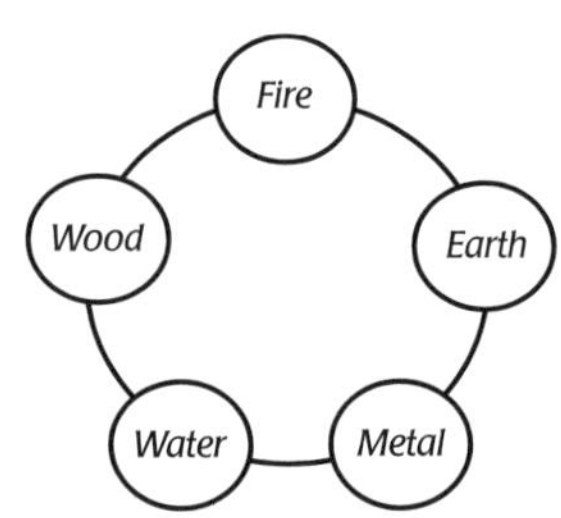

Distillations

December 1

"O wild West Wind, thou breath of Autumn's being..."

- Percy Bysshe Shelley,
Ode to the West Wind

One wonders whether Shelley was familiar with Chinese philosophy when he wrote this poem! For indeed, the direction of the West and the West wind are specifically connected to Autumn in the Chinese classics. In addition, the reference to breath is fascinating in light of the fact that Autumn is associated with the Lungs in Chinese medicine. As the *Nei Jing* says, "The west wind arises in the Fall; its sickness is located in the lungs..."

Of course, the Lungs of Chinese medicine are more than simply bodily organs. They encompass a wide spectrum of functions—physical, mental, emotional, and spiritual. Professor Worsley says of them that they "receive the qi energy from the Heavens." In this aspect, they are close to the idea of "breath" as "spirit," which is a connection found in many cultures (for example, the "prana" of Hindu philosophy).

Exercise

Walk out on a windy day and let the wind push you down the sidewalk.

Note your distillations . . .

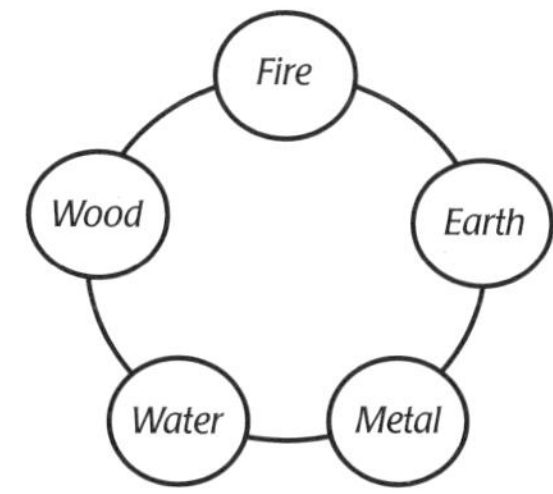

December 2

The Lungs and breath are what connect us to the Divine, to the Heavens, enabling us to receive it into ourselves. With each breath, we receive Divine "inspiration" (from the Greek word *"inspiros"* which means "to breathe in"). Many cultures have religious practices that focus on the breath and specific breathing exercises as a means of attaining that spiritual connection (i.e., yoga and esoteric Taoism, etc.).

In our own culture, some healing modalities such as re-birthing and breathwork, utilize the breath in a way to bring buried emotions to the surface and reconnect us to primal experiences of wholeness and openness. In this age, when many people are no longer affiliated with traditional churches and religions, there is a tremendous longing for some experience of a spiritual dimension. Learning a spiritual practice that includes disciplined breathing exercises can be a way to reconnect to our own spirituality, on the most fundamental level. The connection is there whether we are aware of it or not, since with each in-breath, we draw some of the Universe into ourselves.

Exercise

Learn and practice some "qi gong" exercises—Chinese breathing exercises that help to cultivate energy and discipline the mind —such as the ones in *The Way of Energy,* by Master Lam Kam Chuen.

Note your distillations . . .

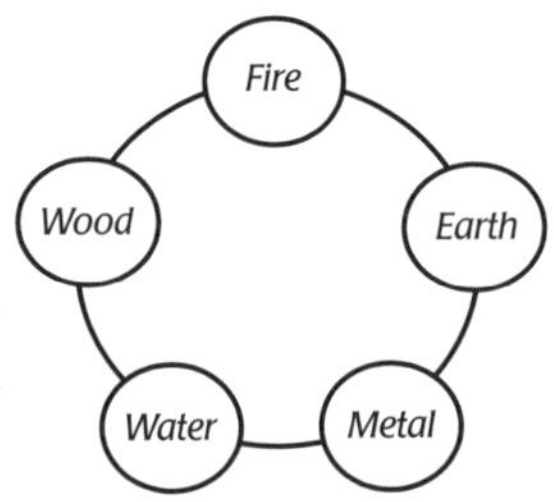

December 3

"You do not do, you do not do
Any more, black shoe
In which I have lived like a foot
For thirty years, poor and white,
Barely daring to breathe or Achoo.

Daddy, I have had to kill you.
You died before I had time – "

- Sylvia Plath,
"Daddy," from *Ariel*

Professor Worsley speaks of the Lungs as "the Official who receives the pure Ch'i from the Heavens." This function of receiving energy from the outside and particularly from the Heavens links the Lungs with fatherly energy. Just as the Spleen takes in energy from the Earth (Yin) and is thus linked with the mother, so the Lungs, which connect us to the Heavens (Yang), are linked with the father. This can refer to one's individual father as well as to Father with a capital "F".

Exercise

List three things you received from your father.

Note your distillations . . .

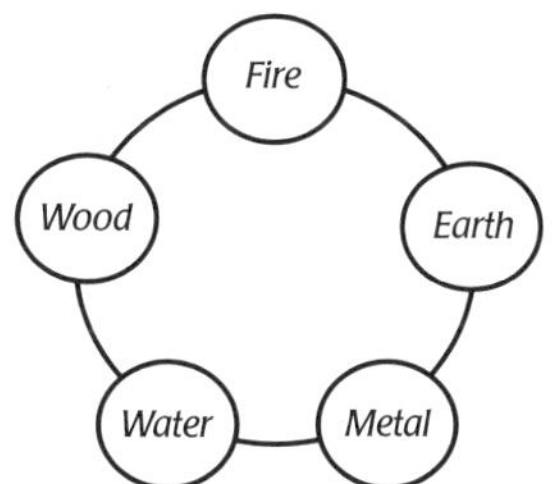

December 4

We look for something special from a father, something we don't get from our mothers. A mother will love you simply because you are her child; she provides the ground of your being. But a father loves you because of some special quality you have, which he acknowledges, draws out, and helps to guide and shape into manifestation. He provides inspiration and a code of honor to follow in life. Thus, a father provides a more "heavenly" kind of sustenance, while a mother provides on the "earthly" plane.

One's relationship to one's own father greatly influences subsequent relationships with father-figures such as teachers, bosses, clergymen, political leaders, policemen, etc.—and any disharmony in these relationships can indicate an imbalance in the Lungs. Often, people who lose their fathers early to divorce or death have deficiencies in their Lung meridians. This can lead to specific symptoms in the lungs, such as asthma or bronchitis, or it can manifest in a more psychological way. These people will seek Metal energy in relationship to another person or institution that offers fatherly acknowledgment and guidance. Many a young woman has sought a father in an older husband, a teacher, or a boss, and many a young man has looked for a father in a football coach, a scout leader, a professor, or the army.

Exercise

Who has fathered you in your life?

Note your distillations . . .

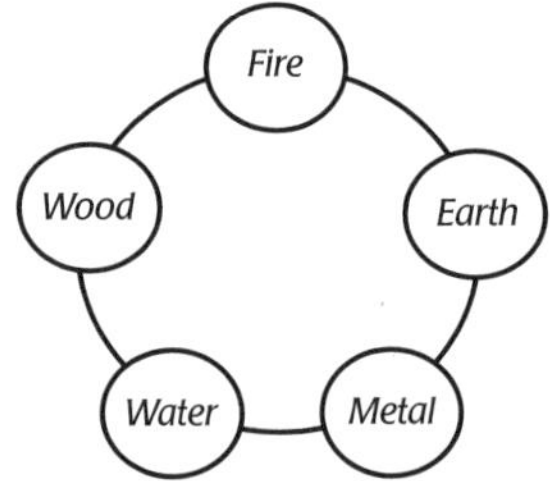

December 5

i am metallic
hard as nails
my mother broke her teeth on me
my father's fingers reached for me
but I blunted them
I would like to be strong as steel
sharp, tempered
but I end up being brittle
as glass
easily shattered by extremes of temperature
at my best, I shine
glittering like a jewel
facets flashing in the white light
at my worst, a cry of anguish
rises from my dry lungs
in my dreams,
I mount a white stag
and fly upward to the heavens
breathing the pure air
of perfection
down below, the abyss opens
rank as a bog
to enfold me

- Janice MacKenzie

Exercise

What kind of metal are you? Is it similar to your father's?

Note your distillations . . .

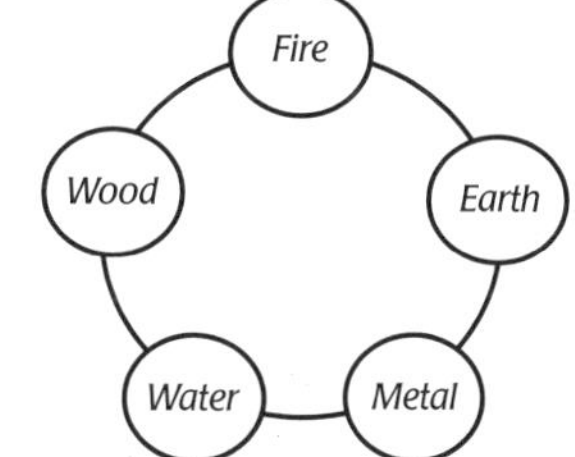

December 6

"The Metal Element is responsible for bringing quality into our lives."

- Professor J.R. Worsley,
The Five Elements and The Officials

Because of the connection of the Metal energies and the Autumn with things precious, there has been a linking of the concepts of Metal and quality. Perhaps, because in the Autumn we let go of everything inessential, there is a sense that what we choose to keep must be too valuable to throw away. Thus, issues of quality come up in the Autumn, and people who are out of balance in Metal will be particularly concerned with quality in their lives.

For example, someone whose sense of inner value and worth is weak might demand that everything around him be of the highest quality. This is the person who would never wear a Timex, but only a Rolex watch; who would never drive a Ford but only a Mercedes or a Porsche; who would live only in the best neighborhood and wear only the best clothes.

Exercise

How do you measure quality in your life? Make a list of your assets, financial and otherwise.

Note your distillations . . .

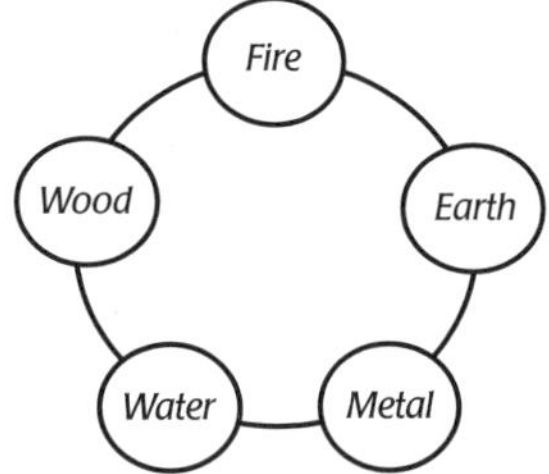

Distillations

December 7

Being surrounded by quality "things" enables some people to feel a sense of quality and value in themselves. This doesn't mean that everyone who wears a Rolex has problems with self-worth! But someone whose whole sense of value comes from the quality of the objects he owns might be indicating an imbalance in the Metal element.

Conversely, someone might have the opposite reaction and feel unworthy of quality things, preferring to wear cheap clothes and jewelry or ignoring personal appearance altogether, even when he can afford better. This person never seems to notice that his clothing is threadbare or torn, that his car is dirty and dented, that the objects around him are Brand X. If the first person's attitude is: "Only the best quality for me!", this one seems to be saying, "I don't deserve to have anything better!"

Exercise

Buy yourself an expensive present and tell yourself you deserve it.

Note your distillations . . .

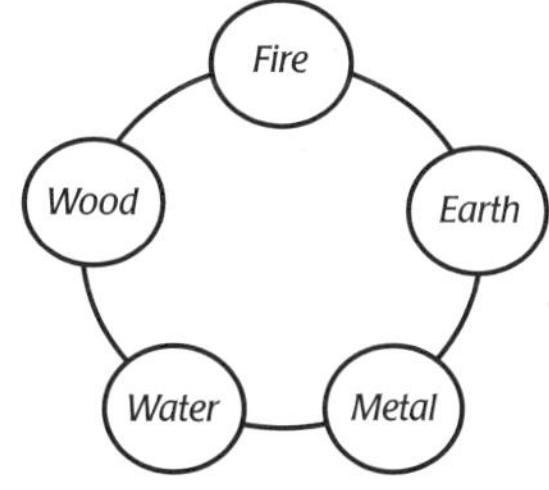

Distillations

December 8

"In trying to be the abstract perfect, we batter, judge, and distort ourselves. No matter what we do or how we try to achieve, it is never enough. We are never enough. Trying too hard and never trying at all are two sides of the coin of perfection. Unfortunately, it is a coin that never pays off."

- Anne Wilson Schaef,
Meditations for Women Who Do Too Much

The function of the Metal element of eliminating everything inessential can be taken to an extreme. Combined with the Metal element's quest for quality, this can result in perfectionism. Perfectionism is epidemic in our society, along with the related problem of workaholism that runs through our culture. Just as being called a workaholic is seen as a compliment, so is being called a perfectionist.

Exercise

Repeat this affirmation: "Today I will do the best I can, easily and effortlessly."

Note your distillations . . .

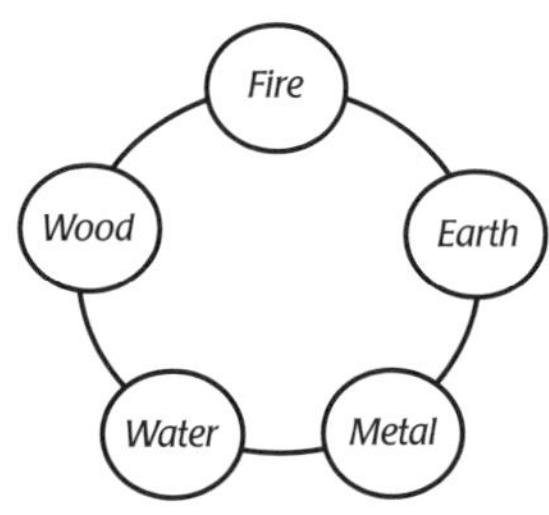

December 9

Being a perfectionist means that you strive for the highest quality of performance in whatever you do, and that if you are making something, you try to make it flawless. This is a good quality to have in an artist, because creating art needs that kind of focused attention to detail. If taken out into everyday life, however, it can create a lot of stress and strain. Those who try to copy Martha Stewart will understand what I mean.

The relentless pursuit of perfection in everything that you do can be a sign that your Metal energies are out of balance. Often, people who are perfectionistic do not have a good sense of self-worth, and only feel value when they do something perfectly. If there are flaws, it nullifies any sense of goodness or worth in the entire enterprise. Perfectionists need to "let go" of the rigid need to be perfect, and allow their quest for quality to be balanced by kindness to themselves.

Exercise

Today, be kind to yourself and allow yourself to be less than perfect. Give yourself permission to just be you.

Note your distillations . . .

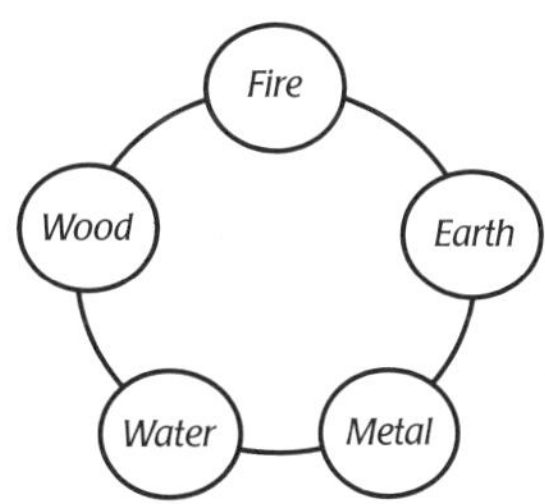

December 10

autumn gallops in
grasses of roan and
dun, the trees
waving dark butter
manes
this forest
holds me
kindled by the
surge of
wind-stallions
everything flames,
falls, sinks
cindered to the earth
to the last
yellow leaves of the
wild grape

- Janice MacKenzie

Exercise

Read some inspiring poetry. Try your hand at writing some.

Note your distillations . . .

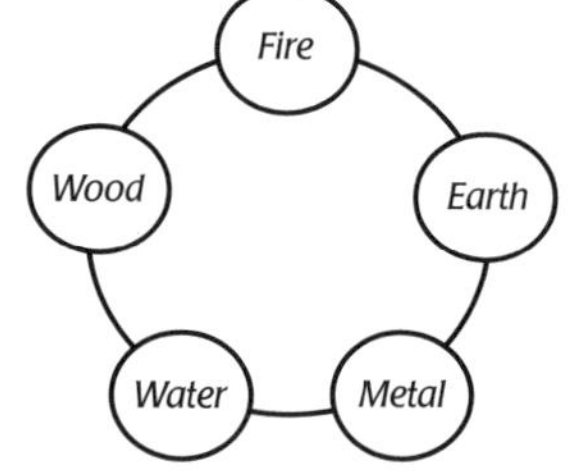

December 11

"To treat and to cure disease means to examine the body..."

- Nei Jing

"The Metal hand...forms a symmetrical oval. The palm is long and so are the fingers...."

- Yves Requena,
Morphotypological Hand Diagnosis in Acupuncture

The Metal hand has a very long palm, with fingers that are also long but not as long as the palm. The fingers are not necessarily slender, unlike the Fire hand, and are often crooked, with the three phalanges not well aligned so that they take on a zig-zag pattern. With age, these irregularities can become accentuated, so that the hand becomes totally deformed with extremely crooked fingers. This is not to be confused with the symptoms of arthritis, but is simply the characteristic of the Metal hand.

Exercise

Using pencil and paper, trace your hand and notice its size and shape, compared to two of your friends'. Is it a Metal hand?

Note your distillations . . .

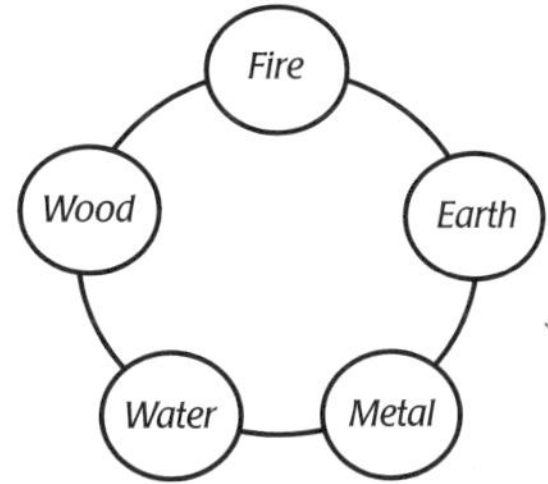

Distillations

December 12

Another specific characteristic of the Metal hand is the presence of three or more folds at the interphalangeal articulations. These folds are called "the triple link."

The Metal fingernail is usually long and rectangular, with sharp angles, and only slight rounding at the base and the tip. It is often marked longitudinally with fine lines, which are not exclusive to the Metal hand but are found there more often than elsewhere. The Metal fingernail is usually convex, but sometimes a Metal hand will have short, wide nails that are convex both in width and in length, resembling a seashell. In these cases, the last phalanx of the finger will be broadened, like a drumstick.

If someone has a hand that is diagnosed as a Metal hand, it doesn't necessarily follow that s/he will have symptoms in the Metal organs or meridians. The hand type simply gives one a sense of the person's basic constitution.

Exercise

Examine the hands of your family and friends. If someone has a Metal hand, do you see other signs and symptoms of the Metal element?

Note your distillations . . .

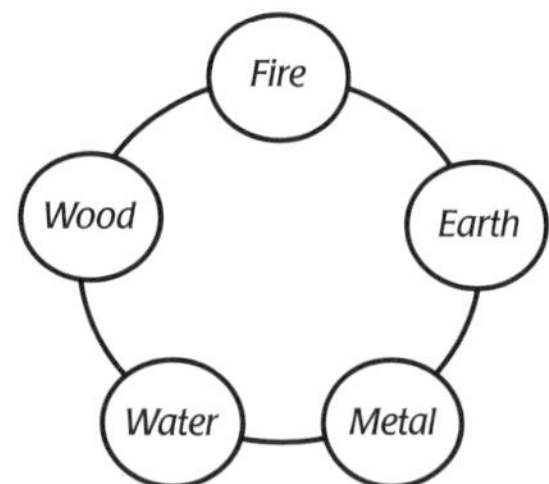

December 13

Elm

the sun grows ill
rising late in the day
the great winds wail their
indifference
it is time for the long sleep
slowly I withdraw myself
from my cells and fibers
leaving dry skins
my fingers stiffen
and my bright green hair
turns brittle and brown
soon my body will become numb
and I will drift and forget
my bones left to creak
in the wind
everything blurs and darkens
I feel the lids close –
down and under, where it is safe
I dream my dark dreams

- Janice MacKenzie

Exercise

Prepare for the coming cold weather by checking your wood or fuel supplies and stocking up on extra food.

Note your distillations . . .

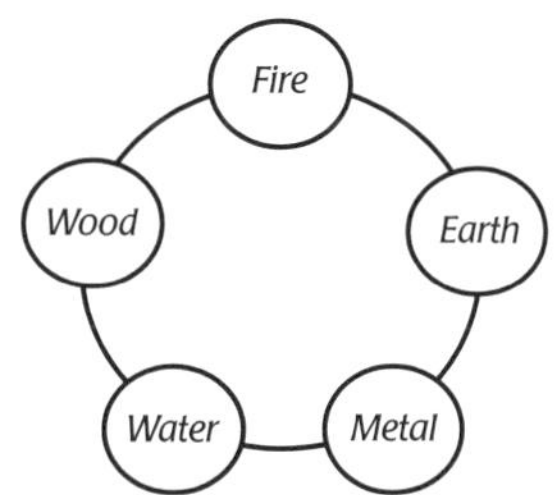

Distillations

December 14

We stand still to hear
Tinkle of far
Temple bell...
Willow-leaves falling
- Basho

Here is the dark tree
Denuded now
Of leafage...
But a million stars
- Shiki

I am growing old...
O sweet bird
Disappearing
Into autumn dusk
- Basho

Exercise

Plan a party or gathering of your friends to reaffirm your connections, and to counteract the sense of loneliness and melancholy that Autumn can bring.

Note your distillations . . .

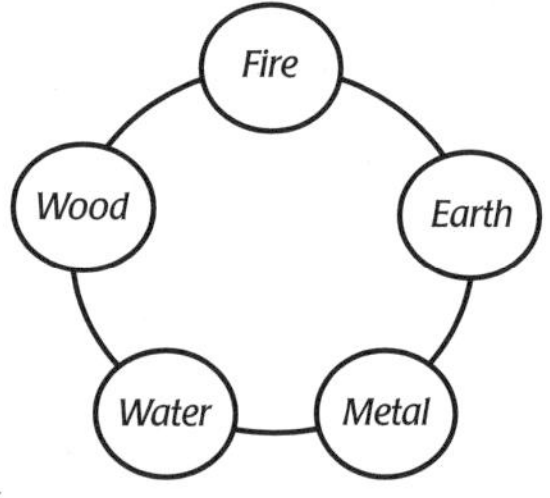

Distillations

December 15

"...its sound is shang *..."*

- Nei Jing

The musical note corresponding to the Autumn season and the Metal energy is *shang*, which resonates with all of the other correspondences of that season. A musical sound is almost impossible to explain in words—we must liken it to other qualities of sound in nature to get the flavor of it. *Shang* was said to correspond to the crashing peals of thunder in Autumn.

Historians of Chinese culture trace the origins of the names of the notes to the ancient practice of war divination, used to ascertain the morale of armies before battle. Each of the five sounds represented a different aspect of an army's qi: "If it is *shang* there will be victory in the fight; the soldiers of the army are strong."

Exercise

Listen to some rousing marches by John Philip Sousa to get your energy going.

Note your distillations . . .

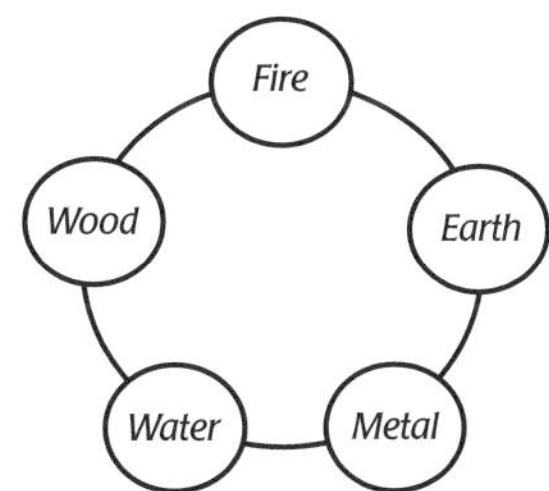

Distillations

December 16

Even the materials with which musical instruments were made corresponded to the five elements, directions, season, and moods. In Autumn, the season when the Yang forces fade, bells and metal instruments were played as the troops were ordered to retire. The tones these instruments produced corresponded to certain emotional as well as martial and political effects: "The sound of bells is clanging. Clangour produces a call as if to arms. Such a call gives rise to wild excitement. Wild excitement produces warlike emotion. When the *chun tzu* (man of breeding) listens to the sound of bells he thinks of heroic military officers. Cheng Hsuan observes that the effect of a bell is that of a warning to rouse the people, and explains that it causes a person's *chih* to become abundant...The sound of ringing-stones is a tinkling. Tinkling sets up a power of discrimination. Discrimination enables men to press on to their deaths. When the man of breeding listens to the sound of ringing-stones he thinks of loyal officials who have died on the frontiers."

Joseph Needham,
Science and Civilization in China, Vol. II

Exercise

Listen to music that makes you feel inspired or elevated.

Note your distillations . . .

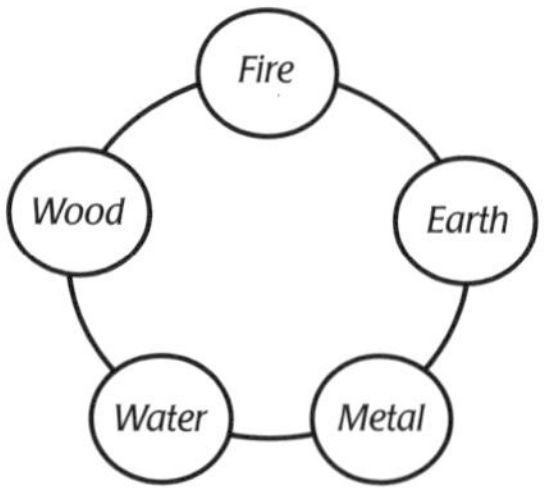

Fire
Wood
Earth
Water
Metal

Distillations

December 17

Listen to the air.
You can hear it, feel it,
smell it, taste it.
Woniya wakan, the holy air,
which renews all by its breath.
Woniya wakan, spirit, life, breath, renewal,
it means all that.
We sit together, don't touch,
but something is there,
we feel it between us,
as a presence.

- John Lame Deer

"Sooner or later every one of us breathes
an atom that has been breathed before
by anyone you can think of
who has lived before us –
Michelangelo or George Washington
or Moses."

- Jacob Bronowski

Exercise

Today, do some vigorous exercise out of doors. Feel how the crisp autumn air invigorates you.

Note your distillations . . .

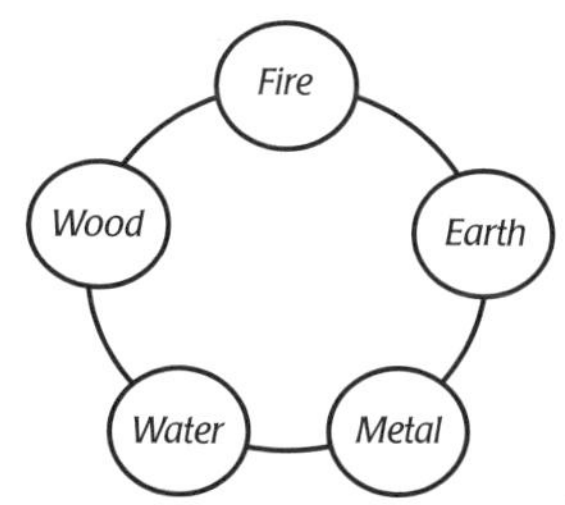

Distillations

December 18

"In Fall the pulse is that of the lungs; and metal is the element of the West. All things in creation approach their harvest, perfection and completion."

- Nei Jing

In an agricultural society, the Autumn was the time of the harvest, and also of taking stock of what had been harvested in order to know whether there was enough to last through the Winter. Thus, the process of taking stock, of evaluating exactly what one has, is a process associated with Autumn and with the Metal element.

If we look at the seasons of a person's life, Autumn would be that season linked with mid-life, in which we "sum up" what we've accomplished so far, and take stock of where we are and where we still want to go. In our culture, this often happens when people are in their late 40's or 50's, after their children are grown but before retirement, when there is a strong drive to evaluate one's life to date, and perhaps strike out in new directions.

Exercise

Make a list of your professional accomplishments. What do you still need to accomplish to feel complete?

Note your distillations . . .

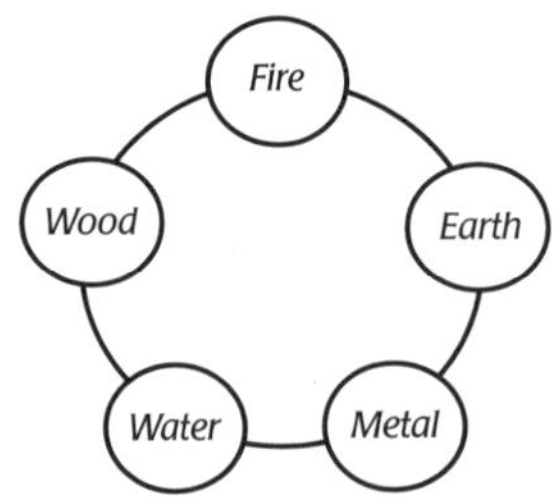

December 19

An example of Metal evaluation is a man in his late 40's who takes stock and realizes that he's never going to be president of his company, or really "make it big." He might be tempted to leave everything, start his own company, run off with his secretary, or become a Buddhist monk in Tibet. A woman in her late 40's, whose children have all grown and left home, might take stock and realize that she always wanted to study painting, or start her own catering business, or travel around the world with a backpack. Of course, some people will take stock and realize they are quite happy right where they are! When these people weigh their accomplishments and sum up their lives, they feel that "perfection and completion" mentioned in the *Nei Jing*.

We can all feel this drive to evaluate things in the Autumn, no matter what our age or life circumstances. As we sum up the year in preparation for Winter, we decide which things were worthwhile and which things we will eliminate next year. During this season, it is easier to weigh and measure things, to see which ones have true value for us.

Exercise

What was worthwhile about this past year? What will you change next year?

Note your distillations . . .

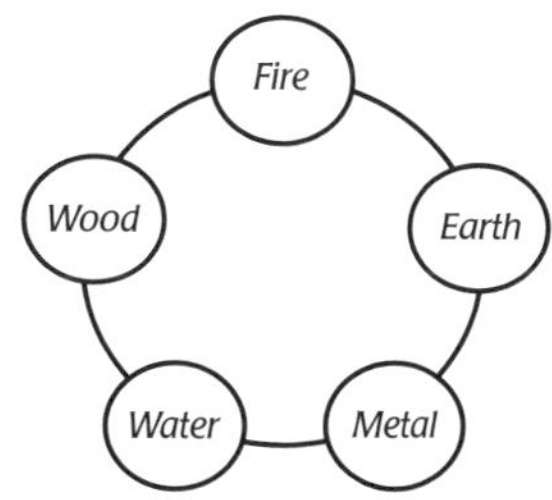

December 20

One leaf left on a branch
and not a sound of sadness
or despair. One leaf left
on a branch and no unhappiness.
One leaf left all by itself
in the air and it does not speak
of loneliness or death.
One leaf and it spends itself
in swaying mildly in the breeze.

- David Ignatow

This poem perfectly captures the poignancy of late Autumn, just before it turns into Winter. It portrays a surrender to what is—without grief or sadness—and so is the perfect reading for the transition from Autumn into Winter, from Metal into Water. When all is stripped away, the essence of what is left can be felt in serene acceptance. This is the point of maximum letting go, when any pain from loss dissolves into the stillness of death. We can feel this serenity when we finally let go of all striving and surrender to the present moment.

Exercise

Try to see the beauty in the starkness of late Autumn, when Nature is stripped to the bare essentials. Buy some watercolors or pastels and attempt painting it, or capture it on film.

Note your distillations . . .

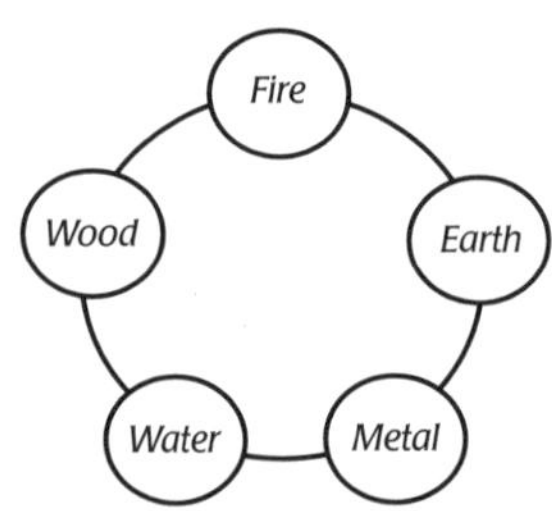

Distillations

December 21

That time of year thou mayst in me behold
When yellow leaves, or none, or few, do hang
Upon those boughs which shake against the cold,
Bare ruined choirs where late the sweet bird sang.
In me thou see'st the twilight of such day
As after sunset fadeth in the west,
Which by and by black night doth take away,
Death's second self, that seals up all in rest.
In me thou see'st the glowing of such fire
That on the ashes of his youth doth lie,
As the deathbed whereon it must expire,
Consumed with that which it was nourished by.
This thou perceiv'st, which makes thy love more strong,
To love that well which thou must leave ere long.

- William Shakespeare

Exercise

Let go of all of your plans for this year, and prepare to rest over the Winter. The Spring will bring new opportunities to fulfill those plans, as well as new ones.

Note your distillations . . .

Distillations

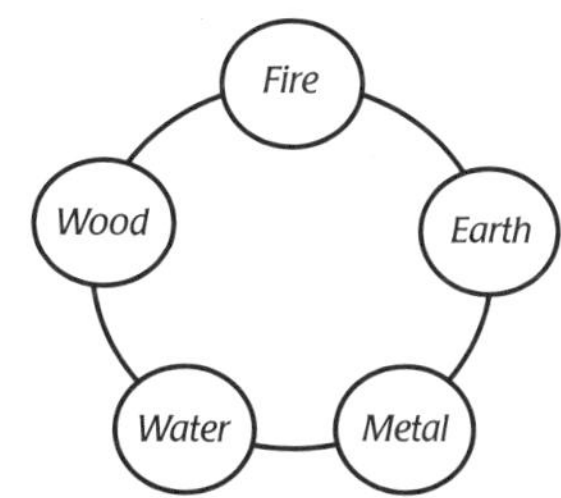

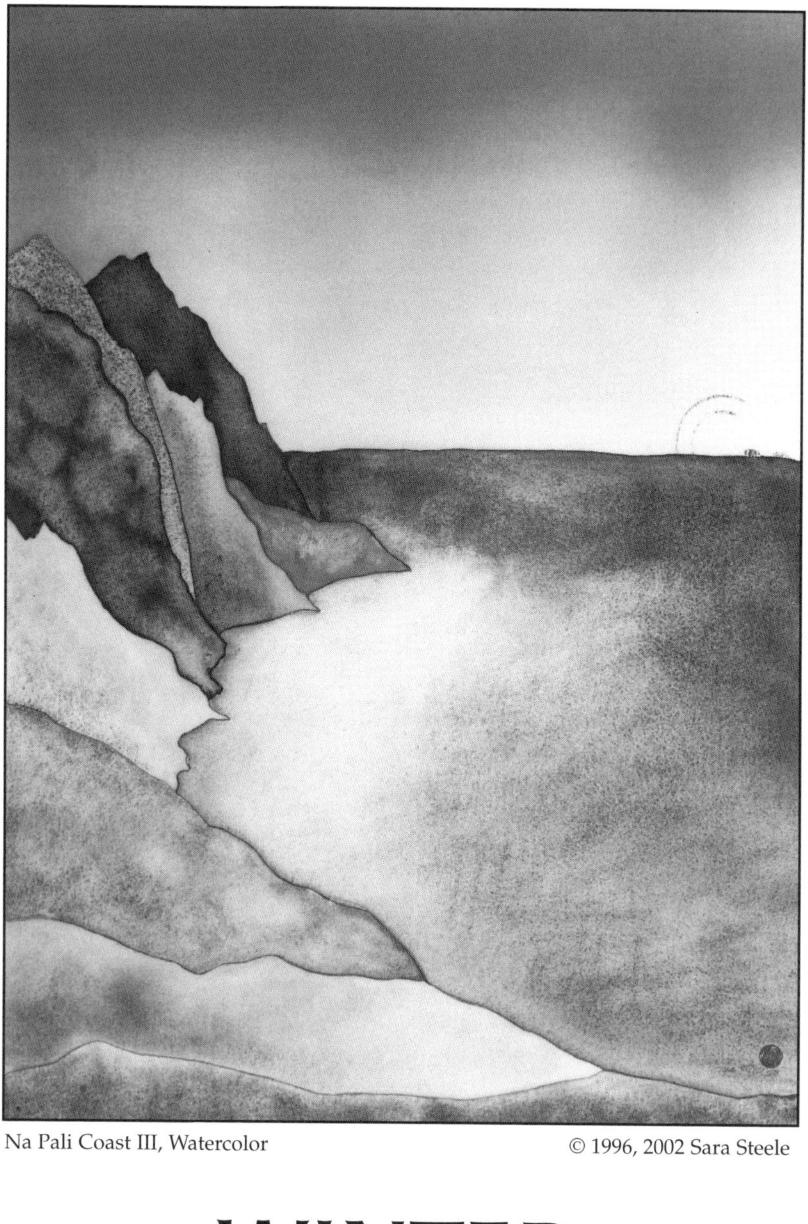

Na Pali Coast III, Watercolor

WINTER

水

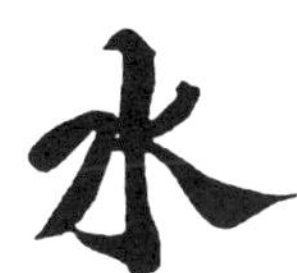

December 22

"The three months of Winter are called the period of closing and storing. Water freezes and the Earth cracks open. One should not disturb one's Yang.

"People should retire early at night and rise late in the morning and they should wait for the rising of the sun. They should suppress and conceal their wishes, as though they had no internal purpose, as though they had been fulfilled. People should try to escape the cold and they should seek warmth, they should not perspire upon the skin, they should let themselves be deprived of breath of the cold.

"All this is in harmony with the atmosphere of Winter and all this is the method for the protection of one's storing.

"Those who disobey (the laws of Winter) will suffer an injury of the kidneys (testicles); for them Spring will bring impotence, and they will produce little."

- Nei Jing

Exercise

As the season changes once again into Winter, practice retiring early and rising with the sun to be in harmony with nature. Feel how your body wants more rest at this time of year.

Write your reflections . . .

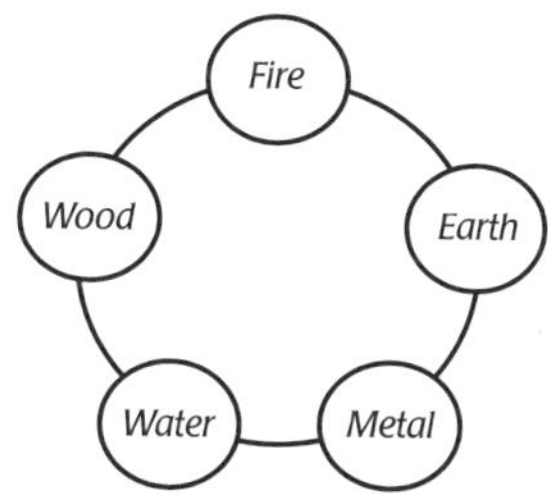

December 23

In the soul, power doesn't work the same way as it does in the ego and will. When we want to accomplish something egotistically, we gather our strength, develop a strategy, and apply every effort. This is the kind of behavior James Hillman describes as heroic or Herculean. He means the word in the bad sense: using brute strength and narrow, rationalistic vision. The power of the soul, in contrast, is more like a great reservoir or, in traditional imagery, like the force of water in a fast-rushing river. It is natural, not manipulated, and stems from an unknown source."

- Thomas Moore,
Care of the Soul

Exercise

Take a trip to the nearest big river. Stand on the banks and watch the rushing water, and imagine that power moving through you. When you follow your soul's direction, you have that kind of power.

Write your reflections . . .

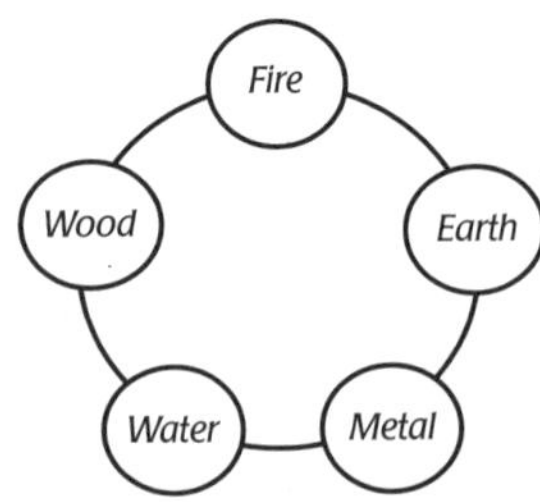

Reflections

December 24

drifting

i long to
plunge myself into
soft curves of
voluptuous snow
as the wind like
time shifts
these forms of
frozen flesh to
new bodies
lean and carven
the wind blowing
away all semblance
of youth
leaving ridged
aristocratic arches
the bones of the
drifts showing
through stretched
white skin
in the precise
definition of
age

- Janice MacKenzie

Exercise

As you shovel snow, notice the crispness of the air, the texture of the snow, and how your muscles flex.

Write your reflections . . .

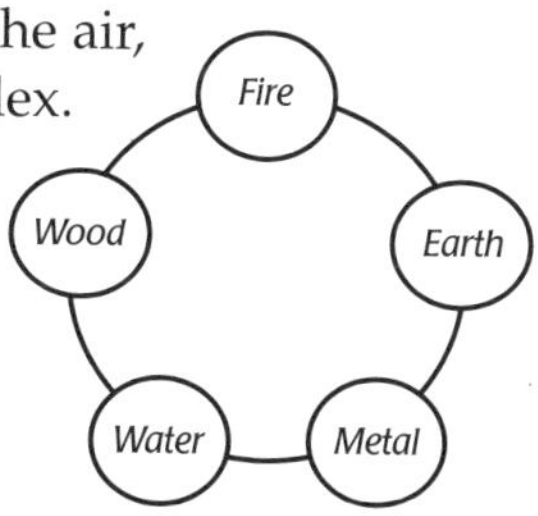

Fire
Wood
Earth
Water
Metal

Reflections

December 25

It is our quiet time.
We do not speak, because the voices are within us.
It is our quiet time.
We do not walk, because the earth is all within us.
It is our quiet time.
We do not dance, because the music has lifted us to a place where the spirit is.
It is our quiet time.
We rest with all of nature. We wake when the seven sisters wake.
We greet them in the sky over the opening of the kiva.

- Nancy Wood,
Hollering Sun

For many of us, this day is a day that is far from quiet. The Christmas holiday is one that is usually full of activity, family gatherings, and celebrations. Often, these gatherings can be stressful, as we cope with disappointed expectations, difficult family dynamics, or just plain overload. This poem calls us to tune into the quietness of Nature at this time of year. Taking time out to be quiet on this day can help us to balance the extra activity of the rest of the day, and put us in touch with a deeper level of spirit.

Exercise

Turn off all the lights, light a candle, and give yourself some quiet time.

Write your reflections . . .

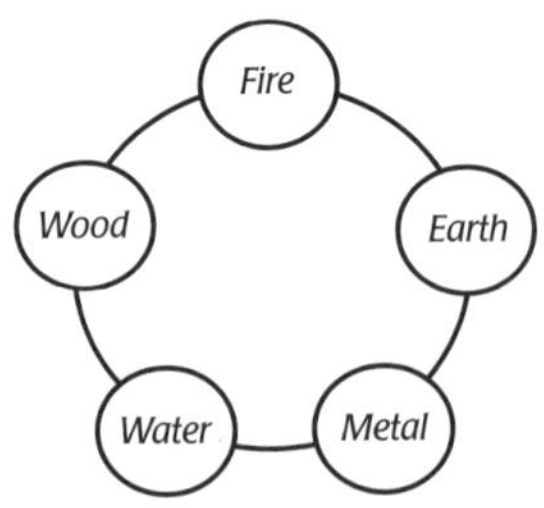

Reflections

December 26

woods in winter
the twisted shapes of vines
rain-blackened trunks of
trees, thickets where
something small and furry
probably lives, tiny trails
leaving and returning
dank smells of wet leaves,
old pine needles, deer scat,
cold earth - the honk of a
wild goose from the swamp
through the trees, then the
annoyed quacking of mallards
in answer –
my heart lifts only
when I see the raindrops
strung along the slim arches
of a wineberry bush
crystal beads, sparkling
as if lit from inside
the only bright things
in this dull and dreary
landscape

- Janice MacKenzie

Exercise

Put birdseed outside your kitchen window, and watch which birds come as you eat your breakfast.

Write your reflections . . .

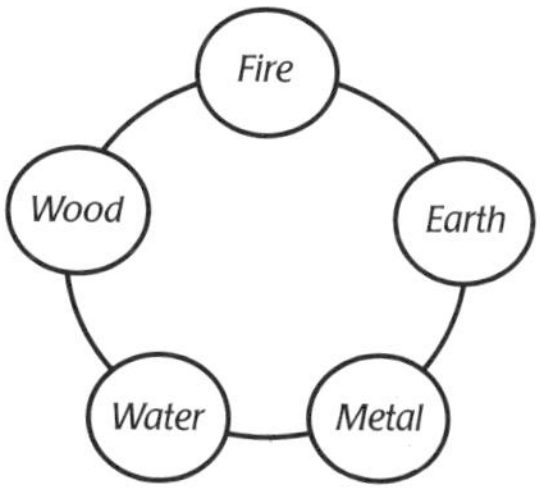

Fire
Wood
Earth
Water
Metal

Reflections

December 27

"Grow old along with me!
The best is yet to be,
The last of life, for which the first was made:"

- Robert Browning

"Every one of us is called upon, probably many times, to start a new life. A frightening diagnosis, a marriage, a move, loss of a job or a limb or a loved one, a graduation, bringing a new baby home: it's impossible to think at first how this all will be possible. Eventually, what moves it all forward is the subterranean ebb and flow of being alive among the living."

- Barbara Kingsolver,
High Tide in Tucson

Exercise

Talk to an older relative and ask them what daily life was like when they were young.

Write your reflections . . .

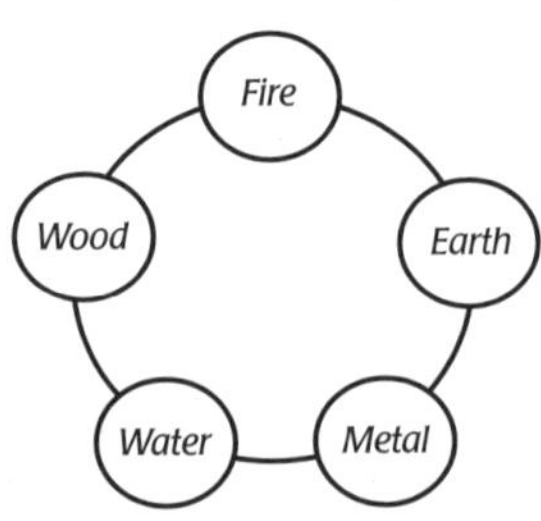

Reflections

December 28

"In the depths of winter, I finally learned that within me lay an invincible summer."

- Albert Camus

This wonderful quote speaks of the invincible nature of the human spirit, but it could also be talking about the spark of Fire that is within the Water energy of each of us. This spark is the Yang within the Yin, like the tiny white dot in the middle of the black half of the yin-yang symbol. The Chinese would call this *"ming men"*—the "Gate of Life" or the "Door of Destiny"—which is the dynamic, life-giving aspect of the Kidney energy. In the dark, cold, lightless depths of the Water energy, there is this powerful spark of Fire that animates us, giving us power and passion.

Exercise

As we move into the dark time of year, keep your Fire burning within by remembering the joys of the past Summer.

Write your reflections . . .

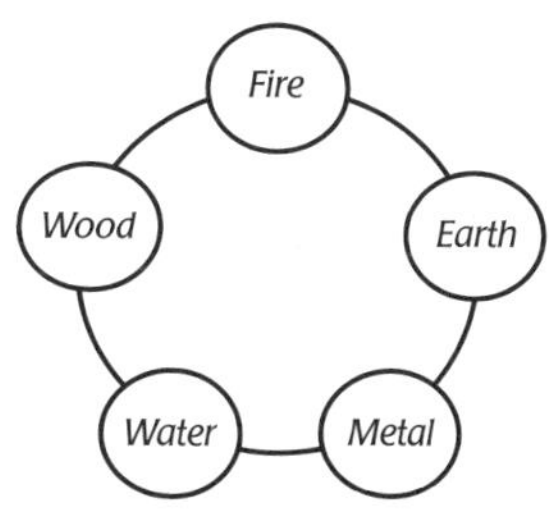

Reflections

December 29

"I feel like some old engine Done lost its drivin' wheel..."

- David Wiffen

Linking the Kidneys with generating power means that the health of our Kidneys determines our capacity to have the energy available for work, play, sex, or initiating projects. Our Kidneys give us our "drive."

When our Kidney energy is weak, deficient, or just temporarily exhausted, we have little desire to begin a new project, play vigorous sports, or have sex. Someone who is chronically "too tired" to play sports, go out on the town, or engage in sexual intercourse is probably suffering from an imbalance in the Kidney energy. Often, someone like this will talk about needing to "recharge my batteries" or "get an energy boost." Actually, the only reliable way to "recharge your batteries" is to get some rest; when the Kidneys have had an opportunity to store up some more energy, you will naturally feel your initiating spark come back.

Exercise

Treat your Kidneys to a brisk massage, or warm them with ginger compresses.

Write your reflections . . .

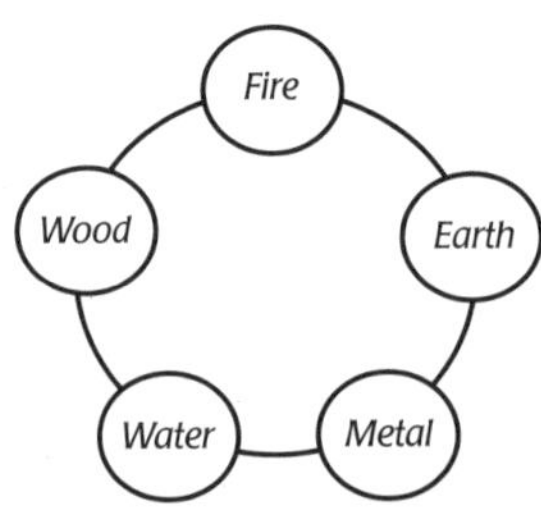

Reflections

December 30

*"Make your ego porous. Will is of little importance,
complaining is nothing, fame is nothing.
Openness, patience, receptivity, solitude is everything."*

- Rainer Maria Rilke

"You do not need to leave the room. Remain sitting at your table and listen. Do not even listen, simply wait. Do not even wait, be quite still and solitary. The world will freely offer itself to you to be unmasked, it has no choice, it will roll in ecstasy at your feet."

- Franz Kafka

"Such is the nature of the ocean that the waters which flow into it can never fill it, nor those which flow from it exhaust it."

- Chuang Tzu

Exercise

Be still and feel the inexhaustible ocean of energy that is available to you.

Write your reflections . . .

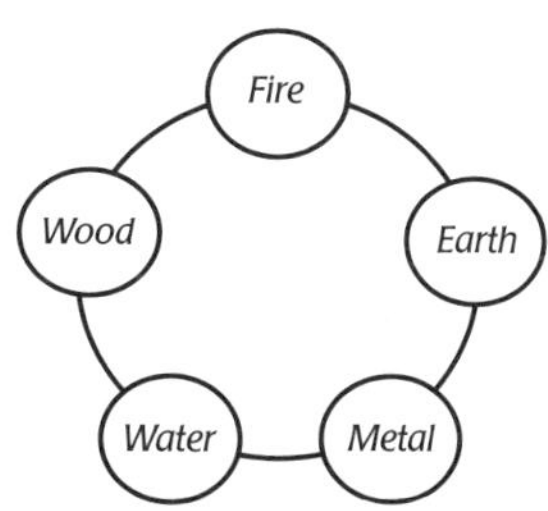

Reflections

December 31

"In Japan we have the phrase Shoshin *, which means "beginner's" mind. The goal of practice is always to keep our beginner's mind. Our "original mind" includes everything within itself. It is always rich and sufficient within itself. This does not mean a closed mind, but actually an empty mind and a ready mind. If your mind is empty, it is always ready for anything; it is open to everything. In the beginner's mind there are many possibilities; in the expert's mind there are few."*

– Shunryu Suzuki

"The most beautiful thing we can experience is the mysterious. It is the source of all true art and science. He to whom the emotion is a stranger, who can no longer pause and stand wrapped in awe, is as good as dead; his eyes are closed."

– Albert Einstein

Exercise

Resolve in the year to come to keep your "beginner's mind" open and ready to experience the mystery.

Write your reflections . . .

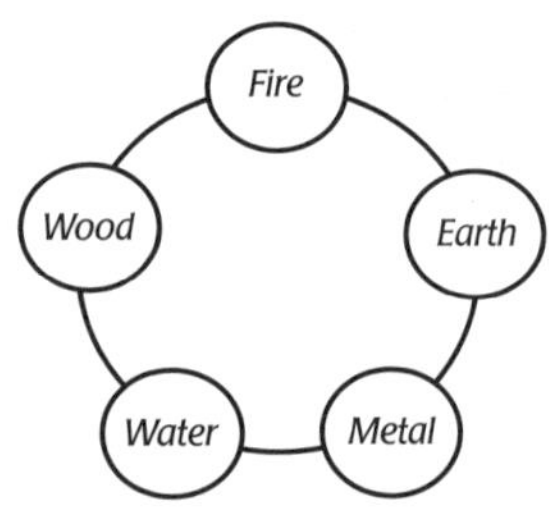

Reflections

Pat's Daylilies, watercolor

EPILOGUE

Epilogue

"The breath of Heaven is pure and light. Heaven always maintains its (original) virtue; thus it never comes to fall. If Heaven opened up completely then sun and moon would never be bright, evil would come during this period of emptiness, the atmosphere of Yang would close up and the Earth would lose its brightness, clouds and fog would be unable to undergo changes and as a consequence white dew would not fall, and the circulation (of the natural elements) would not communicate with the life of everything in creation. This situation would be called "not bestowing," and as a consequence of "not bestowing" all vegetation would perish. Furthermore, the noxious air would not disappear, wind and rain would not be harmonious, white dew would not fall, so that vegetation would never again flourish. There would always be violent winds and sudden squalls of rain, and Heaven and Earth and the four seasons would be unable to protect each other, they would lose Tao and would soon be destroyed."

- Nei Ching

Bibliography

The Yellow Emperor's Classic of Internal Medicine, Ilza Veith, Translator, University of California Press, Berkeley, CA, 1972.

Traditional Acupuncture: The Law of the Five Elements, by Dianne M. Connelly, Traditional Acupuncture Institute, Columbia, MD, 1975.

All Sickness is Home Sickness, by Dianne M. Connelly, Traditional Acupuncture Institute, Columbia, MD, 1993.

Traditional Acupuncture, Vol. II: Traditional Diagnosis, by J.R. Worsley, College of Traditional Acupuncture (U.K.), Royal Leamington Spa, U.K., 1990.

Classical Five-Element Acupuncture, Vol. III: The Five Elements and the Officials, by J.R. Worsley, published by J.R. and J.B. Worsley, 1998.

Staying Healthy with the Seasons, by Elson Haas, Celestial Arts, Millbrae, CA, 1981.

Between Heaven and Earth: A Guide to Chinese Medicine, by Harriet Beinfield and Efrem Korngold, Ballantine Books, NY, 1991.

Nourishing Destiny: The Inner Tradition of Chinese Medicine, by Lonny S. Jarrett, Spirit Path Press, Stockbridge, MA, 1998.

In the Footsteps of the Yellow Emperor, by Peter Eckman, Cypress Book Company, San Francisco, CA, 1996.

Five Elements and Ten Stems: Nan Ching Theory, Diagnostics and Practice, by Kiiko Matsumoto and Stephen Birch, Paradigm Publications, Higganum, CT, 1983.

Healing with Whole Foods, by Paul Pitchford, North Atlantic Books, Berkeley, CA, 1993.

Chinese Medicine from the Classics (whole series including The Lung, The Kidneys, The Spleen and Stomach, The Heart, The Liver, Master of the Heart) by Claude Larre and Elisabeth Rochat de la Vallee, Monkey Press, Cambridge, U.K., 1989–on.

Chinese System of Food Cures, by Henry C. Lu, New York: Sterling Publishing., 1986.

Six Healing Sounds, by Mantak Chia, Healing Tao Books, Huntington, NY, 1986.

The Four Books, by Confucius, trans. by James Legge, Oxford, U.K., Clarendon Press, 1983.

Tao Te Ching, by Lao Tzu, trans. by D.C. Lau, Penguin Books, New York, NY, 1963.

Tao Teh Ching, by Lao Tzu, trans. by Dr. John C.H. Wu, St. John's University Press, New York, 1961.

Tao Te Ching, by Lao Tzu, trans. by Gia-Fu Feng and Jane English, Vintage Books, New York, 1972.

The I Ching, trans. by Richard Wilhelm and Cary Baynes, Bolligen Series XIX, Princeton University Press, Princeton, NJ, 1950.

T'ung Shu: The Ancient Chinese Almanac, Ed. by Martin Palmer, Shambhala Publications, Boston, MA, 1986.

Ch'i: A Neo-Taoist Approach to Life, by R.G.H. Siu, The MIT Press, Cambridge, MA, 1974.

Chuang Tzu: Basic Writings, Trans. by Burton Watson, Columbia University Press, New York, 1964.

Science and Civilization in China, Vol. II, by Joseph Needham, Cambridge University Press, Cambridge, U.K., 1956.

The Silent Pulse, by George Leonard, E.P. Dutton, New York, 1978.

The Foundations of Chinese Medicine, by Giovanni Maciocia, Churchill Livingstone, Edinburgh, U.K., 1989.

Morphotypological Hand Diagnosis in Acupuncture, by Yves Requena, Editions Solal, Marseilles, France, 1986.

The Way of Energy, by Master Lam Kam Chuen, Simon & Schuster, Inc., New York, 1991.

Wise Woman Ways: Menopausal Years, by Susun Weed, Ash Tree Publishing, Woodstock, NY, 1992.

Health Through Balance, by Dr. Yeshi Donden, Snow Lion Publications, Ithaca, NY, 1986.

The Journal of Traditional Acupuncture, Traditional Acupuncture Institute, Columbia, MD: All issues, but especially those after Spring 1981.

Meridians, Traditional Acupncture Institute, Columbia, MD. All issues.

Medicine in China: A History of Ideas, by Paul U. Unschuld, University of California Press, Berkeley, CA, 1985.

A Source Book in Chinese Philosophy, trans. by Wing-Tsit Chan, Princeton University Press, Princeton, NJ, 1963.

Rooted in Spirit: The Heart of Chinese Medicine, trans. by Claude Larre, S.J., Elisabeth Rochat de la Vallee, and Sarah Stang, Institut Ricci and Station Hill Press, Barrytown, NY, 1995.

Chinese Characters, by Dr. L. Wieger, S.J., Paragon Book Reprint Corp. and Dover Publications, 1965.

Notes

Preface: Wallace Stevens, *The Collected Poems of Wallace Stevens*, Alfred A. Knopf, Inc., © 1923, 1931, 1935, 1936, 1942, 1944, 1947, 1954 by Wallace Stevens.

Winter/Water

Intro: Ilza Veith, trans., *The Yellow Emperor's Classic of Internal Medicine*, © 1949 & 1972, The Regents of the University of California, p. 103 and p. 120.

Jan. 1. Ibid., p. 120.

Jan. 2. Joseph Needham, *Science and Civilization in China*, Vol. 2, Cambridge University Press, 1956.

Jan. 3. Veith, 1972, p. 113.

Jan. 5. Ibid., p. 120.

Jan. 6. Ibid., p. 147.

Jan. 7. Ibid., p. 120.

Jan. 9. Ibid., p. 133.

Jan. 11. Ibid., p. 133.

Jan. 12. Tom Robbins, *Even Cowgirls Get the Blues*, Bantam Books, 1977, pp.1-2.

Jan. 13. Veith, 1972, p. 120.

Jan. 14. Claude Larre and Elisabeth Rochat de la Vallee, *Chinese Medicine from the Classics: The Kidneys*, Monkey Press, 1989, p. 73.

Jan. 17. Dylan Thomas, "The Force That Through the Green Fuse Drives the Flower," *The Mentor Book of Major British Poets*, Mentor Books, 1963, p. 563.

Jan. 18. Larre and Rochat de la Vallee, 1989, p. 71.

Jan. 19. Veith, 1972, p. 120 and p. 170.

Jan. 20. Ibid., p. 113.

Jan. 21. Ibid., p. 141.

Jan. 22. Emily Dickinson, *The Complete Poems of Emily Dickinson*, Little, Brown and Company, 1960, p. 118.

Jan. 23. Veith, 1972, p. 120.

Jan. 24. Psalm 32:3, *The Holy Scriptures According to the Masoretic Text*, Jewish Publications Society, 1917.

Jan. 26. Veith, 1972, p. 120 and p. 141.

Jan. 27. Ibid., p. 203.

Jan. 28. Ibid., p.141 and p. 203.

Jan. 29. Henry C. Lu, *Chinese System of Food Cures*, Sterling Publishing Co., 1986, p. 21.

Jan. 30. Veith, 1972, p. 113.

Jan. 31. Ibid., p. 207.

Feb. 1. Robert Frost, "Stopping by Woods on a Snowy Evening," *Complete Poems of Robert Frost*, Henry Holt & Co., 1930, 1947, & 1949.

Feb. 3. Veith, 1972, p. 103 and p. 139.

Feb. 5. Kate Barnes, The Bear Trees," from *Talking in Your Sleep*, Blackberry Books, 1986.

Feb. 6. Veith, 1972, p. 209.

Feb. 8. Mantak Chia, *Six Healing Sounds*, Healing Tao Books, 1986.

Feb. 9. Robert Graves, "A Time of Waiting," from *Man Does, Woman Is*, Doubleday & Company, Inc., 1964.

Feb. 10. Lao Tzu, *Tao Te Ching*, trans. by Gia-Fu Feng and Jane English, Vintage Books, 1972, p. 78.

Feb. 12. Robin Williamson, The Incredible String Band, on *The Hangman's Beautiful Daughter*, Electra Records, 1967.

Feb. 13. Loren Eisley, *The Immense Journey*, Vintage Books, V1959, p. 19.

Feb. 14. Thomas Moore, *Care of the Soul*, HarperCollins Publishers, 1992, p. 121.

Feb. 16. Frost, 1965, p. 240.

Feb. 18. Reprinted by permission of the publishers and the Trustees of Amherst College from *The Poems of Emily Dickinson*, Thomas H. Johnson, ed., Cambridge, Mass.: The Belknap Press of Harvard University Press, Copyright © 1951, 1955, 1979 by the President and Fellows of Harvard College.

Feb. 19. Franz Kafka, *Zen to Go*, ed. by Jon Winokur, Plume/Penguin Books, 1990, p. 110.

Feb. 20. Francis Thompson, from "The Mistress of Vision," *Poetical Works*, Oxford University Press, 1937.

Feb. 21. *The I Ching*, trans. by Richard Wilhelm and Cary F. Baynes, Princeton University Press, 1967, p. 115.

Feb. 22. *The Holy Bible*, King James Version, Westminster Press, 1943, St. Matthew 17:20.

Feb. 26. Veith, 1972, p. 120.

Feb. 27. Needham, 1956, pp. 155-159.

Feb. 28. Yves Requena, *Morphotypological Hand Diagnosis in Acupuncture,* Editions Solal, 1986, p. 84.

Mar. 2. Lao Tzu, *Tao Teh Ching,* trans. by Dr. John C.H. Wu, St. John's University Press, 1961, p. 11 & 21.

Mar. 3. Dianne Connelly, The Journal of Traditional Acupuncture, Vol. 1, No. 2, Winter 1977-1978, p. 6.

Mar. 4. Veith, 1972, p. 206.

Mar. 5. Ibid., p. 206.

Mar. 6. Ibid., p. 139.

Mar. 7. Ibid., p. 208.

Mar. 8. Chuang Tzu, *The Way of Chuang Tzu,* trans. by Thomas Merton, New Directions, 1965, p. 87.

Mar. 9. Veith, 1972, p. 120.

Mar. 12. Ibid., p. 163.

Mar. 13. Ibid., p. 152.

Spring/Wood

Intro: Ibid., p. 102 and p. 118.

Mar. 15. Ibid., p. 110 and 118.

Mar. 16. *T'ung Shu: The Ancient Chinese Almanac,* trans. by Martin Palmer, Shambhala Publications, 1986, p. 43.

Mar. 17. Veith, 1972, p. 112 and 118.

Mar. 19. Ibid., p. 110.

Mar. 21. Ibid., p. 133.

Mar. 23. Ibid., p. 139.

Mar. 24. Ibid., p. 133.

Mar. 27. Wendell Berry, "Another Descent," from *A Part,* North Point Press, 1980.

Mar. 28. Veith, 1972, p. 118.

Mar. 30. Dylan Thomas, *The Mentor Book of Major British Poets,* New American Library, 1963, p. 554.

Mar. 31. Reprinted by permission of the publishers and the Trustees of Amherst College from *The Poems of Emily Dickinson,* Thomas H. Johnson, ed., Cambrdige, Mass.: The Belknap Press of Harvard University Press, Copyright © 1951, 1955, 1979 by the President and Fellows of Harvard College.

Apr. 1. e.e. cummings, *100 Selected Poems,* Grove Press, 1926, p. 5.

Apr. 3. Emily Dickinson, *Selected Poems & Letters of Emily Dickinson*, copyright © 1959 by Robert N. Linscott. Reprinted with the permission of the Estate of Robert N. Linscott.

Apr. 4. Veith, 1972, p. 118.

Apr. 5. Quote attributed to Thomas Edison.

Apr. 6. Veith, 1972, p. 140.

Apr. 7. Ibid., p. 118.

Apr. 8. Ibid., p. 118.

Apr. 9. cummings, 1926, p. 114.

Apr. 10. May Sarton, *Collected Poems: 1930-1973*, W.W. Norton & Co., 1974.

Apr. 11. Veith, 1972, p. 118.

Apr. 15. George Leonard, *The Silent Pulse*, E.P. Dutton, 1978, p. 185.

Apr. 16. Ibid., p. 185-186.

Apr. 17. Veith, 1972, p. 207.

Apr. 19. Ibid., p. 118.

Apr. 20. Ibid., p. 118.

Apr. 21. Ibid., p. 109.

Apr. 22. Elson Haas, *Staying Healthy with the Seasons*, Celestial Arts, 1981.

Apr. 23. Veith, 1972, p. 112.

Apr. 24. Ibid., p. 102.

Apr. 26. Dianne M. Connelly, The Journal of Traditional Acupuncture, Vol. V, No. 1, Spring 1981, p. 17.

Apr. 27. Veith, 1972, p. 102.

Apr. 29. Requena, 1986, p. 44.

Apr. 30. Veith, 1972, p. 118.

May 3. R.G.H. Sui, *Ch'i: A Neo-Taoist Approach to Life*, The MIT Press, 1974, p. 29.

May 4. Walt Whitman, excerpted from *Complete Poetry and Selected Prose of Walt Whitman*, ed. by James E. Miller, Jr. Copyright © 1959 by Houghton Mifflin Company.

May 5. Whitman, p. 93.

May 6. Veith, 1972, p. 112.

May 7. Simon Mills, *The Essential Book of Herbal Medicine*, Arkana Press, 1991, p. 609.

May 9. Veith, 1972, p. 207.

May 10. Giovanni Maciocia, *The Foundations of Chinese Medicine*, Churchill Livingstone, 1989, p. 283.

May 11. Veith, 1972, p. 118.

May 12. Needham, p. 155.

May 13. Opal Whitely, *The Singing Creek Where the Willow Grows: The Rediscovered Diary of Opal Whitely*, Ticknor & Fields, 1986.

May 14. Han-Shan, *Poems of Han-Shan and Shih-te*, trans. by Arthur Tobias, James Sanford and J.P. Seaton, White Pine Press, 1982.

May 20. Antoinette Adam, *Weavings*, Vol. 111, no. 3, May/June 1987.

May 22. Sitting Bull, *Earth Prayers from Around the World*, ed. by Elizabeth Roberts and Elias Amidon, HarperSan Francisco, 1991, p. 296.

May 25. John Matthews, *The Celtic Shaman*, Shaftesbury: Element Books, 1991.

Summer/Fire

Intro: Veith, 1972, p. 102, 110, and 119.

May 26. Ibid., p. 119.

May 28. Ibid., p. 102.

May 30. Ibid., p. 112.

May 31. Robert Burns, *The Complete Poetical Works of Robert Burns*, Cambridge Edition, Houghton Mifflin Co., 1897.

June 1. Veith, 1972, p. 148.

June 2. Ibid., p. 148.

June 3. Ibid., p. 112.

June 4. Stephen Levine, *Guided Meditations, Explorations, and Healings*, Anchor/Doubleday, 1991.

June 5. Veith, 1972, p. 133.

June 7. Ibid., p.P 133.

June 10. Ibid., p. 133.

June 12. Ibid., p. 119.

June 13. Ibid., p. 119.

June 18. William Shakespeare, Sonnet 18, published 1609 by Thomas Thorpe.

June 20. Veith, 1972, p. 102.

June 22. Ibid., p. 169.

June 23. Ibid., p. 119.

June 24. Ibid., p. 112.

June 25. cummings, 1926, p. 114.

June 26. Veith, 1972, p. 140.

June 27. Ibid., p. 119.

June 28. Ibid., p. 119.

June 29. Eddie Cochran and Jerry Capeheart, "Summertime Blues," Jan. 1959.

July 1. Veith, 1972, p. 112.

July 2. Ibid., p. 118.

July 3. Ibid., p. 206.

July 5. Ibid., p. 207.

July 7. Ibid., p. 209.

July 9. cummings, 1926, p. 66.

July 10. Whitely, 1986.

July 11. Moore, p. 164.

July 13. Veith, 1972, p. 102; *The Holy Bible*, First Corinthinians 13, vs. 1-3.

July 15. Elizabeth Barrett Browning, *Love Sonnets*, The Odyssey Press, 1964, p. 35.

July 18. William Shakespeare, *Sonnets to a Dark Lady*, Peter Pauper Press, p. 57.

July 19. cummings, 1926, p. 90.

July 21. Whitman, 1959, p. 115.

July 23. Veith, 1972, p. 133 and p. 222.

July 24. Yeshi Donden, The Journal of Traditional Acupuncture, Vol. VII, No. 3, Spring 1984, p. 36.

July 25. Moore, 1992, p. 157.

July 28. Requena, 1986, p. 54.

July 29. Veith, 1972, p. 184.

July 30. Needham, 1956, p. 141.

July 31. Ibid., p. 155.

Aug. 1. Roberts and Amidon, 1991, p. 158.

Aug. 5. Whitman, 1959, p. 25.

Aug. 6. Veith, 1972, p. 133.

Aug. 7. Ibid., p. 208.

Late Summer/Earth

Intro: Ibid., p. 117, 119, and 148.

Aug. 8. Ibid., p. 112 and p. 199.

Aug. 10. T.S. Eliot, *The American Tradition in Literature*, W.W. Norton & Company, 1962, p. 1457.

Aug. 12. Veith, 1972, p. 112.

Aug. 13. Ibid., p. 141.

Aug. 14. Ibid., p. 119.

Aug. 15. Larre and de la Vallee, *Chinese Medicine from the Classics: Spleen and Stomach*, Monkey Press, 1990, p. 38.

Aug. 16. Veith, 1972, p. 133.

Aug. 18. Ibid., p. 184.

Aug. 19. Ibid., p. 178.

Aug. 20. Ibid., p. 119.

Aug. 26. Federico Garcia Lorca, *Roots and Wings: Poetry from Spain 1900-1975*, trans. by James Wright, HarperCollins, 1976.

Aug. 28 M.C. Richards, *Centering*, Wesleyan University Press, 1989, p. 33.

Aug. 30. Ron Fox, *YO! Magazine*, Fall1993.

Aug. 31. Ibid., 1993.

Sept. 1. Veith, 1972, p. 119.

Sept. 2. Diane Ackerman, *A Natural History of the Senses*, Vintage Books, 1990, p. 138.

Sept. 3. Veith, 1972, p. 119 and p. 202.

Sept. 4. Ibid., p. 206.

Sept. 6. Susun Weed, *Wise Woman Herbal: Healing Wise*, Ash Tree Publishing, 1989, p. 13.

Sept. 7. Veith, 1972, p. 119.

Sept. 8. Claude Larre and Elisabeth Rochat de la Vallee, *Chinese Medicine from the Classics: Spleen and Stomach*, Monkey Press, 1990, p. 24.

Sept. 9. Veith, 1972, p. 141.

Sept. 10. Ibid., p. 139.

Sept. 11. Ibid, p. 119 and p. 169.

Sept. 13. Starhawk, *The Spiral Dance*, Harper & Row, 1979, p. 78.

Sept. 14. Joseph Eppes Brown, *The Sacred Pipe: Black Elk's Account of the Seven rites of the Oglala Sioux*, Penguin, 1971.

Sept. 17. Veith, 1972, p. 112.

Sept. 18. Ibid., p. 119.

Sept. 19. The Traditional Circle of Elders, Navajo-Hopi Joint Council, from their 1982 letter to the United Nations General Assembly.

Sept. 20. Brooke Medicine Eagle, *Buffalo Woman Comes Singing*, Ballantine Books, 1991, p. 284.

Sept. 21. Ibid., p. 284.

Sept. 22. Requena, 1986, p. 64.

Sept. 23. Whitman, 1959, p. 47.

Sept. 24. Danann Parry, *The Earthsteward's Handbook*, Sunstone Publications,

Sept. 25. Veith, 1972, p. 209.

Sept. 26. Pawnee Hako Ceremony, Elizabeth Roberts and Elias Amidon, ed., *Earth Prayers from Around the World*, Harper SanFrancisco, 1991, p.240.

Sept. 27. Veith, 1972, p. 119.

Sept. 28. Shu Hsin-cheng, et al., *Tz'u Hai*, Tai Pei: Tai-wan Chung-hua shu chu, Min kuo, 1976.

Sept. 29. Starhawk, 1979, p. 77.

Sept. 30. Veith, 1972, p. 119.

Oct. 2. Robinson Jeffers, "Return," copyright © 1935 & renewed 1963 by Donnan Jeffers and Garth Jeffers, from *Selected Poetry by Robinson Jeffers.* Used by permission of Random House, Inc.

Oct. 3. Matthews, 1991.

Oct. 4. Veith, 1972, p. 208.

Oct. 5. Larre and Rochat de la Vallee, 1990, p. 52.

Oct. 6. Whitman, 1959, p. 46.

Oct. 8. Ojibway Prayer, Roberts and Amidon, 1991, p. 95.

Oct. 9. Dianne Connelly, *All Sickness is Home Sickness*, Traditional Acupuncture Institute, 1993, p. 124.

Oct. 11. Susan Griffin, *Woman and Nature: The Roaring Inside Her*, Harper and Row, 1978.

Oct. 12. Susan Griffin, from "Our Mother," *She Rises Like the Sun*, The Crossing Press, 1989, p. 45.

Oct. 13. Theokritos, from *Sappho and the Greek Lyric Poets*, translated by Willis Barnstone, copyright © 1962, 1967, 1988 by Willis Barnstone. Used by permission of Schocken Books, a division of Random House, Inc.

Oct. 14. Mary Oliver, *Dream Work*, Atlantic Monthly Press, © 1986, page 14.

Oct. 15. Pierre Teilhard de Chardin, *Hymn of the Universe*, HarperCollins, 1969.

Fall/Metal

Intro: Veith, 1972, p. 110, 103 and 119.

Oct. 16. Ibid, p. 119.

Oct. 18. Ibid., p. 147.

Oct. 19. Claude Larre and Elisabeth Rochat de la Vallee, *Chinese Medicine from the Classics: The Lung*, Monkey Press, 1989, p. 23.

Oct. 20. Veith, 1972, p. 119.

Oct. 22. Ibid., p. 119.

Oct. 24. Ibid., p. 119.

Oct. 26. Ibid., p. 133.

Oct. 27. Ibid., p. 139.

Oct. 29. Alfred, Lord Tennyson, *The Mentor Book of Major British Poets*, Mentor Books, 1963, p. 227.

Oct. 30. Dickinson, 1960, p. 162.

Oct. 31. Clysta Kinstler, *The Moon Under Her Feet*, Harper, 1989.

Nov. 2. Allen Ginsberg, from an interview filmed by Richard Lerner, *What Happened to Kerouac?*

Nov. 6. Veith, 1972, p. 133 and p. 208.

Nov. 7. Ibid., p. 189.

Nov. 8. Ibid., p. 140.

Nov. 9. Ibid., p. 119.

Nov. 10. Ibid., p. 140.

Nov. 11. Ibid., p. 119.

Nov. 12. Ibid., p. 113.

Nov. 13. Ibid., p. 120.

Nov. 15. Ibid., p. 119.

Nov. 16. Ibid., p. 207.

Nov. 17. Lu, 1986, p. 21.

Nov. 19. Veith, 1972, p. 120.

Nov. 21. Wei Ying Wu, *The Great Age of Chinese Poetry*, ed. by Stephen Owen, Yale University Press, 1981.

Nov. 22. Veith, 1972, p. 133.

Nov. 23. Helen Bevington, North Carolina poet and essayist, 1906-2001.

Nov. 24. "Mother of my birth" from *New and Collected Poems 1970-1985*, © 1982 by David Ignatow and reprinted by permission of Wesleyan University Press.

Nov. 25. "I will lie down," from *Nature: Poems Old and New* by May Swenson. Copyright © 1994 by The Literary Estate of May Swenson.

Nov. 26. Veith, 1972, p. 147.

Nov. 28. Larre and Rochat de la Vallee, 1989, p. 10.

Nov. 29. Ibid., p. 12.

Nov. 30. Dickinson, 1960, p. 133.

Dec. 1. Percy Bysshe Shelley, *The Mentor Book of Major British Poets*, Mentor Books, 1963, p. 169.

Dec. 3. Sylvia Plath, *Ariel*, Harper and Row, 1961, p. 49.

Dec. 6. Professor J.R. Worsley, *Classical Five-Element Acupuncture, Vol. III: The Five Elements and the Officials*, Published by J.R. & j.b. Worsley, 1998, p. 9.4.

Dec. 8. Anne Wilson Schaef, *Meditations for Women Who Do Too Much*, Harper and Row, 1990, p. "February 7."

Dec. 11. Veith, 1972, p. 184 ; Requena, 1986, p. 74.

Dec. 14. Basho and Shiki, from *The Four Seasons*, copyright © 1958, Peter Pauper Press; Basho, from *The Cherry Blossoms*, copyright © 1960, Peter Pauper Press. Reprinted by permission.

Dec. 15. Veith, 1972, p. 113.

Dec. 16. Needham, 1956, p. 155.

Dec. 17. "Listen to the air" reprinted with the permission of Simon & Schuster from *Lame Deer Seeker of Visions* by John Fire/Lame Deer and Richard Erdoes. Copyright © 1972 by John Fire/Lame Deer and Richard Erdoes. Jacob Bronowski, "Biography of an Atom and the Universe," New York Times, Oct. 13, 1968.

Dec. 18. Veith, 1972, p. 176.

Dec. 20. "One leaf left on a branch" from *New and Collected Poems 1970-1985*, © 1982 by David Ignatow and reprinted by permission of Wesleyan University Press.

Dec. 21. William Shakespeare, *Sonnets to a Dark Lady*, Peter Pauper Press.

Dec. 22. Veith, 1972, p. 103.

Dec. 23. Moore, 1992, p. 119.

Dec. 25. Nancy Wood, *Hollering Sun*, Simon & Schuster, 1972.

Dec. 27. Robert Browning, *The Mentor Book of Major British Poets*, Mentor Books, 1963, p. 275; Barbara Kingsolver, *High Tide in Tuscon: Essays from now or never*, HarperPerennial, 1996, p. 15.

Dec. 28. Albert Camus, from *Return to Tipasa*, 1954.

Dec. 29. David Wiffen, "Drivin' Wheel," from the album David Wiffen, Fantasy Records, 1971.

Dec. 31. Shunryu Suzuki, *Zen Mind, Beginner's Mind*, Walker/Weatherhill, 1970.

Epilogue

Veith, 1972, p. 103.

An exhaustive effort has been made to locate all rights holders and to clear reprint permissions. This process has been complicated, and if any required acknowledgements have been omitted, or any rights overlooked, it is unintentional and forgiveness is requested. If notified the publisher will be pleased to rectify any omission in future edition.

Biographies

Janice MacKenzie is an acupuncture practitioner and teacher with over 20 years experience in the field. She studied at the College of Traditional Chinese Acupuncture (U.K.) under Professor J.R. Worsley, founder of the school and one of the leading proponents of Five Element acupuncture. In addition, she studied extensively with Simon Mills, M.A., a Master Herbalist from Exeter, England, and Cara Frank, R.Ac., in Philadelphia, and has taken seminars and workshops with most of the leading acupuncturists in the United States, including: Ted Kaptchuk; Mark Seem; Kiiko Matsumoto; Dianne Connelly; Bob Duggan; Leon Hammer; Yves Requena; Bob Flaws; Peter Eckman: and Lonny Jarrett.

Janice is currently a faculty member of the Eastern School of Acupuncture and Traditional Medicine in Montclair, New Jersey. In addition, she has done extensive public lecturing and teaching about acupuncture and Oriental medicine in and around the Philadelphia area.

Janice was a co-founder and vice president of the Pennsylvania Acupuncture Society in 1983, a grass-roots organization created to change the law regarding acupuncture in Pennyslvania. The new law was signed into effect in February, 1986. Subsequently, she became the Secretary of the newly-formed Acupuncture Society of Pennyslvania (ASOP), a professional society of acupuncturists devoted to education and professional development. For several years thereafter she was a member of ASOP's Board of Directors, and was the creator and editor of the ASOP Newsletter, which has been publishing since 1989.

Janice's past writing experiences have included being the Assistant Editor of the *Wharton Magazine* (a national business magazine), and having original poems published in several poetry magazines, including *Earth's Daughters, Niagara, Rapport*, and *Women's Voices*. More recently, Janice has been a contributor to the *Journal of Traditional Acupuncture, Meridians*, and the *ASOP Newsletter*.

When she's not practicing acupuncture, Janice's other interests include bicycling, Tai Chi and photography. She lives in a cabin in the woods in rural Pennsylvania with her husband and two Austrialian Kelpies named Keli and Django.

Sara Steele is a nationally recognized artist based in Philadelphia. Her stunning watercolors are sensual, dynamic, inspiring, and convey a deep admiration for the natural world.

Sara is also an activist in the areas of ecology, peace, social justice, women's issues, and family and intimate violence, using her work to support such organizations as the National Domestic Violence Hotline, the Nature Conservancy, the National Clearinghouse in Defense of Battered Women, SANE/Committee for a Sane Nuclear Policy, and countless others. In 1997, Steele became the first Artist-in-Residence at Friends Hospital, the oldest private psychiatric hospital in the nation. She has led workshops for women survivors of personal violence as part of USArtists for the Pennsylvania Academy of the Fine Arts, and in 1998 and 1999 organized a national juried show for artists with special needs.

Sara's work has appeared on hundreds of products and she has won many awards throughout her career. Her original paintings are included in numerous private and public collections. Her annual calendars have been continuously in print for 23 years and can be found in major bookstores or at www.sarasteele.com. *In Bloom*, a book of Sara's floral paintings, was published in 1994. Sara's work has been exhibited throughout the U.S. In 2000 she had a solo show in Spain, and she is currently working on a retrospective show at the Berman Museum in 2005 and a new book of her paintings.

Sara has an enduring interest in holistic health. She became interested in Taoist philosophy and Chinese language as a teenager, and studied Chinese calligraphy with Cecelia Chiang. She was introduced to acupuncture and Systems Energetics in the late 1980's and her interest in the subject continues to grow.

Sara Steele may be reached at P.O. Box 4002, Philadelphia, PA 19118, (215) 242-4107, or by e-mail at sara@sarasteele.com.

Did You Borrow This Book? Have one of your own!

If you have your own copy of *Discovering the Five Elements One Day at a Time,* you can write in it and use it as your own personal energy diary. You can obtain your personal copy by completing and returning the form below.

For more information contact me at:
Janice MacKenzie, 14 Chapel Road, New Hope, PA 18938;
or call (215) 862-1825; or email me at acujanny@comcat.com.

________YES, I'd like ______copies of

Discovering the Five Elements One Day at at Time.

Please allow 30 days for delivery.

Name____

Address______________________________________

City/State/Zip_________________________________

Phone______________________ Email_____________

__________ book(s) at $19.95 each $_______________

Add sales tax

(7% Philadelphia; 6% PA residents only) $________

Shipping and handling @ $3.00/book $________

Total enclosed $________

Make your check payable to:

Janice MacKenzie
14 Chapel Road
New Hope, PA 18938

Bulk orders invited

For bulk discounts or special handling,
please call (215) 862-1825 or email acujanny@comcat.com.